# THE SPREAD OF FINANCIAL
# SOPHISTICATION THROUGH
# EMERGING MARKETS
# WORLDWIDE

# RESEARCH IN FINANCE

Series Editor: John W. Kensinger

Recent Volumes:

RESEARCH IN FINANCE    VOLUME 32

# THE SPREAD OF FINANCIAL SOPHISTICATION THROUGH EMERGING MARKETS WORLDWIDE

EDITED BY

## JOHN W. KENSINGER
*University of North Texas, Denton, TX, USA*

United Kingdom – North America – Japan
India – Malaysia – China

Emerald Group Publishing Limited
Howard House, Wagon Lane, Bingley BD16 1WA, UK

First edition 2016

**Reprints and permissions service**
Contact: permissions@emeraldinsight.com

**British Library Cataloguing in Publication Data**
A catalogue record for this book is available from the British Library

ISBN: 978-1-78635-156-2
ISSN: 0196-3821 (Series)

Printed and bound by CPI Group (UK) Ltd, Croydon, CR0 4YY

ISOQAR certified
Management System,
awarded to Emerald
for adherence to
Environmental
standard
ISO 14001:2004.

Certificate Number 1985
ISO 14001

INVESTOR IN PEOPLE

# CONTENTS

v

# LIST OF CONTRIBUTORS

| | |
|---|---|
| *Naseem Ahamed* | Department of Accounting and Finance, ICFAI Business School (IBS)-Hyderabad, Hyderabad, India |
| *Salima Ben Ezzeddine* | Ecole Superieure de Commerce de Tunis, Campus Universitaire LaManouba, Tunis, Tunisia |
| *Luis Berggrun* | Department of Finance, Universidad ICESI, Cali, Colombia |
| *Basabi Bhattacharya* | Financial Economics, Department of Economics, Jadavpur University, Kolkata, West Bengal, India |
| *Rita Biswas* | Department of Finance, University at Albany, Albany, NY, USA |
| *Kurt Burneo* | Department of Finance, Accounting and Economics, CENTRUM Católica Graduate Business School, Pontificia Universidad Catolica del Perú, Lima, Peru |
| *Wai Lun (Patrick) Cheung* | ABRS International Consultancy, Hong Kong, China |
| *A. Roy Chowdhury* | High Energy Physics Division, Department of Physics, Jadavpur University, Kolkata, West Bengal, India |
| *Charles P. Cullinan* | Department of Accounting, Bryant University, Smithfield, Rhode Island, MA, USA |
| *Konpanas Dumrongwong* | Xfi Centre for Finance and Investment, University of Exeter Business School, Exeter, UK |

ix

Jordan French            Faculty of Business Administration,
                         Stamford International University,
                         Bangkok, Thailand

Karoll Gómez Portilla    Faculty of Human and Economic Sciences,
                         Universidad Nacional de Colombia,
                         Bogota, Medellín, Columbia

Kousik Guhathakurta      Finance & Accounting, Indian Institute of
                         Management Indore, Indore, India

Reza Habibi              Iran Banking Institute, Central Bank of
                         Iran, Tehran, Iran

Mohamed                  Financial Economics, Kairouan University,
    Rochdi Keffala        Kairouan, Tunisia

Dmitry L. Komyagin       Department of Financial Law, National
                         Research University "Higher School of
                         Economics," Moscow, Russia

Ping-fu (Brian) Lai      Division of Business and Management,
                         United International College, Beijing
                         Normal University, Hong Kong Baptist
                         University, Hong Kong, China

Knut F. Lindaas          School of Management, Boston University,
                         Boston, MA, USA

Edmundo R.               Department of Economics, Finance and
    Lizarzaburu           Risk, Esan Graduate School of Business,
                         Universidad Esan, Lima, Peru

Kamel Naoui              University of Trade of Tunis,
                         Tunis, Tunisia

Elena Precourt           Department of Accounting, Bryant
                         University, Smithfield, Rhode Island,
                         MA, USA

Prodosh Simlai           Department of Economics, University of
                         North Dakota, Grand Forks, ND, USA

| | |
|---|---|
| *Nityanand Tripathi* | Department of Accounting and Finance, ICFAI Business School (IBS)-Hyderabad, Hyderabad, India |
| *Firano Zakaria* | Department of Management, Faculty of Law, Economics and Social Sciences, University Mohammed V Rabat, Rabat, Morocco |
| *Xiaochuan Zheng* | Department of Accounting, Bryant University, Smithfield, Rhode Island, MA, USA |

# INTRODUCTION

The volume starts at the base of economic expansion with an examination of entrepreneurial startups in emerging economies. Then we get insights into using the Capital Asset Pricing Model in the Association of Southeast Asian Nations, compared with the United States. Then follows a cross-sectional analysis of average returns and volatility with focus on the effects of size, value, and momentum risk. Subsequent chapters examine optimal holdings of the United States Treasury securities in multinational portfolios, IPO advertising and possible overvaluation, and the impact of derivatives trading on bank stability in emerging and newly developed countries. We also have studies of currency trading, including the relationship between the cash conversion cycle and corporate businesses in India. There is an interesting study of how demographic change affects economic growth in Hong Kong, plus studies of Corporate Governance among listed companies in Peru. We also have an opportunity to see investments in Russia in a new light – not so much as investments but as the means for transforming public property into the private economy.

John W. Kensinger
*Series Editor*

# TOTAL FACTOR PRODUCTIVITY, GROWTH, AND ENTREPRENEURSHIP IN EMERGING ECONOMIES

Rita Biswas

## ABSTRACT

*This study examines the role of social and cultural acceptance of new ideas and the fear of failure in emerging economies within the context of entrepreneurship and growth (Romer Growth Model, 1986). Using data from the Global Entrepreneurship Monitor and the Panel Regression Analysis methodology for a sample of 22 emerging countries over the period 2008–2014, this study finds that perceived opportunities, knowledge of peers involved in startups, and media attention to startups, all indicators of the social acceptance of entrepreneurship, are statistically significant determinants of growth as measured by per capita Gross Domestic Product and reduction in unemployment. This influence is persistent even after controlling for time effects, despite the liquidity crunch and credit squeeze that occurred during the financial crisis starting in 2008. The fear of failure factor did not have a statistically significant influence on growth, confirming the notion that entrepreneurs in*

The Spread of Financial Sophistication Through Emerging Markets Worldwide
Research in Finance, Volume 32, 1–18
Copyright © 2016 by Emerald Group Publishing Limited
ISSN: 0196-3821/doi:10.1108/S0196-382120160000032001

1

*emerging economy environments, in particular, are prepared to pursue their goals doggedly, even in the face of less than 50:50 odds of succeeding.*

**Keywords:** Entrepreneurship; economic growth; emerging economies; social acceptance of entrepreneurship; fear factor of failure

# INTRODUCTION

"Investment helps countries at all levels of economic development reap productivity gains from new technologies and improve living standards. Investing to support innovation and a skilled workforce is as crucial for China as it is for the U.S.," says Federal Reserve Bank of Dallas senior research economist, Martinez-Garcia (2015). In other words, investing in new technologies and fostering innovation will lead to growth, even in emerging economies. Enhancing entrepreneurship, both at the infrastructure level as well as at the level of the individual's mindset for embarking on an entrepreneurial venture, can facilitate economic development. However, entrepreneurship has risks and it is the serial entrepreneur, undaunted by failure, and impervious to social and cultural biases against failure, whose persistence in the face of all odds will probably succeed. This study is an attempt to identify, through empirical analysis, the extent to which social acceptance of entrepreneurial innovation impacts growth in developing economies. The broader objective of the study is to help develop a research and policy reform agenda for facilitating entrepreneurship-lead growth in developing countries.

Using data from the Global Entrepreneurship Monitor (GEM), Reynolds, Bygrave, Autio, & Cox, 2002, and the panel regression analysis methodology for a sample of 22 emerging countries over the period 2008–2014, this study finds that knowledge of peers involved in startups and media attention to startups, both indicators of the social acceptance of entrepreneurship, are statistically significant determinants of growth as measured by per capita Gross Domestic Product. When controlling for time effects, the availability of financing for entrepreneurs ceases to play a significant role in influencing the per capita GDP. This is consistent with the liquidity crunch and credit squeeze that occurred during the financial crisis starting in 2008.

Traditional economic literature has long established theoretically that apart from the factors of production such as labor and capital (Solow, 1956), ideas play a significant role in achieving long-term sustainable growth (Romer, 1986). There is a wide spectrum of literature providing empirical support for these theories, for instance Bleaney and Nishiyama (2002), Mansfield (1972), Nadiri (1993), Sala-i-Martin (1997) to name a few. The original Solow (1956) growth model established that factors of production labor and capital lead to steady-state growth while Romer (1986) introduced the notion of "non-rivalry of ideas," which allows increasing returns to scale in the production function to lead to long-term sustainable growth in per capita output. Romer's conceptual framework centered round the notion that ideas can be used simultaneously by multiple agents in the economy; use of an idea by one agent does not preclude its use by others.[1] The other two factors of production, capital and labor on the other hand, are "objects" and use of either by an economic agent precludes its use by any other agent.

What role do ideas play in the realm of entrepreneurship? For that matter, what is entrepreneurship? Kilby (1971) once compared entrepreneurship to the imaginary animal, the Heffalump, implying that it could take on different attributes in different contexts.[2] Entrepreneurship, in our context, may be defined as the process of developing an idea into a successful business. The entrepreneur is the generator of the innovative idea and absorbs the risk involved in transforming the idea to a commercially viable production and marketing process. Schumpeter (1911) was the first to establish conceptually that the entrepreneur is indeed an innovator and can be a significant driver of economic development. His later work (Schumpeter, 1942) introduced the notion of innovation as "creative destruction" in the sense that innovation temporarily destabilizes an economic equilibrium. Successful innovators earn economic rents, unsuccessful ones get weeded out and equilibrium is restored once more but in the meantime, development has occurred and the economy has grown. Cole (1942) associated entrepreneurship with purposeful activity and the creation of organizations that employ labor. Not all innovation has to be disruptive globally; innovation could also lead to a slight adaptation of an existing product to facilitate its use by the final consumer or it could lead to a new use for an existing product. Engelbrecht (1997) and Guellec and van Pottelsberghe de la Potterie (2001) are two studies out of a growing body of literature that has provided empirical evidence on the role of innovation in driving economic growth in the spirit of Schumpeter's theories.

Porter (1990), Baumol (1968, 1993) and more recently, Acs (2006), have described theoretically some of the channels through which entrepreneurship can impact the economy. According to Porter, a nation's competitive advantage lies in its industries' capacity to innovate on a sustained basis. Baumol, on the other hand, proves that the longer the gap between the research and development stage of an idea and its transformation to the manufacturing and marketing process, the better is the final product but there is then the tradeoff that competitors might develop a similar product. Wennekers and Thurik (1999) have developed an operational framework for linking entrepreneurship to economic growth. They have drawn attention to the multiple roles played by an entrepreneur. An entrepreneur can not only contribute to the growth of an economy by innovation and the introduction of new ideas but can also foster growth by starting new businesses in new geographical markets. Alfaro and Charlton (2006) provide evidence that entrepreneurship and new firm growth play a significant role in economic development. Entrepreneurial activity has also been shown to stimulate competitiveness and innovativeness and alleviate poverty (Landes, 1998). Finally, for developing countries in particular, a growing body of literature describe the environmental conditions that facilitate entrepreneurship (see Gnyawali & Fogel, 1994; Lingelbach, De la Viña, & Asel, 2005; Manning, Birley, & Norburn, 1989).

Entrepreneurship, however, is difficult to measure (and even define, as seen earlier) and hence empirical studies providing evidence on the various dimensions of entrepreneurship are few. The GEM has changed that the database has developed uniform metrics along several dimensions for measuring entrepreneurial activity, even in less developed countries. Using GEM data, Wong, Ho, and Autio (2005) find that fast growing new firms contribute the most to growth in terms of creating employment opportunities. A second study using GEM data is by van Stel, Carree, and Thurik (2005). They show that entrepreneurial activity by nascent (classified in a stage even prior to early-stage start-ups) entrepreneur and young businesses fosters economic growth as measured by per capita Gross Domestic Product (GDP). They also find that the per capita level of income influences this relation between entrepreneurial activity and growth implying that economies in different stages of development would behave differently.

Despite the existence of the GEM database for more than a decade now, studies on the attributes and social conditioning of the individual entrepreneur and economic growth are nonexistent. This study is an attempt to fill this gap and is unique in three ways: first, it focuses on emerging economies, where the social and cultural acceptance of entrepreneurship and its accompanying high rates of failure, are not the same as in developed countries with consequences on financing issues too. Second, this study takes advantage of the existence of the GEM data for over a decade now; it uses cross-sectional as well as longitudinal data to implement the panel regression methodology, a deviation from the cross-sectional regression methods used in previous studies. Third, it provides evidence during the financial crisis period and its aftermath, spanning 2008 through 2014.

The rest of the chapter is organized as follows: the section "Hypotheses Development, Data, and Methodology" develops the hypotheses and testable implications followed by a description of the data and the panel regression methodology and our specific model. The section "Panel Regression Analysis" presents the results and analysis. The section "Policy Implications, Limitations and Future Research" concludes with a summary of the key findings, their significance and policy implications, the caveats of the current study, and the agenda for future research.

# HYPOTHESES DEVELOPMENT, DATA, AND METHODOLOGY

The social and cultural fabric of developed countries is kind and forgiving to failure, especially in the realm of entrepreneurship. However, this may not be true in several parts of the world. For instance, the Bhide (1996, 2000), strategies, models, and frameworks used for new firms in developed countries do not work in the context of low-income economies and markets (see West, Bamford, & Marsden, 2008, for a discussion of the assumptions that need adjustments in the instance of less developed Latin American economies). Further, as we saw in the previous section, entrepreneurship is about the generation of new ideas, taking the risk for implementing those ideas into a business process, quite likely failing, trying again and again, and possibly succeeding as a persistent serial entrepreneur. Some societies and cultures have beliefs and attitudes that stimulate this risk-taking behavior both at the level of providing an accepting framework for the new venture and at the individual level by not treating the failed entrepreneur as an outcast of society. However, other societies and cultures, primarily in emerging economies, impose an opportunity cost to entrepreneurial activity on individuals and their attempts at starting a new firm. Starting a new business may not be viewed as a desirable career choice due to its instability. An individual who may have failed at her or his first attempt at starting such a firm faces personal ramifications, is held in even lower regard, and will find the sympathy and support of friends and family lacking even further, the second time round.

The financial implications can be even more punitive. To begin with, entrepreneurs in emerging economies struggle to find angel financing, venture capitalists, and private equity funding sources on par with their counterparts in developed countries. Add to that the social stigma and personal ramifications of failure and the scarce financing sources practically dissipate to nothing for a once-failed entrepreneur embarking on a second venture. Intuition suggests that awareness and education at any level about entrepreneurial activity, its inherent risks and uncertainty, and the increased likelihood of success of serial entrepreneurs would reduce this gap between developed and developing countries' attitudes toward entrepreneurship. Rather than focus on total entrepreneurial activity, the focus of this study is to explore the "ideas" generating aspect of entrepreneurship in the spirit of the Romer (1986) growth model. Factors stimulating the idea-generating process in individuals from emerging economies could range from the society's acceptance of failure to angel investors not shying away from previously failed entrepreneurial endeavors and these factors in turn, will lead to higher growth in such countries. However, countries, even in similar stages of economic development, could differ significantly in the beliefs and attitudes toward entrepreneurs and entrepreneurial activity.

Fig. 1 summarizes the conceptual framework in a simple schematic diagram.

We can now posit the following testable implications:

**Testable Implication 1.** Countries with higher social and cultural acceptance of entrepreneurial activity will tend to have higher growth rates.

**Testable Implication 2.** Countries with higher social and cultural acceptance of new venture failure will tend to have higher growth rates.

Precise metrics for these attributes are not easy to come by, especially in developing countries. Fortunately, however, the GEM database has survey data at the national and individual level on certain attributes that can allow us to test our hypothesis about the facilitating and hindering factors behind idea-generation in emerging economies. Further, the GEM data are

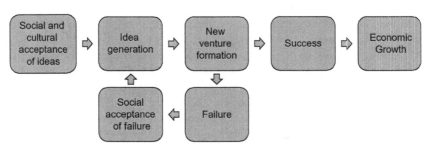

*Fig. 1.* The Flow of the Success or Failure of Ideas to New Venture Formation for Economic Growth.

harmonized across countries and over time, permitting the use of panel regression analysis.

The Global Enterprise Research Association (GERA), in collaboration with London School of Business and Babson College initiated the GEM project in 1997, with the first survey being conducted in 1999 across nine countries. The project has grown in depth and breadth and the 2014 surveys were based on 73 economies. Surveys are conducted toward gathering information on individual beliefs and attitudes from adults aged 18−64 years (the Adult Position Survey or APS database) and about the "eco-system" of entrepreneurship from National Experts (the National Expert Survey or NES database).

For this study, out of the 73 countries for which data were available in 2014, we selected those that were classified as emerging economies by The World Bank. Further, since we wanted to use longitudinal data with a natural cut-off point, we selected a sample period from 2008 through 2014. Our final sample of countries had to satisfy the requirement of having data for all 7 years, which yielded 22 countries.[3]

Next, consistent with the literature, we used natural logarithms of the per capita GDP and the unemployment rates as two alternative proxies for measuring growth. Data on these variables for our sample of 22 countries and 7 years were obtained from The World Bank's World Development Indicators. Finally, we noted that several attributes surveyed in the GEM database, both at the APS and NES levels could be used as reasonable proxies for gauging the varying degrees of social and cultural acceptance of entrepreneurial activities in emerging economies. However, as we note earlier, we selected those that we deemed most relevant for facilitating or inhibiting idea-generation in individuals and be reflective of attitudes and beliefs and social acceptance of entrepreneurship.

Tables 1 and 2 present the correlations between the *complete* set of variables used in each of the GEM APS and NES databases, respectively, as a general reference point. Guided by our overall objective of selecting variables indicative of the social acceptance for generating new ideas and the social acceptance of failure as well as the correlation coefficients to eliminate severe multicollinearity issues, we used inferences from this table to select our final set of independent variables.

For this final subset of independent variables that we used in our regression analysis, Table A1 in the appendix presents the raw data from the APS and NES database for 2008 only, for the purpose of providing the data definitions of All data points for the APS data are expressed as a percentage of population aged 18−64, excluding those individuals

**Table 1.** This table presents the Pearson correlation coefficients of the variables 'GDP per Capita (US$)' and 'Unemployment' with all the variables in the APS dataset.

Column key:
1. GDP per capita (US$)
2. Unemployment (% of Total Labor Force)
3. Perceived capabilities
4. Perceived opportunities
5. Fear of Failure Rate
6. Entrepreneurial Intention
7. Know Startup Entrepreneur Rate
8. Entrepreneurship as Desirable Career Choice
9. High Status Successful Entrepreneurship
10. Media Attention for Entrepreneurship
11. Nascent Entrepreneurship Rate
12. New Business Ownership Rate
13. Total Early-Stage Entrepreneurial Activity (TEA)
14. Established Business Ownership Rate
15. Necessity-Driven Entrepreneurial Activity: Relative Prevalence
16. Improvement-Driven Opportunity Entrepreneurial Activity: Relative Prevalence
17. Total Early-stage Entrepreneurial Activity for Male Working Age Population
18. Total Early-stage Entrepreneurial Activity for Female Working Age Population
19. Informal Investors Rate
20. Growth Expectation Early-stage Entrepreneurial Activity: Relative Prevalence
21. New Product Early-stage Entrepreneurial Activity
22. International Orientation Early-stage Entrepreneurial Activity

| | 1 | 2 | 3 | 4 | 5 | 6 | 7 | 8 | 9 | 10 | 11 | 12 | 13 | 14 | 15 | 16 | 17 | 18 | 19 | 20 | 21 | 22 |
|---|---|---|---|---|---|---|---|---|---|---|---|---|---|---|---|---|---|---|---|---|---|---|
| GDP per capita (US$) | 1 | | | | | | | | | | | | | | | | | | | | | |
| Unemployment (% of total labor force) | -0.16 | 1 | | | | | | | | | | | | | | | | | | | | |
| Perceived capabilities | -0.37 | -0.46 | 1 | | | | | | | | | | | | | | | | | | | |
| Perceived opportunities | -0.42 | -0.47 | 0.62 | 1 | | | | | | | | | | | | | | | | | | |
| Fear of failure rate | 0.35 | 0.16 | -0.22 | -0.31 | 1 | | | | | | | | | | | | | | | | | |
| Entrepreneurial intention | -0.48 | -0.34 | 0.58 | 0.75 | -0.21 | 1 | | | | | | | | | | | | | | | | |
| Know startup entrepreneur rate | -0.14 | -0.38 | 0.56 | 0.40 | -0.23 | 0.15 | 1 | | | | | | | | | | | | | | | |
| Entrepreneurship as desirable career choice | -0.52 | 0.05 | 0.46 | 0.54 | -0.19 | 0.53 | 0.20 | 1 | | | | | | | | | | | | | | |
| High status successful entrepreneurship | -0.26 | -0.08 | 0.31 | 0.30 | -0.13 | 0.27 | 0.35 | 0.42 | 1 | | | | | | | | | | | | | |
| Media attention for entrepreneurship | -0.47 | -0.23 | 0.41 | 0.67 | -0.29 | 0.44 | 0.33 | 0.41 | 0.48 | 1 | | | | | | | | | | | | |
| Nascent entrepreneurship rate | -0.34 | -0.52 | 0.56 | 0.71 | -0.10 | 0.72 | 0.29 | 0.31 | 0.09 | 0.46 | 1 | | | | | | | | | | | |
| New business ownership rate | -0.37 | -0.43 | 0.64 | 0.65 | -0.14 | 0.69 | 0.19 | 0.41 | 0.29 | 0.44 | 0.68 | 1 | | | | | | | | | | |
| Total early-stage entrepreneurial activity (TEA) | -0.38 | -0.53 | 0.64 | 0.76 | -0.13 | 0.77 | 0.28 | 0.38 | 0.17 | 0.49 | 0.96 | 0.86 | 1 | | | | | | | | | |
| Established business ownership rate | -0.02 | -0.24 | 0.50 | 0.16 | 0.25 | 0.32 | 0.09 | 0.15 | 0.19 | 0.09 | 0.37 | 0.68 | 0.50 | 1 | | | | | | | | |
| Necessity-driven entrepreneurial activity: relative prevalence | -0.43 | 0.60 | -0.09 | -0.26 | 0.04 | -0.11 | -0.21 | 0.26 | 0.05 | -0.02 | -0.31 | -0.10 | -0.26 | 0.04 | 1 | | | | | | | |
| Improvement-driven opportunity entrepreneurial activity: relative prevalence | 0.30 | -0.59 | 0.09 | 0.20 | -0.17 | 0.05 | 0.38 | -0.24 | 0.02 | 0.15 | 0.22 | 0.09 | 0.19 | 0.00 | -0.62 | 1 | | | | | | |
| Total early-stage entrepreneurial activity for male working age population | -0.38 | -0.52 | 0.62 | 0.76 | -0.15 | 0.80 | 0.24 | 0.36 | 0.18 | 0.46 | 0.94 | 0.85 | 0.98 | 0.48 | -0.25 | 0.18 | 1 | | | | | |
| Total early-stage entrepreneurial activity for female working age population | -0.35 | -0.53 | 0.64 | 0.73 | -0.11 | 0.71 | 0.29 | 0.40 | 0.14 | 0.50 | 0.94 | 0.83 | 0.98 | 0.50 | -0.27 | 0.20 | 0.92 | 1 | | | | |
| Informal investors rate | -0.21 | -0.32 | 0.42 | 0.53 | -0.16 | 0.57 | 0.34 | 0.23 | 0.11 | 0.12 | 0.57 | 0.45 | 0.58 | 0.12 | -0.17 | 0.23 | 0.59 | 0.55 | 1 | | | |
| Growth expectation early-stage entrepreneurial activity: relative prevalence | -0.03 | 0.01 | -0.26 | 0.13 | -0.24 | 0.20 | -0.27 | 0.12 | -0.03 | 0.01 | -0.09 | -0.08 | -0.09 | -0.42 | 0.06 | 0.23 | -0.09 | -0.01 | -0.15 | 1 | | |
| New product early-stage entrepreneurial activity | 0.17 | -0.31 | 0.41 | 0.37 | -0.05 | 0.23 | 0.03 | 0.13 | 0.09 | 0.23 | 0.30 | 0.15 | 0.28 | -0.10 | 0.39 | 0.27 | 0.28 | 0.27 | 0.38 | 0.40 | 1 | |
| International orientation early-stage entrepreneurial activity | 0.22 | 0.48 | -0.49 | -0.46 | 0.00 | -0.43 | -0.21 | -0.17 | -0.38 | -0.28 | -0.47 | -0.61 | -0.56 | -0.53 | -0.12 | -0.56 | -0.54 | -0.32 | -0.56 | 0.18 | -0.17 | 1 |

*Table 2.*　The table reports the Pearson correlation coefficients of the variables 'GDP per Capita (US$)' and 'Unemployment' with all the variables in the NES dataset.

| | GDP per Capita (US$) | Unemployment (% of Total Labor Force) | Financing for Entrepreneurs | Governmental Support and Policies | Taxes and Bureaucracy | Governmental Programs | Basic School Entrepreneurial Education and Training | Post-School Entrepreneurial Education and Training | R & D Transfer | Commercial and Professional Infrastructure | Internal Market Dynamics | Internal Market Openness | Physical and Services Infrastructure | Cultural and Social Norms |
|---|---|---|---|---|---|---|---|---|---|---|---|---|---|---|
| GDP per capita (US$) | 1 | | | | | | | | | | | | | |
| Unemployment (% of total labor force) | -0.18 | 1 | | | | | | | | | | | | |
| Financing for entrepreneurs | 0.08 | 0.04 | 1 | | | | | | | | | | | |
| Governmental support and policies | -0.06 | -0.11 | 0.52 | 1 | | | | | | | | | | |
| Taxes and bureaucracy | 0.00 | -0.08 | 0.17 | 0.56 | 1 | | | | | | | | | |
| Governmental programs | 0.25 | -0.32 | 0.30 | 0.54 | 0.51 | 1 | | | | | | | | |
| Basic school entrepreneurial education and training | 0.00 | 0.06 | 0.10 | 0.18 | 0.16 | 0.19 | 1 | | | | | | | |
| Post-school entrepreneurial education and training | -0.01 | -0.33 | -0.02 | 0.24 | 0.37 | 0.61 | 0.50 | 1 | | | | | | |
| R&D transfer | 0.44 | -0.21 | 0.17 | 0.28 | 0.26 | 0.68 | 0.29 | 0.54 | 1 | | | | | |
| Commercial and professional infrastructure | 0.24 | 0.13 | 0.06 | 0.08 | 0.31 | 0.21 | 0.46 | 0.38 | 0.42 | 1 | | | | |
| Internal market dynamics | 0.01 | 0.27 | 0.08 | -0.26 | -0.47 | -0.38 | 0.00 | -0.43 | -0.23 | -0.11 | 1 | | | |
| Internal market openness | 0.05 | -0.28 | 0.40 | 0.32 | 0.42 | 0.44 | 0.29 | 0.42 | 0.33 | 0.37 | -0.41 | 1 | | |
| Physical and services infrastructure | 0.27 | -0.28 | 0.02 | 0.14 | 0.42 | 0.41 | -0.11 | 0.21 | 0.31 | 0.15 | -0.24 | 0.20 | 1 | |
| Cultural and social norms | -0.28 | -0.25 | 0.15 | 0.34 | 0.21 | 0.28 | 0.29 | 0.51 | 0.06 | 0.07 | -0.25 | 0.53 | 0.03 | 1 |

already involved in any stage of entrepreneurial activity. The specific definitions for the variables are as follows (quoted from GEM Key Indicators, APS, and NES, respectively, Global Entrepreneurship Monitor, 2008):

1. Perceived opportunities (APS) indicates the percentage of the population, aged 18−64, who "see good opportunities to start a firm in the area where they live."
2. Media attention for entrepreneurship (APS) represents the percentage of the population, aged 18−64, who "agree with the statement that in their country, you will often see stories in the public media about successful new businesses."
3. Know startup entrepreneur rate (APS) represents the percentage of the population, aged 18−64, who "personally know someone who started a business in the past two years."
4. Fear of failure rate (APS) represents the percentage of the population, aged 18−64, who "indicate that fear of failure would prevent them from setting up a business."
5. Financing for entrepreneurs (NES) indicates "the availability of financial resources − equity and debt − for small and medium enterprises (SMEs) (including grants and subsidies)", on a 5-point Likert Scale with 1 implying "completely false" and 5 implying "completely true."[4]

We can now restate our testable implications 1 and 2 as the following hypotheses for our empirical analysis:

**Hypothesis 1.** Countries with higher levels of "perceived opportunities" will tend to have higher per capita GDP levels (or lower levels of unemployment).

**Hypothesis 2.** Countries with higher levels of "media attention for entrepreneurs" will tend to have higher per capita GDP levels (or lower levels of unemployment).

**Hypothesis 3.** Countries with higher levels of "know startup entrepreneur" will tend to have higher per capita GDP levels (or lower levels of unemployment).

**Hypothesis 4.** Countries with lower levels of "fear of failure" will tend to have higher per capita GDP levels (or lower levels of unemployment).

**Hypothesis 5.** Countries with higher scores for "financing for entrepreneurs" will tend to have higher per capita GDP levels (or lower levels of unemployment).

## PANEL REGRESSION ANALYSIS

The regression equation we estimate is:

$$y_{it} = \alpha_i + \beta \cdot X_{it} + \mu_t + \epsilon_{it} \tag{1}$$

where $y_{it}$ is the logarithm of per capita GDP (Table 3) or the unemployment rate (Table 4) as our two alternative measures of growth, depending on the model. $X_{it}$ is a vector of our independent variables; $\mu_t$ is a time specific effect; and $\epsilon_{it}$ is the error term. The subscripts $i$ and $t$ represent country and time-period, respectively.[5]

Eq. (1) was estimated using the Ordinary Least Squares (OLS) regression method and the results are presented in Tables 3 and 4. In Table 3, models (1) through (5) present the univariate results for the impact of each of our five independent variables on per capita GDP, in turn, after controlling for country-fixed effects. Specifically, for instance, models (1) through (5) show that "perceived opportunities" has a statistically significant positive effect (at the 1% level) on per capita GDP while "media attention for entrepreneurs" and "financing for entrepreneurs" also have a statistically significant positive effect (at the 10% level) on per capita GDP. "Fear of failure" has the right sign (negative) but is statistically insignificant.

Table 3, models (6) through (10), shows the influence of each of the independent variables on per capita GDP after controlling for the time effects. The results are stronger. Perceived opportunities, media attention for entrepreneurs, know a startup entrepreneur all exert a statistically significant influence on per capita GDP while financing for entrepreneurs and fear of failure have the right sign but are statistically insignificant.

Table 4 shows the corresponding results with unemployment as the dependent variable. Once again, models (1) through (5) show the univariate results after controlling for country-fixed effects while models (6) through (10) control for time effects too. As expected, the signs are reversed from Table 3. For instance, model (6) in Table 4 shows that after controlling for time effects, perceived opportunities has a statistically significant negative influence on unemployment — the higher the perceived opportunities, the lower the unemployment as more people are encouraged to engage in

*Table 3.* This table presents the coefficients from panel fixed effects models. Specifications (1) to (5) include a vector of country-fixed effects. Specifications (6) to (10) include a vector of country-fixed effects and also a vector of time fixed effects. Variables '2008.year', '2009.year', '2010.year', '2011.year', '2012.year', '2013.year' and '2014.year' are binary, taking the value 1 during the specified year and zero otherwise. The table also gives the number of countries in the sample, the number of observations (N) and within R-squared.

| | (1) | (2) | (3) | (4) | (5) | (6) | (7) | (8) | (9) | (10) |
|---|---|---|---|---|---|---|---|---|---|---|
| | | | | | | Dependent Variable is LN (per Capita GDP) | | | | |
| Perceived opportunities | 0.00813*** (0.00121) | | | | | 0.00829*** (0.00169) | | | | |
| Media attention for entrepreneurship | | 0.00480* (0.00277) | | | | | 0.00601*** (0.00210) | | | |
| Know startup entrepreneur rate | | | -0.00176 (0.00396) | | | | | 0.0106** (0.00380) | | |
| Financing for entrepreneurs | | | | 0.142* (0.0762) | | | | | 0.150 (0.109) | |
| Fear of failure rate | | | | | -0.00418 (0.00349) | | | | | -0.00425 (0.00319) |
| 2008.year | | | | | | -0.0270 (0.0267) | -0.0596** (0.0284) | -0.0412 (0.0334) | -0.0412 (0.0304) | -0.0287 (0.0362) |
| 2009.year | | | | | | -0.0707** (0.0305) | -0.117*** (0.0347) | -0.0978*** (0.0317) | -0.107*** (0.0365) | -0.101** (0.0358) |
| 2011.year | | | | | | 0.128*** (0.0175) | 0.112*** (0.0177) | 0.188*** (0.0312) | 0.109*** (0.0205) | 0.107*** (0.0208) |
| 2012.year | | | | | | 0.0936*** (0.0279) | 0.0727** (0.0300) | 0.175*** (0.0305) | 0.0793** (0.0284) | 0.0889*** (0.0275) |
| 2013.year | | | | | | 0.0912** (0.0333) | 0.0473 (0.0350) | 0.150*** (0.0336) | 0.0551 (0.0419) | 0.0720** (0.0340) |
| 2014.year | | | | | | 0.0560 (0.0425) | 0.00523 (0.0436) | 0.117** (0.0421) | 0.0259 (0.0458) | 0.0365 (0.0434) |
| Country-fixed effects | Y | Y | Y | Y | Y | Y | Y | Y | Y | Y |
| Number of countries | 22 | 22 | 22 | 22 | 22 | 22 | 22 | 22 | 22 | 22 |
| N | 128 | 125 | 128 | 131 | 128 | 128 | 125 | 128 | 131 | 128 |
| R-squared | 0.201 | 0.067 | 0.006 | 0.044 | 0.019 | 0.456 | 0.352 | 0.357 | 0.298 | 0.275 |

*** denotes statistical significance at the 1% level, ** at the 5% level and * at the 10% level, respectively.

**Table 4.** This table presents the coefficients from panel fixed effects models. Specifications (1) to (5) include a vector of country-fixed effects. Specifications (6) to (10) include a vector of country-fixed effects and also a vector of time fixed effects. Variables '2008.year', '2009.year', '2010.year', '2011.year', '2012.year', '2013.year' and '2014.year' are binary, taking the value 1 during the specified year and zero otherwise. The table also gives the number of countries in the sample, the number of observations (N) and within R-squared.

| | (1) | (2) | (3) | (4) | (5) | (6) | (7) | (8) | (9) | (10) |
|---|---|---|---|---|---|---|---|---|---|---|
| | Dependent Variable is Unemployment Rate | | | | | | | | | |
| Perceived opportunities | -0.117** | | | | | -0.117*** | | | | |
| | (0.0445) | | | | | (0.0354) | | | | |
| Media attention for entrepreneurship | | -0.0773** | | | | | -0.0792** | | | |
| | | (0.0336) | | | | | (0.0367) | | | |
| Know startup entrepreneur rate | | | -0.178* | | | | | -0.227** | | |
| | | | (0.0907) | | | | | (0.0895) | | |
| Financing for entrepreneurs | | | | -3.966* | | | | | -4.189* | |
| | | | | (2.158) | | | | | (2.085) | |
| Fear of failure rate | | | | | 0.135 | | | | | 0.144 |
| | | | | | (0.0924) | | | | | (0.0849) |
| 2008.year | | | | | | -1.350*** | -0.913** | -1.100*** | -1.058*** | -1.441*** |
| | | | | | | (0.397) | (0.374) | (0.388) | (0.363) | (0.422) |
| 2009.year | | | | | | -1.110** | -0.442 | -0.816* | -0.688 | -0.865 |
| | | | | | | (0.474) | (0.501) | (0.453) | (0.521) | (0.572) |
| 2011.year | | | | | | -0.259 | 0.0777 | -1.733*** | -0.0834 | -0.0395 |
| | | | | | | (0.314) | (0.325) | (0.562) | (0.328) | (0.429) |
| 2012.year | | | | | | 0.225 | 0.514 | -1.643*** | 0.405 | 0.0309 |
| | | | | | | (0.738) | (0.759) | (0.363) | (0.668) | (0.538) |
| 2013.year | | | | | | 0.247 | 0.828 | -1.174** | 0.940 | 0.441 |
| | | | | | | (0.880) | (1.050) | (0.437) | (1.139) | (0.967) |
| 2014.year | | | | | | 0.476 | 1.269 | -1.007*** | 0.830 | 0.680 |
| | | | | | | (0.845) | (1.047) | (0.337) | (0.966) | (0.777) |
| Country-fixed effects | Y | Y | Y | Y | Y | Y | Y | Y | Y | Y |
| Number of countries | 22 | 22 | 22 | 22 | 22 | 22 | 22 | 22 | 22 | 22 |
| N | 128 | 125 | 128 | 131 | 128 | 128 | 125 | 128 | 131 | 128 |
| R-squared | 0.138 | 0.058 | 0.203 | 0.115 | 0.066 | 0.226 | 0.152 | 0.247 | 0.211 | 0.163 |

*** denotes statistical significance at the 1% level, ** at the 5% level and * at the 10% level, respectively.

entrepreneurial activities. As in Table 3, here too, the results are stronger after controlling for time effects and the fear of failure factor has the correct sign (positive) but is statistically insignificant.

Finally, not surprisingly, when controlling for time effects (models (6) through (10) in both Tables 3 and 4), we note that the impact on the per capita GDP switches from negative to positive by 2011 but unemployment is more sluggish in its response and does not become positive till 2012 (Table 4, models 6 through 10). The financial crisis which started in 2008 played out longer in terms of unemployment and the evidence in this analysis supports that notion.

In sum, the results of our panel regression analyses suggest that hypotheses 1 through 4 are supported empirically while there is no empirical support for hypothesis 5. The intuitive interpretation is that emerging economies in which individuals perceive that entrepreneurial opportunities exist or know of a peer who has started a firm in the preceding two years or know that the media (and hence society perhaps) accepts entrepreneurship, tends to show higher rates of growth in terms of both per capita GDP as well as reduction in unemployment. At the infrastructure level, the availability of financing for entrepreneurs exerts a positive influence on growth by both measures, especially reduction in unemployment. Surprisingly, but fortunately perhaps, negative beliefs about failure, the fear factor, does not seem to exert any influence on hindering growth.

## POLICY IMPLICATIONS, LIMITATIONS, AND FUTURE RESEARCH

This study used panel data on 22 emerging economies during the period 2008 through 2014 to test the influence of several individualistic factors and one infrastructure-related factor on the growth of the economy. Based on the panel regression analysis, the results suggest that an individual's awareness of the existence of entrepreneurial opportunities and peer and social acceptance of entrepreneurship play a significant role in determining the growth of an economy through the channel of innovative ideas and new firm formation. Policy-makers could focus on enhancing these societal factors along with continuing to provide public-private partnerships to foster financing for entrepreneurs as that continues to play a significant role in influencing a country's growth. Individuals who embark on the entrepreneurship path in emerging markets are typically those who are willing to beat the less than 50:50 odds of succeeding in a challenging environment. This is consistent with Zahra and Wright's (2011) call for future research in entrepreneurship to focus on the microfoundations. Academicians, policy-makers, and practitioners can foster that individual determination by providing financing, drawing media attention to the pros and cons of entrepreneurial activities, and making it more socially acceptable.

While this study is one of the first to use the panel regression methodology to the GEM data, some caveats are in order. Future research could control for multicollinearity and perform a multivariate analysis. Further, GEM provides data on entrepreneurial activity classified by gender. Since such differences should be narrowing over time in general, it would be interesting to see how the social acceptance of gender equality varies cross-sectionally, with respect to entrepreneurial activity.

# NOTES

1. This excludes patented ideas.
2. In Kilby's own words, "It is a large and important animal which has been hunted by many individuals using various ingenious trapping devices … All who claim to have caught sight of him report that he is enormous, but they disagree on his particularities. Not having explored his current habitat with sufficient care, some hunters have used as bait their own favorite dishes and have then tried to persuade people that what they caught was a Heffalump. However, very few are convinced, and the search goes on."
3. The list of countries in the final sample are: Argentina, Bolivia, Bosnia, Brazil, Chile, Colombia, Croatia, Dominican Republic, Ecuador, Egypt, Greece, Iran, Jamaica, Macedonia, Mexico, Perú, Russia, Serbia, Slovenia, South Africa, Turkey, and Uruguay.
4. GEM requires at least 36 experts in each country complete their closed questionnaire for assessing the national environment for entrepreneurship. The statements are carefully crafted so that a response of 4 or 5 would imply that, in the expert's opinion, factor may be regarded as a facilitator for entrepreneurship while a score of 1 or 2 would imply that the habitat in that country, during that year, was inhibiting entrepreneurial activity.
5. Based on the correlation matrix, there were some concerns about multicollinearity even within our small subset of variables. However, to test our notion of social acceptance, we wanted to include at least these five variables so only univariate regression analyses were conducted on each of the five independent variables, in turn.

# ACKNOWLEDGMENTS

The author wishes to thank Richa Saraf for research assistance and Andrew McAlpine and Kaita Albanese for data extraction assistance. Financial support was provided by the Center for Institutional Investment Management, University at Albany.

# REFERENCES

Acs, Z. (2006). How is entrepreneurship good for economic growth? *Innovations, 1*(1), 97–107.

Alfaro, L., & Charlton, A. (2006). *International financial integration and entrepreneurship.* CEPDP, 755. Centre for Economic Performance, London School of Economics and Political Science, London. ISBN 0753020610.

Baumol, W. J. (1968). Entrepreneurship in economic theory. *American Economic Review Papers and Proceedings, 58,* 64–71.

Baumol, W. J. (1993). *Entrepreneurship, management and the structure of payoffs.* Cambridge, MA: MIT Press.

Bhide, A. (1996). The questions every entrepreneur must answer. *Harvard Business Review, 74*(6), 119–130.

Bhide, A. (2000). *The origin and evolution of new businesses.* New York, NY: Oxford University Press.

Bleaney, M., & Nishiyama, A. (2002). Explaining growth: A contest between models. *Journal of Economic Growth, 7,* 43–56.

Bosma, N., Acs, Z. J., Autio, E., Coduras, A., & Levie, J. (2008). Global Entrepreneurship Monitor. Executive Report.

Cole, A. H. (1942). Entrepreneurship as an area of research. *The Journal of Economic History, 2*(S1), 118–126.

Engelbrecht, H.-J. (1997). International R&D spillovers amongst OECD economies. *Applied Economics Letters, 4,* 315–319.

Gnyawali, D. R., & Fogel, D. S. (1994). Environments for entrepreneurship development: Key dimensions and research implications. *Entrepreneurship Theory and Practice, 18,* 43–62.

Guellec, D., & van Pottelsberghe de la Potterie, B. (2001). *R&D and productivity growth: Panel data analysis of 16 OECD countries.* STI Working Paper 2001/3. Directorate for Science, Technology and Industry, OECD, Geneva.

Kilby, P. (1971). Hunting the Heffalump. *Entrepreneurship and Economic Development,* 1–40.

Landes, D. (1998). *The wealth and poverty of nations: Why some are so rich and some so poor.* New York, NY: W.W. Norton and Publishing.

Lingelbach, D., De la Viña, L., & Asel, P. (2005). *What's distinctive about growth-oriented entrepreneurship in developing countries?* Center for Global Entrepreneurship Working Paper. UTSA College of Business, San Antonio, Texas.

Manning, K., Birley, S., & Norburn, D. (1989). Developing new ventures strategy. *Entrepreneurship Theory and Practice, 14*(1), 69–76.

Mansfield, E. (1972). Contribution of research and development to economic growth of the United States. *Papers and proceedings of a colloquium on research and development and economic growth productivity,* National Science Foundation, Washington, DC.

Martinez-Garcia, E. (2015). Investment enhances emerging economies' living standards. *Economic Letter,* Federal Reserve Bank of Dallas, *10*(5), 1–4.

Nadiri, I. (1993). *Innovations and technological spillovers.* Working Paper 423. National Bureau of Economic Research, Cambridge, MA.

Porter, M. E. (1990). The competitive advantage of notions. *Harvard Business Review, 68*(2), 73–93.

Reynolds, P. D., Bygrave, W. D., Autio, E., & Cox, L. W. (2002). *Global entrepreneurship monitor, 2002 executive report.* Wellesley, MA: Babson College.

Romer, P. M. (1986). Increasing returns and long-run growth. *Journal of Political Economy*, *94*(5), 1002–1037.

Sala-i-Martin, X. (1997). I just ran two million regressions. *American Economic Review*, *87*, 178–183.

Schumpeter, J. A. (1911). Theorie der wirtschaftlichen Entwicklung. Eine Untersuchung ueber Unternehmergewinn, *Kapital, Kredit, Zins und den Konjunkturzyklus*, Berlin: Duncker und Humblot; Translated by R. Opie (1934 & 1963), *The Theory of Economic Development: An Inquiry into Profits, Capital, Credit, Interest and the Business Cycle*. Oxford: Oxford University Press.

Schumpeter, J. A. (1942). *Capitalism, socialism and democracy*. New York, NY: Harper and Row.

Solow, R. M. (1956). A contribution to the theory of economic growth. *Quarterly Journal of Economics*, *70*, 65–94.

The World Bank, World Development Indicators. Several years. Retrieved from http://databank.worldbank.org/data/reports.aspx?source = world-development-indicators&preview = on

van Stel, A., Carree, M., & Thurik, R. (2005). The effect of entrepreneurial activity on national economic growth. *Small Business Economics*, *24*, 311–321.

Wennekers, S., & Thurik, R. (1999). Linking entrepreneurship and economic growth. *Small Business Economics*, *13*(1), 27–55.

West, G. P., Bamford, C. E., & Marsden, J. W. (2008). Contrasting entrepreneurial economic development in emerging Latin American economies: Applications and extensions of resource-based theory. *Entrepreneurship Theory and Practice*, *32*(1), 15–36.

Wong, P. K., Ho, Y. P., & Autio, E. (2005). Entrepreneurship, innovation and economic growth: Evidence from GEM data. *Small Business Economics*, *24*, 335–350.

Zahra, S. A., & Wright, M. (2011). Entrepreneurship's next act. *The Academy of Management Perspectives*, *25*(4), 67–83.

# APPENDIX

*Table A1.*   This table shows the raw GEM data for our final sample of 22 countries but for 2008 only, for illustrative purposes.

| Economy | APS Perceived opportunities | APS Fear of failure rate | APS Know startup entrepreneur rate | APS Media attention for entrepreneurship | NES Financing for entrepreneurs |
|---|---|---|---|---|---|
| Argentina | 47.33 | 29.89 | 35.19 | 79.80 | 1.94 |
| Bolivia | 54.02 | 38.16 | 46.19 | 60.17 | 2.02 |
| Bosnia and Herzegovina | 45.59 | 22.61 | 42.54 | 60.10 | 2.20 |
| Brazil | 41.44 | 37.98 | 47.89 | 78.00 | 2.30 |
| Chile | 27.34 | 26.54 | 45.93 | 44.18 | 2.42 |
| Colombia | 61.28 | 31.59 | 41.22 | 77.58 | 2.07 |
| Croatia | 44.38 | 34.18 | 52.20 | 61.26 | 2.78 |
| Dominican Republic | 53.56 | 28.08 | 57.34 | 63.31 | 1.86 |
| Ecuador | 41.31 | 30.33 | 38.30 | 56.63 | 1.79 |
| Egypt | 34.87 | 20.35 | 43.79 | 57.40 | 2.27 |
| Greece | 28.11 | 45.50 | 39.15 | 54.86 | 2.76 |
| Iran | 33.72 | 20.47 | 46.28 | 53.41 | 2.14 |
| Jamaica | 51.09 | 26.21 | 50.08 | 70.78 | 2.14 |
| Macedonia | 46.74 | 33.32 | 51.40 | 66.18 | 2.41 |
| Mexico | 47.35 | 27.76 | 52.69 | 52.03 | 2.40 |
| Peru | 56.67 | 34.17 | 56.12 | 71.31 | 2.29 |
| Russia | 30.06 | 56.94 | 35.52 | 50.29 | 2.34 |
| Serbia | 51.22 | 25.84 | 54.02 | 66.80 | 2.71 |
| Slovenia | 44.75 | 25.44 | 53.60 | 67.43 | 2.72 |
| South Africa | 37.23 | 33.50 | 44.86 | 69.22 | 2.73 |
| Turkey | 36.19 | 34.01 | 31.10 | 62.89 | 1.94 |
| Uruguay | 51.00 | 29.24 | 45.13 | 66.53 | 2.10 |

The first four attributes are from the APS database and each number is expressed as a percentage of population aged 18−64 who are not involved in any entrepreneurial activity. The last column is from the NES database and represents the availability of financial resources − equity and debt − for small and medium enterprises (SMEs), including grants and subsidies.

# ESTIMATING TIME-VARYING BETA COEFFICIENTS: AN EMPIRICAL STUDY OF US AND ASEAN PORTFOLIOS

Jordan French

## ABSTRACT

*As the Association of Southeast Asian Nations (ASEAN) becomes an emerging market, US investors will want to know how their favorite method of calculating asset pricing fits into this new undeveloped market. Also, as the ASEAN becomes more internationalized, managers within will look for ways in which the capital asset pricing model (CAPM) can be applied for their needs. This research looks at the capabilities of the CAPM using ex-post time varying and compares it with the traditional constant beta model. The data include five US sectors and five ASEAN countries, for 10 total portfolios. Find that using a simple nonparametric method that allows for time variation is not statistically different from the traditional constant beta model for portfolios. This research provides additional support for the constant beta.*

**Keywords:** CAPM; empirical; time-varying beta; nonparametric; systematic risk; generalized additive model

**JEL classifications:** C22; C52; C53; G12; G15

The Spread of Financial Sophistication Through Emerging Markets Worldwide
Research in Finance, Volume 32, 19–34
Copyright © 2016 by Emerald Group Publishing Limited
ISSN: 0196-3821/doi:10.1108/S0196-382120160000032002

# INTRODUCTION

In the financial literature, there exists a community that uses a constant model approach for studying asset pricing and portfolio decisions. This theory is based on the traditional capital asset pricing model (CAPM) proposed by Markowitz (1952) and Sharpe's (1964) key papers. Another community prefers an intertemporal approach known as the consumption based model, yet it does not work well in practice. Whether using the traditional or consumption based model, the beta coefficient has always been used as a measure of risk in cost of capital, project evaluation, and portfolio analysis.

One of the earliest tests of the CAPM was performed by Black, Jensen, and Scholes (1972). Their study found a positive relationship between returns and beta, in support of the CAPM. However, the difference in returns between high and low beta stocks was found to have created a security market line (SML) that was too flat over time. The flat line, in turn, escalated the evidence that the CAPM had serious shortcomings. Fama and MacBeth (1973) published results showing that while there is a relationship between beta and returns, it was unstable from one five-year period to the next.

The traditional CAPM today remains on top as the most commonly used model to measure and manage risk and portfolio evaluation. Among the econometric alternatives to the CAPM is to use a Kalman filter. This alternative approach is often modeled as a process that calculates today's beta from its overall mean or to its last period beta values in an effort to pursue more accurate estimates. However the Kalman filter is much more difficult to implement than the constant beta models and improved accuracy is questionable. This may be just part of the reason why the simple, straightforward constant model prevails in practice of modern finance. For more on the Kalman filter, see Schaefer, Brealey, Hodges, and Thomas (1975). Thus, for this study instead of the Kalman filter a simpler, nonparametric, time-varying method is used.

Graham and Harvey (2001) interviewed 392 CFOs and found that three-fourths almost always or always use the standard CAPM. With its widespread use on the rise, this research seeks to determine if a simple time-varying model is more appropriate than the constant model for practitioners within the US and ASEAN community, using the recent 10-year period of 2005–2014.

Beta estimates are used as a price for risk that justifies the return for an asset. The CAPM also makes it possible to obtain a discount factor in linear form from the beta coefficients. Betas have always been used as a measure of risk in modern finance and aid in a variety of applications such as testing of asset pricing theories, cost of capital, hedging market risk, as well as in portfolio performance measurement. Betas also assist corporate managers to learn how investors judge the riskiness of potential investments, so that they may use their resources efficiently. Owners (shareholders) communicate with managers indirectly through the stock market by the selling if they disapprove and buying when they like the actions of management. The board of directors see the share price going down or up as a result of the owners' aggregated opinions and turn to management to make corrective action. Managers then try to maximize shareholder wealth by making decisions based on the net present value of an endeavor. The key input to that process is the cost of capital, which depends on the individual project and the risk that goes with it. Managers must understand how investors assess that risk and what risk premium they demand. Estimating the cost of capital and net present value for every project under consideration requires a vast amount of resources to evaluate possible projects. The CAPM remains a simple, straightforward approach to estimate the cost of capital and use historical data to capture investors' behavior toward required returns and their betas.

# LITERATURE REVIEW

As to the significance of the single-factor beta risk models, there is a plethora of studies that support the CAPM. Fama and MacBeth (1973) empirically find a relationship between risk, as measured by beta, and returns. Breen and Korajczyk (1993) claim that tests performed in an attempt to prove factors (i.e., book-to-market) other than beta are significant, suffer from selection bias. Jagannathan and McGrattan (1995) pose that the CAPM may be useful for long-run estimates. Kothari, Shanken, and Sloan (1995) find betas and returns to be significant when using portfolio returns and also demonstrate the book-to-market factor to be insignificant. Lastly, Eisenbeiss, Kauermann, and Semmler (2007) find using a nonparametric varying coefficient model to be both powerful and easy to implement. They used seven replicative portfolios to represent different sectors of the German market. Instead of a Kalman filter, they use a technique that allows the beta coefficient to be an unspecified function of time.

This chapter is structured as follows: the section "Data and Methodology" provides an overview of the data before discussing the methodology for time-varying nonparametric model. The section "Results of Non-Parametric, Time Varying Beta" reveals the main results. The final section draws the main conclusions.

## DATA AND METHODOLOGY

The CAPM defines the relationship between risk and return.

Let, $E(R_i)$ = The expected return investors require for asset $i$, $R_f$ = Risk-free rate of return, using the historical period average, $R_m$ = Market portfolio return, using the historical period average

$$E(R_i) = R_f + \beta_i(R_m - R_f) \tag{1}$$

Main assumptions of the CAPM include the following: Many buyers and sellers who are price takers; all investors invest over the same time frame; no taxes or transaction costs; borrow and lend at the risk-free rate; investors only care about expected return (like high) and variance (like low); and market consists of all publicly traded assets.

*Data*

*Market Return (*$R_m$*) and Risk-Free Rate (*$R_f$*)*
The data in this study use each ASEAN country's own market exchange index to be the market return. Each of the Southeast Asian countries used only has the one exchange and thus accurately represents the market return. For the five US sector portfolios, the Wilshire 5000 index is used to represent the market return. The Wilshire 5000 is a market-capitalization weighted index that includes over 3,500 companies that are all headquartered in the United States (American Depositary Receipts and stocks of extremely small companies are excluded). The index currently includes over 22 trillion dollars of US capital. Thus, the Wilshire 5000 has more diversity than the New York Stock Exchange's (NYSE) some 1,800 companies and a larger capitalization than the NYSE and the S&P500.

Best practices of CAPM are to use a risk-free instrument that corresponds to the length of time the investor wishes to hold the asset. In this study, it is assumed that the investors will be a buy-and-holder and invest for a period of 10 years, hence the 10-year US Treasury bond is then used in all calculations when a risk-free rate is required.


*Asset Returns (*$R_i$*)*

The countries that are ASEAN member nations and have been selected to represent the ASEAN include the following: Indonesia, Malaysia, Philippines, Singapore, and Thailand. The other exchanges of ASEAN member states were not included because their exchanges did not have at least 50 publicly traded companies and/or did not span back to 2005. The five sectors that have been selected to represent the US market include: basic materials, healthcare, industrial goods, real estate, and utilities. Each of the five ASEAN and US sector portfolios has a random sample of 50 individual stocks for a total of 250 stocks for ASEAN and 250 stocks for the United States, 500 in total.

A total of 520 weeks of returns are used for the 500 stocks, six indexes and the US 10-year Treasury bond for a grand total of 263,640 observations used in this research. The stocks were randomly selected by selecting every *i*th company. The companies that were recently listed and do not have the full 10 years of trading history were excluded. Historical data consisting of the weekly adjusted close from the first week of 2005 to the last of 2014 are used. Weekly data are used, instead of daily or monthly, as is best-practice. Over 33% of US companies on exchanges are not traded daily and the ASEAN exchanges contain stocks that are traded even less often. Therefore, using daily data would be inappropriate because it would include the days that the assets are not traded and the value of the asset is not known until a sale is made. The non-traded days would generate returns of 0% and would be incorrectly included in the average, skewing results. This problem is exacerbated within the less frequently traded ASEAN companies. On the other hand, the monthly data are not used because they provide too few data points for statistical importance and would smooth out the variations in price change.

In the selecting of the portfolios, an accurate way would be to use several industry and country specific stock indexes. However, due to lack of information, replicating portfolios were created from 50 randomly selected stocks. This approach is justified by the fact that companies within a sector or developing market share characteristics such as business cycles, tariffs, country risk, technological development, and raw material availability. This method is also commonly performed in CAPM studies and also benefits from the law of large numbers. The correlation between the market indexes and replicating portfolios is 0.8412, indicating well diversified portfolios and increasing assurance in the sample used.

When testing CAPM, most agree to use portfolios and never individual stocks as test assets, as this overcomes the errors-in-variables, data snooping, and information loss issues. The errors-in-variables problem is caused by sensitivity to the risk factors that are specified by the pricing models, which are estimated from data that contain sampling errors. Because factor sensitivities for portfolios are estimated more accurately, than for individual stocks, the factor risk premium estimates will be less biased due to the errors-in-variables problems. Thus, it is best if one uses portfolios and not individual stocks. Portfolios built on characteristics known to predict returns, however, pose a problem. These sorted portfolios, even with weakly correlated factors to returns, are able to explain differences in average returns across test portfolios regardless of economic merit of the factors. A study demonstrating the pitfalls of portfolios built around factors was famously conducted by Lewellen, Nagel, and Shanken (2010). In this research, portfolios are not sorted by any fundamental characteristics. The portfolio method that aggregates firm weekly adjusted returns into an equally weighted portfolio was used, as recommended by Jaffe (1974), and not the capitalization weighted method. As capitalization based portfolios weigh the data with overvalued stocks the market has bid up.

*Time Varying Beta*

Most studies use an elaborate Kalman filter to estimate the time path of beta. In this study, an accessible nonparametric method is used to estimate the time movement of beta. Just as the market beta is more intuitive and easy to fit to data than the intricate consumption beta, so is the nonparametric model to the Kalman filter. The model follows the philosophy of Hastie and Tibshirani (1990, 1993). The approach used in this study was devised by Eisenbeiss et al. (2007). In their study, they find their approach to have "more reliable estimates ... [and] a better manageability compared to the existing econometric approaches dealing with time-varying beta-coefficients." The market model (1) can be generalized to account for the time-variation beta by

$$R_{jt} = a_j + \beta_j R_{mt} + \tilde{\beta}_j(t) R_{mt} + \varepsilon_{jt}$$

$\tilde{\beta}_j(t)$ captures the time-effect within the systematic risk component and the coefficients are identifiable under $\int \tilde{\beta}_j(t) dt = 0$. Therefore, the parametric beta estimate is regarded as the mean value of beta for the whole time period used. The nonparametric approach allows coefficients to no longer be treated as constants, but functions of other variables; though predictor variables are still linear with response variables. $\tilde{\beta}_j(t)$ functions as the multiplicative interaction of the influence of RMT. For fitting data using a varying coefficient, the smoothing parameter ($\lambda_j$) controls the trade-off between bias and variance of the fit. For $\lambda \to 0$ the impact of the penalty disappears and the function bounces between the observations. For $\lambda \to \infty$ it forces the penalty term to dominate and will yield a simple linear regression fit. In this study, an algorithm, proposed by Wood (2000), which determines the "optimal" level of smoothing is used.

As further discussed in the results, the adjusted R2, standard errors, and four different out of sample forecasts were used of differing in-sample input lengths in comparison of the two betas. Additionally, graphs were constructed of the time-varying beta for visual inspection of the effectiveness of the model when used in practice.

# RESULTS OF NONPARAMETRIC, TIME VARYING BETA

In order to further address the major econometric problem of imposing a linear constraint on returns and betas, a time-varying approach is used. Model residuals may suffer from serial correlation and heteroscedasticity. If the first is true, the smoothing parameter selection by Wood (2000) would fail. In the data, autocorrelation was not found based on the Durbin–Watson statistics and a graphical investigation. Some of the portfolios exhibit heteroscedastic errors, as financial data often do, based on the Breuch Pagan statistics and visual inspection of the graphs, Table 1 for statistics. The heteroscedasticity does not bias the beta coefficients and only presents an issue with the efficiency of the coefficient standard errors. The problem with the errors is relaxed using the generalized additive model which iteratively fits weights and will smooth the errors (Nelson, 1991). By plotting the autocorrelation function (ACF), it is possible to check with the eye that the models do not suffer from correlated errors. The ACF plots are available in Fig. 3. Because heteroscedasticity is not correlated with the explanatory variable, the results are not misleading (see Greene & Silverman, 1994, for a proof).

Using the replicating portfolios, the mean values of systematic risk is far below unity, indicating that the portfolios on average are affected by macroeconomic events less than their market index. The Singapore, Malaysia, and Philippines' beta move in opposite direction of their economies, as measured by GDP. Within 2008, these portfolio betas all increase and by 2011 the betas have begun decreasing. This beta movement suggests that when the economy declines their risk premiums increase, and vice versa. US Basic Materials' beta has decreased in risk over the entire 10-year period. Indonesia's beta moves in the same direction as their economy, up, signifying the market may believe there to be a bubble atmosphere and are requiring higher risk premiums as the economy enlarges. Thailand, USA Industrial Goods, Healthcare, and Utilities remain fairly constant and unperturbed by changes in their GDPs. USA Real Estate portfolio beta, on the other hand, increases ever slightly over the 10-year period indicating that it has increased in risk, possibly due to the housing meltdown. Graphs available in Figs. 1 and 2. The portfolios for Indonesia and the Philippines exhibit the least constant betas of the 10 portfolios. Interestingly enough, they are also the least developed markets as far as market capitalization and the most recently opened exchanges.

For performance evaluation, the adjusted $R^2$, Generalized Cross Validation (GCV), and standard errors are used as a measure of overall fit. The GCV approximates the mean-squared error and can account for both bias and the variance of an estimate. In Table 2, the adjusted $R^2$ and standard error are used to measure overall fit of the model, as were used in Eisenbeiss,

**Table 1.** Time-Varying Beta Durbin−Watson (Autocorrelation) and Breuch Pagan Test (Heteroscedasticity).

| Diagnostics | DW Statistic ($p$ value) | BP Statistic ($p$ value) |
|---|---|---|
| Indonesia | 2.2101 (0.9909) | 8.2285 (0.0163) |
| Thailand | 2.3466 (0.9999) | 0.3887 (0.8233) |
| Malaysia | 2.1130 (0.8948) | 4.9085 (0.0859) |
| Singapore | 2.1529 (0.9561) | 8.6359 (0.0133) |
| Philippines | 2.3516 (0.9999) | 5.5491 (0.0623) |
| USA Basic | 2.0475 (0.6934) | 3.6827 (0.1586) |
| USA Healthcare | 2.1223 (0.9131) | 10.4191 (0.0054) |
| USA Industrial | 1.9666 (0.3378) | 6.2376 (0.0442) |
| USA Real Estate | 1.9551 (0.2911) | 8.8021 (0.0122) |
| USA Utilities | 2.0945 (0.8514) | 11.0472 (0.0039) |

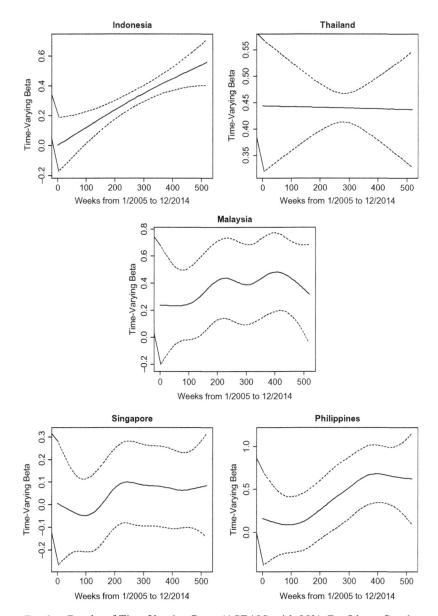

*Fig. 1.* Graphs of Time-Varying Betas (ASEAN) with 95% Confidence Bands.

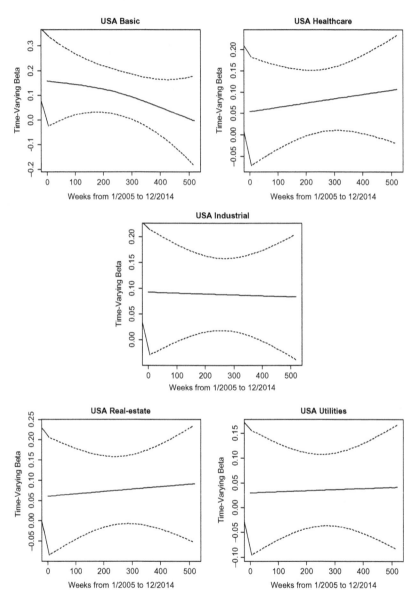

*Fig. 2.*   Graphs of Time-Varying Betas (USA) with 95% Confidence Bands.

Kauermann, and Semmler's research when they compared the constant and time-varying models. The constant beta had a slight edge within ASEAN group, whereas the reverse is true for the USA group; though a *t*-test reveals a failure to reject the null of no difference between the adjusted $R^2$ and standard errors. All of this equates to no statistical improvement in the accessible time-varying approach, and supports the findings of Roenfeldt, Griepentrong, and Pflaum (1978) with contemporary research.

From the results over 10 years, the betas change ever slightly and the trivial changes would equate to less than a 0.01% difference in the expected returns. The 10 time-varying betas are graphed and can be seen in Figs. 1 and 2, along with the graphs inspecting autocorrelation (Fig. 3), and heteroscedasticity (Fig. 4). Thus, for calculation purposes the constant beta models will suffice and the time-varying model is abandoned.

Recommendation for application of the constant beta in developing markets is to use a shorter time period of historical data input. From the graphs (Fig. 1), it can be seen that the ASEAN beta gives the most time-variation. Similarly, Table 3 of the average differences between in-sample expected returns and out of sample actual returns for the constant beta model show a shorter period is better for ASEAN portfolios. Student's *t*-tests also indicate significance between the amount of years used and region for the constant model. Using differing lengths of years as inputs, years 1 (2013), 3 (2011−2013), and 9 (2005−2013) were used with 2014 as the out of sample. Year 5 (2005−2009) was used to predict the out of sample 5 years into the future. In many influential CAPM articles, 5 years of data

***Table 2.*** Performance of Time-Varying and Constant Beta Estimates.

| Portfolio | Time-Varying $\beta$ | | | Constant Beta | |
|---|---|---|---|---|---|
| | $R^2$ (adj) | GCV | Std. error | $R^2$ (adj) | Std. error |
| Indonesia | 0.552 | 0.001 | 0.0137 | 0.5312 | 0.027 |
| Thailand | 0.67 | 0.001 | 0.0142 | 0.6770 | 0.027 |
| Malaysia | 0.886 | 0.0002 | 0.1438 | 0.8904 | 0.014 |
| Singapore | 0.0367 | 0.0001 | 0.087 | 0.0124 | 0.009 |
| Philippines | 0.539 | 0.0012 | 0.1685 | 0.4979 | 0.031 |
| USA Basic | 0.0168 | 0.002 | 0.0493 | 0.0137 | 0.077 |
| USA Healthcare | 0.006 | 0.002 | 0.0361 | 0.0075 | 0.073 |
| USA Industrial | 0.0083 | 0.002 | 0.0345 | 0.0102 | 0.070 |
| USA Real Estate | 0.0026 | 0.003 | 0.0411 | 0.0045 | 0.083 |
| USA Utilities | −0.0019 | 0.002 | 0.0358 | −0.0001 | 0.072 |

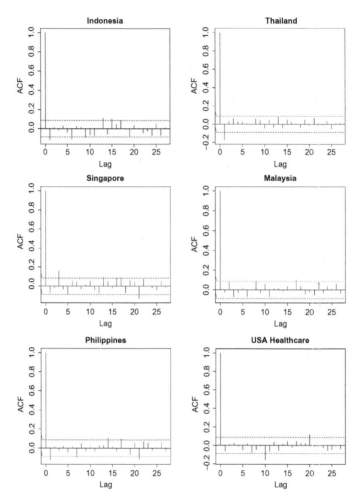

*Fig. 3.* ACF for the Various Portfolios (Time Varying).

are used to forecast out 5 years. As can be seen, the result with this 5 year method is worse than using 9 or 3 years to forecast out only 1 year. For years and regions, it can be seen that using 3 to 1 years of data input is preferred in the ASEAN region, whereas in the developed markets of the United States, more data is better.

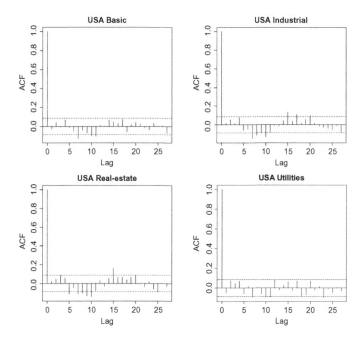

*Fig. 3.* (*Continued*)

# CONCLUSIONS

The most famous coefficient in financial economics and corporate finance is the beta and the constant beta constantly remains the most famed. The accessible nonparametric method for a time-varying beta model proved fruitless compared with the traditional constant beta model. Seven out of ten portfolios had higher adjusted $R^2$s using the constant model rather than time varying. The $t$-tests fail to reject the null hypothesis of no difference between the constant and more involved time-varying model fits. Graphs also indicate over a 10-year period the betas remain fairly constant for the portfolios and actual change is very slight. The simple constant beta method is most widely used by finance practitioners and the like. The results in this research conclude there is no reason to suggest the more complicated time-varying method that does not offer superior performance. The traditional beta model remains a viable tool in estimating the risk coefficients and this research provides additional evidence in the stationarity of portfolio betas.

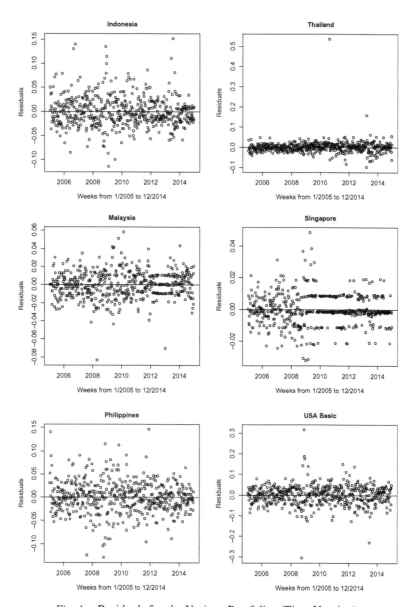

*Fig. 4.*   Residuals for the Various Portfolios (Time Varying).

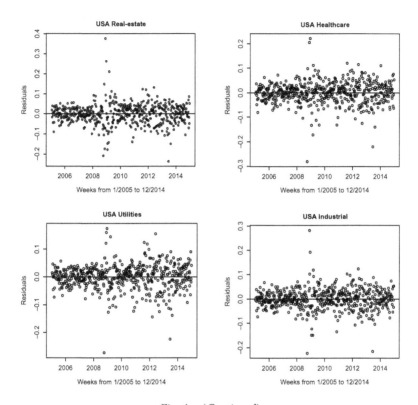

*Fig. 4.* (*Continued*)

***Table 3.*** Average Forecast Errors with Differing Lengths of in-Sample Data.

| | Years and Regions | | | |
|---|---|---|---|---|
| | 1 | 3 | 9 | 5 |
| ASEAN | −0.00209 | −0.00113 | −0.00251 | −0.00253 |
| USA | 0.00997 | 0.00328 | 0.00275 | −0.00305 |

*Notes:* Years: 1 = 2013; 3 = 2011−2013; 9 = 2005−2013 and all use 2014 for out of sample to calculate the forecast error with actual returns. 5 = 2005−2009 and uses 2010−2014 for out of sample forecast.

# REFERENCES

Black, F., Jensen, M. C., & Scholes, M. (1972). The capital asset pricing model: Some empirical tests. In M. C. Jensen (Ed.), *Studies in the theory of capital markets* (pp. 79–121). New York, NY: Praeger.

Breen, W., & Korajczyk, R. (1993). *On selection biases in book-to-market based tests of asset pricing models.* Working Paper, Vol. 163.

Eisenbeiss, M., Kauermann, G., & Semmler, W. (2007). Estimating beta-coefficients of German stock data: A non-parametric approach. *European Journal of Finance, 13,* 503–522.

Fama, E. F., & MacBeth, J. D. (1973). Risk, return, and equilibrium: Empirical tests. *Journal of Political Economy, 81*(3), 607–636.

Graham, J., & Harvey, C. (2001). The theory and practice of corporate finance: Evidence from the field. *Journal of Financial Economics, 60*(2), 187–243.

Greene, P., & Silverman, B. (1994). *Nonparametric regression and generalized linear models. Monographs on statistics and applied probability.* London: Chapman and Hall.

Hastie, T., & Tibshirani, R. (1990). *Generalized additive models. Monographs on statistics and applied probability.* London: Chapman and Hall.

Hastie, T., & Tibshirani, R. (1993). Varying-coefficient models. *Journal of the Royal Statistical Society B, 55,* 757–796.

Jaffe, J. F. (1974). The effect of regulation changes on insider trading. *Bell Journal of Economics and Management Science, 5,* 93–121.

Jagannathan, R., & McGrattan (1995). The CAPM debate. *Federal Reserve Bank of Minneapolis Quarterly Review, 19*(4), 2–17.

Kothari, S., Shanken, J., & Sloan, R. (1995). Another look at the cross-section of expected stock returns. *The Journal of Finance, 50*(1), 185–224.

Lewellen, J., Nagel, S., & Shanken, J. (2010). A skeptical appraisal of asset pricing tests. *Journal of Financial Economics, 96,* 175–194.

Markowitz, H. (1952). Portfolio selection. *The Journal of Finance, 12,* 77–91.

Nelson, D. B. (1991). Conditional heteroskedasticity in asset returns: A new approach. *Econometrica, 59*(2), 347–370.

Roenfeldt, R., Griepentrong, G. L., & Pflaum, C. C. (1978). Further evidence on the stationarity of beta coefficients. *Journal of Financial and Quantitative Analysis, 13,* 117–121.

Sharpe, W. R. (1964). Capital asset prices: A theory of market equilibrium under conditions of risk. *The Journal of Finance, 19*(3), 425–442.

Schaefer, S., Brealey, R., Hodges, S., & Thomas, H. (1975). Alternative models of systematic risk. In E. Elton & M. Gruber (Eds.), *International capital markets* (pp. 150–161). Amsterdam: North Holland.

Wood, S. (2000). Modelling and smoothing parameter estimation with multiple quadratic penalties. *Journal of the Royal Statistical Society, 62*(2), 413–428.

# COMPARATIVE ANALYSIS OF ASSET PRICING MODELS BASED ON LOG-NORMAL DISTRIBUTION AND TSALLIS DISTRIBUTION USING RECURRENCE PLOT IN AN EMERGING MARKET

Kousik Guhathakurta, Basabi Bhattacharya and
A. Roy Chowdhury

## ABSTRACT

*It has long been challenged that the distributions of empirical returns do not follow the log-normal distribution upon which many celebrated results of finance are based including the Black−Scholes Option-Pricing model. Borland (2002) succeeds in obtaining alternate closed form solutions for European options based on Tsallis distribution, which allow for statistical feedback as a model of the underlying stock returns. Motivated by this, we simulate two distinct time series based on initial data from NIFTY daily close values, one based on the Gaussian return distribution and the other on non-Gaussian distribution. Using techniques*

The Spread of Financial Sophistication Through Emerging Markets Worldwide
Research in Finance, Volume 32, 35−73
ISSN: 0196-3821/doi:10.1108/S0196-382120160000032003

*of non-linear dynamics, we examine the underlying dynamic characteristics of both the simulated time series and compare them with the characteristics of actual data. Our findings give a definite edge to the non-Gaussian model over the Gaussian one.*

**Keywords:** Recurrence plot; non-linear dynamics; option pricing; stock market; non-Gaussian; Geometric Brownian Motion

# INTRODUCTION

The daily movement of the stock indices in a particular market indicates the financial dynamics of that market. There have been several attempts to have an approximate idea about the future behaviour of the market. One major attempt to model the stock price behaviour was by the French mathematician Louis Bachelier, who in his thesis on 'Theory of Speculation' in 1901 (Bachelier, 1901) presented a model that pre-empted the Brownian motion. This was further modified by Samuelson to Geometric Brownian Motion (Samuelson, 1965). One of the corollaries of the same is that the stock price follows a log-normal distribution. This hypothesis is one of the foundations of modern financial economic theories, one of the most famous of which is the Option-Pricing model of Black and Scholes (1973) and Merton (1973). Our endeavour was to simulate a Geometric Brownian Motion (GBM) based on data from stock indices of India and examine its validity with respect to actual price. To evaluate the efficacy of the model, we decided to choose an alternative model and compare the relative performance of the two models, using specific tools. The choice of alternative model was critical. Our selection was based on one major consideration. The Black–Scholes–Merton Option-Pricing model gives a closed end solution which makes it so easy to comprehend and use. This implies that the model alternative to the Geometric Brownian Motion model must result in an Option-Pricing model which gives a closed end solution. This is done keeping in view the utility of the model for the investor.

That the distributions of empirical returns of stock do not follow the log-normal distribution have been challenged by many empirical findings. While the derivations are of great importance and widely used, such theoretical option prices do not quite match the observed ones. In particular, the Black–Scholes model underestimates the prices of away-from-the-money options.

This means that the implied volatilities of options of various strike prices form a convex function, rather than the expected flat line. This is known as the 'volatility smile'. Indeed, there have been several modifications to the standard models in an attempt to correct for-omit these discrepancies. One approach is to introduce a stochastic model for the volatility of the stock price, as was done by Hull and White (1987), or via a generalised autoregressive conditional heteroskedasticity (GARCH) model of volatility.

Another class of models includes a Poisson jump diffusion term (Merton, 1976) which can describe extreme price movements. The DVF (Deterministic Volatility Function) approach by Dupire (1994), as well as combinations of some of these different approaches, like that of Anderson and Andreasen (2000), has also been studied. A quite different line of thought is offered in Bouchaud, Iori, and Sornette (1996) and Bouchaud and Potters (2000), where it is argued that heavy non-Gaussian tails and finite hedging time make it necessary to go beyond the notion of risk-free option prices. They obtain non-unique prices, associated with a given level of risk. More recently, other techniques along the lines of Eberlein, Keller and Prause (1988) lead to option prices based on an underlying hyperbolic distribution.

To the best of our knowledge, none of these methods result in manageable closed form solutions, which is a useful result of the Black and Scholes approach. However, Borland (2002) succeeds in obtaining closed form solutions for European options. Their approach is based on a new class of stochastic processes, which allow for statistical feedback as a model of the underlying stock returns. Their stochastic model derives from a class of processes (Borland, 1998) which have been recently developed within the framework of statistical physics, namely within the very active field of Tsallis non-extensive thermo statistics (Curado & Tsallis, 1991; Tsallis, 1988). These stochastic processes can be interpreted as if the driving noise follows a generalised Wiener process governed by a fat-tailed Tsallis distribution of index $q > 1$. For $q = 1$, the Tsallis distribution coincides with a Gaussian and the standard stock price model is recovered. However, it has been seen for $q > 1$ these distributions exhibit fat tails and appear to be good models of real data.

Motivated by this, we simulate two distinct time series based on initial data from NIFTY daily close values. One is based on the classical Gaussian model where stock price follows Geometric Brownian Motion. The other is based on the non-Gaussian model based on Tsallis distribution as proposed by Borland (2002). Using techniques of non-linear dynamics, we examine the underlying dynamic characteristics of both the simulated time series and compare them with the characteristics of actual data.

We find out whether the Tsallis distribution better captures the non-linear dynamics of the index returns.

## DATA

Our analyses are based on S & P CNX NIFTY (NIFTY) index from the NSE (National Stock Exchange, India) website database and SENSEX index from the Bombay stock exchange database. S & P CNX NIFTY is a well-diversified 50 stock index accounting for 25 sectors of the Indian economy. SENSEX is a 30 stock index based on stocks traded in BSE. The data are for the period July 1990−January 2006. The choice of these two indices is obvious as they represent the two largest stock exchanges of India contributing to the majority of stock trading in the country.

## THEORETICAL BACKGROUND OF PRICING MODELS

Theoretical underpinning and algorithm for simulating the pricing models is discussed in this section. Pricing models of GBM is discussed under the Gaussian model. After that, NIG and Tsallis models are described under the non-Gaussian models framework.

The standard representation of pricing model can be given by:

$$S(t) = S(0)e^{X(t)} \qquad (1)$$

where $X(t)$ = stochastic process that governs the stock price dynamics under equivalent martingale measure. $S(0)$ = initial price. The below sections will discuss about the algorithm for all the above mentioned pricing models.

*Geometrical Brownian Motion (GBM)*

The stochastic differential equations for GBM is given by, $\frac{dS_t}{S_t} = \mu dt + \sigma dW_t$, where $\mu$ = percentage drift and assumed to be constant for the period of study. Similarly, $\sigma$ = percentage volatility and again assumed to be constant for the period of study. $dW_t$ is a Wiener (Brownian Motion) process. The solution to the SDE is given by,

$$X(t) = \left( \mu - \frac{\sigma^2}{2} \right) t + \sigma W_t \tag{2}$$

Eq. (1) is used to simulate the GBM pricing.

### Tsallis Distribution

The Tsallis distribution considers the generalised return model as given below, $\frac{dS_t}{S_t} = \mu dt + \sigma d\Omega$, where the noise component $\Omega$ is given by the equation, $d\Omega = P_q(\Omega)^{\frac{1-q}{2}} dW_t$ and $dW_t$ = is a standard Brownian motion and $P(\Omega)$ = probability distribution of the variable $\Omega$, and $q$ is entropic distribution index of generalised Tsallis entropy. Moreover, $\mu$ = percentage drift and assumed to be constant for the period of study and similarly, $\sigma$ = percentage volatility and again assumed to be constant for the period of study. The pricing equation of the Tsallis can be simulated via the following equation:

$$X(t) = \left( \mu + \frac{\sigma^2}{2} P_q(\Omega)^{1-q} \right) t + \sigma\Omega \tag{3}$$

Eq. (3) is used to simulate Tsallis prices.
  The above pricing models are simulated by the $X(t)$ as mentioned earlier. The $S(0)$ is taken as the first day price of the period.

## METHODOLOGY AND APPROACH

We first test all the three series for non-linearity using various established methods for testing non-linearity in data. Once the non-linearity in the data sets is established, we examine the non-linear dynamic properties of each of the simulated time series using recurrence analysis. We now proceed to explain the theoretical background of each of the techniques used.

## Non-Linearity Tests Based on Neural Networks and Taylor Series Approximations

Let us consider a non-linear autoregression involving the last $p$ lags of the variable $u_t$ as follows:

$$u_t = F(u_{t-1}, \ldots, u_{t-p}) + \varepsilon_t \qquad (4)$$

Implementation of the ANN testing framework specifies that the non-linear part of $F(\cdot)$ in [4] is given by $\sum_{j=1}^{q} \beta_j \times \varphi(\sum_{i-1}^{p} \gamma_{ij} \hat{u}_{t-i})$, where $\varphi(\lambda)$ is the logistic function, given by $[1 + \exp(-\lambda)]^{-1}$. As noted by Lee, White, and Granger (1993), this functional form can approximate any continuous function arbitrarily well. The coefficients $\gamma_{ij}$ are randomly generated from a uniform distribution over $[\gamma_l, \gamma_h]$. It should be noted that using random $\gamma_{ij}$ has two purposes. First, it bypasses the need for computationally expensive estimation techniques; second, and most importantly, it solves the identification problem for $\gamma_{ij}$ because these parameters are not identified under the null hypothesis of linearity. For a given $q$, the constructed regressors $\varphi(\sum_{i=1}^{p} \gamma_{ij} \hat{u}_{t-i})$, $j = 1, \ldots, q$, may suffer from multicollinearity. Following a suggestion of Lee et al. (1993), the $\tilde{q}$ in this study is taken to be the largest principle components of the constructed regressors excluding the largest one used as regressors in

$$\hat{u}_t = \alpha_0 + \sum_{i=1}^{p} \alpha_i \hat{u}_{t-i} + \sum_{i=1}^{\tilde{q}} \beta_j \tilde{\varphi}_{j,t} + \varepsilon_t \qquad (5)$$

where $\tilde{\varphi}_{j,t}$ denotes the $(j + 1)$th principal component. A standard LM test is then be performed; Lee et al. (1993) suggested constructing the test statistic as $TR^2$, where $R^2$ is the uncentered squared multiple correlation coefficient of a regression of $\hat{\varepsilon}_t$ on a constant; $\hat{u}_{t-i}, i = 1, \ldots, p$, $\tilde{\varphi}_{j,t}, j = 1, \ldots, \tilde{q}$, where $\hat{\varepsilon}_t$ is the residual of the regression of $\hat{u}_t$ on a constant; and $\hat{u}_{t-i}, i = 1, \ldots, p$. Under the null hypothesis, this test statistic has an asymptotic $\chi_{\tilde{q}}^2$ distribution. Under the alternative hypothesis, this test is consistent, as discussed by Stinchcombe and White (1998).

An alternative two-step approach is to apply the logistic neural network test proposed by Teräsvirta, Lin, and Granger (1993) and Teräsvirta (1994) to the fractionally filtered series. This test approximates the logistic neural network by a Taylor series expansion and tests for the significance of the additional terms when they are subsequently substituted into the model for

$\hat{u}_t$ (see Blake & Kapetanios, 2003 for an alternative interpretation of the logistic neural network test without long memory). The appropriate order of terms will typically depend on the degree of non-linearity in the data. The second-order expansion is

$$\hat{u}_t = \beta_0 + \sum_{i=1}^{p} \beta_i \hat{u}_{t-i} + \sum_{i=1}^{p} \gamma_{0,i,2} \hat{u}_{t-i}^2 + \sum_{i=1}^{p-1} \sum_{j=i+1}^{p} \gamma 1, i, j \, \hat{u}_{t-i} \hat{u}_{t-j} + \varepsilon_t \qquad (6)$$

The third-order expansion, which was recommended by Teräsvirta et al. (1993), is of the form

$$\hat{u}_t = \beta_0 + \sum_{i=1}^{p} \beta_i \hat{u}_{t-i} + \sum_{j=2}^{3} \sum_{i=1}^{p} \gamma_{0,i,2} \hat{u}_{t-i}^j + \sum_{i=1}^{p-1} \sum_{j=i+1}^{p} \gamma 1, i, j \, \hat{u}_{t-i} \hat{u}_{t-j}$$
$$+ \sum_{s=0}^{1} \sum_{i=1}^{p-1} \sum_{j=i+1}^{p} \gamma 2, s, i, j \hat{u}_{t-i}^{2-s} \hat{u}_{t-j}^{s+1} + \varepsilon_t \qquad (7)$$

Clearly, these are all very general approximations with a considerable number of terms and interactions. For the purpose of this study, we decided to restrict the number of parameters in the third- and fourth-order Taylor series expansions by considering only cross-products and powers of up to two lags. Given this restriction, the null hypothesis corresponding to the absence of non-linearity is equivalent to the $\gamma$ coefficients being zero.

### Recurrence Plot (RP)

The initial purpose of RPs is the visual inspection of higher dimensional phase space trajectories. The view on RPs gives hints about the time evolution of these trajectories. The advantage of RPs is that they can also be applied to rather short non-stationary data. The RPs exhibit characteristic large scale and small scale patterns. The first patterns were denoted by Eckmann, Kamphorst, and Ruelle (1987) as typology and the latter as texture. The typology offers a global impression which can be characterised as homogeneous, periodic, drift, and disrupted.

The closer inspection of the RPs reveals small scale structures (the texture) which are single dots, diagonal lines, as well as vertical and horizontal lines (the combination of vertical and horizontal lines obviously forms rectangular clusters of recurrence points).

Single, isolated recurrence points can occur if states are rare, if they do not persist for any time or if they fluctuate heavily. However, they are not a unique sign of chance or noise (e.g., in maps).

A diagonal line $R_{i+k,j+k} = 1$ (for $k = 1 \ldots l$, where $l$ is the length of the diagonal line) occurs when a segment of the trajectory runs parallel to another segment, that is, the trajectory visits the same region of the phase space at different times. The length of this diagonal line is determined by the duration of such similar local evolution of the trajectory segments. The direction of these diagonal structures can differ. Diagonal lines parallel to the line of identity (LOI) (angle $\pi$) represent the parallel running of trajectories for the same time evolution. The diagonal structures perpendicular to the LOI represent the parallel running with contrary times (mirrored segments; this is often a hint for an inappropriate embedding). Since the definition of the Lyapunov exponent uses the time of the parallel running of trajectories, the relationship between the diagonal lines and the Lyapunov exponent is obvious.

A vertical (horizontal) line $R_{i+k,j+k} = 1$ (for $k = 1 \ldots v$, where $v$ is the length of the vertical line) marks a time length in which a state does not change or changes very slowly. It seems that the state is trapped for some time. This is a typical behaviour of laminar states (intermittency).

These small scale structures are the base of a quantitative analysis of the RPs. The visual interpretation of RPs requires some experience. The study of RPs from paradigmatic systems gives a good introduction into characteristic typology and texture. However, their quantification offers a more objective way for the investigation of the considered system. With this quantification, the RPs have become more and more popular within a growing group of scientists who use RPs and their quantification techniques for data analysis. A detailed discussion on the application and interpretation of RP and the various structures revealed by RP is found in Marwan, Romano, Thiel, and Kurths (2007).

The most natural question relates to the way of choosing an appropriate value for the time delay $d$ and the embedding dimension $m$. Several methods have been developed to best guess $m$ and $d$.

The most often used methods are the average mutual information function (AMI) for the time delay, as introduced by Fraser and Swinney (1986) and the false nearest neighbours (FNN) method for the embedding dimension developed by Kennel, Brown, and Abarbanel (1992).

First of all, the time delay has to be estimated. In the first one, the value for which the autocorrelation function $C(d)$ first passes through zero is searched, which gives $d$. In the second, one chooses the first minimum location of the average mutual information function, where the mutual information function $S(d)$ is defined in the usual manner. The value $d$ that firstly minimises the quantity $S(d)$ is the method choice for finding a reasonable time delay.

The difference between these two methods resides in the fact that while the first looks for linear independence, the second measures a general dependence of two variables. For this reason, the second method seems to be preferred in non-linear time series analysis.

On the other hand, the method used to find the embedding dimension is based on the concept of a false neighbour. A false neighbour is a point in the data set that looks like a neighbour to another because the orbit is seen in an overly small embedding space. For example, two points on a circle can appear close to each other, even though they are not, if, for example, the circle is seen sideways (as a projection), thus is appearing as a line segment. Therefore, increasing by one the dimension $m$ of the reconstructed space often permits one to differentiate between the points of the orbit, that is, those which are true neighbours and those which are not.

*Quantification of Recurrence Plots (Recurrence Quantification Analysis) with Confidence Intervals*

The recurrence quantification analysis (RQA) is a method of non-linear data analysis which quantifies the number and duration of recurrences of a dynamical system presented by its phase space trajectory.

A quantification of RPs was developed by Zbilut and Webber Jr. (1992) and extended with new measures of complexity by Marwan (2003). Measures that are based on diagonal structures are able to find chaos-order transitions (Trulla, Giuliani, Zbilut, & Webber, 1996), and measures based on vertical (horizontal) structures are able to find chaos-chaos transitions (laminar phases) (Marwan & Kurths, 2002).

These measures can be computed in windows along the main diagonal. This allows us to study their time dependence and can be used for the detection of transitions (Trulla, Giuliani, Zbilut, & Webber, 1996). Another possibility is to define these measures for each diagonal parallel to the main diagonal separately (Marwan & Kurths, 2002). This approach enables the study of time delays, unstable periodic orbits (UPOs; Gilmore, 1998; Lathrop & Kostelich, 1989), and by applying to cross RPs, the assessment of similarities between processes (Marwan & Kurths, 2002). The complexity measures the RQA provides have been useful in describing and analysing a broad range of data. But one key question in empirical research concerns the confidence bounds of measured data. However, Schinkel, Marwan, Dimigen, and Kurths (2009) have recently presented one for RQA measures. We have used the following RQA measures: (a) Determinism (DET), (b) average lengths of the diagonal lines ($L$), (c) Laminarity (LAM), (d) Trapping Time (TT). For a detailed discussion of these measures, we recommend Marwan, Romano, Thiel, and Kurths (2007) and Schinkel, Marwan, Dimigen, and Kurths (2009).

We have used 95% confidence level for computation of these measures. Our next section deals with discussion of the results of our tests.

# EMPIRICAL RESULTS

## Test for Non-Linearity

### White's Neural Network Test

Tables 1 and 2 summarise the findings of White's neural network test for non-linearity in data.

**Table 1.** Results of White's Neural Network Test for NIFTY Data Set and the Corresponding Simulations based on GBM and Borland Model.

Data: Brownian
$X$-squared = 8.1479, d$f$ = 2, $p$-value = 0.01701
Data: Borland
$X$-squared = 12.9638, d$f$ = 2, $p$-value = 0.001865
Data: NIFTY
$X$-squared = 13.1307, d$f$ = 2, $p$-value = 0.001408

**Table 2.** Results of White's Neural Network Test for SENSEX Data Set and the Corresponding Simulations Based on GBM and Borland Model.

Data: SENSEX
$X$-squared = 7.5072, d$f$ = 2, $p$-value = 0.02343
Data: Brownian
$X$-squared = 6.1086, d$f$ = 2, $p$-value = 0.04716
Data: Borland
$X$-squared = 6.3873, d$f$ = 2, $p$-value = 0.04102

**Table 3.** Results of Teräsvirta Neural Network Test for NIFTY Data Set and the Corresponding Simulations Based on GBM and Borland Model.

Data: Brownian
$X$-squared = 10.8971, d$f$ = 2, $p$-value = 0.004303
Data: Borland
$X$-squared = 12.061, d$f$ = 2, $p$-value = 0.002404
Data: NIFTY
$X$-squared = 13.4945, d$f$ = 2, $p$-value = 0.001174

**Table 4.** Results of Teräsvirta Neural Network Test for SENSEX Data Set and the Corresponding Simulations Based on GBM and Borland Model.

Data: SENSEX
$X$-squared = 7.5677, d$f$ = 2, $p$-value = 0.02273
Data: Brownian
$X$-squared = 6.5633, d$f$ = 2, $p$-value = 0.03757
Data: Borland
$X$-squared = 7.6876, d$f$ = 2, $p$-value = 0.02141

As is evident from the results earlier, both simulated series, as well as the original time series representing the daily close of NIFTY and SENSEX reject the hypothesis of linearity.

*Teräsvirta Neural Network Test*
We now present the test results of Teräsvirta Neural Network test (Table 3 and 4).

We can clearly see that like all the previous tests before, this test also establishes the fact that there is presence of significant non-linearity in the time series representing the daily close values of NIFTY and SENSEX. We also see that both the simulated series depict a significant presence of non-linearity. But we cannot comment on whether the nature of non-linearity is same in all the time series or not. Thus, understanding the necessity of further investigation we proceed with recurrence analysis of the respective series.

*Recurrence Plot and Recurrence Quantification Analysis*

For an economic time series, a RP will reveal the changes in dynamics of the time series. By examining the structures in the RP, one can decipher in what state the system was during a particular time regime. Our purpose is to compare the time states of the respective time series representing the original data set and the simulations thereof and find out how much of the different dynamic states as revealed by the RP of the original data set match with those in the simulated data series. Through our comparison, we can then reach a conclusion as to which simulation captures the dynamics of the original data set much better.

Using the methods mentioned above we have used an embedding dimension of 2 and a delay parameter of 1 for NIFTY data set and SENSEX data set. We used the unthresholded RP so that we can capture all minute changes. For RQA, we used the same embedding parameters and a threshold value of 0.1. We used a bootstrap sample size of 500 and confidence level of 95%.

Figs. 1–3 show the trend graph of NIFTY daily closing, the corresponding simulated time series based on Geometric Brownian Motion (Eq. (2)), and Borland model (Eq. (3)), respectively. Figs. 4–6 show the trend graph of SENSEX daily closing, the corresponding simulated time series based on Geometric Brownian Motion (Eq. (2)), and Borland model (Eq. (3.3)), respectively. Fig. 7 represents the RP of NIFTY, Fig. 8 represents the RP of simulated time series based on Geometric Brownian Motion given by Eq. (2) and Fig. 9 represents the RP of simulated time series based on Borland model given by Eq. (3.3). Fig. 10 represents the RP of SENSEX,

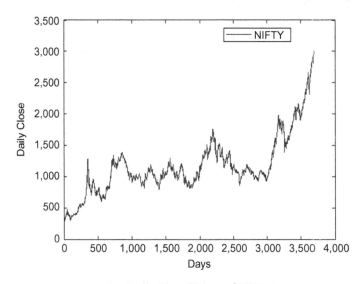

*Fig. 1.* Daily Close Values of NIFTY.

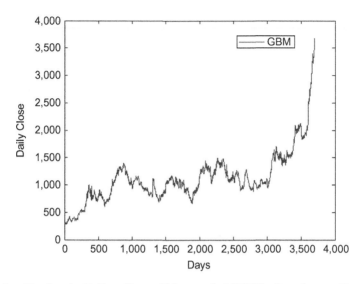

*Fig. 2.* Simulated Daily Close Values of NIFTY Based on Geometric Brownian Motion.

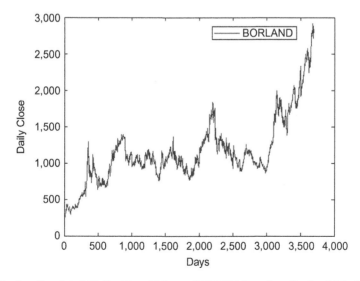

*Fig. 3.* Simulated Daily Close Values of NIFTY Based on Borland Model.

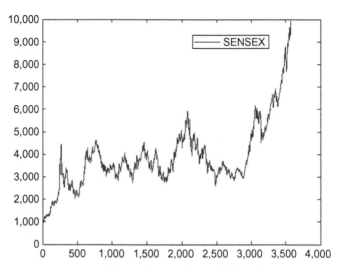

*Fig. 4.*   Daily Close Values of SENSEX.

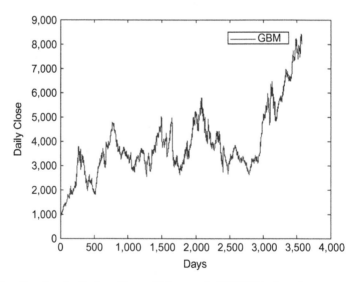

*Fig. 5.*   Simulated Daily Close Values of SENSEX Based on Geometric Brownian Motion.

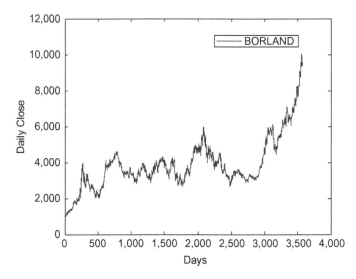

*Fig. 6.* Simulated Daily Close Values of SENSEX Based on Borland Model.

Fig. 11 represents the RP of simulated time series based on Geometric Brownian Motion given by Eq. (2), and Fig. 12 represents the RP of simulated time series based on Borland model given by Eq. (3.3). The colour patterns in RP represents the recurrence distance which in turn indicates the level of complexity moving from pure random at the yellow or lightest colour to highly complex at blue or darkest colour. The presence of any dark band indicates a phase change which is analogous to a formation of a trend in economic systems (Guhathakurta, Bhattacharya, & Roychowdhury, 2010a, 2010b).

We find both the simulated models represent the basic non-linear dynamics of the actual data as shown by a dark band toward the end indicating emergence of a trend, a bubble, in this case, preceded by lighter areas representing random behaviour. The similar colour patterns indicate that the recurrences of states are similar. If we look closely at the RPs, we can see that a large part in the middle is red and yellow in case of NIFTY indicating randomness. A first look suggests that both the models capture the dynamics of the original data set rather properly.

However, a closer inspection tells us that the simulation based on the Borland model almost replicates the original data set in its RP while the GBM based simulation differs in colour pattern in certain places. For example, the dark blue band emanates from the point $x = 3,500$ suggesting

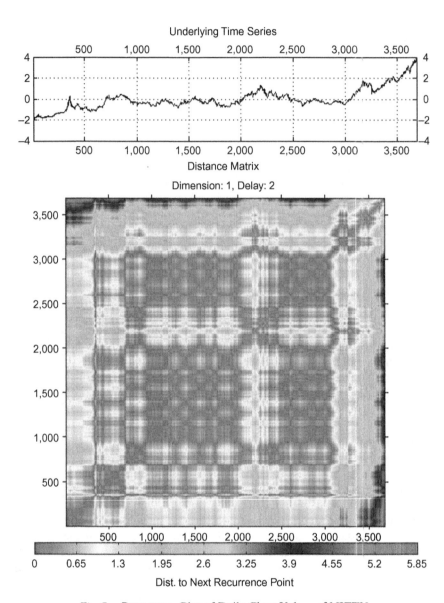

*Fig. 7.*   Recurrence Plot of Daily Close Values of NIFTY.

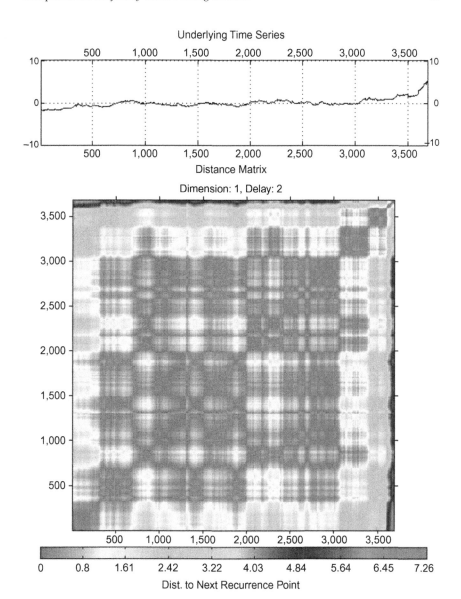

*Fig. 8.* Recurrence Plot of Simulated Daily Close Values of NIFTY Based on Geometric Brownian Motion.

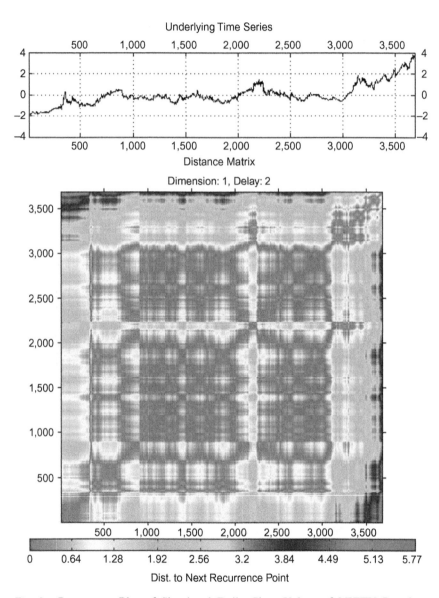

*Fig. 9.*  Recurrence Plot of Simulated Daily Close Values of NIFTY Based on Borland Model.

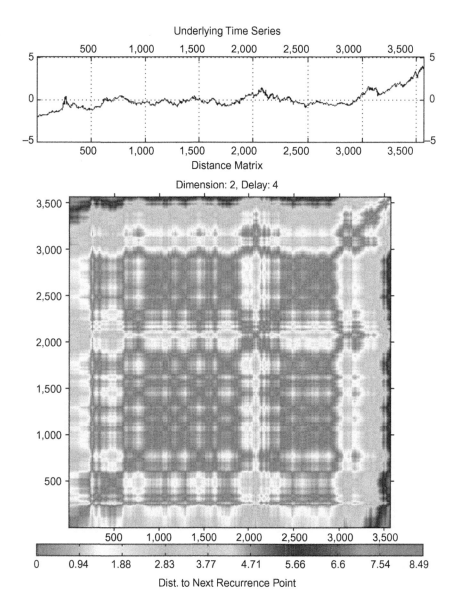

*Fig. 10.*    Recurrence Plot of Daily Close Values of SENSEX.

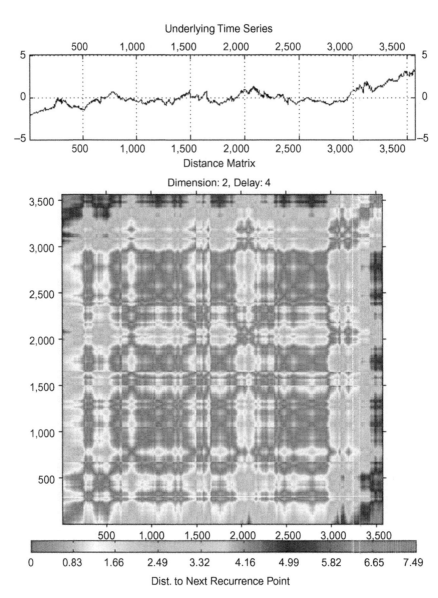

*Fig. 11.* Recurrence Plot of Simulated Daily Close Values of SENSEX Based on Geometric Brownian Motion.

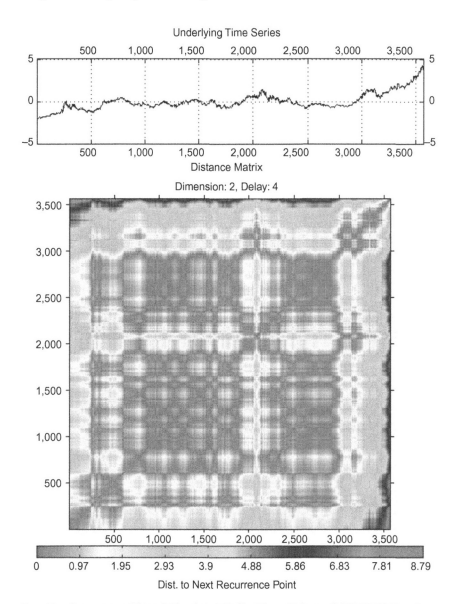

*Fig. 12.* Recurrence Plot of Simulated Daily Close Values of SENSEX Based on Borland Model.

a change in trend from day 3,500 in original Nifty data set (Fig. 7). We find
the same occurrence in the RP of the simulated data series based on
Borland model (Fig. 9). In case of the simulation based on GBM (Fig. 8),
however, we find the dark band emanating at a much later period which
suggests that this model fails to capture the same dynamics as closely as the
Borland model. In case of SENSEX, a similar picture emerges. Again we
find that although both the models capture the essential dynamics of the
original data set as suggested by their respective RPs, the Borland model
(Fig. 12) almost replicates the RP of the original data set (Fig. 10) while
there are some differences in the recurrence pattern of the data set representing simulation based on GBM model (Fig. 11).

A close look at the RQA results (Figs. 13−20) reveals a similar story.
We do not concentrate on the absolute values of the DET, $L$, LAM, and
TT measures. Instead we try to look at the comparative analysis of the
values. We specifically try to detect whether the RQA measures of a simulated series closely resembles those of the original series.

If we see the emergence of the values of DET, $L$, LAM, and TT for
NIFTY and Borland model, we find that though there are some differences
the values change in a similar pattern and is much more synchronised when
compared to NIFTY and GBM model. This shows that the changes in

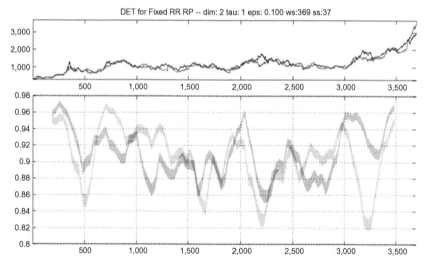

*Fig. 13.*   DET Values of NIFTY (Upper) and Simulated Series Based on GBM
Model (Lower).

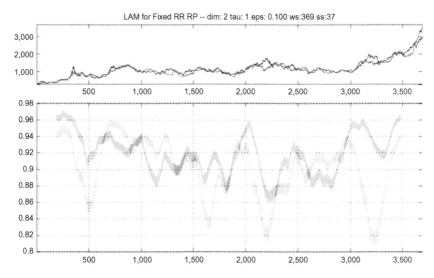

*Fig. 14.* LAM Values of NIFTY (Upper) and Simulated Series Based on GBM Model (Lower).

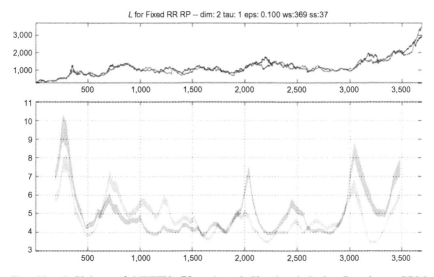

*Fig. 15.* L Values of NIFTY (Upper) and Simulated Series Based on GBM Model (Lower).

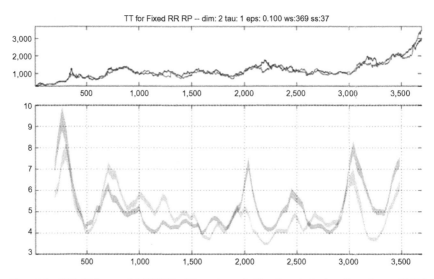

*Fig. 16.* TT Values of NIFTY (Upper) and Simulated Series Based on GBM Model (Lower).

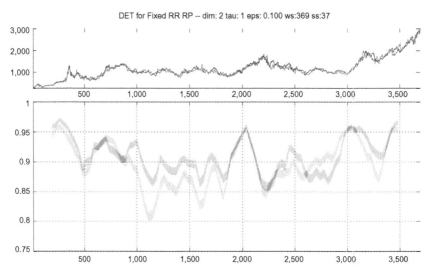

*Fig. 17.* DET Values of NIFTY (Upper) and Simulated Series Based on Borland Model (Lower).

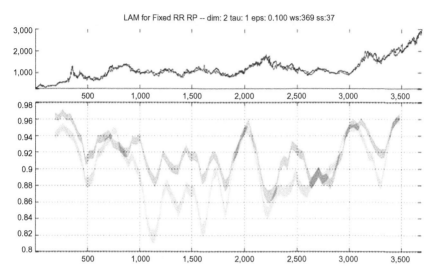

*Fig. 18.* LAM Values of NIFTY (Upper) and Simulated Series based on Borland Model (Lower).

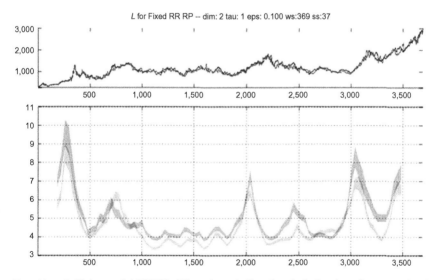

*Fig. 19.* L Values of NIFTY (Upper) and Simulated Series based on Borland Model (Lower).

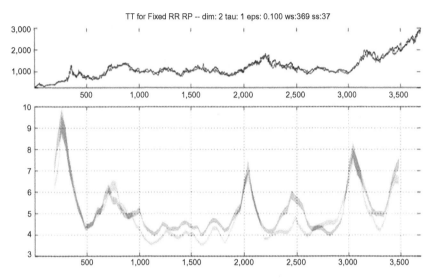

*Fig. 20.* TT Values of NIFTY (Upper) and Simulated Series Based on Borland
Model (Lower).

underlying dynamics of the original data set are much better captured by
the Borland model than the classical GBM model. If we look at the RQA
values for SENSEX data (Figs. 21–28), a similar picture emerges. Here
again, we find that the RQA values of original data set and simulation
based on Borland model appear much more synchronised than the RQA
values in case of the original data set and GBM combination. We find that
in case of NIFTY data set during the epoch between day 2,500 and day
3,000, there is a dip in the DET values showing a decrease in Determinism.
But in case of the GBM model, it is just the opposite. However, the
Borland model almost replicates this phenomenon. A similar picture
emerges in case of SENSEX data set as well. If we look carefully at
the change in values, the DET values take a dip between day 2,500 and day
3,000, whereas the opposite happens in case of the simulated data set based
on GBM. On the other hand, the values for the data set of simulation
based on Borland model more or less follow the same path as the original
data set. Our findings lead to the conclusion that the dynamic behaviour of
the time series as revealed by the RQA statistics is better captured by the
Borland model than the GBM model both in case of NIFTY and SENSEX
because the latter is based on a statistical distribution that allows for statistical feedback.

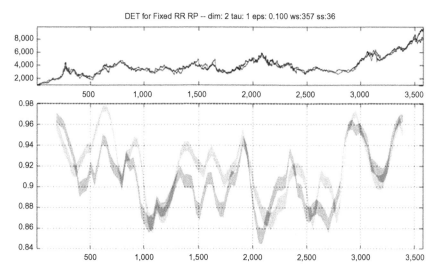

*Fig. 21.* DET Values of SENSEX (Upper) and Simulations Based on GBM Model (Lower).

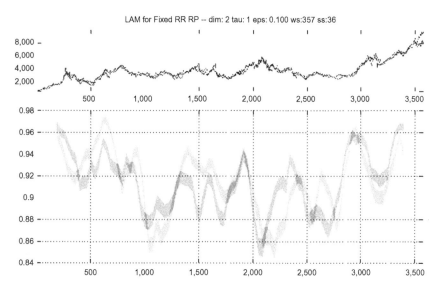

*Fig. 22.* LAM Values of SENSEX (Upper) and Simulations Based on GBM Model (Lower).

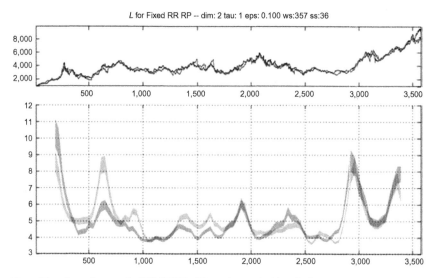

*Fig. 23.* *L* values of SENSEX (Upper) and Simulations Based on GBM Model (Lower).

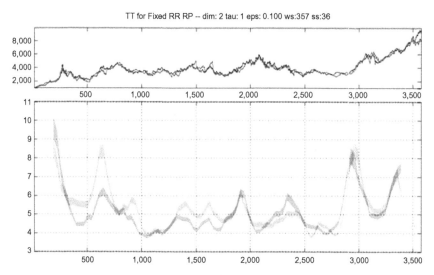

*Fig. 24.* TT Values of SENSEX (Upper) and Simulations Based on GBM Model (Lower).

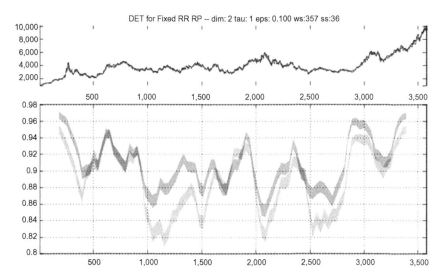

*Fig. 25.* DET Values of SENSEX (Upper) and Simulations Based on Borland
Model (Lower).

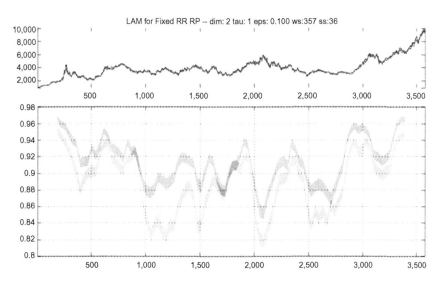

*Fig. 26.* LAM Values of SENSEX (Upper) and Simulations Based on Borland
Model (Lower).

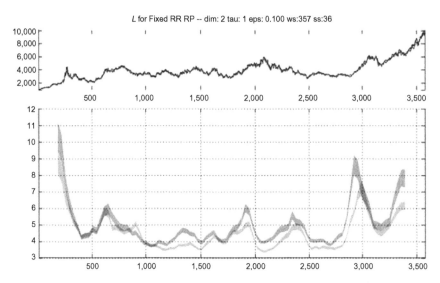

*Fig. 27.* *L* values of **SENSEX** (Upper) and Simulations Based on Borland
Model (Lower).

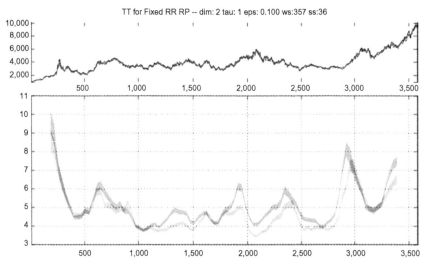

*Fig. 28.* TT Values of **SENSEX** (Upper) and Simulations Based on Borland
Model (Lower).

# EMPIRICAL EVIDENCE ON BORLAND AND GBM MODEL

Our findings enable us to comment on the efficacy of the Borland (2002) proposed model over the Black–Scholes model. Our RP analysis showed that out of the two, Borland model captures the essential dynamics of the original data set much better. An inspection of the RQA revealed a similar picture. Our findings indicate that at micro epoch level the pricing model using Tsallis distribution captures the time series dynamics of the actual data set better than the simulation using Geometric Brownian Motion assumption.

This acts as an empirical validation of the underlying theoretical framework of the Option-Pricing model. The Borland model being a major closed end solution to Option-Pricing can become an alternative to the BS model as a benchmark tool for the investors. Taking all findings into account, we can propose that the Geometric Brownian Motion assumption needs to be replaced by the model based on Tsallis distribution. This means that for the data set representing the Indian market, the return distribution is indeed fat tailed and using a Tsallis distribution, therefore, we are able to catch the non-linear dynamics of the original data set. The implication for Option-Pricing model is that the same assumption from the Black–Scholes–Merton pricing theory is to be replaced by the new one based on Tsallis distribution. This further means that the solution derived by Borland (2002) may be considered as a viable alternative, at least for Indian conditions.

# REFERENCES

Anderson, L., & Andreasen, J. (2000). Jump-diffusion processes: Volatility smile fitting and numerical methods for pricing. *Review of Derivatives Research, 4*, 231–262.

Bachelier, L. (1901). Théorie mathématique du jeu. *Annales Scientifiques de l'Ecole Noemale Supéreure, 18*, 143–210.

Black, F., & Scholes, M. (1973). The valuation of option contracts in a test of market efficiency. *Journal of Finance, 27*, 399–417.

Blake, A. P., & Kapetanios, G. (2003). A radial basis function artificial neural network test for neglected nonlinearity. *Econometrics Journal, 6*, 357–373.

Borland, L. (1998). Microscopic dynamics of the nonlinear Fokker-Planck equation: A phenomenological model. *Physical Review E, 57*, 6634.

Borland, L. (2002). A theory of non-Gaussian option pricing. *Quantitative Finance, 2*, 415–431.

Bouchaud, J.-P., Iori, G., & Sornette, D. (1996). Real-world options. *Risk, 9*(3), 61–65.

Bouchaud, J.-P., & Potters, M. (2000). *Theory of financial risks.* New York, NY: Cambridge University Press.

Curado, E., & Tsallis, C. (1991). Generalized statistical mechanics connection with thermodynamics. *Journal of Physics A, 24,* L 69.

Dupire, B. (1994). Pricing with a smile. *Risk, 7,* 18–20.

Eberlein, E., Keller, U., & Prause, K. (1988). New insights into smile, mispricing and value at risk: The hyperbolic model. *Journal of Business, 71,* 371.

Eckmann, J., Kamphorst, S., & Ruelle, D. (1987). Recurrence plot of dynamical system. *Europhysics Letters, 4,* 973–977.

Fraser, A., & Swinney, M. L. H. (1986). Independent coordinates for strange attractors from mutual information. *Physical Review A, 33,* 1134–1140.

Gilmore, R. (1998). Topological analysis of chaotic dynamical systems. *Review of Modern Physics, 70*(4), 1455–1529.

Guhathakurta, K., Bhattacharya, B., & Roychowdhury, A. (2010a). An examination of critical periods of stock price movements using recurrence plot. In B. Bhattacharya & M. Roy (Eds.), *Essays in finance* (pp. 98–111). New Delhi: Allied Publishers.

Guhathakurta, K., Bhattacharya, B., & Roychowdhury, A. (2010b). Using recurrence plot analysis to distinguish between endogenous and exogenous stock market crashes. *Physica A, 389*(9), 1874–1882.

Hull, J., & White, A. (1987). The pricing of options on assets with stochastic volatility. *Journal of Finance, 42,* 281–300.

Kennel, M. B., Brown, R., & Abarbanel, H. D. (1992). Determining embedding dimension for phase-space reconstruction using a geometrical construction. *Physical Review A, 45,* 3403–3411.

Lathrop, D. P., & Kostelich, E. J. (1989). Characterization of an experimental strange attractor by periodic orbits. *Physical Review A, 40*(7), 4028–4031.

Lee, T. H., White, H., & Granger, C. W. (1993). Testing for neglected nonlinearity in time series models. *Journal of Econometrics, 56,* 269–290.

Marwan, N. (2003). *Encounters with neighbours – Current developments of concepts based on recurrence plots and their applications.* Potsdam: University of Potsdam.

Marwan, N., & Kurths, J. (2002). Nonlinear analysis of bivariate data with cross recurrence plots. *Physics Letters A, 302*(5–60), 299–307.

Marwan, N., Romano, M. C., Thiel, M., & Kurths, J. (2007). Recurrence plots for the analysis of complex systems. *Physics Reports, 438*(5–6), 237–329.

Merton, R. (1973). The theory of rational option-pricing. *The Bell Journal of Economics and Management Science, 4,* 141–183.

Merton, R. (1976). Option-pricing when underlying stock returns are discontinuous. *Journal of Financial Economics, 3,* 125–144.

Samuelson, P. (1965). Proof that property anticipated prices fluctuate randomly. *Industrial Management Review, VI,* 41–49.

Schinkel, S., Marwan, N., Dimigen, O., & Kurths, J. (2009). Confidence bounds of recurrence-based complexity measures. *Physics Letters A, 373*(26), 2245–2250.

Stinchcombe, M. B., & White, H. (1998). Consistent specification testing with nuisance parameters present only under the alternative. *Econometric Theory, 14,* 295–325.

Teräsvirta, T., Lin, C. F., & Granger, C. (1993). Power of the neural network test. *Journal of Time Series Analysis, 14*(2), 209–220.

Teräsvirta, T. T. (1994). Aspects of modelling nonlinear time series. In R. F. Engle & D. L. McFadden (Eds.), *Handbook of econometrics* (Vol. 4). Amsterdam: Elsevier.

Thistleton, W. J., Marsh, J. A., Nelson, K., & Tsallis, C. (2007). Generalized box–Müller method for generating q-Gaussian random deviates. *IEEE Transactions on Information Theory, 53*(12), 4805–4810.

Trulla, L. L., Giuliani, A., & Zbilut, J. P., & Webber, C. L., Jr. (1996). Recurrence quantification analysis of the logistic equation with transients. *Physics Letters A, 223*(4), 255–260.

Tsallis, C. (1988). Possible generalization of Boltzmann-Gibbs statistics. *Journal of Statistical Physics, 52*, 47.

Zbilut, J. P., & Webber, C. L. (1992). Embeddings and delays as derived from quantification of recurrence plots. *Physics Letters A, 171*(3–4), 199–203.

# APPENDIX

*MATLAB Program for Simulation*

Program: Simopti (Finding the Optimum simulation based on threshold root mean square error for either Geometric Brownian Motion or Tsallis Modified distribution based on user's choice.)

```
%Function to optimally simulate time series following Geometric
Brownian
%Motion or Tsallis Modified Geometric Brownian Motion based on
correlation
%coefficient of the actual data series to replicate
%y =Simopti(x,init, endvalue, m, sig, dt,q,type,c )
%INPUT DATA
%x = actual data series to be replicated
%init = initial value
%endvalue = series length
%m = Mean value of time
%series to simulate(In case of Financial time series
like Stock
or index values this is generally taken
%as annual average return)
%sig = Standard Deviation of time series (In case of Financial
time series
%like Stock or index values this generally taken as Standard
Deviation of
%annual return)
%dt = unit of time (for daily dt = 1/365 and so on)
% q = q-factor for Tsallis distribution
%type = 'GBM' for Geometric Brownian Motion; 'TSALLIS' for
Tsallis modified
%Brownian Motion
%c = threshold value for root mean square error
%OUTPUT
% A single column vector 'y' of length 'endvalue' representing a
discrete
% version of Geometric Brownian Motion or Modified Geometric
Brownian
% Motion based on Tsallis Distribution with initial value 'init'
optimised
```

```
% based on rmse between x and y
%
%A joint plot of actual and simulated data series
%
%OTHER MATLAB FUNCTIONS
%Uses the function randn.m and corrcoef.m from MATLAB functions.
%Uses the functions GBMsim and Tsallisim
%Uses Function_q.m
%Uses Function gfit.m% {Copyright 2004-2005 by Durga Lal
%Shrestha.}%
%Ref: Borland L(2002), "A theory of non-Gaussian option
pricing " Quantitative Finance 2 No. 6 (June),Pages: 415-431
% John C Hull, Options, Futures and other Derivatives,
Pearson Education.
% Tsallis C., (1988), "Possible Generalization of
Boltzmann-Gibbs
% Statistics", Journal of Statistical Physics. 52,
479Tsallis C.,
% (1988), "Possible Generalization of Boltzmann-Gibbs
Statistics", Journal of Statistical Physics. 52, 479
%
%Function created by Kousik Guhathakurta (kousikg@gmail.com)
function y = Simopti(x,init, endvalue, m, sig, dt, q,type, c)
switch upper(type)
case 'GBM'
for i = 1:5000
y = GBMsim(x,init, endvalue, m, sig, dt);
if gfit(x,y,'3')<c break
end
end
case 'TSALLIS'
for i = 1:5000
y = Tsallisim(x,init, endvalue, m, sig, dt,q);
if gfit(x,y,'3')<c break
end
end
otherwise
error(' Unrecognized type! type is either "GBM" or
"TSALLIS"')
end
```

## Program: GBMsim(Simulating Geometric Brownian Motion)

```
%Function to simulate time series following Geometric Brownian
Motion
%y = GBMsim(x,init, endvalue, m, sig, dt)
%INPUT DATA
%x = actual data series to replicate
%init = initial value
%endvalue = series length
%m = Mean value of time
%series to simulate(In case of Financial time series like Stock
or index values this is generally taken
%as annual average return)
%sig = Standard Deviation of time series (In case of Financial
time series
%like Stock or index values this generally taken as Standard
Deviation of
%annual return)
%dt = unit of time (for daily dt = 1/365 and so on)
%
%OUTPUT
% A single column vector 'y' of length 'endvalue' representing a
discrete
% version of Geometric Brownian Motion with initial value 'init'
%%
%A joint plot of actual and simulated data series
%
%OTHER MATLAB FUNCTIONS
%Uses the function randn() from MATLAB functions.
%
% Reference: John C Hull, Options, Futures and other
Derivatives, Pearson
% Education.
%
%Function created by Kousik Guhathakurta (kousikg@gmail.com)
function y = GBMsim(x,init, endvalue, m, sig, dt)
for i = 2:endvalue
y(1)=init;
ds(i)=m*y(i-1)*dt + sig*y(i-1)*sqrt(dt)*randn();
y(i)=y(i-1)+ds(i);
```

```
end
plot (x, 'DisplayName', 'x', 'YDataSource', 'x'); hold all; plot
(y, 'DisplayName', 'y', 'YDataSource', 'y'); hold off;
figure(gcf)
```

Program: Tsallisim (Program to simulate time series following Tsallis Modified Geometric Brownian Motion)

```
%Function to simulate time series following Tsallis Modified
Geometric Brownian Motion
%y =Tsallisim(x,init, endvalue, m, sig, dt,q)
%INPUT DATA
%x = actual data series to replicate
%init = initial value
%endvalue = series length
%m = Mean value of time
%series to simulate(In case of Financial time series like Stock
or index values this is generally taken
%as annual average return)
%sig = Standard Deviation of time series (In case of Financial
time series
%like Stock or index values this generally taken as Standard
Deviation of
%annual return)
%dt = unit of time (for daily dt = 1/365 and so on)
% q = q-factor for Tsallis distribution
%OUTPUT
% A single column vector 'y' of length 'endvalue' representing a
discrete
% version of Modified Geometric Brownian Motion based on Tsallis
Distribution with initial value 'init'
%
%A joint plot of actual and simulated data series
%
%OTHER MATLAB FUNCTIONS
%Uses the function randn.m from MATLAB functions.
%Uses Function_q.m
%
%Ref: Borland L(2002), "A theory of non-Gaussian option
pricing " Quantitative Finance 2 No. 6 (June),Pages: 415-431
```

% Tsallis C., (1988), "Possible Generalization of
Boltzmann-Gibbs Statistics", Journal of Statistical Physics. 52,
479
%
% Function created by Kousik Guhathakurta (kousikg@gmail.com)

```
function y = Tsallisim(x, init, endvalue, m, sig, dt, q)
for i = 2:endvalue
y(1)=init;
ds(i)=m*y(i-1)*dt + sig*y(i-1)*sqrt(dt)*Function_q(1,q);
y(i)=y(i-1)+ds(i);
end
plot (x, 'DisplayName', 'x', 'YDataSource', 'x'); hold all; plot
(y, 'DisplayName', 'y', 'YDataSource', 'y'); hold off;
figure(gcf)
```

Program: Function_q (Program to generate q-Gaussian random
  number)

% This function generates random drawings from a Tsallis
distribution.
%This is created according to code given in William J.
% Thistleton, John A. Marsh, Kenric Nelson, and Constantino
Tsallis (2007),
%"Generalized Box–Müller Method for Generating q-Gaussian Random
Deviates",
%IEEE Transactions On Information Theory, Vol. 53, No. 12,
December 2007
% For this function contact Kousik Guhathakurta
(kousikg@gmail.com)

```
function qGaussian = qGaussianDist(nSamples, qDist)
```

%
% Returns random deviates drawn from a q-Gaussian
% distribution.
% The number of samples returned is nSamples.
% The q that characterizes the q-Gaussian is given
% by qDist
%
% Check that q < 3
if qDist < 3
% Calculate the q to be used on the q-log
qGen = (1 + qDist)/(3 - qDist);
% Initialize the output vector

```
qGaussian = zeros(1, nSamples);
% Loop through, populate the output vector
for k = 1 : nSamples
% Get two uniform random deviates
% from built-in rand function
u1 = rand;
u2 = rand;
% Apply the q-Box-Muller algorithm,
% taking only one of two possible values
R = sqrt(-2*log_q(u1, qGen));
qGaussian(k) = R*sin(2*pi*u2);
end
% Return 0 and give a warning if q >= 3
else
warning('q value must be less than 3')
qGaussian = 0;
end
end
function a = log_q(x, q)
%
% Returns the q-log of x, using q
%
% Check to see if q = 1 (to double precision)
if abs(q - 1) < 10*eps
% If q is 1, use the usual natural logarithm
a = log(x);
else
% If q differs from 1, use def of the q-log
a = (x.^(1-q) -1)./(1 - q);
end
end
```

# DOES LIQUIDITY RISK PREMIUM AFFECT OPTIMAL PORTFOLIO HOLDINGS OF U.S. TREASURY SECURITIES?

Karoll Gómez Portilla

## ABSTRACT

*This chapter focuses on examining how changes in the liquidity differential between nominal and TIPS yields influence optimal portfolio allocations in U.S. Treasury securities. Based on a nonparametric estimation technique and comparing the optimal allocation decisions of mean-variance and CRRA investor, when investment opportunities are time varying, I present evidence that liquidity risk premium is a significant risk-factor in a portfolio allocation context. In fact, I find that a conditional allocation strategy translates into improved in-sample and out-of-sample asset allocation and performance. The analysis of the portfolio allocation to U.S. government bonds is particularly important for central banks, specially in developing countries,*

The Spread of Financial Sophistication Through Emerging Markets Worldwide
Research in Finance, Volume 32, 75–108
Copyright © 2016 by Emerald Group Publishing Limited
ISSN: 0196-3821/doi:10.1108/S0196-382120160000032004

*given the fact that, collectively they have accumulate a large holdings of U.S. securities over the last 15 years.*

**Keywords:** Liquidity risk; optimal portfolio allocation; bond risk premia; nonparametric estimation; foreign-exchange reserves

**JEL classifications:** C13; C52; G11; G32

Foreign-exchange reserves, as a key part of the asset side of the central bank's sheet, play a fundamental role in monetary management. Almost all foreign-exchange reserves are held in five currencies: the U.S. dollar, the euro, the Japanese yen, the British pound, and the Swiss franc; accounting dollar reserve holdings for 61 percent of the total at the end 2014 (BIS). The dollar commands a high share in global reserves because the deep and highly liquid market for the U.S. Treasury bonds. Indeed, over the last 15 years, foreign official holdings of U.S. Treasuries reached unprecedented levels, increasing from $600 billion in January 2000 to about $4.142 billion in January 2015. Foreign Official Institutions (FOIs), such as central banks, were the first to significantly increase their holdings, as part of their reserve accumulation policies. The pattern of the foreign demand for U.S. Treasury securities is showed in Fig. 1(a). Panel (b) shows that on average 82% of the FOIs holdings correspond to Treasury notes (with maturities between 1 and 10 years) and T-bonds (more than 10-year maturity), while 18% is held in bonds with less than 1-year maturity.

Most of this growth is accounted for by the emerging market economies, where besides China, Latin American countries have played an important role. As Fig. 1(c) shows, over the past 15 years, China has steadily increased its U.S. Treasury holdings to become the largest U.S. holder, with about 30% of the total. Similarly, Latin American countries noticeably increased the level of international reserves. Indeed, official holdings of U.S. Treasuries increased from $17 billion in January 2000 to almost $413.9 billion in January 2015, representing 10% of the total. Holdings by the Oil Exporters (which include Venezuela and Ecuador) have also grown in the past few years, representing 7% of the total in January 2015. Finally, Panel (d) depicted the market share of the Latin American major foreign holders of U.S. Treasury securities by year. Until 2007 only Mexico and Brazil appeared in the group of major foreign holders, however, since 2008 other countries, such as Colombia, Chile, Peru, and Uruguay, have significantly increased their holdings. In such a context, the foreign officials' portfolio of U.S. Treasury securities became in a "self-insurance" strategy against

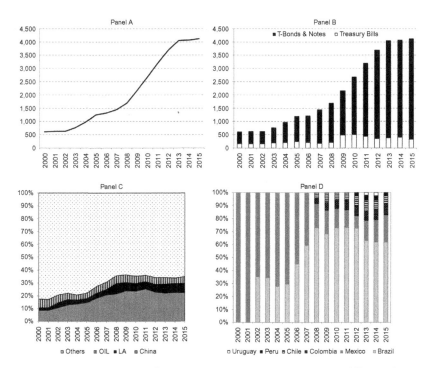

*Fig. 1.* Foreign Holdings of U.S. Treasury Securities. (a) U.S. Billions of FOIs Holdings, (b) FOIs Holdings by Type, (c) % of FOIs by Group of Countries, and (d) % of FOIs by Latin America Country. *Notes*: The data in each panel include foreign holdings of U.S. Treasury bills, bonds, and notes reported every January under the Treasury International Capital (TIC) reporting system for the years 2000–2015. OIL represents Oil Exporters, which include Ecuador, Venezuela, Indonesia, Bahrain, Iran, Iraq, Kuwait, Oman, Qatar, Saudi Arabia, the United Arab Emirates, Algeria, Gabon, Libya, and Nigeria. L.A. represents Latin American countries (except Ecuador and Venezuela).

potential external shocks, or resulted as a by-product of interventions by Latin American central banks in foreign-exchange markets, especially in the context of surges of capital inflows that characterized part of this period.

Investment portfolios traditionally have been constructed with a focus on what asset classes to invest in and how much to invest in each. Recent research, however, has shown that focusing on risk-factor allocations, rather than asset class allocations, can result in better risk-adjusted portfolio performance. This chapter contributes to this debate. In particular, I focus on examining how a change in the liquidity differential between nominal and TIPS yields influences optimal portfolio allocations in U.S. Treasury securities. There are a series of ways in which this study contributes to the literature. First, it incorporates financial information (liquidity premium) in an asset allocation context, and shows how this can be of significance for both a mean-variance and a CRRA investor. Second, it focuses on a bond portfolio choice that is relatively unexplored in the literature, since the majority of the studies on asset allocation examine stock-only portfolios. Additionally, portfolios of U.S. Treasury securities are singularly important for central banks, especially in developing countries. Third, I examine portfolio choice among multiple government bonds with different maturities. More so, I consider both the U.S. Treasury bonds and Treasury Inflation-Protected Securities (TIPS) in the investor's asset menu.

Government debt of the United States includes Treasury bonds and TIPS. The U.S. Treasury Department typically has issued debt in the form of Treasury bonds, including T-bills, T-notes, and T-bonds (according with its maturity). These securities, simply called Treasuries, are widely regarded to be the safest investments because the deep and highly liquid market added to its lack significant default risk. Therefore, it is no surprise that investors turn to U.S. Treasuries during times of increased uncertainty as a safe haven for their investments (flight to quality). In addition to Treasuries, in 1997, the U.S. Treasury Department started its Treasury Inflation-Protected Securities (TIPS) program. The program is intended to provide investors with protection against inflation.[1] TIPS has shown a consistent growth since its inception in 1997. In fact, the market capitalization has grown by more than 30 times, from $33 billion in 1997 to over $1.200 billion in 2013. However, it has been characterized by be less liquid than nominal Treasury bond market. As a consequence, the lack of liquidity is thought to result in TIPS yields having a liquidity premium relative to nominal securities.

Liquidity risk in Treasury markets, arise from the fact that investor may need to make portfolio adjustments due to some unforeseen events, after the initial auction or before the maturity of a Treasury security. Thus, investors care about the likely costs associated with such trading, and in response, demand a higher yield to compensate the cost to buy or sell the security in a secondary market. Even though, nominal Treasuries and TIPS have similar trading costs (such as brokerage fees and commissions), the cost related to the ease and convenience of trading is not the same for both securities, and it might be related to the differences in liquidity market conditions. Hence, the additional yield to compensate the incremental risks and higher costs of trading is referred as liquidity risk premium. The existence of this liquidity premium in TIPS yields has been well documented in the academic literature by Campbell, Shiller, and Viceira (2009), Dudley, Roush, and Steinberg (2009), Christensen and Gillan (2011), Gurkaynak, Sack, and Wright (2010), Pflueger and Viceira (2012), Gomez (2015), among others.

   Focusing on a conditional allocation technique and comparing the optimal allocation decisions of mean-variance and CRRA investor, when investment opportunities are time varying, I present evidence that liquidity risk premium is a significant risk-factor in a portfolio allocation context. Throughout this chapter, I assume that the investor makes decisions in real terms where the investment horizon is one-month, one-quarter, and one-year. I only consider a short-term investor in the empirical analysis. The reason for this is related to the fact that for a buy-and-hold long-term investor, whose investment horizon perfectly matches the maturity of the bond, TIPS offer full protection against inflation if held until maturity.[2] Similarly, an investor who adopts a buy-and-hold strategy for TIPS mitigates risk arising from illiquidity, given that he/she does not face higher costs of buying or selling the bond before it reaches maturity. However, TIPS are currently issued with only a few specific maturities: 5-year, 10-year, and 30-year, therefore the investment horizon over which I consider investors who hold assets does not match the maturity of any outstanding TIPS.[3] Hence, I study a short-term investor who maximizes real wealth but is not able to invest in a risk-less asset in real terms (given that TIPS are a risky asset both in nominal and in real terms), and also faces liquidity risk. Notice, however, that a short-term investor benefits from the availability of TIPS in terms of a wider investment opportunity set that allows an increase in the returns per unit of risk, investing even a small fraction of his wealth in TIPS (Cartea, Saul, & Toro, 2012).

   The investor's problem is to choose optimal allocations to the risky asset as a function of predictor variable: the TIPS liquidity premium. As risky assets, I consider equally weighted bond portfolios on short-term bonds (1−10 years maturity); and on long-term bonds (11−20 years maturity), each of them are computed for Treasury bonds and for TIPS. I identify the liquidity component in TIPS yields through the difference between inflation-linked and nominal bond asset swap spreads. This difference is capturing of the relative financing cost, the specialness and the balance sheet cost of TIPS over nominal Treasury bonds. These characteristics influence the ease of liquidating some securities and the attractiveness by which to hold them with respect to others. Therefore, this is a market-based measure of the market perception (current and expected) of relative liquidity in the bond market. The particular choice of this measure for the liquidity premium is motivated by the fact that: (i) it is highly correlated with other measures of the TIPS liquidity premium available in the literature, which suggests that they are all capturing similar information about the liquidity differential between nominal and TIPS yields; (ii) U.S. bond excess returns can be predicted by this liquidity measure (see Gomez, 2015); and (iii) it is a market-based measure of liquidity which is straightforward to compute.

   In summary, I consider the portfolio policy of an investor who is able to invest in only one risky asset, and I differentiate various portfolio alloca-tion problems: first, where the investor chooses between the portfolio of short-term or long-term Treasury bonds and a risk-free asset; and second, where the investor chooses between a portfolio of short-term or long-term TIPS and a risk-free asset. I also study an investor with mean-variance (MV) and constant relative risk aversion (CRRA), with different degrees of risk aversion, in order to test the sensitivity of the optimal portfolio choice to the higher moments.

   I make use of an econometric framework based on a portfolio choice problem of a single-period investor, where the investor's problem is set up as a statistical decision problem, with asset allocations as parameters and the expected utility as the objective. The allocations are estimated by direct maximization of expected utility proposed by Brandt (1999). A number of key results emerge from this analysis. First, the liquidity premium seems to be a significant determinant of the portfolio allocation of U.S. government bonds. In fact, conditional allocations in risky assets decrease as liquidity conditions worsen. In particular, an increase in the liquidity differential between nominal and TIPS bonds leads to lower optimal portfolio alloca-tions for nominal Treasury bonds, and also to lower optimal portfolio allocations in TIPS, but at different levels of liquidity. Additionally, the effect of liquidity is a decreasing function of investment horizons, in the sense that for the same degree of risk aversion the investor reacts less abruptly to an increase in the liquidity premium when he/she has a longer investment horizon. Furthermore, as the investment horizon becomes longer, the smaller the optimal portfolio weight, and so, the less is invested in the risky asset.

   The above conclusions are not determined by the level of risk aversion or the investors preferences. The relation between optimal portfolio weights and the liquidity premium remains the same for different values of risk aversion, and also across investor preferences. These characteristics mainly change the level of the portfolio function, having a small impact on the shape of the function. In addition, results do not depend on a particular choice of the maturity of the liquidity premium (similar results are found when considering 10-year or 20-year liquidity premium), nor on a specific way to proxy liquidity (I have similar results with both liquidity premium measures).

From the standpoint of practical advice to U.S. Treasury security investors, a final natural question to ask is whether or not a conditional strategy translates into improved (in- and out-of-sample) asset allocation and performance. To answer this question, I compare the performance of the optimal portfolio choices of two investors: one investor who makes portfolio allocations conditional upon observing a particular liquidity signal (conditional strategy); and the other who ignores any change in liquidity in making his/her portfolios allocation choices (unconditional strategy). I conclude that the conditional strategy outperforms the unconditional strategy, improving not only the in-sample, but also the out-of-sample asset allocation and performance.

The rest of this chapter is organized as follows. Section 2 defines the conditional portfolio choice problem and presents the nonparametric estimation technique used. I describe the data and provide some basic statistics in Section 3. Section 4 presents the empirical results for different bond portfolios, different types of investors, and different investment horizons. Section 5 concludes.

# THE CONDITIONAL OPTIMAL PORTFOLIO PROBLEM

The traditional problem of optimal portfolio choice considers an investor which maximizes the conditional expected utility of next period's wealth under a budget constraint. Merton (1969) provides the solution, where the investor can trade continuously in a finite set of stocks and bank account. However, given that the stocks and bonds differ in many ways, the theory of portfolio management does not apply as it stands to bond portfolios (see Ekeland & Taflin, 2005 for a discussion of this point). For the bond market, Schroder and Skiadas (1999), Ekeland and Taflin (2005), Ringer and Tehranchi (2006), and Liu (2007) have studied this problem using a theoretical approach. In particular, Ekeland and Taflin (2005) and Ringer and Tehranchi (2006) set up and solve the problem of managing a bond portfolio by optimizing (over all self-financing trading strategies for a given initial capital) the expected utility of the final wealth. Thus, optimal portfolio at time $t$ is a linear combination of self-financing instruments, each one with a fixed time to maturity. Under this setup, the value of the portfolio changes only because the bond prices change. Price bonds behave like price stocks, that is, it depends only on the risk it carries and not on time to maturity.

The impact of inflation on portfolio choice has also been considered in the literature. An initial extension of the Markowitz problem was introduced in the 1970s by Biger (1975), Friend, Landskroner, and Losq (1976), Lintner (1975), and Solnik (1978), among others. Intertemporal portfolio choice problem under inflation risk was studied by Campbell and Viceira (2001) in discrete time and by Brennan and Xia (2002) in continuous time. Both works tell us that a long-term, risk-averse investor prefers the indexed bond or a perfect substitution of indexed bond in order to hedge against the inflation risk. However, in these papers all relevant state variables are assumed observable and the probability distributions of all processes are assumed known. Bensoussan, Keppo, and Sethi (2009) and Chou, Han, and Hung (2010) relax that restriction by assuming that the expected inflation rate is unobservable to the investor.

Most of the existing studies on portfolio choice (with or without inflation risk) focus on stock-only portfolio (Barberis, 2000; Viceira & Campbell, 1999; Wachter, 2002) or examine the stock-bond mix portfolio choice (Munk, Sorensen, & Nygaard Vinther, 2004). Given the extensive literature for equity markets, it is surprising to note that no effort has been undertaken to examine the influence of liquidity in government bond portfolio choice. Filling this gap is one contribution of this chapter. To follow, I define the investor's maximization problem, describe the conditioning information, and finally, introduce the estimation technique.

*Investor Utility Maximization*

*Portfolio Choice without Inflation*
Ekeland and Taflin (2005) and Ringer and Tehranchi (2006) express the solution of optimal portfolio choice as portfolios of self-financing trading strategies that naturally include stocks and bonds. In particular, they fix a utility function $u$ and a planning horizon $T > 0$, and consider the functional $J(\varphi) = \mathbb{E}^{\mathbb{P}}\left[u\left(W_T^{\varphi}\right)\right]$, where $W_T^{\varphi}$ is the accumulated wealth at time $T$ generated by the self-financing trading strategy $\varphi$. The goal is to characterize the strategy that maximizes $J$.

Following on from this literature, I consider the problem of optimal portfolio choice when the traded instruments are a set of risky bonds and a risk-less bond. In particular, and without loss of generality, I consider a bond market where only zero-coupon bonds are available. Fixing a utility function $u(W_{t+1})$ and a planning horizon $T > 0$, I consider an investor who maximizes the conditional expected utility of next period's wealth, subject to the budget constraint:

$$\max_{\alpha_t \in \mathscr{A}(\varphi)} \mathbb{E}[u(W_{t+1})|Z_t]$$
$$\text{subject to: } W_{t+1} = W_t\left(R_{f,t+1} + \alpha_t\left(R_{b,t+1} - R_{f,t+1}\right)\right) \tag{1}$$

where $W_{t+1}$ is the accumulated wealth at time $t + 1$ generated by the self-financing trading strategy $\varphi$ (which belongs to the set of admissible self-financing strategies denoted by $\mathscr{A}$), $\alpha_t$ represents the proportion of wealth invested in a risky bond with return $R_{b,t+1}$ and the remaining proportion $1 - \alpha_t$ is invested in risk-free bond with return $R_{f,t+1}$. The expectation is conditional on a state variable $Z_t$. The investor can have three different horizons: one-month, one-quarter, or one-year (this represents the difference between $t$ and $t + 1$).

The weight that maximizes the expected utility function is the solution to the following Euler optimality condition:

$$\mathbb{E}\left[\frac{\partial u(W_{t+1})}{\partial W_{t+1}}\frac{\partial W_{t+1}}{\partial \alpha}|Z_t\right] = 0 \tag{2}$$

In particular, the solution of the investor's problem is the mapping from the state variable $Z_t$ to the portfolio weights

$$\alpha_t = \alpha(Z_t) \tag{3}$$

and it denotes the portfolio choice of observing a signal $Z_t = z$.

The relation between the portfolio policy and the predictability of individual moments of the returns given the predictor $Z_t$ depends on the specification of the utility function. I consider two types of investor preferences: MV and power utility (CRRA) preferences. An investor with MV preferences maximizes

$$\max_{\alpha_t \,\in\, \mathscr{A}(\varphi)} \mathbb{E}[W_{t+1}|Z_t] - \frac{\gamma}{2} \mathbb{V}\left[W_{t+1}^2|Z_t\right]$$

where $\gamma > 0$ represents the coefficient of absolute risk aversion. The reason I consider MV preferences is because it can be stated as a primitive, or can be derived as a special case of expected utility theory. Also, under MV preferences, portfolio weights depend exclusively and analytically on the two first moments of returns, which serve as benchmark case in this study.[4]

I also consider the most popular objective function in the portfolio choice literature, which is an investor with CRRA or power utility. In this case, the investor solves the following problem:

$$\max_{\alpha_t \,\in\, \mathscr{A}(\varphi)} \begin{cases} \mathbb{E}\left[\dfrac{W_{t+1}^{1-\gamma}}{1-\gamma}|Z_t\right] & \text{if } \gamma > 1 \\ \mathbb{E}[\log(W_{t+1}|Z_t)] & \text{if } \gamma = 1 \end{cases}$$

subject to the budget constraint in Eq. (1), and where $\gamma > 0$ now measures the coefficient of relative risk aversion. As is well known, unlike MV preferences, CRRA does not permit a closed-form solution to the investor's portfolio problem. However, I consider CRRA preferences to be able to test whether or not an investor cares about higher order moments of the return distribution.

*Portfolio Choice with Inflation*
In this section, I follow Cartea et al. (2012), who solve the optimal portfolio choice problems for investors concerned with maximizing real wealth. Here, I assume that investors make allocation decisions in real terms, and are worried about the purchasing power of their terminal wealth, and do not suffer from money illusion. As before, I consider the optimal investment allocation of investors who are not worried about what may happen beyond the immediate next period but rather, care about the purchasing power of their wealth.

To avoid exposure to inflation risk, investors can: (i) invest in a risk-less asset in real terms and/or (ii) invest in assets that covary with inflation. However, in this empirical analysis, I only consider investors who have a maximum investment horizon of one-year; they cannot find TIPS with this maturity and thus they are not able to invest in a risk-less real asset. Additionally, given that real interest rate changes affect TIPS returns, investors consider TIPS as a risky asset in both nominal and real terms.

An investor with MV or CRRA preferences maximizes the same problem in Eqs. (4) and (5), respectively, but are now subject to the budget constraint

$$W_{t+1}^R = W_t^R \left( R_{f,t+1} + \alpha_t \left( R_{b,t+1} - R_{f,t+1} \right) \right)$$

where $W_{t+1}^R$ is now the real terminal wealth and $R_{b,t+1}$ and $R_{f,t+1}$ are the risky and risk-free bond returns, as already seen.[5] In the absence of a real risk-free asset, investors face inflation risk and deal with this through the covariances between the returns of risky assets and inflation. Securities that are correlated with inflation help to hedge against inflation, reducing the portfolio variance in real terms.

### Nonparametric Estimation

I use the methodology proposed by Brandt (1999) and Ait-Sahalia and Brandt (2001). They apply a standard generalized method of moments (GMM) technique to the conditional Euler equation that characterizes the investor's portfolio choice problem. In particular, it consists of replacing the conditional expectation with sample analogues, computed only with returns realized in a given state of nature where the forecasting variable level is $Z_t = \bar{z}$ (which is liquidity premium). Brandt (1999) suggests estimating the conditional expectation with a standard nonparametric regression. Ait-Sahalia and Brandt (2001) suggest a semiparametric approach to address the issue of which predictors are important for the portfolio choice when a large number of them are available.

Let a neighborhood of $Z$ be $Z \pm h$ for some bandwidth $h > 0$. When the investor is characterized by the power utility, a simple nonparametric estimator of the conditional Euler equation is given by the Nadaraya–Watson estimator, where the moment condition is given by:

$$\hat{\mathbb{E}} \left[ \frac{\partial u(W_{t+1})}{\partial W_{t+1}} \frac{\partial W_{t+1}}{\partial \alpha} | Z_t = \bar{z} \right] = \frac{1}{Th} \frac{\sum_{t=1}^T \frac{\partial u(W_{t+1})}{\partial W_{t+1}} \frac{\partial W_{t+1}}{\partial \alpha} k\left(Z_t, \bar{z}, h\right)}{\sum_{t=1}^T k\left(Z_t, \bar{z}, h\right)} = 0$$

where $k(Z_t, \bar{z}, h)$ is the kernel function which is assumed to be Gaussian. I apply exactly identified GMM to Eq. (2) to obtain $\alpha(\hat{Z})$ which is a consistent estimate for the unknown optimal portfolio choice (see Ait-Sahalia and

Brandt (2001) for asymptotic properties of this estimators). The conventional solution to optimize the classical trade-off between variance and bias is to choose a bandwidth of the form $h = \lambda \sigma_z T^{-1/K+4}$, where $\lambda$ is a constant, $K$ is the number of predictor variables, and $\sigma_z$ is the standard deviation of the predictor $Z$ (see Hardle & Marron, 1985).

Finally, the optimal unconditional portfolio weight is compute by applying a standard GMM procedure to the unconditional Euler equation. In this case, the moment condition is

$$\hat{\mathbb{E}}\left[\frac{\partial u(W_{t+1})}{\partial W_{t+1}}\frac{\partial W_{t+1}}{\partial \alpha}\right] = \frac{1}{T}\sum_{t=1}^{T}\frac{\partial u(W_{t+1})}{\partial W_{t+1}}\frac{\partial W_{t+1}}{\partial \alpha} = 0$$

which yields the same results that directly compute weights from Eq. (3).

## THE DATA AND BASIC STATISTICS

I am interested in the analysis of the empirical time-series relationship between optimal bond portfolio allocations and alternative measures of liquidity. To that end, I calculate monthly, quarterly, and annual holding period returns from daily observations of zero-coupon nominal and real Treasury bond yields constructed by Gurkaynak, Sack, and Wright (2007) and Gurkaynak et al. (2010) for observed bond yields, respectively, available through the Federal Reserve website. This data set contains constant maturity yields for maturities of 2–20 years. I construct equally weighted bond portfolios on short-term bonds (1–10 years maturity) and on long-term bonds (11–20 years maturity), each of them computed for Treasury bonds and for TIPS, ending up with four risky assets. The sample period is from January 2, 2004 to December 31, 2012.

For the same period, I also collect information on one-year Treasury bills from the Federal Reserve Board statistical releases. Following Ait-Sahalia and Brandt (2001) and Ghysels and Pereira (2008), I assume Treasury bill is risky-free, and I fix the risk-free rate at its historical average. They argue that the constant risk-free rate assumption guarantees that any difference in the optimal portfolio functions across frequencies is solely due to the relation between returns and liquidity. In summary, the asset universe consists of the short-term Treasury bonds (weight $\alpha_{NS}$), the long-term Treasury bonds (weight $\alpha_{NL}$), the short-term

TIPS (weight $\alpha_{RL}$), the long-term Treasury bonds (weight $\alpha_{RL}$), and the risk-free assets (weight $\alpha_{rf}$).

I calculate liquidity premium for 10- and 20-years to maturity as the residual spread between TIPS and nominal $z$-spread asset swaps using daily data from January 2004 to December 2011, I using daily nominal and TIPS $z$-spread asset swaps data from Barclays Live. I denote this measure by $L_{n,t}^{z-asw}$ and it is going to be the predictor variable $Z_t$. I find that this variable is highly correlated and shares the same dynamic pattern with other measures of relative bond liquidity premium proposed in the literature by Christensen and Gillan (2011) and Pflueger and Viceira (2012). Additionally, it is strictly positive for all maturities and shows a peak in the late 2008 during the financial crisis.

Table 1 shows descriptive statistics of the liquidity predictor and holding period government bond portfolio returns, for the three investment

***Table 1.*** Descriptive Statistics for the Portfolio Measures of Liquidity and Bond Returns.

| | Short-Term | | | Long-Term | | |
|---|---|---|---|---|---|---|
| | $L_{10,t}^{z-asw}$ | $R_{t+1}^{N}$ | $R_{t+1}^{TIPS}$ | $L_{20,t}^{z-asw}$ | $R_{t+1}^{N}$ | $R_{t+1}^{TIPS}$ |
| *Panel A: Monthly frequency* | | | | | | |
| Mean | 0.00 | 1.04 | 1.02 | 0.00 | 1.06 | 1.03 |
| Stdev | 1.00 | 0.02 | 0.02 | 1.00 | 0.04 | 0.03 |
| Skewness | 2.58 | 0.03 | −0.34 | 1.91 | 0.49 | 0.10 |
| Kurtosis | 11.15 | 3.70 | 6.30 | 8.36 | 5.60 | 5.91 |
| Percentiles | | | | | | |
| 5% | −0.95 | 1.01 | 0.99 | −1.17 | 0.99 | 0.98 |
| 50% | −0.19 | 1.05 | 1.02 | −0.18 | 1.06 | 1.03 |
| 95% | 2.15 | 1.07 | 1.05 | 2.06 | 1.11 | 1.07 |
| Cross-correlations | | | | | | |
| $L_t^{z-asw}$ | 1.00 | | | 1.00 | | |
| $R_{t+1}^{N}$ | 0.05 | 1.00 | | −0.13 | 1.00 | |
| $R_{t+1}^{TIPS}$ | 0.33 | 0.46 | 1.00 | 0.18 | 0.59 | 1.00 |
| Auto-correlations | | | | | | |
| 1-day | 0.99 | 0.95 | 0.96 | 0.99 | 0.95 | 0.94 |
| 2-day | 0.98 | 0.91 | 0.92 | 0.98 | 0.90 | 0.89 |
| 5-day | 0.95 | 0.80 | 0.78 | 0.95 | 0.77 | 0.72 |
| 22-day | 0.76 | 0.07 | 0.06 | 0.77 | −0.06 | −0.11 |
| Unit root test | | | | | | |
| DF $p$-value | 0.02 | 0.01 | 0.01 | 0.14 | 0.01 | 0.01 |

## Table 1. (Continued)

| | Short-Term | | | Long-Term | | |
|---|---|---|---|---|---|---|
| | $L_{10,t}^{z-asw}$ | $R_{t+1}^N$ | $R_{t+1}^{TIPS}$ | $L_{20,t}^{z-asw}$ | $R_{t+1}^N$ | $R_{t+1}^{TIPS}$ |
| **Panel B: Quarterly frequency** | | | | | | |
| Mean | 0.00 | 1.05 | 1.02 | 0.00 | 1.06 | 1.03 |
| Stdev | 1.00 | 0.03 | 0.03 | 1.00 | 0.07 | 0.05 |
| Skewness | 2.58 | 0.04 | −0.55 | 1.91 | 0.28 | −0.26 |
| Kurtosis | 11.15 | 2.80 | 6.78 | 8.36 | 3.32 | 4.27 |
| Percentiles | | | | | | |
| 5% | −0.95 | 1.00 | 0.98 | −1.17 | 0.95 | 0.95 |
| 50% | −0.19 | 1.04 | 1.02 | −0.18 | 1.06 | 1.04 |
| 95% | 2.15 | 1.09 | 1.07 | 2.06 | 1.17 | 1.11 |
| Cross-correlations | | | | | | |
| $L_{10,t}^{z-asw}$ | 1.00 | | | 1.00 | | |
| $R_{t+1}^N$ | −0.14 | 1.00 | | −0.23 | 1.00 | |
| $R_{t+1}^{TIPS}$ | 0.37 | 0.28 | 1.00 | 0.23 | 0.59 | 1.00 |
| Auto-correlations | | | | | | |
| 1-day | 0.99 | 0.98 | 0.99 | 0.99 | 0.98 | 0.98 |
| 2-day | 0.98 | 0.96 | 0.97 | 0.98 | 0.96 | 0.95 |
| 5-day | 0.95 | 0.92 | 0.93 | 0.95 | 0.91 | 0.89 |
| 22-day | 0.90 | 0.86 | 0.86 | 0.90 | 0.85 | 0.81 |
| Unit root test | | | | | | |
| DF $p$-value | 0.02 | 0.01 | 0.01 | 0.14 | 0.01 | 0.01 |
| **Panel C: Monthly frequency** | | | | | | |
| Mean | 0.00 | 1.06 | 1.04 | 0.00 | 1.10 | 1.06 |
| Stdev | 1.00 | 0.04 | 0.05 | 1.00 | 0.09 | 0.08 |
| Skewness | 2.58 | −0.14 | 0.02 | 1.91 | 0.16 | 0.06 |
| Kurtosis | 11.15 | 2.33 | 3.06 | 8.36 | 3.70 | 2.76 |
| Percentiles | | | | | | |
| 5% | −0.95 | 0.99 | 0.96 | −1.17 | 0.94 | 0.93 |
| 50% | −0.19 | 1.06 | 1.04 | −0.18 | 1.09 | 1.07 |
| 95% | 2.15 | 1.12 | 1.11 | 2.06 | 1.29 | 1.21 |
| Cross-correlations | | | | | | |
| $L_{10,t}^{z-asw}$ | 1.00 | | | 1.00 | | |
| $R_{t+1}^N$ | −0.50 | 1.00 | | −0.60 | 1.00 | |
| $R_{t+1}^{TIPS}$ | 0.36 | −0.04 | 1.00 | 0.00 | 0.46 | 1.00 |
| Auto-correlations | | | | | | |
| 1-day | 0.99 | 0.99 | 1.00 | 0.99 | 0.99 | 0.99 |
| 2-day | 0.98 | 0.98 | 0.99 | 0.98 | 0.98 | 0.98 |
| 5-day | 0.95 | 0.96 | 0.97 | 0.95 | 0.95 | 0.95 |
| 22-day | 0.76 | 0.83 | 0.86 | 0.77 | 0.78 | 0.82 |
| Unit root test | | | | | | |
| DF $p$-value | 0.02 | 0.23 | 0.09 | 0.14 | 0.05 | 0.02 |

*Notes:* The liquidity measure corresponds to the TIPS Liquidity proposed by Christensen and Gillan (2011). U.S. daily data from January 1, 2004 to December 30, 2012 in basis points.

horizons: one-month, one-quarter, and one-year. The first lines in each panel show the mean, standard deviation, skewness, and kurtosis for each liquidity measure and returns. By construction, and to facilitate the interpretation of the results, liquidity measure has a mean zero and standard deviation equal to one (i.e., they have been standardized). Also, there is evidence of fat tails in returns, especially at the shorter investment horizon. This tail risk suggests that the distribution is not normal, but skewed, and has fatter tails. The fatter tails increase the probability that an investment will move beyond three standard deviations. Nominal returns are negatively correlated with liquidity, while TIPS returns are positively correlated. This means that as liquidity conditions worsen (higher liquidity premium), TIPS returns rise in order to compensate for the higher risk in bad times.

The following lines show the autocorrelation coefficients for different lags, which do not suggest persistence in most of the variables, especially at any frequency. The last line shows the *p*-value for the Dickey and Fuller test. The *p*-value for the Dickey and Fuller tests suggest the rejection of the null of a unit root for both short-term and long-term returns, and Christensen and Gillan (2011) 10-year liquidity.

# EMPIRICAL RESULTS

## *Unconditional Portfolio Weights*

The goal in this section is to characterize the unconditional portfolio choice, which serves as a benchmark for the conditional problem. Table 2 presents estimates of unconditional portfolio choices of investors with MV and CRRA preferences with different risk aversion degrees of $\gamma = 2, 5, 10$, and 20, and for three investment horizons. The entries in each column correspond to a portfolio choice between Treasury bills (assumed as risk-free) and one of the four different equally weighted portfolio bonds: short-term nominal bonds (NS), long-term nominal bonds (NL), short-term TIPS (RS), or long-term TIPS (RL). That they do not impose short-sell constraints suggests a less realistic environment, mainly because the Markowitz portfolio tends to have very large quantities of individual assets (sometimes unreasonably so), I do not impose this restriction to make my results comparable with previous papers.

Several well-known features of optimal portfolio choice emerge. Consider the MV portfolio choice weights. First, risk aversion affects how much wealth the investor allocates to risky securities instead of to

**Table 2.** Unconditional Portfolio Weights.

| | Mean-Variance Investor | | | | Power Utility Investor | | | |
|---|---|---|---|---|---|---|---|---|
| | Treasury | | TIPS | | Treasury | | TIPS | |
| | Short-term | Long-term | Short-term | Long-term | Short-term | Long-term | Short-term | Long-term |
| **Monthly frequency** | | | | | | | | |
| 2 | 79.75 [29.70] | 15.58 [3.48] | 33.53 [5.73] | 12.32 [1.80] | 139.32 [5.91] | 10.15 [0.77] | 7.26 [1.16] | 6.57 [0.45] |
| 5 | 31.90 [11.88] | 6.23 [1.39] | 13.41 [2.29] | 4.93 [0.72] | 64.58 [10.65] | 5.11 [0.65] | 7.26 [1.16] | 3.63 [0.59] |
| 10 | 15.95 [5.94] | 3.12 [0.70] | 6.71 [1.15] | 2.46 [0.36] | 30.15 [6.50] | 2.79 [0.41] | 3.97 [0.72] | 1.95 [0.35] |
| 20 | 7.98 [2.97] | 1.56 [0.35] | 3.35 [0.57] | 1.23 [0.18] | 14.51 [3.60] | 1.43 [0.22] | 2.06 [0.39] | 1.00 [0.19] |
| **Quarterly frequency** | | | | | | | | |
| 2 | 29.45 [6.30] | 6.54 [0.81] | 10.11 [1.93] | 5.31 [0.80] | 29.35 [1.57] | 6.94 [0.64] | 6.00 [0.92] | 4.00 [0.58] |
| 5 | 11.78 [2.52] | 2.61 [0.33] | 4.05 [0.77] | 2.12 [0.32] | 14.04 [1.45] | 3.01 [0.36] | 2.88 [0.60] | 1.82 [0.35] |
| 10 | 5.89 [1.26] | 1.31 [0.16] | 2.02 [0.39] | 1.06 [0.16] | 6.98 [0.77] | 1.50 [0.18] | 1.51 [0.33] | 0.94 [0.19] |
| 20 | 2.95 [0.63] | 0.65 [0.08] | 1.01 [0.19] | 0.53 [0.08] | 3.44 [0.39] | 0.75 [0.09] | 0.77 [0.17] | 0.47 [0.09] |
| **Annual frequency** | | | | | | | | |
| 2 | 13.91 [1.60] | 4.71 [0.64] | 3.45 [0.73] | 3.23 [0.37] | 14.78 [1.34] | 3.62 [0.39] | 3.45 [0.84] | 3.20 [0.49] |
| 5 | 5.57 [0.64] | 1.88 [0.26] | 1.38 [0.29] | 1.29 [0.15] | 6.30 [0.73] | 1.77 [0.28] | 1.41 [0.36] | 1.35 [0.23] |
| 10 | 2.78 [0.32] | 0.94 [0.13] | 0.69 [0.15] | 0.65 [0.07] | 3.11 [0.37] | 0.92 [0.15] | 0.71 [0.18] | 0.68 [0.12] |
| 20 | 1.39 [0.16] | 0.47 [0.06] | 0.35 [0.07] | 0.32 [0.04] | 1.54 [0.18] | 0.46 [0.08] | 0.35 [0.09] | 0.34 [0.06] |

*Notes:* This table shows estimates of the optimal unconditional portfolio choice of investors. This is computed by applying a standard GMM procedure to the unconditional euler equation (9). Each panel shows a different investment horizon: monthly, quarterly, and annual. I consider four portfolio allocation problems: two where the investor chooses between the portfolio of short-term or long-term nominal Treasury bonds and a risk-free asset and another two where he chooses between a portfolio of short-term or long-term TIPS and a risk-free asset. Weights in the table correspond to the risky asset. In brackets are the Newey-West (12 lags) standard errors. I used U. S. data from January 1, 2004 to December 30, 2011.

the risk-free Treasury bill. The more risk-averse the investor, the less they will invest in the risky bond, so that long positions in risky bonds go down with a higher degree of risk aversion. Second, given that this investor is forming his portfolio using only bonds and the risk-free Treasury bill, he/she will not want to short-sell the risky asset but rather will want to buy it on the margin (i.e., $\alpha > 1$). That means investors borrow money at risk-free rates and go long in risky bonds. For instance, an investor with an annual investment horizon and $\gamma = 20$ borrows 39% of wealth at the risk-free rate to invest a total of 139% in short-term nominal bonds portfolios. Finally, we see less large quantities of short-sales $1 - \alpha$ or, in some cases, no short-sales for the risk-free Treasury bill, for the same degree of risk aversion as the investment horizon increases. For example, an investor with $\gamma = 20$ goes short in the risk-free bond at the monthly frequency but goes long in both long-term nominal bonds and the risk-free bond at longer investment horizons. The same situation occurs with long-term bonds with respect to short-term ones in the sense that we see less large quantities for a portfolio of long-term versus short-term bonds. This indicates that a smaller portion of the portfolio is devoted to risky assets as investment horizons increase or when long-run assets are available.

Results for CRRA preferences are very similar to those for MV. In theory, what differentiates an MV investor from a CRRA investor is that the latter has a preference for higher order moments and not only for the expected return and its variance, thus their risky position depends on relative risk aversion. However, empirical results in Table 2 show that investors seem not to be primarily affected in their decisions by the first two return moments. So, the effect of higher order moments of CRRA investors seems not to be strong enough, especially for TIPS. The biggest holding difference is for short-term nominal bonds at the monthly frequency, where CRRA investors with different levels of risk aversion tend to hold larger quantities.

There are important differences in the optimal portfolio weights between short-term and long-term nominal bonds with both types of preferences. In fact, equally risk-averse investors tend to hold bigger positions on short-term bonds relative to long-term ones, that is, the short-term bond weight typically exceeds the long-term weight for the same kind of bond. However, these differences become smaller when the investment horizon become longer. Bonds with a longer maturity will usually pay a higher interest rate than shorter-term bonds. However, long-term bonds have greater duration than short-term bonds, so interest rate changes will have a greater effect on long-term bonds than on short-term bonds. As a result, investors are more conservative holding smaller positions in long-term bonds relative to short-term bonds, given that they would offer greater stability and lower risk.

Investors also hold bigger positions in nominal bonds relative to TIPS bonds. These differences could be attributed, at least in the case of CRRA investor, to the negative skewness in short-term TIPS bond returns for monthly and quarterly frequency, as Table 1 shows. Investors prefer positive skewness, because it implies a low probability of obtaining a large negative return. Then, investors tend to the extreme portfolios (Sharpe ratio driven, skewness driven, or kurtosis driven) and avoid being stuck in the middle.

### Conditional Portfolio Weights

*Nonparametric Optimal Portfolio Function*
In this section, I present the optimal portfolio weights as a function of the liquidity differential between inflation-indexed bonds and nominal bonds (liquidity premium), represented by $Z_t$. I apply the utility maximization framework presented above with respect to $Z_t$. For each kernel grid point,[6] I optimize the portfolio weight by maximizing the representative agent's marginal utility in that state using a GMM inference technique. The portfolio weights that follow from the optimization of the expected utility under MV and CRRA preferences are presented in this section.

Table 3 shows estimates of the optimal conditional portfolio choice of investors (Weight) and their corresponding standard errors (Std) obtained by applying the Politis and Romano (1994) bootstrap procedure. I use this stationary bootstrap procedure to preserve autocorrelation properties of the data in the bootstrap samples.[7] The standard errors are presented only in order to assess the precision of the nonparametric method used. Each panel shows a different investment horizon (monthly, quarterly, and annual), and they present the portfolio allocation problems considered before: two where the investor chooses between the portfolio of short-term or long-term nominal Treasury bonds and a risk-free asset, and another two where the investor chooses between a portfolio of short-term or long-term TIPS and a risk-free asset, with each of them considering an MV and a CRRA investor.

Fig. 2 is the companion graphs to Table 3. Each figure shows the optimal portfolio weight as a function of liquidity $\alpha(Z_t)$ represented by the bold line. Additionally, in each figure the thinner horizontal line represents the optimal unconditional allocation. The bars in the background represent the histogram of liquidity premium (scaled to add up to 30). Results

**Table 3.** Conditional Portfolio Weights ($\gamma = 20$).

| | Mean-Variance Investor | | | | | | | | Power Utility Investor | | | | | | | |
|---|---|---|---|---|---|---|---|---|---|---|---|---|---|---|---|---|
| | Treasury | | | | TIPS | | | | Treasury | | | | TIPS | | | |
| | Short-term | | Long-term | | Short-term | | Long-term | | Short-term | | Long-term | | Short-term | | Long-term | |
| Z | Weight | Stdev | Weight | Stdev | Weight | Stdev | Weight | Stdev | Weight | Stdev | Weight | Stdev | Weight | Stdev | Weight | Stdev |
| **Monthly frequency** | | | | | | | | | | | | | | | | |
| −1 | 9.41 | 0.72 | 2.05 | 0.17 | 3.80 | 0.50 | 1.31 | 0.19 | 7.00 | 0.00 | 2.21 | 0.26 | 2.13 | 0.52 | 0.99 | 0.18 |
| 0 | 9.07 | 0.72 | 2.02 | 0.17 | 3.68 | 0.55 | 1.33 | 0.19 | 7.00 | 0.00 | 2.10 | 0.24 | 2.01 | 0.52 | 0.98 | 0.18 |
| 2 | 7.06 | 0.93 | 1.42 | 0.20 | 3.61 | 0.66 | 1.38 | 0.21 | 7.00 | 0.00 | 1.51 | 0.23 | 1.90 | 0.57 | 1.03 | 0.18 |
| 4 | 2.99 | 0.95 | 0.41 | 0.17 | 3.15 | 0.50 | 0.82 | 0.20 | 7.00 | 0.00 | 0.55 | 0.32 | 2.56 | 0.77 | 1.19 | 0.26 |
| 5 | 2.31 | NaN | 0.27 | NaN | 3.16 | NaN | 0.65 | NaN | 7.00 | 0.00 | 0.33 | 0.42 | 3.33 | 1.06 | 1.12 | 0.43 |
| **Quarterly frequency** | | | | | | | | | | | | | | | | |
| −1 | 1.46 | 0.16 | 0.75 | 0.07 | 0.24 | 0.07 | 0.51 | 0.08 | 3.48 | 0.36 | 0.88 | 0.10 | 0.74 | 0.15 | 0.46 | 0.08 |
| 0 | 1.63 | 0.16 | 0.73 | 0.07 | 0.30 | 0.08 | 0.49 | 0.09 | 3.48 | 0.36 | 0.85 | 0.09 | 0.71 | 0.16 | 0.43 | 0.08 |
| 2 | 1.68 | 0.21 | 0.61 | 0.08 | 0.60 | 0.10 | 0.58 | 0.11 | 3.51 | 0.39 | 0.68 | 0.08 | 0.79 | 0.16 | 0.49 | 0.09 |
| 4 | 0.24 | 0.21 | 0.07 | 0.11 | 1.41 | 0.19 | 0.76 | 0.21 | 2.43 | 1.05 | 0.08 | 0.14 | 1.38 | 0.28 | 0.84 | 0.17 |
| 5 | −0.21 | NaN | −0.03 | NaN | 1.65 | NaN | 0.77 | NaN | 2.15 | 1.44 | −0.03 | 0.19 | 1.88 | 0.47 | 1.04 | 0.27 |
| **Annual frequency** | | | | | | | | | | | | | | | | |
| −1 | 0.24 | 0.08 | 0.59 | 0.06 | 0.24 | 0.08 | 0.29 | 0.04 | 1.63 | 0.17 | 0.71 | 0.07 | 0.23 | 0.08 | 0.31 | 0.05 |
| 0 | 0.30 | 0.08 | 0.62 | 0.06 | 0.30 | 0.09 | 0.30 | 0.05 | 1.78 | 0.17 | 0.72 | 0.07 | 0.30 | 0.08 | 0.32 | 0.05 |
| 2 | 0.60 | 0.09 | 0.50 | 0.08 | 0.60 | 0.11 | 0.39 | 0.06 | 1.72 | 0.17 | 0.42 | 0.08 | 0.52 | 0.09 | 0.38 | 0.06 |
| 4 | 1.41 | 0.21 | −0.18 | 0.08 | 1.41 | 0.22 | 0.68 | 0.12 | 0.26 | 0.31 | −0.18 | 0.07 | 1.20 | 0.16 | 0.76 | 0.12 |
| 5 | 1.65 | NaN | −0.32 | NaN | 1.65 | NaN | 0.67 | NaN | −0.23 | 0.42 | −0.35 | 0.10 | 1.71 | 0.25 | 1.08 | 0.20 |

*Notes*: This table shows estimates of the optimal conditional portfolio choice of investors. This is computed by applying a standard GMM procedure to the conditional euler equation (8). Each panel shows a different investment horizon: monthly, quarterly, and annual. I consider four portfolio allocation problems: two where the investor chooses between the portfolio of short-term or long-term nominal Treasury bonds and a risk-free asset and another two where he chooses between a portfolio of short-term or long-term TIPS and a risk-free asset. Weights correspond to the risky asset. Standard errors (Std) are obtained applying the Politis and Romano (1994) bootstrap procedure. I used U.S. data from January 1, 2004 to December 30, 2011.

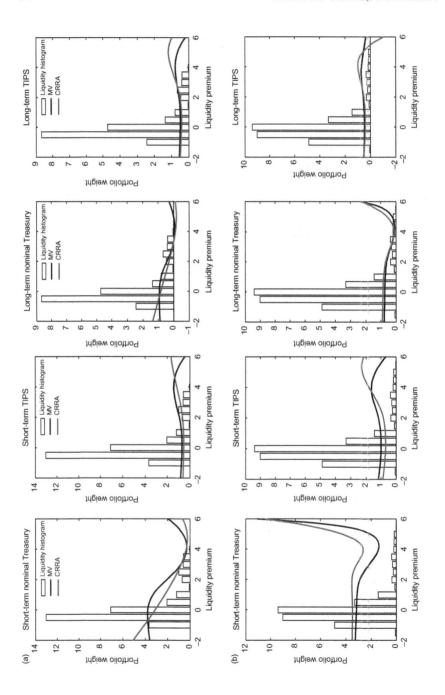

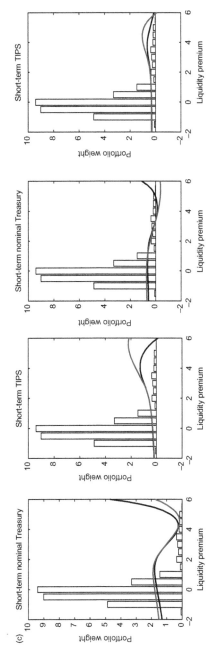

*Fig. 2.* Optimal Portfolio Weights as a Function of 10-Year Liquidity Premium. (a) Monthly Frequency, (b) Quarterly Frequency, and (c) Annual Frequency. *Notes*: In each panel, the thinner horizontal lines represents the optimal unconditional allocation. The bars in the background represent the histogram (scaled to add up to 30) of liquidity premium. The bold line represents the optimal fraction of wealth allocated to the respective equally weighted U.S. bond return portfolios as a function of liquidity premium calculated using daily data from January 2, 2004 to December 30, 2012. In the first row, both the investment horizon and the rebalancing frequency are one-month; in the second row, one-quarter; and in the third, one-year.

presented in Table 3 and Fig. 2 corresponds to the case when the coefficient of relative risk aversion is equal $\gamma = 20$. A number of results emerge from this analysis. First, the liquidity premium seems to be a significant determinant of the portfolio allocation to U.S. government bonds. For instance, for an MV investor and at the monthly horizon, liquidity is a strong determinant of the allocation to short-term and long-term nominal bonds, with the optimal weight ranging from 9.41 at Liquidity = $(-1)$ to 2.31 at Liquidity = 5, as Table 3 shows. This indicates that an increase in the liquidity premium (i.e., liquidity conditions worsen) is accompanied by a strong decrease in the optimal allocation in short-term nominal bonds.

I have a similar result for the long-term nominal bonds with weights ranging from 2.05 to 0.27. Furthermore, liquidity also seems to be an important determinant of the allocation to TIPS. In this case, an increase in liquidity premium produces a decrease in the optimal allocation to both short-term, and long-term TIPS bonds. However, the effect is less strong with weights ranging from 3.80 to 3.16 for short-term, and from 1.31 to 0.65 for long-term for liquidity ranging between $-1$ and 5, respectively.

At quarterly and annual frequencies, optimal allocation still responds to changes in liquidity but mainly at high levels of liquidity premium. What we see is that the conditional weight is very close to the unconditional weight for low levels of liquidity (i.e., liquidity = $-1$ to 2), however optimal allocation starts to respond to changes in the liquidity when market liquidity conditions worsen (i.e., liquidity > 2). Interestingly, the investor tends to substitute cash for nominal bonds, and TIPS bonds for cash when the liquidity rises above its mean plus about 4 standard deviations, as Fig. 2 shows.

Second, conditional allocations in risky assets decrease as liquidity conditions worsen. In particular, an increase in the liquidity differential between nominal and TIPS bonds leads to: lower optimal portfolio allocations on nominal Treasury bonds, and also lower optimal portfolio allocations in TIPS, but at different levels of liquidity. When the liquidity premium is low (i.e., the liquidity differential between nominal and TIPS bonds is small), we see that the optimal allocation to either nominal or TIPS bonds is mostly unresponsive to liquidity premium, and it is very close to unconditional allocation. This occurs in the negative range of liquidity and also in the center of the distribution.

When the liquidity premium is high (i.e., in the presence of big liquidity differentials between nominal and TIPS bonds), portfolio allocation on both nominal bonds and TIPS bonds decreases. However, this occurs at different levels of liquidity. In particular, the investor starts to decrease their position in nominal bonds at liquidity = 2, but when there is insufficient liquidity, the investor holds a larger position in nominal bonds. On the other hand, portfolio allocation on TIPS bonds behaves in the reverse direction. That is, the investor only decreases asset allocation to TIPS in the upper positive part of liquidity (i.e., when the liquidity premium is very high), while between liquidity = 2 and liquidity = 4 TIPS bonds allocations increases, being above the unconditional value. Thus, in general, portfolio allocation for each type of bonds (nominal and TIPS) moves in cycles and each of them has its own cycle. Typically, when one type of bond is performing well, the other may not be performing as well in terms of liquidity, and the allocation rule reflects this situation.

Third, I find in general that the shape of the optimal portfolio policy functions of MV and CRRA investors, with the same degree of risk aversion, are similar even though they have different levels. This suggests that investors seem to be primarily affected in their decisions by the first two return moments. Thus, the effect of higher order moments of CRRA investors exists but it seems not to be strong enough. However, this is not true at the monthly frequency. In this case, portfolio policies differ substantially which can be attributed to time variation in the higher order moments of the return distribution. This result is not induced by the choice of the kernel bandwidth, given that I explicitly control for it by constraining the kernel to be the same for the MV and the CRRA preferences.[8]

Fourth, the effect of liquidity is a decreasing function of the investment horizon. For a given degree of risk aversion, the size of the optimal portfolio weight differs considerably across investment horizons. I find that as investment horizons became longer, the smaller the optimal portfolio weight, and the less that is invested in the risky asset. In particular, for the same degree of risk aversion investors react less abruptly to an increase in the liquidity premium when the investment horizon is one-year, than when the investment horizon is one-month.

For instance, we can see from Table 3 that when liquidity is equal to its mean ($Z_t = 0$) an MV investor with $\gamma = 20$ reduces the cash holdings from 2.02 to 0.62 when the investment horizon increases from one-month to one-year. This means that the investor borrows 102% of wealth at the risk-free rate to invest a total of 202% in short-term nominal bonds when the investment horizon is one-month. However, when the investment horizon becomes larger, the investor takes a long position in both assets holding 62% of their wealth in short-term nominal bonds and 38% in cash. The same occurs when I consider a CRRA investor. For example, considering the same case, but for long-term

TIPS bonds, a CRRA investor reduces their bonds positions from 98% to 32%, as Table 3 shows.

Fifth, different degrees of risk aversion mainly change the level of the portfolio function but have little impact on the shape of this function, as is shown in Fig. 3. In this figure, I only plot the portfolio policies for the long-term nominal (left column) and TIPS bonds (right column) for a one-year investment horizon. The first row in the figure corresponds to an MV

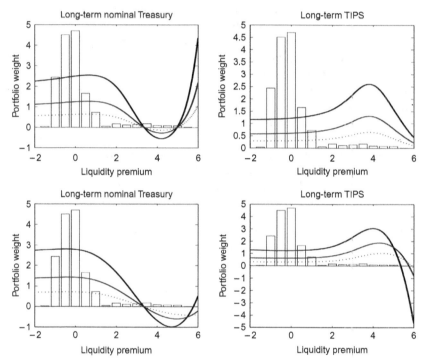

*Fig. 3.* Optimal Portfolio Weights as a Function of 10-Year Liquidity Premium (Mean-Variance and CRRA Investor with Different Values for $\gamma$). *Notes*: The bars in the background represent the histogram (scaled to add up to 30) of liquidity premium. The lines represent the optimal fraction of wealth allocated to the respective equally weighted U.S. bond return portfolios as a function of liquidity premium calculated using daily data from January 2, 2004 to December 30, 2012. Bold black line represent an investor with $\gamma = 5$, the bold grey line for $\gamma = 10$, and dotted line for $\gamma = 20$. The first row corresponds to the case of MV investor and the second row to the CRRA investor. The investment horizon and the rebalancing frequency in this figure correspond to one-year.

investor, and the second row to a CRRA investor. Finally, in each panel bold black lines represent an investor with $\gamma = 5$, the bold gray line with $\gamma = 10$ and the dotted line with $\gamma = 20$. Looking at Fig. 3, we see that the more risk-averse the investor becomes, the smaller the optimal portfolio weight, so the less that is invested in the risky asset. Furthermore, more risk-averse investors react less abruptly to an increase in the liquidity premium.

To summarize, and in general, results consistently show that the optimal allocation to short-term or long-term bonds is mostly unresponsive to changes in liquidity conditions at low levels (i.e., at liquidity $= -1$ to 4). However, once liquidity reaches certain levels (liquidity $> 4$), which indicates that market liquidity conditions have worsened, then the investor starts to respond by decreasing the positions in TIPS and increasing the position in nominal bonds.

Additionally, the above conclusion is not determined by the level of risk aversion, the investment horizon, or the investor preferences. The relation between optimal portfolio weights and liquidity premium remains the same for different values of risk aversion, different investment horizons, and also across investors' preferences. The characteristics mainly change the level of the portfolio function that have a small impact on the function shape, except for the monthly frequency.

*Do Weights Really Respond to Changes in Liquidity?*
The main question of this chapter is whether or not the weights respond to changes in liquidity. To test whether or not a portfolio weight is statistically different from zero is pointless in this context, simply because it does not provide an answer for the question asked above. What I do next, following Ghysels and Pereira (2008), is to statistically test this question by using the following approximation:

$$H_0 : \frac{\partial \alpha(Z)}{\partial Z} : Z = \bar{z} \simeq \frac{\alpha(Z + 0.1) - \alpha(Z - 0.1)}{0.2} = 0 \qquad (4)$$

where the first derivative of $\alpha(Z)$ is approximated by a finite difference which allows me to compute the slope of the optimal portfolio weight function at each value of the predictor variable.

Table 4 shows the point estimate slopes and $t$-stat computed using the standard errors obtained also from the Politis and Romano (1994) stationary bootstrap procedure. I draw one main conclusion from this table which is consistent with the results presented above. It is clear that optimal

**Table 4.** Point Estimates for the Slope of the Conditional Portfolio Weight Function.

| | Mean-Variance Investor | | | | | | | | Power Utility Investor | | | | | | | |
|---|---|---|---|---|---|---|---|---|---|---|---|---|---|---|---|---|
| | Treasury | | | | TIPS | | | | Treasury | | | | TIPS | | | |
| | Short-term | | Long-term | | Short-term | | Long-term | | Short-term | | Long-term | | Short-term | | Long-term | |
| $Z$ | Slope | t-stat | Slope | t-stat | Slope | t-stat | Slope | t-stat | Slope | t-stat | Slope | t-stat | Slope | t-stat | Slope | t-stat |
| *Monthly frequency* | | | | | | | | | | | | | | | | |
| −1 | −0.30 | −1.62 | −0.01 | −0.31 | −0.15 | −1.14 | 0.01 | 0.18 | 0.00 | −0.03 | −0.08 | −1.49 | −0.14 | −2.02 | −0.01 | −0.53 |
| 0 | −0.40 | −2.19 | −0.06 | −1.10 | −0.08 | −0.58 | 0.03 | 0.76 | 0.00 | −0.26 | −0.15 | −2.39 | −0.11 | −1.63 | 0.00 | −0.05 |
| 2 | −2.08 | −3.33 | −0.67 | −4.76 | −0.07 | −0.35 | −0.07 | −0.62 | 0.00 | 0.07 | −0.47 | −3.96 | 0.05 | 0.58 | 0.06 | 1.42 |
| 4 | −1.01 | −2.01 | −0.19 | −1.64 | −0.14 | −0.52 | −0.24 | −2.75 | 0.00 | 0.61 | −0.31 | −2.06 | 0.66 | 1.68 | −0.01 | −0.03 |
| 4.5 | −0.71 | −1.67 | −0.14 | −1.27 | −0.03 | −0.05 | −0.18 | −2.51 | 0.00 | −1.76 | −0.23 | −1.62 | 0.76 | 1.77 | −0.07 | −0.31 |
| 6.0 | 2.43 | 4.31 | −0.10 | −1.30 | −0.01 | −0.05 | −0.13 | −2.35 | 0.00 | 0.65 | 0.42 | 0.93 | 0.91 | 2.24 | −0.06 | −0.28 |
| *Quarterly frequency* | | | | | | | | | | | | | | | | |
| −1 | 0.17 | 4.26 | −0.03 | NaN | 0.06 | 3.08 | −0.03 | −1.60 | −0.02 | −0.24 | −0.03 | −1.08 | −0.05 | −2.43 | −0.03 | −1.06 |
| 0 | 0.18 | 2.81 | −0.02 | −1.00 | 0.08 | 3.95 | 0.00 | −0.05 | 0.01 | 0.10 | −0.03 | −1.04 | −0.02 | −1.10 | −0.01 | −0.72 |
| 2 | −0.35 | −2.85 | −0.18 | −4.56 | 0.28 | 6.51 | 0.10 | 2.42 | −0.08 | −0.33 | −0.23 | −3.31 | 0.13 | 3.78 | 0.08 | 3.26 |
| 4 | −0.62 | −3.18 | −0.17 | −1.98 | 0.31 | 2.52 | 0.01 | 0.04 | −0.55 | −1.05 | −0.18 | −2.29 | 0.46 | 2.21 | 0.24 | 1.84 |
| 4.5 | −0.53 | −2.82 | −0.13 | −1.61 | 0.27 | 2.18 | 0.00 | 0.03 | −0.44 | −0.84 | −0.14 | −1.79 | 0.48 | 2.18 | 0.23 | 1.71 |
| 6.0 | 0.93 | 2.76 | 0.65 | 1.65 | −0.31 | 1.96 | −0.05 | −0.91 | 0.57 | 0.54 | 0.45 | 1.68 | 0.53 | 2.07 | −0.43 | −1.08 |
| *Annual frequency* | | | | | | | | | | | | | | | | |
| −1 | 0.06 | 3.23 | 0.03 | 3.00 | 0.06 | 2.78 | 0.01 | 0.66 | 0.14 | 5.12 | 0.02 | 1.12 | 0.05 | 3.06 | 0.00 | −0.15 |
| 0 | 0.08 | 4.26 | 0.03 | 1.48 | 0.08 | 3.39 | 0.02 | 1.46 | 0.15 | 3.41 | −0.02 | −0.61 | 0.07 | 3.74 | 0.01 | 0.64 |
| 2 | 0.28 | 6.16 | −0.26 | −4.02 | 0.28 | 5.94 | 0.10 | 4.41 | −0.45 | −3.13 | −0.29 | −5.80 | 0.19 | 5.90 | 0.08 | 3.34 |
| 4 | 0.31 | 1.83 | −0.21 | −3.64 | 0.31 | 2.04 | 0.04 | 0.54 | −0.65 | −3.75 | −0.24 | −4.48 | 0.48 | 3.96 | 0.30 | 2.78 |
| 4.5 | 0.24 | 1.26 | −0.15 | −2.61 | 0.24 | 1.54 | −0.01 | −0.21 | −0.52 | −3.04 | −0.18 | −3.45 | 0.50 | 3.66 | 0.31 | 2.55 |
| 6.0 | 0.87 | 1.45 | 0.54 | 2.34 | −0.33 | 1.98 | −0.11 | −0.76 | 0.37 | 1.92 | 0.06 | 1.57 | 0.12 | 3.25 | −0.34 | −2.48 |

*Notes:* This table shows the point estimates slopes and their standard errors obtained from Politis and Romano (1994) stationary bootstrap procedure. This is computed by approximating the first derivative of $\alpha(Z)$ by Eq. (4). Each panel shows a different investment horizon: monthly, quarterly, and annual. I consider four portfolio allocation problems: two where the investor chooses between the portfolio of short-term or long-term nominal Treasury bonds and a risk-free asset and another two where he chooses between a portfolio of short-term or long-term TIPS and a risk-free asset. I used U.S. data from January 1, 2004 to December 30, 2011.

portfolio policy is not linear or constant in liquidity. For the two investor preferences, the short-term nominal and the TIPS bonds portfolio policy respond to changes in liquidity. This conclusion is derived from the fact that the null hypothesis is rejected indicating that all slopes are statistically significant at the 10% level or less. The only case where slopes are not statistically significant is for short-term TIPS bonds with MV preferences. The other case where we cannot reject the null hypothesis is for short-term nominal bonds with CRRA preferences. In this case, the optimal portfolio function is constant but smaller than the unconditional weight.

For long-term TIPS, $\alpha(Z_t)$ is almost constant and statistically not different from zero over the negative range of liquidity until $Z_t = 2$. After that, the slopes are positive and over the last range of liquidity they are negative and statistically significant. I find the same results for both investor preferences. The optimal portfolio function for long-term nominal bonds goes in the opposite way. It starts by being flat and statistically not different from zero, then slopes become negative, and over the end range of liquidity, slopes are positive and statistically significant.

Overall, I can conclude that optimal portfolio choice is unresponsive over the negative and first positive range of liquidity, however portfolio allocations start to react as liquidity conditions worsen. This conclusion regarding the general shape of the portfolio weight functions is reliable in the sense that nonparametric techniques used here produce a consistent estimator of the portfolio functions.

### *Does a Conditional Allocation Strategy Imply Improved Asset Allocation and Performance?*

From the standpoint of practical advice to portfolio investors, an additional natural question to ask is whether or not to follow a conditional strategy translates into improved out-of-sample asset allocation and performance. The idea is that at the start of each period (one-month, one-quarter, or one-year), one investor makes portfolio allocations conditional upon observing a particular liquidity signal (conditional strategy). I compare his/her performance to that of another investor who ignores any change in liquidity in making his/her portfolios allocation choices (unconditional strategy).

I used rolling estimation approach, which consists of estimating a series of out-of-sample portfolio returns by using a rolling estimation window over the entire data set. Specifically, I choose an estimation window of length $M = 260$ days (one year). In each day, starting from $t = M + 1$, I use the data in the previous $M$ days to estimate the optimal portfolio weights. In other words, each investor has an investment horizon of one-year and uses all data available until period $T - M$ to choose his/her first portfolio weights. Next, I use those weights to compute the portfolio returns. Repeating this procedure, involve adding the information for the next period in the data set and dropping the earliest period (keeping the window length fixed), until the end of the data set is reached. In this way, I obtain a time series of portfolio returns for each (unconditional and conditional) strategy.

To compute out-of-sample performance of these two different strategies, I compute the out-of-sample Sharpe ratio of strategy $j$, defined as the sample mean of out-of-sample excess returns (over the risk-free asset), $\mu_j$, divided by their sample standard deviation, $\sigma_j$, for strategy $j = C,U$.

$$SR_j = \frac{\mu_j}{\sigma_j}$$

In addition, I calculate the certainty equivalent rates of return (CER) for each strategy to judge its relative performance. The CER represents the risk-free rate of return that investor is willing to accept instead of undertaking the risky portfolio strategy. Formally, I compute the CER of strategy $j$ as

$$CER_j = \mu_j + \frac{\gamma}{2}\sigma_j^2$$

where $\mu_j$ and $\sigma_j$ are the mean and variance of out-of-sample excess returns for strategy $j = C,U$. To test whether or not the Sharpe ratios and the certainty equivalent returns of two strategies are statistically distinguishable, I test the following null hypothesis $H_0$: $SR_U - SR_C$ and $H_0$: $CER_U - CER_C$. This difference represents the gain (or loss) in returns from investing in unconditional strategy versus conditional strategy. I compute the $p$-value of the differences by using the Politis and Romano (1994) stationary bootstrap procedure ($pv$-$boot$).[9] Finally, a useful benchmark are the in-sample Sharpe ratios and the certainty equivalent returns (to assess the effect of estimation error), calculated for the different portfolio strategies by using the entire time series of excess returns.

Table 5 shows results assuming both investors are MV optimizer with a one-year investment horizon, and $\gamma = 10$. Panel A shows the CER and the SR calculated with the entire data set (in-sample analysis). The in-sample Sharpe ratios are all positive (except for short-term nominal bonds), being the performing of the conditional strategy better than the unconditional strategy for all portfolios. For instance, for a nominal long-term portfolio

**Table 5.** Sharpe Ratios and Certainty Equivalent Returns (Mean-Variance Investor with $\gamma = 10$).

| | Unconditional | | Conditional | | Differential | | $H_0$: differential = 0 | |
|---|---|---|---|---|---|---|---|---|
| | SR | CER | SR | CER | $SR_U - SR_C$ | $CER_U - CER_C$ | pv-boot | pv-boot |
| *Panel A: In-Sample Results* | | | | | | | | |
| Treasury Short-term | 0.289 | 1.501 | 0.191 | 0.344 | 0.481 | 1.155 | 0.046 | 0.048 |
| Long-term | 0.128 | 0.535 | 0.363 | 0.601 | −0.234 | −0.065 | 0.047 | 0.001 |
| TIPS Short-term | 0.218 | 0.360 | 0.411 | 0.954 | −0.192 | −0.593 | 0.048 | 0.000 |
| Long-term | 0.139 | 0.350 | 0.810 | 0.811 | −0.6703 | −0.460 | 0.040 | 0.000 |
| *Panel B: Out-of-Sample Results* | | | | | | | | |
| Treasury Short-term | 0.282 | 1.588 | 0.226 | 0.320 | 0.508 | 1.268 | 0.055 | 0.054 |
| Long-term | 0.122 | 0.554 | 0.341 | 0.645 | −0.219 | −0.091 | 0.050 | 0.004 |
| TIPS Short-term | 0.208 | 0.335 | 0.352 | 1.133 | −0.143 | −0.798 | 0.054 | 0.000 |
| Long-term | 0.129 | 0.289 | 0.752 | 0.884 | −0.755 | −0.595 | 0.046 | 0.000 |

*Notes:* This table reports the out-of-sample CER returns for two different investor strategies: unconditional (bond returns are i.i.d.) and conditional (bond returns are predictable) strategy. The *p-values* of the difference between SR, and CER from each strategy are obtained applying the Politis and Romano (1994) bootstrap procedure. The complete data set correspond to U.S. data from January 1, 2004 to December 30, 2011.

the Sharpe ratio of unconditional strategy is equal to 0.12 versus 0.36 of the conditional strategy, indicating that with the conditional strategy the investor takes on less risk to achieve the same return. For the same portfolio, the $CER_U$ is equal to 0.53 versus 0.60 of the $CER_C$. This means that an investor requires a higher risk-free return to give up the opportunity to invest in the portfolio following a conditional strategy.

Similarly, the difference between the in-sample SR for the unconditional and conditional strategy shows the loss (given that I obtain negative values) from investing, based on the belief that bond returns are i.i.d. This means that the bond return predictability translates into improved in-sample asset allocation and performance. The comparison of in-sample certainty equivalent returns and their differences confirms the conclusions from the analysis of Sharpe ratios. Finally, the difference between the Sharpe ratios and certainty equivalent returns of each strategy is statistically significant in all cases, as *pv-boot* values indicate.

Next, I assess the magnitude of the potential gains that can actually be realized by an investor, using the out-of-sample performance of the strategies. From Panel B of Table 5, we see that in all cases the SR for the portfolios from the conditional strategy is much higher than for the unconditional strategy. I find the same results for CER. This means that a conditional strategy outperforms the unconditional strategy. This suggests also that conditional strategy might improve, not only in-sample but also out-of-sample performance. The significance of the CER differential and the SR differential, which is measure using the stationary bootstrap technique proposed by Politis and Romano (1994), implies that this result is statistically significant.

Finally, the difference between the in-sample and out-of-sample strategies allows me to gauge the severity of the estimation error. From the out-of-sample Sharpe ratio, reported in Panel B of Table 5, the unconditional strategy does not have a substantially lower Sharpe ratio and certainty equivalent returns out-of-sample than in-sample. This means that the effect of estimation error seems not to be so large. Consequently, it does not erodes the gains from optimal diversification given that differences turn out not to be economically important.

## CONCLUSIONS

I consider the portfolio problem of an MV and a power utility investor whose portfolio choices are between the asset of interest and a risk-free asset. The investor's problem is to choose optimal allocations to the risky asset as a function of predictor value: liquidity premium. The goal is to assess whether or not liquidity changes influence optimal portfolio allocations in the U.S. government bond market. While these issues have been well studied for stock-only portfolios, in general, less has been done to provide empirical evidence for the optimal portfolio choice of Foreign Official Institutions investing in U.S. Treasury securities, conditional upon observing a particular liquidity signal. This analysis is particularly important for central banks, especially in developing countries, given that collectively they have accumulated large holdings of U.S. securities during the last 15 years.

Overall, results show that optimal portfolios vary substantially with regards to predictor value. In particular, the effect of liquidity is a decreasing function of the investment horizon. Additionally, conditional allocations in risky assets decrease as liquidity conditions worsen. However, once the liquidity differential between U.S. nominal Treasury and TIPS bonds is sufficiently large, it leads to: (i) lower optimal portfolio allocations in TIPS; and (ii) higher optimal portfolio allocations on nominal bonds with respect to the risk-free bond. To summarize, this chapter suggests that market liquidity signals could provide valuable guidance to central banks as one of the main FOIs investing in U.S. Treasury securities, and adds to the evidence found for stock portfolios by Ghysels and Pereira (2008), which suggests the existence of a dependence of the optimal portfolio choices on changes in liquidity.

# NOTES

1. TIPS help to guard against inflation by adjusting the face value with changes in the rate of inflation. Interest is then paid on the adjusted face value of the bond.
2. TIPS are an useful hedge against inflation, but they do not guarantee a real rate of return. This is because the mechanics of adjusting for inflation for TIPS limit the exactness of the inflation adjustment and allow only approximate inflation hedges especially at high inflation levels. In fact, for TIPS, the reference price index is the non-seasonally adjusted CPI-U, and the indexation lag is three months. Therefore, TIPS operate with an indexation lag of three months. In other words, it takes three months from the incidence of price inflation (the month when a reference index reading is recorded) until it is incorporated into the coupon payment of the inflation-linked bond. Consequently, the indexation lag affects how well TIPS compensate for contemporaneous inflation, and prevents TIPS from guaranteeing a specified real return.

3. TIPS bonds have been offered in 5-, 10-, 20-, and 30-year denominations. However, TIPS that have less than one-year remaining to maturity are not easy to find in the secondary market, given that they have extremely high transaction costs.

4. Although the limitations of mean-variance analysis are well established in portfolio theory, its relative simplicity and easy intuition contribute to its continued use among investment professionals, in theoretical and empirical studies.

5. In this case, the real risk-free bond returns is calculated as $R_{f, t+1} - \pi_{t+1}$; $\pi_{t+1}$ which is inflation rate.

6. I define 15 not evenly spaced realizations of the liquidity ranging from its mean minus one standard deviation to its means plus three standard deviations, which correspond to the interior 95% of the empirical distribution of the liquidity premium. Alternatively, I also define 15 not evenly spaced realizations of the liquidity ranging between its minimum and maximum value, however results are broadly the same with both grids.

7. This method is a variation of the standard block bootstrap that manages to create bootstrap series that are strictly stationary which accounts for the autocorrelation in the data.

8. Non-parametric methods are typically indexed by a bandwidth or tuning parameter which controls the degree of complexity. The choice of bandwidth is often critical to implementation. In this application, the bandwidth is given by $h = \lambda \sigma_z T^b$, where $b = -1/k + 4$ and $K = 1$ which is the dimension of $Z$ (I am considering only one predictor variable which is liquidity), $O(Z)$ is the standard deviation of the predictor variable, $T = 2,086$ is the sample size and $A$ is a constant. For a big enough value of $A$, I obtain a flat portfolio weight and small $A$ produce a very noise portfolio weight function. I consider values ranging from 9 to 3 for $A$. These values guarantee bigger weight to an observation located at the mean of liquidity variable (which is zero), smaller weights to observations located one standard deviation away from the mean ($Z_t = \pm 1$), and even smaller weights to observations located two standard deviation away from the mean, etc. The results presented in this section correspond to $A = 6$.

9. I replicate the Politis and Romano procedure 1,000 times. For each such replication, I compute the optimal allocations for each investor through one year (260 days). At every point in time, the investors are allowed to utilize just the information available up to that point in time. I calculate the difference in certainty equivalent between the two strategies and the adjusted Sharpe ratio for each replication. Finally, I count the proportion of times in 1,000 replications that these differences exceed the certainty equivalent and adjusted Sharpe ratio based on the original data for a given set of results.

# REFERENCES

Ait-Sahalia, Y., & Brandt, M. W. (2001). *Variable selection for portfolio choice.* Technical Report.

Barberis, N. (2000). Investing for the long run when returns are predictable. *Journal of Finance, 55*, 225–264.

Bensoussan, A., Keppo, J., & Sethi, S. P. (2009). Optimal consumption and portfolio decisions with partially observed real prices. *Mathematical Finance, 19*(2), 215−236.

Biger, N. (1975). The assessment of inflation and portfolio selection. *Journal of Finance, 30*(2), 451−467.

Brandt, M. (1999). Estimating portfolio and consumption choice: A conditional euler equations approach. *Journal of Finance, 54*, 1609−1645.

Brennan, M. J., & Xia, Y. (2002). Dynamic asset allocation under inflation. *Journal of Finance, 57*(3), 1201−1238.

Campbell, J., Shiller, R., & Viceira, L. (2009). *Understanding inflation-indexed bond markets.* Technical Report 1696, Cowles Foundation for Research in Economics, Yale University.

Campbell, J., & Viceira, L. (2001). Who should buy long-term bonds? *American Economic Review, 91*(1), 99−127.

Cartea, A., Saul, J., & Toro, J. (2012). Optimal portfolio choice in real terms: Measuring the benefits of tips. *Journal of Empirical Finance, 19*(5), 721−740.

Chou, Y., Han, N., & Hung, M. (2010). Optimal portfolio-consumption choice under stochastic inflation with nominal and indexed bonds. *Applied stochastic models in Business and Industry, 27*(6), 691−706.

Christensen, J., & Gillan, J. (2011). *A model-independent maximum range for the liquidity correction of tips yields.* Working Paper Series 2011−16, Federal Reserve Bank of San Francisco.

Dudley, W., Roush, J., & Steinberg, M. (2009). The case for tips: An examination of the costs and benefits. *Economic Policy Review, 89*(428), 1−17.

Ekeland, I., & Taflin, E. (2005). A theory of bond portfolios. *Annals of Applied Probability, 15*(2), 1260−1305.

Friend, I., Landskroner, Y., & Losq, E. (1976). The demand for risky assets under uncertain inflation. *Journal of Finance, 31*(5), 1287−1297.

Ghysels, E., & Pereira, J. P. (2008). Liquidity and conditional portfolio choice: A nonparametric investigation. *Journal of Empirical Finance, 15*(4), 679−699.

Gomez, K. (2015). *Essays on bond return predictability and liquidity risk.* PhD Dissertation, Toulouse School of Economics.

Gurkaynak, R., Sack, B., & Wright, J. (2007). The U.S. treasury yield curve: 1961 to the present. *Journal of Monetary Economics, 54*(8), 2291−2304.

Gurkaynak, R., Sack, B., & Wright, J. (2010). The tips yield curve and inflation compensation. *American Economic Journal: Macroeconomics, 2*(1), 70−92.

Hardle, W., & Marron, J. S. (1985). Optimal bandwidth selection in nonparametric regression function estimation. *Annals of Statistics, 13*(4), 1465−1481.

Lintner, J. (1975). Inflation and security returns. *Journal of Finance, 30*(2), 259−280.

Liu, J. (2007). Portfolio selection in stochastic environments. *Review of Financial Studies, 20*, 1−39.

Merton, R. (1969). Lifetime portfolio selection under uncertainty: The continuous-time case. *The Review of Economics and Statistics, 51*(3), 247−257.

Munk, C., Sorensen, C., & Nygaard Vinther, T. (2004). Dynamic asset allocation under mean-reverting returns, stochastic interest rates, and inflation uncertainty: Are popular recommendations consistent with rational behavior? *International Review of Economics and Finance, 13*(2), 141−166.

Pflueger, C., & Viceira, L. (2012). *An empirical decomposition of risk and liquidity in nominal and inflation-indexed government bonds.* Technical Report, Harvard Business School.

Politis, D., & Romano, J. (1994). The stationary bootstrap. *Journal of the American Statistical Association, 89*(428), 1303–1313.

Ringer, N., & Tehranchi, M. (2006). Optimal portfolio choice in the bond market. *Finance and Stochastics, 10*(4), 553–573.

Schroder, M., & Skiadas, C. (1999). Optimal consumption and portfolio selection with stochastic differential utility. *Journal of Economic Theory, 89*, 68–126.

Solnik, B. (1978). Inflation and optimal portfolio choice. *Journal of Financial and Quantitative Analysis, 13*(5), 903–925.

Viceira, L. M., & Campbell, J. Y. (1999). Consumption and portfolio decisions when expected returns are time varying. *Quarterly Journal of Economics, 114*, 433–495.

Wachter, J. (2002). Portfolio and consumption decisions under mean-reverting returns: An exact solution for complete markets. *Journal of Finance and Quantitative Analysis, 37*(1), 63–91.

# SIZE, VALUE, AND MOMENTUM RISK IN THE CROSS-SECTION OF AVERAGE RETURNS AND VOLATILITY

Knut F. Lindaas and Prodosh Simlai

## ABSTRACT

*We examine the incremental cross-sectional role of several common risk factors related to size, book-to-market, and momentum in size-and-momentum-sorted portfolios. Unlike the existing literature, which focuses on the conditional mean specification only, we evaluate the common risk factors' incremental explanatory power in the cross-sectional characterization of both average return and conditional volatility. We also investigate the role of ex-ante market risk in the cross-section. The empirical results demonstrate that the size-and-momentum-based risk factors explain a significant portion of the cross-sectional average returns and cross-sectional conditional volatility of the benchmark equity portfolios. We find that the Fama—French (1993) factors and the ex-ante market risk are priced in the cross-sectional conditional volatility. We conclude that the size-and-momentum-based factors provide a source of risk that is independent of the Fama—French factors as well as*

The Spread of Financial Sophistication Through Emerging Markets Worldwide
Research in Finance, Volume 32, 109–144
Copyright © 2016 by Emerald Group Publishing Limited
All rights of reproduction in any form reserved
ISSN: 0196-3821/doi:10.1108/S0196-382120160000032005

*ex-post and ex-ante market risk. Our results bolster the risk-based explanation of the size and momentum effects.*

**Keywords:** Common risk factors; beta; factor models; average returns; volatility; cross-section

**JEL classifications:** G12; G14

# INTRODUCTION

There exists an extensive literature suggesting that, on average, stocks with high book-to-market ratios (value stocks) outperform stocks with low book-to-market ratios (growth stocks), and stocks with high 12-month past returns (high momentum) outperform stocks with low 12-month past returns (low momentum).[1] Researchers have argued that momentum returns are not driven by market risk (Jegadeesh & Titman, 1993) or by common risk factors related to size-and-book-to-market equity ($BE/ME$) (Fama & French, 1996). The existing literature suggests several possible explanations for price momentum, such as data mining, behavioral patterns, and risk.[2] Despite the enormity of the literature, three shortcomings are worthy of attention.

First, even though the use of common risk factors related to firm-level characteristics and past-behavior are widely known in empirical works (see, e.g., Fama & French, 2015a, 2015b; Harvey, Liu, & Zhu, 2014), no prior studies offer a formal examination of their incremental role in the cross-section of average returns of size-and-momentum-sorted portfolios. Furthermore, the existing works explore the common risk structures associated with size, value, and momentum separately.[3] Second, the literature evaluates the cross-sectional pricing of various common risk factors using the conditional mean specification only.[4] Not much is known a priori about the role of common risk factors in the conditional volatility of cross-sectional stock returns. Finally, most of the work is focused on the role of ex-post market risk in the cross-sectional pricing. It is not clear what role ex-ante market risk, which is not independent of aggregate economic conditions, plays in the cross-section. In this chapter, we address all of these issues and examine the relative role of common risk factors related to size, value, and momentum in a unified setting.

In this chapter, our objective is to investigate the incremental explanatory power of various common risk factors in the cross-sectional characterization of both average return and conditional volatility. We use 25 size-and-momentum-sorted benchmark equity portfolios as our testing assets and conduct cross-sectional pricing tests using Fama and MacBeth (1973) two-pass regression approach. Following Kogan (2004), we define the conditional volatility of returns as the conditional expectation of the absolute value of returns.[5] We use several common risk factors related to market, size, book-to-market, and momentum. The list includes a traditional ex-post version of excess market returns, two factors related to size-and-book-to-market-sorted value-weighted portfolios (denoted by $SMB^0$ and $HML^0$ respectively), and two factors formed on value-weighted portfolios sorted by size and short-term prior (2–12 months) returns (denoted by $SMB^1$ and $MOM^1$, respectively). Both $SMB^0$ and $HML^0$ were introduced by Fama and French (FF, 1993), and $MOM^1$ originated in the work of Carhart (1997). In addition to the incorporation of ex-post market risk ($EPM$), we also empirically evaluate the role of an ex-ante version of market risk in the cross-section. The ex-ante market risk ($EAM$) is obtained by fitting a regression of the realized market return at time $t$ on a set of four macroeconomic variables from period $t - 1$. We use the market segmentation procedures advocated by Pettengill, Sundaram, and Mathur (1995) and provide support for the existence of a significant relationship between average returns and factor betas in up and down markets.

It is widely known that momentum is not explained by the FF three-factor (3F) model (Cochrane, 2005, chapter 20). Since momentum stocks move together, one possible way we can explain momentum returns is by creating factors that are organized on the same characteristic as the portfolios.[6] In this chapter, we evaluate the sensitivity of the specifics of factor construction in the cross-sectional asset pricing tests for the size-and-momentum-sorted benchmark equity portfolios. We find that since the spread in average returns corresponds to the spread in size and momentum factor betas, they are more acceptable as performance attribution factors. This also reveals the incremental cross-sectional pricing power of size and momentum in the presence of traditional FF common risk factors, as well as the ex-post and ex-ante market risk.

Altogether, we find surprisingly strong support for $SMB^1$ and $MOM^1$ factors in the cross-section, as a sizeable portion of average returns and conditional volatility in our testing assets can be explained by the corresponding variation in exposure to those risk factors. We find that the ability of the FF three-factor (FF3F) model to explain the cross-sectional differences is related to shared characteristics of size-momentum-sorted portfolios. When we complement the traditional FF size by the new size factor, we capture a unique dimension of risk. We find that most of the variation in the average returns of our testing assets can be explained by the corresponding variation in exposure to $SMB^1$ and $MOM^1$ factors. Even though there is substantial variation in the corresponding premium, both $SMB^1$ and $MOM^1$ show empirical relevancy in the cross-section. Another surprising part of our findings is that both $SMB^1$ and $MOM^1$ factors seem to be distinct from $Mktrf$, $SMB^0$, and $HML^0$ — suggesting an independent source of risk. It is also interesting that the FF value factor — the role of which is limited in the case of average momentum returns — helps to explain the cross-sectional conditional volatility of the size-and-momentum-sorted portfolios. The economically significant role of $HML^0$ even in the presence of $SMB^1$ and $MOM^1$, which are based on the same set of securities as the test assets themselves, suggests a strong correlation structure, albeit in second moments, among value and momentum strategies.

This chapter addresses a potentially interesting point not clearly understood in the empirical asset pricing literature. Although various risk factors have been widely used in empirical studies, to the best of our knowledge, no prior studies offer a formal synthesis of the incremental asset pricing role of the risk factors for a standard set of testing assets. In addition, the inclusion of a measure of $EAM$ risk in our analysis demonstrates whether the incremental cross-sectional pricing power is sensitive to the inclusion of macroeconomic conditions. Furthermore, this study potentially adds a new dimension to the cross-sectional analysis of average stock returns in the standard asset pricing framework, which is almost always based on first moments. Even though the nexus between conditional volatility and systematic risk of stock returns is implicit in theoretical models (Leahy & Whited, 1996), the link is rarely explored empirically in the literature. The observation that the common risk factors are relevant in the cross-sectional characterization of conditional volatility is not quite known in the existing works.

The remainder of the chapter is organized as follows: The section "Related Literature and Our Contribution in Perspective" reviews the prior literature and explains what motivates our idea, the section "Data and Methodology" describes the methodology and models of performance measurement used throughout the chapter, the section "Empirical Results and Interpretations" presents our main empirical results and in the section "Conclusion" we conclude with some brief comments.

# RELATED LITERATURE AND OUR CONTRIBUTION IN PERSPECTIVE

Asset pricing models and the common risk factors serve as benchmarks for evaluating performance of active investments. In particular, performance is measured by the intercept (alpha) in the time-series regression of excess fund (or portfolio) returns on a set of benchmarks. There is an abundance of studies in corporate finance that use four benchmarks for mutual funds and a variety of other factors for hedge funds to adjust asset returns.[7] In one of the earlier works, Carhart (1997) extends the FF3F model and proposes a four-factor (4F) model to evaluate performance of equity mutual funds, where the set of four factors[8] include $EPM$, $SMB^0$, $HML^0$, and $MOM^1$. Carhart (1997) shows that the profitability of "hot hands" based trading strategies – documented by Hendricks, Patel, and Zeckhauser (1993) – disappears when investment payoffs are adjusted by $MOM^1$. It is also known that the profitability of "smart money" based trading strategies – documented by Zheng (1999) – also disappears in the presence of $MOM^1$. Following the seminal contribution of Fama and French (1993) and Carhart (1997), a number of works emerged on the evaluation of alternative common risk factors.

In the literature, in addition to proposals for new common risk factors, the investigation into the momentum effect has continued. Among others, Hung (2008a, 2008b) investigates the association between the return on the momentum, size and book-to-market portfolios, and the higher-order co-moments of these portfolios with the market return.[9] Chen, Novy-Marx, and Zhang (CNZ, 2011) propose an alternative 3F model where the factors are the market portfolio, an investment factor, and a return on equity factor. The CNZ model is claimed to explain short run reversal, earnings momentum, accrual, and stock valuation ratios, among several other anomalies. Recently, Novy-Marx (2012) examines intermediate and short horizon momentum, and finds that the former, rather than the latter, is the driver behind the momentum effect investigated in the previous literature.[10] The study also shows that this same result can be observed in international equity index, commodity, and currency markets. Novy-Marx (2012) concludes that the ability of intermediate horizon past performance to drive momentum challenges the popular behavioral (Barberis et al., 1998; Daniel et al., 1998; Hong & Stein, 1999) and rational (Johnson, 2002; Sagi & Seasholes, 2007) explanations of momentum.

In a related work, Du and Denning (2005) investigate the sources of the momentum observed in industry portfolio returns and use an augmented version of the delayed-reaction model of Jegadeesh and Titman (1993). By including contemporaneous and lagged market factors, as well as contemporaneous and lagged size and book-to-market factors, Du and Denning (2005) find that the common risk factors are important in explaining the industry momentum effect. This finding contradicts previous research, which indicates that industry-specific risk, rather than common factor risk, explains industry momentum (Lewellen, 2002; Moskowitz & Grinblatt, 1999). Liu and Zhang (2008) find evidence in support of a risk-based explanation of momentum. The authors find that the risk associated with the growth rate in industrial production (*GIP*) plays an important role in explaining momentum profits. This result contradicts Griffin, Ji, and Martin (2003), who found no macroeconomic risk explanation of momentum. By altering the design of the empirical tests conducted by Griffin et al. (2003), Liu and Zhang (2008) are able to show that the *GIP* factor explains a significant portion of the momentum profits.

Compared to the existing works, we find that a significant part of the cross-sectional variability is potentially due to some sources of variation, which are not independent of firm size and momentum factors. This view is related to Stivers and Sun (2010), who show that the variation in the value and momentum premia over time is related to changes in the stock markets cross-sectional return dispersion. More specifically, Stivers and Sun (2010) indicate that during their sample period from 1962 to 2005, the return dispersion in recent stock returns is positively related to value payoffs and negatively related to momentum payoffs. The authors also conclude that the relationship between return dispersion and value and momentum premia remains strong even in the presence of macroeconomic state variables.

The intuition of this chapter is closely related to the work of Asness et al. (2013), who investigate the joint returns to value and momentum strategies across different asset classes and countries. The authors find that the combined value and momentum strategy produces stronger results, statistically and economically, than the individual strategies studied in the previous literature. The authors indicate that "Value strategies are positively correlated with other value strategies across otherwise unrelated markets, and momentum strategies are positively correlated with other momentum strategies globally. However, value and momentum are negatively correlated with each other within and across asset classes" (p. 930).[11] It is instructive that, due to the presence of correlation, studies of value and momentum should be done jointly rather than examining each in isolation. In this chapter, we follow the same intuition. The evidence we uncover elucidates the source of common risk structure. The findings also demonstrates the importance of risk characterization by utilizing a combination of multiple factors related to size, value, and momentum for a set of standard testing assets. In the following section, we describe our data and methodology for analyzing the relative role of the common risk factors.

## DATA AND METHODOLOGY

Let $R_{i,t}$ be the return to the $i$th asset ($i = 1, 2, ..., N$) and $R_{f,t}$ be the risk free rate. Given the market risk premium and the risk premia of the systematic factors, we assume the following model for the determinants of expected returns for asset $i$:

$$E(R_{i,t} - R_{f,t}) = \lambda_1 \beta_{i,1} + \lambda_2 \beta_{i,2} + \cdots + \lambda_K \beta_{i,K} \qquad (1)$$

where $\lambda_j (j = 1, 2, ..., K)$ has the interpretation of the expected return to a portfolio (price of risk) with unit sensitivity to factor $j$ and zero sensitivity to all other factors, and $\beta$s are the slope coefficients from the return-generating process. For example, for market model, $K = 1$, $F_{1t} = R_{M,t} - R_{f,t}$, $\lambda_1 = E(R_{M,t} - R_{f,t})$, $\beta_{i1} = Cov(R_{i,t} - R_{f,t}, R_{M,t} - R_{f,t})/Var(R_{M,t} - R_{f,t})$. Similarly, for FF3F $K = 3$, $F_{1,t} = R_{M,t} - R_{f,t}$, $F_{2,t} = SMB_t^0$, $F_{3,t} = HML_t^0$, $\lambda_j = E(F_{j,t}) \forall j$.

The market risk premium, which has its foundation in the CAPM, is the reward for exposure to market risk. Unlike the market portfolio, the size and value portfolios are empirically motivated.[12] It has been argued that the size factor proxies for the illiquidity of the stock and that the value factor proxies for the "distress risk" (Fama & French, 1996). It is also well-known that $SMB^1$ and $HML^0$ contain information above and beyond that of the market factor for forecasting GDP growth (Lettau & Ludvigson, 2001; Liew & Vassalou, 2000; Vassalou, 2003).

To evaluate the relative importance of common risk factors, we conduct cross-sectional pricing tests using the Fama and MacBeth (1973) two-pass regression approach. We first obtain the factor betas in the first pass and risk premia in the second pass. More specifically, the factor exposures are obtained from the following first-pass time-series regressions:

$$R_{i,t} - R_{f,t} = \alpha_i + \beta_{i,1} F_{1,t-1} + \beta_{i2} F_{2,t-1} + \cdots + \beta_{i,K} F_{K,t-1} + \varepsilon_{i,t} \qquad (2)$$

where $F_{j,t}$s are factors ($j = 1, 2, ..., K$), $\beta_{i,j}$s are factor loadings or sensitivities, $E(\varepsilon_{i,t}) = 0 \ \forall i, Var(\varepsilon_{i,t}) = \sigma_i^2 \ \forall i, Cov(\varepsilon_{i,t}, \varepsilon_{k,t}) = 0 \ \forall \ i \neq k$, and

$Cov(\varepsilon_{i,t}, F_{j,t-1}) = 0$ $\forall i$ and $j$. In the second pass, betas are used as explanatory variables in the following cross-sectional regression:

$$R_{i,t} - R_{\mathrm{f},t} = \gamma_0 + \gamma_1\hat{\beta}_{i,1} + \gamma_2\hat{\beta}_{i,2} + \cdots + \gamma_K\hat{\beta}_{i,K} + e_{i,t} \qquad (3)$$

If the portfolio's loadings with respect to the risk factors $F_{j,t-1}$ ($j = 1, 2, \ldots,$ $K$) are important determinants of average returns, the slope coefficients of $\hat{\beta}_{i,j}$'s from Eq. (3) should be statistically significant.

In order to measure the relationship between conditional volatility and the systematic risk of portfolio returns, we follow Kogan (2004) and specify the following time-series model:

$$\left|r_{i,t} - \bar{r}_i\right| = \alpha_i + \beta_{i,1}F_{1,t-1} + \beta_{i2}F_{2,t-1} + \cdots + \beta_{i,K}F_{K,t-1} + \varepsilon_{i,t} \qquad (4)$$

where $r_{i,t}$ is the excess monthly return over the one-month T-bill rate for asset $i$, and $\bar{r}_i$ is the sample mean (or sample median). As mentioned by Kogan (2004, p. 426), "At a high frequency of observation, the conditional expectation of the absolute value of return should provide a reasonable measure of the conditional volatility of returns." We estimate the cross-sectional relation between conditional volatility and systematic risk of portfolio returns by the following model:

$$\left|r_{i,t} - \bar{r}_i\right| = \gamma_0 + \gamma_1\hat{\beta}_{i,1} + \gamma_2\hat{\beta}_{i,2} + \cdots + \gamma_K\hat{\beta}_{i,K} + e_{i,t} \qquad (5)$$

where we use the $\hat{\beta}_{i,j}$'s obtained from Eq. (4). If our cross-sectional tests using Eq. (5) reject $H_0 : \gamma_j = 0$ against $H_1 : \gamma_j \neq 0, \forall j = 1, \ldots, K$, it should predict a significant relation between common risk factors and conditional volatility, which is time-varying by nature.

We use 25 size-and-momentum-sorted benchmark equity portfolios as our testing assets. Our sample commences in January 1963 and extends through December 2011. We use six value-weighted portfolios formed on size and prior (2–12 months) returns to construct $SMB^1$ and $MOM^1$. The underlying portfolios, which are formed monthly, are the intersections of two portfolios formed on size (Small and Big) and three portfolios formed on prior returns (Low, Medium, and High). The monthly size breakpoint is the median NYSE market equity. The monthly prior (2–12) return breakpoints are the 30th and 70th NYSE percentiles. $SMB^1$ is the average return on the three small portfolios minus the average return on the three big portfolios:

$$SMB^1 = \frac{1}{3}(\text{Small/Low} + \text{Small/Medium} + \text{Small/High})$$
$$- \frac{1}{3}(\text{Big/Low} + \text{Big/Medium} + \text{Big/High})$$

$MOM^1$ is the average return on the two high prior return portfolios, minus the average return on the two low prior return portfolios:

$$MOM^1 = \frac{1}{2}(\text{Small/High} + \text{Big/High}) - \frac{1}{2}(\text{Small/Low} + \text{Big/Low})$$

Following Fama and French (2015a), we also use two sets of orthogonalized factors. The orthogonalized size factor, which we naturally call $SMB^2$, is the sum of the intercept and residual from the regression of $SMB^1$ on $EPM$, $SMB^0$, $HML^0$, and $MOM^1$. The orthogonalized momentum factor, which we identify as $MOM^2$, is equal to the sum of the intercept and residual from the regression of $MOM^1$ on $EPM$, $SMB^0$, $HML^0$, and $SMB^1$. Finally, by replacing $EPM_t$ with $EAM_t$ in the orthogonalized framework, we obtain two additional size and momentum factors, which we identify as $SMB^3$ and $MOM^3$, respectively.

The ex-post version of market return is the return of CRSP's value-weighted index on all NYSE, AMEX, and NASDAQ stocks. We obtain all double-sorted portfolio returns and value-weighted market returns from Ken French's website.[13] We estimate the ex-ante market risk factor by the following specification:

$$R_{M,t} - R_{f,t} = \delta_0 + \delta_1\left(R_{M,t-1} - R_{f,t-1}\right) + \delta_2 DIV_{t-1} + \delta_3 DEF_{t-1} + \delta_4 TERM_{t-1} + \delta_5 R_{f,t-1} + \varepsilon_{Mt}$$

$$(6)$$

where $DIV$ is the aggregate dividend yield, $DEF$ is the default spread (between Moody's Baa and Aaa corporate bonds), $TERM$ is the term spread (between the ten-year Treasury note and the one-year Treasury bill), and $R_f$ is the short-term interest rate (one-month Treasury bill rate). We obtain the bond yields from the Federal Reserve Bank of St. Louis. The estimated expected market risk premium, which we denote by $EAM_t$, is the fitted value from Eq. (6). In the next section, we detail all the empirical results.

# EMPIRICAL RESULTS AND INTERPRETATIONS

## *Descriptive Statistics*

We start the analysis with Table 1, which depicts the summary statistics and correlations of various risk factors. The means of both the ex-post and

*Table 1.* Factor Summary Statistics (Sample Period: January 1963–December 2011).

*Panel A: Descriptive Statistics*

| Variable | Portfolio | Orthogonalized | Mean | Median | Std. dev. | Min | Max | Skew | Kurtosis |
|---|---|---|---|---|---|---|---|---|---|
| $EPM$ | All three markets | No | 0.45 | 0.78 | 4.53 | −23.14 | 16.05 | −0.54 | 4.96 |
| $EAM$ | All three markets | Yes | 0.45 | 0.51 | 0.73 | −1.79 | 2.99 | −0.08 | 3.57 |
| $SMB^0$ | Six value-weighted size and BE/ME | No | 0.26 | 0.08 | 3.14 | −16.62 | 22.06 | 0.53 | 8.52 |
| $HML^0$ | Six value-weighted size and BE/ME | No | 0.39 | 0.41 | 2.91 | −12.87 | 13.88 | −0.02 | 5.52 |
| $SMB^1$ | Six value-weighted size and momentum | No | 0.27 | 0.18 | 2.98 | −10.27 | 16.34 | 0.49 | 5.42 |
| $MOM^1$ | Six value-weighted size and momentum | No | 0.72 | 0.83 | 4.29 | −34.76 | 18.40 | −1.44 | 14.08 |
| $SMB^2$ | Six value-weighted size and momentum | Yes | −0.03 | −0.03 | 0.91 | −4.18 | 3.97 | 0.09 | 5.52 |
| $MOM^2$ | Six value-weighted size and momentum | Yes | 0.91 | 0.95 | 4.16 | −29.90 | 15.47 | −1.23 | 11.27 |
| $SMB^3$ | Six value-weighted size and momentum | Yes | −0.05 | −0.06 | 0.91 | −4.07 | 3.95 | 0.15 | 5.50 |
| $MOM^3$ | Six value-weighted size and momentum | Yes | 1.09 | 1.30 | 4.19 | −30.31 | 15.85 | −1.34 | 11.65 |

*Panel B: Correlation*

| | $EPM$ | $EAM$ | $SMB^0$ | $HML^0$ | $SMB^1$ | $MOM^1$ | $SMB^2$ | $MOM^2$ | $SMB^3$ | $MOM^3$ | $VIX$ |
|---|---|---|---|---|---|---|---|---|---|---|---|
| $EPM$ | 1.00 | | | | | | | | | | |
| $EAM$ | 0.16*** | 1.00 | | | | | | | | | |
| $SMB^0$ | 0.31*** | 0.22*** | 1.00 | | | | | | | | |
| $HML^0$ | −0.29*** | −0.05 | −0.23*** | 1.00 | | | | | | | |
| $SMB^1$ | 0.27*** | 0.22*** | 0.94*** | −0.05 | 1.00 | | | | | | |
| $MOM^1$ | −0.12*** | −0.11*** | −0.00 | −0.16*** | −0.05 | 1.00 | | | | | |
| $SMB^2$ | −0.00 | 0.04 | 0.00 | −0.00 | 0.30*** | −0.00 | 1.00 | | | | |
| $MOM^2$ | 0.01 | −0.09** | 0.00 | 0.00 | 0.00 | 0.97*** | 0.08* | 1.00 | | | |
| $SMB^3$ | 0.03 | −0.00 | 0.00 | 0.00 | 0.30*** | −0.00 | 1.00*** | 0.08** | 1.00 | | |
| $MOM^3$ | −0.15*** | −0.01 | 0.00 | 0.00 | 0.00 | 0.98*** | 0.08*** | 0.98*** | 0.08* | 1.00 | |
| $VIX$ | −0.66*** | −0.04 | −0.19*** | 0.14 | −0.19*** | 0.13 | −0.05 | 0.06 | −0.07 | 0.15 | 1.00 |

*Notes: EPM* is the excess market return of the value-weighted CRSP portfolio in excess of the 3-month Treasury bill rate. *EAM* is the ex-ante market return calculate using the fitted component from the regression of *Mktrf* on lagged *Mktrf* and four lagged conditioning variables – the dividend yield, the default spread, the term spread, and the short-term Treasury bill rate.

$SMB^0$ and $HML^0$ are Fama and French (1993) size (old) and value factors based on six value-weight portfolios sorted by size and book-to-market. $SMB^1$ and $MOM^1$ are size (new) and momentum factors related to six value-weight portfolios formed on size and prior (2–12 months) returns. $SMB^2$ is the orthogonalized size (new) factor and is equal to the sum of the intercept and residual from the regression of $SMB^1$ on $Mktrf$, $SMB^0$, and $HML^0$.

$MOM^2$ is the orthogonalized momentum factor and is equal to the sum of the intercept and residual from the regression of $MOM^1$ on $Mktrf$, $SMB^0$, and $HML^0$.

$SMB^3$ is the orthogonalized size (new) factor and is equal to the sum of the intercept and residual from the regression of $SMB^1$ on $exMkt$, $SMB^0$, and $HML^0$.

$MOM^3$ is the orthogonalized momentum factor and is equal to the sum of the intercept and residual from the regression of $MOM^1$ on $exMkt$, $SMB^0$, and $HML^0$.

$VIX$ represents the returns to the Chicago Board Options Exchange Volatility Index. The correlations involving $VIX$ are based on data from the period between February 1990 and December 2011.

*, **, and *** denote a rejection of zero null hypothesis at the 10%, 5%, and 1% levels, respectively.

the ex-ante market returns are 0.45% per month, and the correlation between $EPM_t$ and $EAM_t$ is only around 0.16. Thus, a high downside ex-post market risk does not necessarily imply a high downside ex-ante market risk exposure. Compared to $EPM_t$, the standard deviation of $EAM_t$ is very small. Also, compared to $Mktrf_t$, the distribution of $EAM_t$ is much closer to a normal distribution. The average returns for the FF size and value factors are 0.26% and 0.39% per month, respectively. Both of our new size and momentum factors — $SMB^1$ and $HML^1$ — generate strong and economically significant premia. Not surprisingly, the new size factor $SMB^1$ is highly correlated with the FF size factor $SMB^0$, with a correlation equal to 0.94. The correlation between the momentum factor $MOM^1$ and $SMB^0$ and $HML^0$ are −0.00 and −0.16, respectively. Altogether, the descriptive statistics indicate that $SMB^1$ and $MOM^1$ capture unique aspects of risk, and are not reflective of the ex-post and ex-ante market factors.

When we inspect the orthogonalized factors, we find that the correlation between $SMB^1$ and $SMB^2$ is quite high, while the correlation between $SMB^2$ and $SMB^0$ is almost zero.[14] After also introducing the orthogonalized momentum factor, we observe that both $SMB^2$ and $MOM^2$ have about zero correlation with $EPM$, $SMB^0$, and $HML^0$. The average return of $SMB^2$ is very small (−0.03% per month), while the average return of $MOM^2$ is considerably higher (0.91% per month). Finally, when we incorporate $EAM_t$ in the orthogonalized framework, the resulting factors $SMB^3$ and $MOM^3$ have about zero correlation with $EAM$, $SMB^0$, and $HML^0$. As a result of the orthogonalizations, we obtain very low cross-correlations across competing sets of risk factors and this framework enables us to quantify the incremental role of $SMB^1$ and $MOM^1$ in the cross-section. The orthogonalized factors, by construction, also aid us in avoiding the multicollinearity problem. As we expect, the $EPM$ risk factor has significant negative correlation with $VIX$ measure during post-$VIX$ introduction period. The size factor is the only common risk factor significantly correlated with $VIX$. Interestingly, the $EAM$ risk factor is not related to $VIX$ at all.

Table 2 summarizes the average excess returns of the testing portfolios that we use as dependent variables in regressions (2) and (3). The set of 25 size-momentum portfolios produce a wide range of average excess returns, from −0.04% to 1.37% per month. The return summary indicates that high-momentum stocks have higher returns than low-momentum stocks and small-size stocks have lower returns than big stocks. In all but the lowest-momentum quintile, the average excess returns tend to decrease from the small-size to the big-size portfolios. Furthermore, the average

**Table 2.** Summary Statistics for the Average Excess Returns on 25 Size and Momentum Sorted Portfolios (Sample Period: January 1963–December 2011).

| Portfolio | Mean | Median | Std. Dev. | Min | Max | Skewness | Kurtosis |
|---|---|---|---|---|---|---|---|
| 11 | −0.04 | −0.21 | 8.13 | −29.71 | 47.33 | 0.89 | 8.49 |
| 12 | 0.64 | 0.68 | 5.97 | −27.41 | 36.78 | 0.10 | 7.37 |
| 13 | 0.88 | 1.25 | 5.52 | −28.65 | 30.94 | −0.29 | 6.70 |
| 14 | 1.03 | 1.40 | 5.58 | −30.86 | 24.18 | −0.57 | 6.03 |
| 15 | 1.37 | 1.82 | 6.89 | −33.34 | 31.55 | −0.44 | 5.63 |
| 21 | 0.09 | −0.04 | 7.98 | −28.09 | 57.48 | 0.65 | 8.65 |
| 22 | 0.61 | 0.83 | 5.95 | −27.87 | 34.03 | 0.03 | 7.19 |
| 23 | 0.78 | 1.12 | 5.31 | −30.29 | 26.56 | −0.45 | 6.68 |
| 24 | 0.97 | 1.31 | 5.47 | −31.38 | 23.60 | −0.61 | 6.21 |
| 25 | 1.21 | 1.62 | 6.85 | −32.91 | 30.11 | −0.41 | 5.32 |
| 31 | 0.21 | 0.08 | 7.47 | −25.74 | 44.75 | 0.46 | 6.15 |
| 32 | 0.55 | 0.61 | 5.59 | −23.54 | 27.03 | −0.07 | 5.99 |
| 33 | 0.67 | 0.87 | 5.13 | −26.26 | 24.70 | −0.36 | 6.37 |
| 34 | 0.75 | 1.24 | 5.06 | −32.02 | 18.45 | −0.75 | 6.76 |
| 35 | 1.17 | 1.51 | 6.40 | −33.41 | 26.05 | −0.52 | 5.21 |
| 41 | 0.13 | −0.14 | 7.36 | −25.11 | 46.41 | 0.42 | 6.95 |
| 42 | 0.52 | 0.50 | 5.60 | −24.97 | 28.87 | −0.02 | 5.79 |
| 43 | 0.59 | 0.84 | 4.92 | −25.30 | 21.32 | −0.30 | 5.60 |
| 44 | 0.76 | 0.89 | 4.86 | −26.28 | 20.14 | −0.51 | 5.55 |
| 45 | 1.01 | 1.37 | 5.98 | −29.97 | 24.42 | −0.54 | 5.13 |
| 51 | 0.10 | −0.02 | 6.85 | −25.83 | 30.94 | 0.19 | 5.72 |
| 52 | 0.40 | 0.30 | 4.96 | −20.60 | 24.69 | 0.15 | 5.33 |
| 53 | 0.31 | 0.34 | 4.43 | −21.74 | 17.34 | −0.30 | 5.04 |
| 54 | 0.50 | 0.66 | 4.38 | −21.10 | 19.96 | −0.17 | 4.99 |
| 55 | 0.74 | 1.28 | 5.34 | −25.48 | 21.22 | −0.42 | 4.90 |

*Note*: Each representative asset (*ij*) is a portfolio sorted by *i*th size and *j*th momentum.

portfolio returns ranges from 0.78% per month for the smallest-size quintile to 0.41% per month for the biggest-size quintile, moving in a perfectly decreasing pattern. The difference between the average excess returns for the highest- and lowest-momentum portfolios in each size category ranges from 1.41% to 0.64% per month. The summary statistics regarding the median estimates suggests that the distributions of the 25 size-momentum portfolio excess returns are not symmetric. In fact, none of the median excess returns are equal to the mean counterparts.[15] The range of median excess returns is from −0.21% to 1.82% per month. The relationship between median returns and momentum is consistent with our expectation, in that for every size quintile, median excess returns tend to increase with momentum.

The median excess returns of the long-short portfolio based on the highest-and lowest-momentum portfolios ranges from 2.03% to 1.30% per month. The summary statistics regarding higher moments such as standard deviation, skewness, and kurtosis, as well as the minimum and maximum values, are given in the last five columns of Table 2. It is worth noting that the small-size portfolios appear more volatile than the big-size portfolios. The average standard deviations of the smallest and the biggest-size quintiles are 6.41% and 5.18% per month, respectively. For 17 out of 25 portfolios, the average return is smaller than the median return and the result is considerable negative skewness. The extreme winner portfolios produce the highest average returns, which are associated with large negative skewness, and therefore have the possibility of large losses. All the five extreme loser portfolios on the other hand are positively skewed and include the possibility of large returns. There is also significant excess kurtosis, especially for small-size and low-momentum portfolios.

In order to visually supplement our findings, Fig. 1 depicts the historical average returns of our testing assets and several common risk factors against their historical average volatility. The vertical axis measures the average returns, and the horizontal axis represents the average volatility. We observe that except for the extreme five loser portfolios (the low-momentum quintile), for all other assets there is positive trade-off between

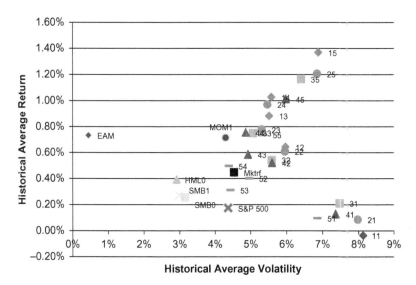

*Fig. 1.* Historical Trade-off between Risk and Return (Using Observed Values).

historical average return and average volatility. The portfolios consisting of the smallest size and highest momentum stocks have the highest returns, but also have very high volatility. We also plot the prediction of average returns and volatility in Fig. 2 using a multifactor model, which includes the new and the old size factors as well as the value and momentum factors. We see that, except for the extreme loser quintile portfolios, most of the portfolios lie closer to the 45° line, suggesting that the multifactor model is indeed successful in explaining the variability in average stocks returns.

We continue the visual supplementation by plotting the observed returns and observed volatilities using a three dimensional format, and the results are shown in Figs. 3 and 4. The average portfolio returns show an increasing trend as we move from the lowest to the highest momentum quintile. With the exception of the low-momentum quintile, there is also an increasing trend as we move from the largest to the smallest-size quintile. The average portfolio volatility on the other hand exhibits more of a U-shaped pattern. In other words, the volatility is generally higher in the highest and lowest-momentum quintiles, but for each momentum quintile the returns tend to increase as we move from the largest to the smallest-size quintile. Altogether, any variation in momentum quintile produces nonlinear association between return and volatility. Given these preliminary findings,

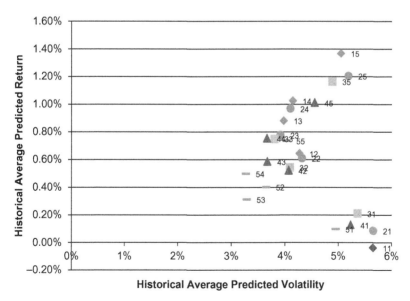

*Fig. 2.* Historical Trade-off between Risk and Return (Using Predicted Values).

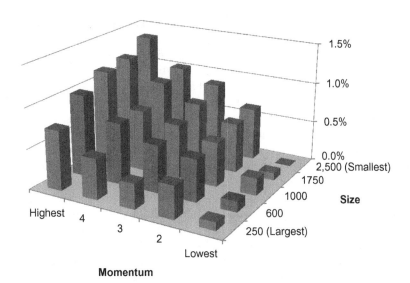

*Fig. 3.*   Observed Portfolio Returns by Size and Momentum.

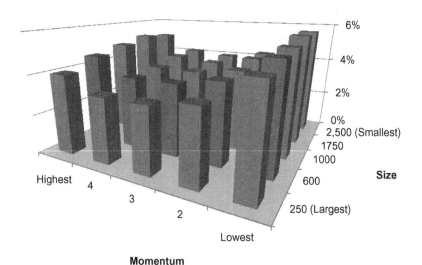

*Fig. 4.*   Mean Portfolio Volatility by Size and Momentum (Median in the Conditional Volatility Specification).

we are in a position to examine the cross-sectional relationship between average portfolio returns or volatility on the one hand, and factor loading estimates on the other. We will do so in the following two sections.

### Cross-Sectional Regressions Using Conditional Mean Specification

We start with Table 3 and report the familiar standard set of Fama and MacBeth (1973) cross-sectional regressions (CSRs) of excess returns to 25 size-and-momentum-sorted portfolios on realized betas associated with various sources of risk. The results from model 1 allow us to investigate the exclusive role of the traditional market risk in our testing assets. We find that the $EPM$ beta carries a negative coefficient of $-0.40$ and it is not statistically significant ($t$-statistic $= -0.70$). The inability of the market model to explain the cross-section of stock returns for size-and-momentum-sorted portfolios supports the findings of Jegadeesh and Titman (1993). In models 2−4, we examine the cross-sectional role of the traditional FF size and value factors. The estimated slope coefficients show that $SMB^0$ is significantly priced in the cross-section in all the models. $HML^0$ on the other hand, appear to be priced only in the absence of $SMB^0$. As such, in the FF3F specification (i.e., model 4), only $SMB^0$ is priced in the cross-section. Given the correlation structure reported in Panel B of Table 1, the result is not entirely surprising and corroborates previous findings that momentum is not explained by the FF3F model (Cochrane, 2005, chapter 20).

In models 5 through 10, we evaluate the cross-sectional role of $SMB^1$ and $MOM^1$ separately and jointly, with and without the presence of the FF factors. First of all, the coefficients on $SMB^1$ and $MOM^1$ appear to be individually significant in the cross-section. When used along with $EPM$ (i.e., model 5), the coefficient on the new size factor $SMB^1$ is positive (slope $= 3.18$) and highly significant ($t$-statistic $= 4.24$). When $MOM^1$ is used in conjunction with $EPM$ (i.e., model 6), the momentum factor carries a positive coefficient of 5.52 and a $t$-statistics of 3.79. The multifactor specifications 7−10 imply that there is a positive premium to size and negative premium to momentum. When we include all three FF factors in the model specifications, the coefficients on both $SMB^1$ and $MOM^1$ remain significant at the 1% level. As we already observed in Fig. 3, the high-momentum quintiles have higher returns than the low-momentum quintiles, and small-size firms with high momentum tend to have higher returns than large size firms with high momentum. Therefore, it is not surprising to see that, once we control for size, the CSR predicts low average returns of

*Table 3.* Fama–MacBeth Regressions with Returns on 25 Size and Momentum Portfolios as Independent Variable, Using Lagged Factors Including Lagged Ex-Post Market Factor (January 1963–December 2011).

| Model | $\gamma_0$ Int | $\gamma_1$ EPM | $\gamma_2$ $SMB^0$ | $\gamma_3$ $HML^0$ | $\gamma_4$ $SMB^1$ | $\gamma_5$ $MOM^1$ | $\gamma_6$ $SMB^2$ | $\gamma_7$ $MOM^2$ | RMSE | $R^2(\bar{R}^2)$ |
|---|---|---|---|---|---|---|---|---|---|---|
| 1 | 0.71*** (3.73) | −0.40 (−0.70) | | | | | | | 2.12 | 0.22 (0.19) |
| 2 | 0.72*** (3.77) | −1.25** (−1.93) | 3.39*** (4.41) | | | | | | 1.85 | 0.39 (0.34) |
| 3 | 0.58*** (3.03) | 0.06 (0.10) | | −3.69*** (−3.96) | | | | | 1.85 | 0.40 (0.34) |
| 4 | 0.69*** (3.86) | −1.01 (−1.40) | 2.96*** (4.02) | −1.03 (−1.02) | | | | | 1.77 | 0.46 (0.38) |
| 5 | 0.73*** (3.81) | −1.57** (−2.25) | | | 3.18*** (4.24) | | | | 1.86 | 0.39 (0.33) |
| 6 | 0.86*** (4.58) | 0.29 (0.52) | | | | 5.52*** (3.79) | | | 1.99 | 0.32 (0.26) |
| 7 | 0.49** (2.54) | −3.82*** (−3.68) | | | | 6.30*** (4.44) | −8.78*** (3.96) | | 1.80 | 0.44 (0.36) |
| 8 | 0.44** (2.31) | −3.09*** (−3.11) | 6.61*** (4.72) | | | 6.01*** (4.34) | −9.17*** (−4.03) | | 1.74 | 0.50 (0.40) |
| 9 | 0.45** (2.36) | −3.21*** (−3.32) | | 0.52 (0.62) | 5.22*** (4.41) | −8.02*** (−4.08) | | | 1.70 | 0.52 (0.42) |
| 10 | 0.48** (2.49) | −3.52*** (−3.62) | 7.83*** (6.32) | 1.60* (1.83) | 7.13*** (5.62) | −10.19*** (−4.89) | | | 1.69 | 0.55 (0.43) |
| 11 | 0.48** (2.49) | −3.52*** (−3.62) | 7.83*** (6.32) | 1.60* (1.83) | | −10.19*** (−4.89) | −0.51** (−2.49) | | 1.69 | 0.55 (0.43) |
| 12 | 0.48** (2.49) | −3.52*** (−3.62) | 7.83*** (6.32) | 1.60* (1.83) | | | −0.51** (−2.49) | −10.50*** (−4.88) | 1.69 | 0.55 (0.43) |

*Notes*: The table presents second-stage cross-sectional regressions results, including the intercepts and slopes in percent per month. $EPM$ is the lagged excess market return. $SMB^0$ and $HML^0$ are lagged size (old) and value factors based on six value-weight portfolios sorted by size and book-to-market. $SMB^1$ and $MOM^1$ are lagged size (new) and momentum factors related to six value-weight portfolios formed on size and prior (2–12 months) returns. $SMB^2$ is the lagged orthogonalized size (new) factor and is equal to the sum of the intercept and residual from the regression of $SMB^1$ on $EPM$, $SMB^0$, $HML^0$, and $MOM^1$. $MOM^2$ is the lagged orthogonalized momentum factor and is equal to the sum of the intercept and residual from the regression of $MOM^1$ on $EPM$, $SMB^0$, $HML^0$, and $SMB^1$. Figures in parenthesis are the Fama–MacBeth *t*-statistics.
*, **, and *** denote a rejection of the null hypothesis at the 10%, 5%, and 1% levels, respectively.

high-momentum stocks. This observation also holds true in the presence of $SMB^0$ and $HML^0$.

In the last two regressions of Table 3, we show that the orthogonalized versions of $SMB^1$ and $MOM^1$, which are represented by $SMB^2$ and $MOM^2$, respectively, strongly capture common variation in average returns left by $EPM$, $SMB^0$, and $HML^0$. The coefficient of $SMB^2$ is significant with or without the presence of $MOM^2$, indicating that the premium to the momentum factor doesn't dominate in the cross-section. In the presence of the FF factors and $SMB^2$ (i.e., model 12), the coefficient on $MOM^2$ remains negative and highly significant. In the presence of other factors than $EPM$, the significance of $HML^0$ never reaches 5% level. This continues to hold true when we introduce the orthogonalized size and momentum factors. Interestingly, even after the orthogonalization, the $EPM$ risk does play a significant role in the cross-section. In terms of overall performance, models 10–12 produce the highest $\overline{R}^2$ and lowest root-mean-squared errors.

Altogether, the results in Table 3 suggest that momentum is economically significant and commands an average negative risk premium. It is natural to ask where the momentum premium comes from. If we think of the $\lambda_j$ associated with $MOM^1$ as a risk premium, then we need to understand the real, economic, and nondiversifiable risk that is proxied by the $MOM^1$ portfolio. In particular, why are investors so concerned about holding stocks that perform poorly at times when the $MOM^1$ portfolio does poorly, even though the market does not fall? One possible explanation is that $MOM^1$ proxies for variables that forecast time-varying investment opportunities or time-varying risk aversion. As we saw in Table 2, the low expected return momentum portfolios (losers) have higher skewness than high expected return portfolios (winners). If portfolio returns have systematic skewness, expected returns should include rewards for accepting this risk (Harvey & Siddique, 2000). Echoing similar argument, Conrad, Dittmar, and Ghysels (2013) recently suggest that "more negatively skewed securities have higher subsequent returns" (p. 87). We already observed in Table 2, that in our testing assets, there is positive (negative) skewness for 8 out of 25 (17 out of 25) portfolios. All five quintiles corresponding to the lowest-momentum category display positive skewness. In addition, small-size portfolios have a higher average excess kurtosis than that of the big-size firms (3.92 compared to 2.20), and on average, the winner quintile display much lower excess kurtosis than the loser quintile (2.24 compared to 4.26). Therefore, consistent with the existing literature, what we observe in the CSRs appears to be the fallout of a negative relationship between skewness and subsequent returns of size-momentum-sorted portfolios.

Table 4 contains similar Fama—MacBeth CSRs as in Table 3 with the exception that the *EPM* factor is now replaced by the *EAM* factor. As in the ex-post case, the *EAM* beta in model 1 carries a statistically insignificant negative coefficient and explains around 20% of overall variability. Unlike *EPM*, the *EAM* beta however is significantly priced in all the CSRs except models 1 and 6. Among the most notable results in Table 4, both $SMB^0$ and $SMB^1$ always remain statistically significant at the 5% level. This indicates that, in the presence of the ex-ante market factor, both of the size related factors appear positively priced in the cross-section. Unlike the situation in Table 3, $MOM^1$ is not always statistically significant in Table 4. The value factor $HML^0$ carries negative slope coefficients that are significant only at the 5% level. It should also be noted that the $SMB^1$ factor loses its statistical significance after orthogonalization. In the presence of *EAM*, $MOM^1$ remains economically significant with an average positive risk premium only for model 6. For models 7—11, the premium to $MOM^1$ is negative and statistically insignificant. After orthogonalization (i.e., model 12), the significance of the premium reappears, which suggests that we adequately dealt with multicollinearity. As in Table 3, the presence of size-and-momentum-based factors produces the best overall performance. Continuing with the central theme of the chapter, in the next section, we elaborate on our next set of results using the conditional volatility in the cross-sections.

*Cross-Sectional Regressions Using Conditional Volatility Specification*

Table 5 contains results from Fama—MacBeth CSRs similar to those in Table 3, but the independent variable is now the absolute difference between the monthly return and the sample mean, as outlined in the left-hand sides of Eqs. (4) and (5). Kogan (2004) has previously employed the absolute value of de-meaned excess returns as the dependent variable in time-series regressions, but we are the first to analyze absolute value of excess returns as the dependent variable in cross-sectional regressions.

The estimated models in Table 5 portray an intuitive picture of the common risk factors relative role in the cross-section of conditional volatility. In model 1, the slope coefficient on *EPM* is negative and highly significant (slope = −3.55 and *t*-statistic = −4.64). In models 2—4, both $SMB^0$ and $HML^0$ are significantly priced. More generally, $SMB^0$ is negatively priced and $HML^0$ is positively priced in all the CSRs. As such, it appears that smaller size firms display smaller conditional volatility than bigger size

***Table 4.*** Fama–MacBeth Regressions with Returns on 25 Size and Momentum Portfolios as Independent Variable, Using Lagged Factors Including Lagged Ex-Ante Market Factor (January 1963–December 2011).

| Model | $\gamma_0$ Int | $\gamma_1$ EAM | $\gamma_2$ SMB$^0$ | $\gamma_3$ HML$^0$ | $\gamma_4$ SMB$^1$ | $\gamma_5$ MOM$^1$ | $\gamma_6$ SMB$^3$ | $\gamma_7$ MOM$^3$ | RMSE | $R^2(\overline{R}^2)$ |
|---|---|---|---|---|---|---|---|---|---|---|
| 1 | 0.81*** (4.20) | −0.19 (−1.00) | | | | | | | 2.15 | 0.20 (0.17) |
| 2 | 1.13*** (5.80) | −0.89*** (−3.55) | 3.18*** (4.79) | | | | | | 1.94 | 0.35 (0.29) |
| 3 | 0.88*** (4.55) | −0.68*** (−2.95) | | −4.37*** (−4.41) | | | | | 1.90 | 0.37 (0.31) |
| 4 | 1.06*** (5.94) | −0.87*** (−3.52) | 2.40*** (3.85) | −2.16** (−1.99) | | | | | 1.83 | 0.44 (0.36) |
| 5 | 1.16*** (5.92) | −0.92*** (−3.53) | | | 2.95*** (4.65) | | | | 1.93 | 0.35 (0.29) |
| 6 | 0.82*** (4.27) | 0.08 (0.43) | | | | 4.39*** (3.10) | | | 2.01 | 0.31 (0.25) |
| 7 | 1.23*** (6.49) | −1.24*** (−4.79) | | | 3.57*** (4.96) | −2.03 (−1.52) | | | 1.85 | 0.43 (0.34) |
| 8 | 1.17*** (6.41) | −1.16*** (−4.37) | | | 3.09*** (4.37) | −1.62 (−1.21) | | | 1.81 | 0.48 (0.37) |
| 9 | 1.13*** (6.39) | −1.32*** (−5.00) | | −2.29** (−2.18) | 2.19*** (3.05) | −2.18 (−1.64) | | | 1.73 | 0.51 (0.42) |
| 10 | 1.13*** (6.39) | −1.28*** (−4.40) | 2.81*** (4.21) | −2.23** (−2.07) | 2.28*** (3.18) | −2.03 (−1.59) | | | 1.70 | 0.55 (0.43) |
| 11 | 1.13*** (6.39) | −1.28*** (−4.40) | 2.81*** (4.21) | −2.23** (−2.07) | | −2.03 (−1.59) | 0.11 (0.39) | | 1.70 | 0.55 (0.43) |
| 12 | 1.13*** (6.39) | −1.28*** (−4.40) | 2.81*** (4.21) | −2.23** (−2.07) | | −2.03 (−1.59) | 0.11 (0.39) | −3.30*** (−2.59) | 1.70 | 0.55 (0.43) |

*Notes*: The table presents second-stage cross-sectional regressions results, including the intercepts and slopes in percent per month. *EAM* is the lagged ex-ante excess market return. $SMB^0$ and $HML^0$ are lagged size (old) and value factors based on six value-weight portfolios sorted by size and book-to-market. $SMB^1$ and $MOM^1$ are lagged size (new) and momentum factors related to six value-weight portfolios formed on size and prior (2–12 months) returns. $SMB^3$ is the lagged orthogonalized size (new) factor and is equal to the sum of the intercept and residual from the regression of $SMB^1$ on *EAM*, $SMB^0$, $HML^0$, and $MOM^1$. $MOM^3$ is the lagged orthogonalized momentum factor and is equal to the sum of the intercept and residual from the regression of $MOM^1$ on *EAM*, $SMB^0$, $HML^0$, and $SMB^1$. Figures in parenthesis are the Fama–MacBeth *t*-statistics.
** and *** denote a rejection of the null hypothesis at the 5% and 1% levels, respectively.

*Table 5.* Fama–MacBeth Regressions with Volatility (Mean Specification) of 25 Size and Momentum Portfolios as Independent Variable, Using Lagged Factors Including Lagged Ex-Post Market Factor (January 1963–December 2011).

| Model | $\gamma_0$ Int | $\gamma_1$ EPM | $\gamma_2$ $SMB^0$ | $\gamma_3$ $HML^0$ | $\gamma_4$ $SMB^1$ | $\gamma_5$ $MOM^1$ | $\gamma_6$ $SMB^2$ | $\gamma_7$ $MOM^2$ | RMSE | $R^2(\bar{R}^2)$ |
|---|---|---|---|---|---|---|---|---|---|---|
| 1 | 3.81*** (20.60) | −3.55*** (−4.64) | | | | | | | 2.05 | 0.10 (0.06) |
| 2 | 2.69*** (19.62) | −7.06*** (−10.35) | −11.01*** (−13.47) | | | | | | 1.87 | 0.26 (0.19) |
| 3 | 4.45*** (20.51) | −5.56*** (−7.70) | | 19.16*** (15.23) | | | | | 1.87 | 0.24 (0.17) |
| 4 | 4.27*** (19.36) | −5.85*** (−8.43) | −5.18*** (−6.02) | 18.07*** (12.30) | | | | | 1.77 | 0.34 (0.25) |
| 5 | 3.35*** (20.77) | −4.93*** (−6.89) | | | −5.52*** (−7.71) | | | | 1.90 | 0.25 (0.18) |
| 6 | 3.67*** (20.52) | −4.94*** (−6.66) | | | | −11.89*** (−9.06) | | | 1.79 | 0.26 (0.20) |
| 7 | 3.13*** (20.92) | −6.55*** (−9.58) | | | −6.20*** (−8.72) | −11.90*** (−9.07) | | | 1.60 | 0.41 (0.33) |
| 8 | 2.35*** (15.08) | −8.36*** (−11.84) | −11.50*** (−13.17) | | −7.40*** (−9.94) | −0.10 (−0.07) | | | 1.58 | 0.45 (0.34) |
| 9 | 3.94*** (23.94) | −6.06*** (−8.91) | | 12.92*** (12.40) | −2.48*** (−3.57) | −9.47*** (−6.85) | | | 1.56 | 0.46 (0.35) |
| 10 | 2.85*** (16.21) | −7.79*** (−11.02) | −9.80*** (−11.04) | 9.89*** (9.49) | −5.59*** (−6.99) | −1.44 (−1.18) | | | 1.55 | 0.49 (0.36) |
| 11 | 2.85*** (16.21) | −7.79*** (−11.02) | −9.80*** (−11.04) | 9.89*** (9.49) | | −1.44 (−1.18) | 1.78*** (9.16) | | 1.55 | 0.49 (0.36) |
| 12 | 2.85*** (16.21) | −7.79*** (−11.02) | −9.80*** (−11.04) | 9.89*** (9.49) | | −1.44 (−1.18) | 1.78*** (9.16) | 0.95 (0.71) | 1.55 | 0.49 (0.36) |

*Notes:* The table presents second-stage cross-sectional regressions results, including the intercepts and slopes in percent per month. *EPM* is the lagged excess market return. $SMB^0$ and $HML^0$ are lagged size (old) and value factors based on six value-weight portfolios sorted by size and book-to-market. $SMB^1$ and $MOM^1$ are lagged size (new) and momentum factors related to six value-weight portfolios formed on size and prior (2–12 months) returns. $SMB^2$ is the lagged orthogonalized size (new) factor and is equal to the sum of the intercept and residual from the regression of $SMB^1$ on *EPM*, $SMB^0$, $HML^0$, and $MOM^1$. $MOM^2$ is the lagged orthogonalized momentum factor and is equal to the sum of the intercept and residual from the regression of $MOM^1$ on *EPM*, $SMB^0$, $HML^0$, and $SMB^1$. Figures in parenthesis are the Fama–MacBeth *t*-statistics.
** and *** denote a rejection of the null hypothesis at the 5% and 1% levels, respectively.

firms, and that growth firms are more volatile than the value firms. The momentum factor is negatively priced in models 6, 7, and 9, suggesting that the high-momentum firms may have lower volatility compared to the low-momentum firms. However, when we include the dimension of risk characterized by $SMB^0$, momentum loses its significance. This implies that most of the conditional volatility in average returns are related to the size of the firms, and appear independent of whether the firms are recent winners or losers. This is indeed supported by the mean portfolio volatility estimates displayed in Fig. 4. On average, the mean conditional volatility monotonically decreases over size quintiles but displays a U-shaped pattern over momentum quintiles. Similar observation holds when we redefine conditional volatility with respect to median. Finally, we notice that the significance of $HML^0$ remains intact even in the presence of the orthogonalized versions of the size-and-momentum-based factors.

In Table 6, we replicate the CSRs of Table 5, but we replace $EPM$ with the $EAM$ risk factor. The CSR results show that the slope coefficient on the $EAM$ factor is always negative and significantly priced when we employ the conditional volatility specification. When the market is up in the ex-ante sense, the volatility decreases, and when the market is down in ex-ante sense, the volatility increases. In other words, the conditional volatility of size-and-momentum-sorted portfolios appears to be procyclical. In all models 2–5, the introduction of $EAM$ does not alter the significance of $SMB^0$ and $HML^0$. Even in the presence of $EAM$, both $SMB^0$ and $SMB^1$ are negatively priced. For the subsequent specifications, models 6–12, it is interesting to note that the introduction of $EAM$ doesn't force a change to the positive sign of $SMB^3$ or its significance. This observation suggests that the conditional volatility of the size-momentum-sorted portfolios is stochastic and is not only a function of the state of the economy but also of the firm size. When it comes to explanatory power, models 10–12 have the lowest RMSE and highest $\bar{R}^2$ in both Tables 5 and 6.

Due to the asymmetry of the portfolio return distribution, we also redefine the conditional volatility by utilizing the median returns and replicate the two-stage tests presented in Tables 5 and 6. The CSR results when using median returns in the conditional volatility specification are reported in Tables 7 and 8. Even after modifying the definition of conditional volatility, across all 12 models, the coefficients on $EPM$ and $EAM$ continue to be negative and remain highly significant (at the 1% level). In both Tables 7 and 8, model 1 explains 10% of the overall conditional volatility. The slope coefficients of the traditional size and value factors are similar to those in

*Table 6.* Fama–MacBeth Regressions with Volatility (Mean Specification) of 25 Size and Momentum Portfolios as Independent Variable, Using Lagged Factors Including Lagged Ex-Ante Market Factor (January 1963–December 2011).

| Model | $\gamma_0$ Int | $\gamma_1$ EAM | $\gamma_2$ SMB$^0$ | $\gamma_3$ HML$^0$ | $\gamma_4$ SMB$^1$ | $\gamma_5$ MOM$^1$ | $\gamma_6$ SMB$^3$ | $\gamma_7$ MOM$^3$ | RMSE | $R^2$ ($\bar{R}^2$) |
|---|---|---|---|---|---|---|---|---|---|---|
| 1 | 4.07*** (30.61) | −1.60*** (−14.18) | | | | | | | 2.03 | 0.10 (0.06) |
| 2 | 3.11*** (26.13) | −1.60*** (−14.16) | −9.33*** (−10.29) | | | | | | 1.84 | 0.27 (0.20) |
| 3 | 3.96*** (31.08) | −0.39*** (−2.46) | | 17.11*** (10.67) | | | | | 1.90 | 0.23 (0.16) |
| 4 | 3.59*** (27.00) | −0.74*** (−6.62) | −6.88*** (−8.17) | 12.89*** (10.53) | | | | | 1.84 | 0.30 (0.20) |
| 5 | 3.55*** (28.61) | −1.79*** (−16.64) | | | −5.97*** (−8.21) | | | | 1.88 | 0.25 (0.18) |
| 6 | 4.35*** (28.08) | −0.97*** (−8.02) | | | | −7.55*** (−5.40) | | | 1.79 | 0.26 (0.19) |
| 7 | 3.77*** (26.93) | −1.13*** (−9.78) | | | −5.99*** (−8.24) | −7.98*** (−5.67) | | | 1.60 | 0.41 (0.33) |
| 8 | 2.73*** (18.48) | −0.88*** (−7.23) | −10.80*** (−11.09) | | −7.18*** (−9.24) | 0.45 (0.37) | | | 1.57 | 0.45 (0.34) |
| 9 | 3.95*** (27.65) | −0.51*** (−4.10) | | 10.44*** (11.93) | −3.21*** (−4.81) | −8.54*** (−6.04) | | | 1.60 | 0.44 (0.33) |
| 10 | 2.99*** (19.47) | −0.61*** (−5.04) | −9.54*** (−9.84) | 9.24*** (11.12) | −5.59*** (−7.19) | −1.22 (−1.04) | | | 1.58 | 0.47 (0.34) |
| 11 | 2.99*** (19.47) | −0.61*** (−5.04) | −9.54*** (−9.84) | 9.24*** (11.12) | | −1.22 (−1.04) | 1.66*** (7.91) | | 1.58 | 0.47 (0.34) |
| 12 | 2.99*** (19.47) | −0.61*** (−5.04) | −9.54*** (−9.84) | 9.24*** (11.12) | | −1.22 (−1.04) | 1.66*** (7.91) | 1.03 (0.90) | 1.58 | 0.47 (0.34) |

*Notes:* The table presents second-stage cross-sectional regressions results, including the intercepts and slopes in percent per month. *EAM* is the lagged ex-ante excess market return. $SMB^0$ and $HML^0$ are lagged size (old) and value factors based on six value-weight portfolios sorted by size and book-to-market. $SMB^1$ and $MOM^1$ are lagged size (new) and momentum factors related to six value-weight portfolios formed on size and prior (2–12 months) returns. $SMB^3$ is the lagged orthogonalized size (new) factor and is equal to the sum of the intercept and residual from the regression of $SMB^1$ on $EAM$, $SMB^0$, $HML^0$, and $MOM^1$. $MOM^3$ is the lagged orthogonalized momentum factor and is equal to the sum of the intercept and residual from the regression of $MOM^1$ on $EAM$, $SMB^0$, $HML^0$, and $SMB^1$. Figures in parenthesis are the Fama–MacBeth $t$-statistics.
*** denotes a rejection of the null hypothesis at the 1% level.

**Table 7.** Fama–MacBeth Regressions with Volatility (Median Specification) of 25 Size and Momentum Portfolios as Independent Variable, Using Lagged Factors Including Lagged Ex-Post Market Factor (January 1963–December 2011).

| Model | $\gamma_0$ Int | $\gamma_1$ EPM | $\gamma_2$ $SMB^0$ | $\gamma_3$ $HML^0$ | $\gamma_4$ $SMB^1$ | $\gamma_5$ $MOM^1$ | $\gamma_6$ $SMB^2$ | $\gamma_7$ $MOM^2$ | RMSE | $R^2(\bar{R}^2)$ |
|---|---|---|---|---|---|---|---|---|---|---|
| 1 | 3.92*** (20.10) | −2.73*** (−3.40) | | | | | | | 2.06 | 0.10 (0.06) |
| 2 | 2.78*** (18.54) | −6.26*** (−8.60) | −10.51*** (−12.74) | | | | | | 1.87 | 0.26 (0.20) |
| 3 | 4.49*** (20.26) | −5.12*** (−6.84) | | 19.38*** (16.44) | | | | | 1.89 | 0.23 (0.16) |
| 4 | 4.34*** (19.15) | −5.35*** (−7.18) | −4.91*** (−5.52) | 18.60*** (14.05) | | | | | 1.77 | 0.35 (0.25) |
| 5 | 3.52*** (19.60) | −3.80*** (−4.85) | | | −4.69*** (−6.23) | | | | 1.89 | 0.26 (0.19) |
| 6 | 3.56*** (19.92) | −5.60*** (−7.58) | | | | −11.89*** (−9.36) | | | 1.80 | 0.26 (0.20) |
| 7 | 3.02*** (19.84) | −7.15*** (−10.31) | | | −6.27*** (−8.53) | −12.26*** (−9.66) | | | 1.59 | 0.42 (0.34) |
| 8 | 2.28*** (14.35) | −8.69*** (−12.15) | −11.44*** (−12.83) | | −7.36*** (−9.61) | −1.06 (−0.79) | | | 1.57 | 0.46 (0.35) |
| 9 | 3.88*** (23.62) | −6.32*** (−9.22) | | 13.33*** (12.50) | −2.47*** (−3.43) | −9.99*** (−7.46) | | | 1.54 | 0.48 (0.37) |
| 10 | 2.97*** (16.68) | −7.78*** (−11.01) | −9.08*** (−10.02) | 11.01*** (10.03) | −4.97*** (−6.02) | −3.21*** (−2.92) | | | 1.53 | 0.51 (0.38) |
| 11 | 2.97*** (16.68) | −7.78*** (−11.01) | −9.08*** (−10.02) | 11.01*** (10.03) | | −3.21*** (−2.92) | 1.51*** (7.66) | | 1.53 | 0.51 (0.38) |
| 12 | 2.97*** (16.68) | −7.78*** (−11.01) | −9.08*** (−10.02) | 11.01*** (10.03) | | | 1.51*** (7.66) | −0.54 (−0.44) | 1.53 | 0.51 (0.38) |

*Notes:* The table presents second-stage cross-sectional regressions results, including the intercepts and slopes in percent per month. *EPM* is the lagged excess market return. $SMB^0$ and $HML^0$ are lagged size (old) and value factors based on six value-weight portfolios sorted by size and book-to-market. $SMB^1$ and $MOM^1$ are lagged size (new) and momentum factors related to six value-weight portfolios formed on size and prior (2–12 months) returns. $SMB^2$ is the lagged orthogonalized size (new) factor and is equal to the sum of the intercept and residual from the regression of $SMB^1$ on *EPM*, $SMB^0$, $HML^0$, and $MOM^1$. $MOM^2$ is the lagged orthogonalized momentum factor and is equal to the sum of the intercept and residual from the regression of $MOM^1$ on *EPM*, $SMB^0$, $HML^0$, and $SMB^1$. Figures in parenthesis are the Fama–MacBeth *t*-statistics.
*** denotes a rejection of the null hypothesis at the 1% level.

*Table 8.*  Fama–MacBeth Regressions with Volatility (Median Specification) of 25 Size and Momentum Portfolios as Independent Variable, Using Lagged Factors Including Lagged Ex-Ante Market Factor (January 1963–December 2011).

| Model | $\gamma_0$ Int | $\gamma_1$ EAM | $\gamma_2$ $SMB^0$ | $\gamma_3$ $HML^0$ | $\gamma_4$ $SMB^1$ | $\gamma_5$ $MOM^1$ | $\gamma_6$ $SMB^3$ | $\gamma_7$ $MOM^3$ | RMSE | $R^2\left(\bar{R}^2\right)$ |
|---|---|---|---|---|---|---|---|---|---|---|
| 1 | 4.02*** (30.05) | -1.65*** (-14.83) | | | | | | | 2.04 | 0.10 (0.06) |
| 2 | 3.06*** (25.25) | -1.69*** (-15.28) | -9.23*** (-10.22) | | | | | | 1.85 | 0.27 (0.20) |
| 3 | 3.90*** (30.48) | -0.33* (-1.96) | | 17.68*** (10.98) | | | | | 1.91 | 0.23 (0.16) |
| 4 | 3.56*** (26.96) | -0.68*** (-5.89) | -6.67*** (-7.94) | 13.86*** (12.27) | | | | | 1.85 | 0.30 (0.20) |
| 5 | 3.53*** (27.43) | -1.84*** (-17.36) | | | -5.62*** (-7.50) | | | | 1.88 | 0.25 (0.18) |
| 6 | 4.32*** (27.70) | -1.05*** (-8.64) | | | | -7.38*** (-5.48) | | | 1.79 | 0.26 (0.20) |
| 7 | 3.72*** (26.11) | -1.22*** (-10.36) | | | -6.10*** (-8.14) | -8.11*** (-5.97) | | | 1.58 | 0.42 (0.34) |
| 8 | 2.75*** (18.62) | -0.96*** (-7.74) | -10.57*** (-10.91) | | -7.11*** (-9.01) | -0.43 (-0.37) | | | 1.56 | 0.46 (0.35) |
| 9 | 3.93*** (27.26) | -0.45*** (-3.53) | | 11.47*** (12.31) | -2.98*** (-4.48) | -9.15*** (-6.71) | | | 1.58 | 0.45 (0.34) |
| 10 | 3.10*** (20.84) | -0.57*** (-4.61) | -8.90*** (-9.50) | 10.28*** (11.54) | -5.02*** (-6.69) | -2.84*** (-2.65) | | | 1.56 | 0.49 (0.35) |
| 11 | 3.10*** (20.84) | -0.57*** (-4.61) | -8.90*** (-9.50) | 10.28*** (11.54) | | -2.84*** (-2.65) | 1.43*** (6.72) | | 1.56 | 0.49 (0.35) |
| 12 | 3.10*** (20.84) | -0.57*** (-4.61) | -8.90*** (-9.50) | 10.28*** (11.54) | | -2.84*** (-2.65) | 1.43*** (6.72) | -0.36 (-0.35) | 1.56 | 0.49 (0.35) |

*Notes*: The table presents second-stage cross-sectional regressions results, including the intercepts and slopes in percent per month. *EAM* is the lagged ex-ante excess market return. $SMB^0$ and $HML^0$ are lagged size (old) and value factors based on six value-weight portfolios sorted by size and book-to-market. $SMB^1$ and $MOM^1$ are lagged size (new) and momentum factors related to six value-weight portfolios formed on size and prior (2–12 months) returns. $SMB^3$ is the lagged orthogonalized size (new) factor and is equal to the sum of the intercept and residual from the regression of $SMB^1$ on *EAM*, $SMB^0$, $HML^0$, and $MOM^1$. $MOM^3$ is the lagged orthogonalized momentum factor and is equal to the sum of the intercept and residual from the regression of $MOM^1$ on *EAM*, $SMB^0$, $HML^0$, and $SMB^1$. Figures in parenthesis are the Fama–MacBeth *t*-statistics.
* and *** denote a rejection of the null hypothesis at the 10% and 1% levels, respectively.

Tables 5 and 6 – both being significantly priced in the CSRs. The FF3F model that includes $EPM$ risk explains around 25% of overall cross-sectional volatility, and the same estimate for the FF3F model that includes $EAM$ risk is 20%. Across models 5 through 10, the unorthogonalized size factors are predominantly negatively priced, $HML^0$ is positively priced, while $MOM^1$ is always negatively priced. These observations indicate that the conditional volatility of portfolios comprised of small firms is higher compared to that of portfolios comprised of big firms. Similarly, value stocks appear to be less volatile than growth stocks. In contrast, the result that portfolios consisting of low-momentum stocks display higher volatility than high-momentum portfolios doesn't hold after orthogonalization. It is interesting to note that in the presence of $EAM$, the CSR results are largely unaffected by the change in the specification of conditional volatility. In both Tables 7 and 8, models 10–12 appear strongest in terms of $\overline{R}^2$ and RMSE.

Next, in order to evaluate whether our reported results are simply an artifact of the underlying methodology, we conduct several robustness tests. In the next section, we report some of those robustness results.

## Robustness Tests

In the literature, it is known that when the factor betas have little variation across the testing assets, one may obtain poorly estimated factor premia.[16] According to Jagannathan and Wang (2007), such a lack of variation may create a near multicollinearity problem between the vector of ones and the vector of $EPM$ betas. The easiest way to check the assertion is to impose a restriction on the model by omitting the intercept and reestimating the CSRs. In our first set of robustness test, therefore, we follow Savov (2011) and repeat the Fama–MacBeth procedure in the absence of an intercept in the cross-section. The idea is to see whether such tests involving free intercepts can produce insignificant slope coefficients on the betas. In the two panels of Table 9, we report the results of such an experiment for the three best models of Tables 3 and 4.

The reported results suggests that omitting the intercept results in positive slope coefficient for both $EPM$ and $EAM$ beta, but only the $EAM$ beta becomes significant in the cross-section. The coefficient on the value factor is always positive, but becomes significant in Panel A and not in Panel B. The momentum factor generates a significant positive risk premium

*Table 9.* Fama–Macbeth Regressions with Returns on 25 Size and Momentum Portfolios as Independent Variable and Without Cross-Sectional Intercept (January 1963–December 2011).

*Panel A: Regressions Using Ex-Post Market Factor*

| Model | $\gamma_1$ EPM | $\gamma_2$ $SMB^0$ | $\gamma_3$ $HML^0$ | $\gamma_4$ $SMB^1$ | $\gamma_5$ $MOM^1$ | $\gamma_6$ $SMB^2$ | $\gamma_7$ $MOM^2$ | RMSE | $R^2\left(\overline{R}^2\right)$ |
|---|---|---|---|---|---|---|---|---|---|
| 1 | 0.36* | 0.68*** | 0.62*** | 0.24* | 0.72*** | | | 1.34 | 0.87 (0.84) |
|   | (1.90) | (4.12) | (3.04) | (1.89) | (3.99) | | | | |
| 2 | 0.36* | 0.68*** | 0.62*** | | 0.72*** | −0.49*** | | 1.34 | 0.87 (0.84) |
|   | (1.90) | (4.12) | (3.04) | | (3.99) | (−4.71) | | | |
| 3 | 0.36* | 0.68*** | 0.62*** | | | −0.49*** | 0.79*** | 1.34 | 0.87 (0.84) |
|   | (1.90) | (4.12) | (3.04) | | | (−4.71) | (4.23) | | |

*Panel B: Regressions Using Ex-Ante Market Factor*

| Model | $\gamma_1$ EAM | $\gamma_2$ $SMB^0$ | $\gamma_3$ $HML^0$ | $\gamma_4$ $SMB^1$ | $\gamma_5$ $MOM^1$ | $\gamma_6$ $SMB^3$ | $\gamma_7$ $MOM^3$ | RMSE | $R^2\left(\overline{R}^2\right)$ |
|---|---|---|---|---|---|---|---|---|---|
| 1 | 0.44*** | 1.10*** | 0.24 | 0.20 | 0.66*** | | | 1.43 | 0.86 (0.83) |
|   | (2.61) | (5.88) | (1.17) | (1.59) | (3.64) | | | | |
| 2 | 0.44*** | 1.10*** | 0.24 | | 0.66*** | −0.87*** | | 1.43 | 0.86 (0.83) |
|   | (2.61) | (5.88) | (1.17) | | (3.64) | (−5.90) | | | |
| 3 | 0.44*** | 1.10*** | 0.24 | | | −0.87*** | 0.71*** | 1.43 | 0.86 (0.83) |
|   | (2.61) | (5.88) | (1.17) | | | (−5.90) | (3.73) | | |

*Notes*: The table presents second-stage cross-sectional regressions results, including the intercepts and slopes in percent per month. These regressions were estimated with no cross-sectional intercept. *EPM* is the excess market return and *EAM* is the ex-ante excess market return. $SMB^0$ and $HML^0$ are size (old) and value factors based on six value-weight portfolios sorted by size and book-to-market. $SMB^1$ and $MOM^1$ are size (new) and momentum factors related to six value-weight portfolios formed on size and prior (2−12 months) returns. $SMB^2$ is the orthogonalized size (new) factor and is equal to the sum of the intercept and residual from the regression of $SMB^1$ on $EPM$, $SMB^0$, $HML^0$, and $MOM^1$. $MOM^2$ is the orthogonalized momentum factor and is equal to the sum of the intercept and residual from the regression of $MOM^1$ on $EPM$, $SMB^0$, $HML^0$, and $SMB^1$. $SMB^3$ is the orthogonalized size (new) factor and is equal to the sum of the intercept and residual from the regression of $SMB^1$ on $EAM$, $SMB^0$, $HML^0$, and $MOM^1$. $MOM^3$ is the orthogonalized momentum factor and is equal to the sum of the intercept and residual from the regression of $MOM^1$ on $EAM$, $SMB^0$, $HML^0$, and $SMB^1$. Figures in parenthesis are the Fama−Macbeth $t$-statistics.
\* and \*\*\* denote a rejection of the null hypothesis at the 10% and 1% levels, respectively.

irrespective of any specification we consider. Even though the new size factor beta is not significant in both panels, after orthogonalization, the negative slope of the corresponding beta reveals an economically meaningful pattern. As the new size captures a different dimension of risk than $SMB^0$, the negative slope coefficients of the $SMB^2$ (and $SMB^3$) beta in models 2 and 3 suggest that small firms with recent past winners result in high average returns in the cross-section.

Next, we test whether the model performances are related to the shared characteristics of risk factors identified through different sorts. We follow Fama and French (2015a, 2015b) and construct a combined size factor $SMB^4$, which is the simple average of $SMB^0$ and $SMB^1$. The results are reported in Table 10. The modified size factor doesn't provide any major improvement in the description of cross-sectional average returns and volatility. The $SMB^4$ beta yields a significant positive slope for average returns and significantly negative slope for conditional volatility. The $HML^0$ beta stays redundant for describing cross-sectional average returns, but continues to be relevant for describing conditional volatility. The role of EPM, EAM, and $MOM^1$ remain unaltered compared to the best models of Tables 3–6. Therefore, we conclude that the inferences about the cross-sectional role of common risk factors do not seem to be sensitive to the way factors are defined.

***Table 10.*** Fama–MacBeth Regressions with Combined $SMB^0$ and $SMB^1$ Factor (January 1963–December 2011).

*Panel A: Regressions Using Ex-Post Market Factor*

| Dependent Variable | $\gamma_0$ Int | $\gamma_1$ EPM | $\gamma_2$ $HML^0$ | $\gamma_3$ $SMB^4$ | $\gamma_4$ $MOM^1$ | RMSE | $R^2\left(\overline{R}^2\right)$ |
|---|---|---|---|---|---|---|---|
| Return | 0.44** | −3.62*** | 1.22 | 6.14*** | −9.50*** | 1.70 | 0.52 (0.42) |
| | (2.34) | (−3.74) | (1.40) | (4.95) | (−4.59) | | |
| Volatility | 3.82*** | −6.24*** | 12.28*** | −4.30*** | −9.18*** | 1.56 | 0.46 (0.36) |
| | (23.58) | (−9.20) | (11.73) | (−5.84) | (−6.68) | | |

*Panel B: Regressions Using Ex-Ante Market Factor*

| Dependent Variable | $\gamma_0$ Int | $\gamma_1$ EAM | $\gamma_2$ $HML^0$ | $\gamma_3$ $SMB^4$ | $\gamma_4$ $MOM^1$ | RMSE | $R^2\left(\overline{R}^2\right)$ |
|---|---|---|---|---|---|---|---|
| Return | 1.13*** | −1.29*** | −2.23*** | 2.51*** | −2.08*** | 1.73 | 0.51 (0.41) |
| | (6.39) | (−5.10) | (−2.10) | (3.62) | (−1.56) | | |
| Volatility | 3.85*** | −0.56*** | 9.81*** | −4.77*** | −8.03*** | 1.59 | 0.44 (0.33) |
| | (26.65) | (−4.58) | (11.54) | (−6.50) | (−5.75) | | |

*Notes*: The table presents second-stage cross-sectional regressions results, including the intercepts and slopes in percent per month. These regressions were estimated using return and conditional volatility (mean specification) as dependent variables. *EPM* is the excess market return and *EAM* is the ex-ante excess market return. $SMB^0$ and $HML^0$ are size (old) and value factors based on six value-weight portfolios sorted by size and book-to-market. $SMB^1$ and $MOM^1$ are size (new) and momentum factors related to six value-weight portfolios formed on size and prior (2–12 months) returns. $SMB^4$ is defined as the simple average of $SMB^0$ and $SMB^1$. Figures in parenthesis are the Fama–MacBeth *t*-statistics.
*, **, and *** denote a rejection of the null hypothesis at the 10%, 5%, and 1% levels, respectively.

As part of the robustness tests, we also implement two additional alternative sets of CSRs. First, instead of the lagged factor betas (used in Tables 3–8), we incorporate contemporaneous factor betas in the CSRs. Second, as an additional step in the cross-sectional analysis of conditional volatility, we substantially alter our specification of conditional volatility. In this second set of tests, we essentially replicate the Fama–MacBeth CSRs discussed in the section "Cross-Sectional Regressions Using Conditional Volatility Specification" by using the predicted variance from a GARCH(1,1) model as the dependent variable. We find that the results of these additional tests are qualitatively similar to those reported in the chapter.[17]

*Price of Factor Risk in Up and Down Market*

Finally, to better understand the nature of the factor loadings in the cross-section, we investigate whether the price of factor risk varies over market conditions and business cycles.[18] In order to investigate such asymmetric risk characterization, we utilize the market segmentation procedures of Pettengill et al. (1995) and reestimate models 5–7 of Tables 3 and 4 by incorporating up and down market dummy variables in the CSR. We define two sets of dummy variables, one using the $EPM$ return and another using expected market risk premium or $EAM$ return. We report the mentioned results in Table 11. In Panel A, we define $\delta = 1$ if $EPM_t > 0$, and $\delta = 0$ if $EPM_t \leq 0$. In Panel B, we define $\delta^* = 1$ if $EAM_t \leq 0$, and $\delta^* = 0$ if $EAM_t > 0$. The end results are that we are able to utilize several new variables. For example, for *Mktrf*, we have $EPM^+ = \delta^* \ EPM$ and $EPM^- = (1 - \delta) * EPM$.

Panel A of Table 11 indicates that the size-and-momentum-sorted portfolios have more downside $EPM$ risk than upside. In model 1, the slope of coefficient of $SMB^1$ beta is 2.35 ($t$-statistic $= 4.16$) in the up-market and 0.84 ($t$-statistic $= 1.67$) in the down market. Therefore, the influence of the size factor is more pronounced in the up-market than in the down market. Model 2 indicates that the positive relationship between average return and momentum that we saw in model 6 of Table 3 is not evenly distributed over up and down markets. When we include both size and momentum factors, the negative relationship between portfolio returns and the momentum factor is stronger in up markets. Furthermore, looking at the results of Panel B provides us with an idea about the influence of $EAM$ risk in up and down markets. Here model 1 suggests that for the

***Table 11.*** Fama−MacBeth Regressions with Returns on 25 Size and Momentum Portfolios as Independent Variable and Up and Down Market Versions of the Lagged Market, Size, and Momentum Factors as Independent Variables (January 1963−December 2011).

*Panel A: Regressions Using Ex-Post Market Factor*

| Model | $\gamma_0$ Int | $\gamma_1$ $EPM^+$ | $\gamma_2$ $EPM^-$ | $\gamma_3$ $SMB^{1+}$ | $\gamma_4$ $SMB^{1-}$ | $\gamma_5$ $MOM^{1+}$ | $\gamma_6$ $MOM^{1-}$ | RMSE | $R^2\left(\overline{R}^2\right)$ |
|---|---|---|---|---|---|---|---|---|---|
| 1 | 0.73*** | 1.02* | −2.59*** | 2.35*** | 0.84* | | | 1.86 | 0.39 (0.33) |
| | (3.81) | (1.89) | (−5.96) | (4.16) | (1.67) | | | | |
| 2 | 0.86*** | 2.19*** | −1.90*** | | | 3.31*** | 2.21** | 1.99 | 0.32 (0.26) |
| | (4.58) | (5.29) | (−5.48) | | | (3.00) | (2.29) | | |
| 3 | 0.49** | −0.27 | −3.54*** | 4.12*** | 2.17** | −5.26*** | −3.52** | 1.80 | 0.44 (0.36) |
| | (2.54) | (−0.33) | (−5.55) | (3.84) | (2.30) | (−3.12) | (−2.41) | | |

*Panel B: Regressions Using Ex-Ante Market Factor*

| Model | $\gamma_0$ Int | $\gamma_1$ $EAM^+$ | $\gamma_2$ $EAM^-$ | $\gamma_3$ $SMB^{1+}$ | $\gamma_4$ $SMB^{1-}$ | $\gamma_5$ $MOM^{1+}$ | $\gamma_6$ $MOM^{1-}$ | RMSE | $R^2\left(\overline{R}^2\right)$ |
|---|---|---|---|---|---|---|---|---|---|
| 1 | 1.16*** | −0.47*** | −0.45** | 0.94** | 2.00*** | | | 1.93 | 0.35 (0.29) |
| | (5.94) | (−2.82) | (−2.22) | (2.38) | (3.98) | | | | |
| 2 | 0.82*** | −0.12 | 0.20 | | | 1.52* | 2.87** | 2.01 | 0.31 (0.25) |
| | (4.27) | (−1.06) | (1.45) | | | (1.73) | (2.56) | | |
| 3 | 1.23*** | −0.62*** | −0.62*** | 1.24*** | 2.33*** | −0.93 | −1.10 | 1.85 | 0.43 (0.34) |
| | (6.49) | (−3.52) | (−3.21) | (2.89) | (3.97) | (−1.21) | (−1.00) | | |

*Notes*: The table presents second-stage cross-sectional regressions results, including the intercepts and slopes in percent per month. $\delta = 1$ when $EPM \geq 0$ and 0 otherwise. $\delta^* = 1$ when $EAM < 0$ and 0 otherwise. $EPM^+ = EPM * \delta$, where $EPM$ is the lagged ex-post market factor. $EAM^+ = EAM * \delta^*$, where $EAM$ is the lagged ex-ante market factor. $EPM^- = (1 - \delta) * EPM$ and $EAM^- = (1 - \delta^*) * EAM$. The same construction is used for $SMB^{1+}$, $SMB^{1-}$, $MOM^{1+}$, and $MOM^{1-}$, where $SMB^1$ and $MOM^1$ are size (new) and momentum factors related to six value-weight portfolios formed on size and prior (2−12 months) returns. Figures in parenthesis are the Fama−MacBeth *t*-statistics.
*, **, and *** denote a rejection of the null hypothesis at the 10%, 5%, and 1% levels, respectively.

CSRs which includes the *EAM* beta, the aggregate risk exposure is evenly distributed over up and down markets. In the presence of *EAM* risk, the size factor continues to play a strong role in both up and down markets, while the momentum factor fails to influence the cross-section of average returns. This evidence, in conjunction with the previously reported results in the sections "Descriptive Statistics," "Cross-Sectional Regressions Using Conditional Mean Specification," "Cross-Sectional Regressions Using Conditional Volatility Specification," "Robustness Tests," suggests an important incremental role of the size and momentum factors that is not clearly understood in the existing literature.

## CONCLUSIONS

In this chapter, we use 25 size-and-momentum-sorted benchmark equity portfolios as testing assets, and conduct various cross-sectional pricing tests using average returns and conditional volatility of returns as dependent variables. We incorporate both ex-post and ex-ante market risk factors, and alternative sets of common risk factors that are related to size, value, and momentum. We illustrate the sensitivity of the specifics of risk factor construction in asset pricing tests. Since various common risk factors are widely used and serve as benchmarks for evaluating the performance of active investments, our study complements the existing literature by providing a formal synthesis of the incremental asset pricing implications of size, value, and momentum factors.

Altogether, we introduce a new dimension to the cross-sectional analysis of average returns in the standard asset pricing framework, which almost always focuses on conditional mean. We highlight whether the incremental cross-sectional pricing power is sensitive to the inclusion of aggregate economic conditions in the cross-section of average returns and conditional volatility. The challenge for future research is to reconcile the two sets of relations for other types of testing assets. A clear understanding of the role of firm-level size, book-to-market, past return, and turnover when individual stock returns are adjusted by various common risk factors should be another avenue of potential future research.

## NOTES

1. Early work on the value effect and the momentum effect include Stattman (1980), Fama and French (1992), Jegadeesh and Titman (1993), Asness (1994), Grinblatt and Moskowitz (2004). Studies confirming the presence of size, value, and momentum in individual stocks across global stock markets includes Fama and French (2012) and Asness, Moskowitz, and Pedersen (2013). A recent paper by Geczy and Samonov (2013) examine U.S. security prices during the period 1801 through 1926 and suggests that momentum profits remain positive and statistically significant during the pre-1927 period.

2. The superior performance of price momentum strategies has been confirmed by a large number of works and has generated a great deal of interest among scholars studying behavioral (Barberis, Shleifer, & Vishny, 1998; Daniel, Hirshleifer, & Subrahmanyam, 1998; Hong, Lim, & Stein, 2000) as well as rational (Berk, Green, & Naik, 1999; Choi & Kim, 2014; Johnson, 2002) theories.

3. Fama and French (2015a, 2015b) discuss the incremental role of value factor in the time-series regressions.

4. For example, recently Harvey et al. (2014) report 313 papers in a selection of journals and a large number of factors that attempt to explain the cross-section of expected returns.

5. There is a view in the literature that the resulting conditional volatility of stock returns is a convenient empirical proxy for the uncertainty of the firm's environment (Leahy & Whited, 1996).

6. Starting with Carhart (1997), there is a large number of works who use this type of momentum factor. But as mentioned by Cochrane (2005, p. 447) "This is obviously so ad hoc that nobody wants to add it as a risk factor." Recently, Fama and French (2015a) argued that if the testing assets originate from finer versions of the sorts that produce the common risk factors, the test are (p. 3) "home games."

7. The performance of common risk factors explaining hedge fund performance is different to account for nonlinear payoffs generated by hedge funds (see Avramov, Kosowski, Naik, & Teo, 2011).

8. Carhart's (1997) original version of zero-investment factor mimicking portfolio for momentum is based on one-year momentum in stock returns.

9. Hung (2008a, 2008b) also confirms previous findings of Chung, Johnson, and Schill (2006), by indicating that the SMB and HML factors act as proxies for higher-order systematic co-moments. Furthermore, the author finds that the momentum factor also acts as a proxy for higher-order systematic co-moments. Hung (2008a, 2008b) therefore concludes that these three factors "proxy for market risk not captured by the traditional mean-variance CAPM" (p. 17).

10. Intermediate horizon momentum is based on performance measured over the 12 to seven months prior to portfolio formation, while short horizon momentum is based on performance measured over the past six months (Novy-Marx, 2012).

11. Asness et al. (2013) discover the presence of common global factors related to value and momentum and construct a 3F model similar to those of Fama and French (1993) and Carhart (1997). Their 3F model however, does not contain a size factor. It is important to note that despite the popularity of various common risk factors from an empirical perspective, they don't explain all anomalies and the underlying statistical tests are successful only for equity portfolios and not for individual securities. For example, Ferson and Harvey (1999) show that the alpha in multifactor models varies with business conditions. Avramov, Chordia, and Goyal (2006) show that firm-level size, book-to-market, past return, and turnover are still important when individual stock returns are adjusted by the $SMB^0$, $HML^0$, $MOM^1$, and liquidity factors.

12. Under the CAPM, the vector of expected returns and the covariance matrix are given by $\beta \mu^e_{Mkt}$ and $\beta \beta' \sigma^2_{Mkt} + \Sigma$, respectively, where $\Sigma$ is the covariance matrix of the residuals in the time-series asset pricing regression. The corresponding quantities under the Carhart (1997) model are $\beta_{Mkt} \mu^e_{Mkt} + \beta_{SMB} \mu^e_{SMB} + \beta_{HML} \mu^e_{HML} + \beta_{MOM} \mu^e_{MOM}$ and $\beta \Sigma_F \beta' + \Sigma$, respectively, where $\Sigma_F$ is the covariance matrix of the factors.

13. See http://mba.tuck.dartmouth.edu/pages/faculty/ken.french/

14. We also create an orthogonalized size factor from the regression of $SMB^2$ on the $SMB^1$ factor alone and our results are qualitatively similar.

15. The observation is important because of the way we define the conditional volatility in Eq. (4). The wide range of median excess returns and its relation with size and momentum presents potential challenges for competing risk factors.

16. In some of the existing work, it is quite common to have a negative market risk premium for the 25 size- and book-to-market-sorted portfolios in the presence of a free constant (Jagannathan & Wang, 2007; Kang, Kim, Lee, & Min, 2011).
17. The detailed summary of this additional set of results can be found in the supplementary materials submitted with the chapter.
18. Recent work that tests whether market states are relevant for predicting momentum profits includes Galariotis, Holmes, Kallinterakis, and Ma (2014).

# REFERENCES

Asness, C. S. (1994). *Variables that explain stock returns.* Ph.D. dissertation, University of Chicago.

Asness, C. S., Moskowitz, T. J., & Pedersen, L. H. (2013). Value and momentum everywhere. *Journal of Finance, 68,* 929–985.

Avramov, D., Chordia, T., & Goyal, A. (2006). Liquidity and autocorrelations in individual stock returns. *Journal of Finance, 61,* 2365–2394.

Avramov, D., Kosowski, R., Naik, N. Y., & Teo, M. (2011). Hedge funds, managerial skill, and macroeconomic variables. *Journal of Financial Economics, 99,* 672–692.

Barberis, N., Shleifer, A., & Vishny, R. (1998). A model of investor sentiment. *Journal of Financial Economics, 49,* 307–343.

Berk, J. B., Green, R. C., & Naik, V. (1999). Optimal investment, growth options, and security returns. *Journal of Finance, 54,* 1553–1607.

Carhart, M. M. (1997). On persistence in mutual fund performance. *Journal of Finance, 52,* 57–82.

Chen, L., Novy-Marx, R., & Zhang, L. (2011). *An alternative three-factor model.* SSRN. Retrieved from http://ssrn.com/abstract=1418117. doi:10.2139/ssrn.1418117

Choi, S. M., & Kim, H. (2014). Momentum effect as part of a market equilibrium. *Journal of Financial and Quantitative Analysis, 49,* 107–130.

Chung, Y. P., Johnson, H., & Schill, M. J. (2006). Asset pricing when returns are nonnormal: Fama-French factors versus higher-order systematic co-moments. *Journal of Business, 79,* 923–940.

Cochrane, J. H. (2005). *Asset pricing.* Princeton, NJ: *Princeton University Press.*

Conrad, J., Dittmar, R. F., & Ghysels, E. (2013). Ex ante skewness and expected stock returns. *Journal of Finance, 68,* 85–124.

Daniel, K., Hirshleifer, D., & Subrahmanyam, A. (1998). Investor psychology and security market under- and overreactions. *Journal of Finance, 53,* 1839–1885.

Du, D., & Denning, K. (2005). Industry momentum and common factors. *Finance Research Letters, 2,* 107–124.

Fama, E. F., & French, K. R. (1992). The cross-section of expected stock returns. *Journal of Finance, 47,* 427–465.

Fama, E. F., & French, K. R. (1993). Common risk factors in the returns on stocks and bonds. *Journal of Financial Economics, 33,* 3–56.

Fama, E. F., & French, K. R. (1996). Multifactor explanations of asset pricing anomalies. *Journal of Finance, 51,* 55–84.

Fama, E. F., & French, K. R. (2012). Size, value, and momentum in international stock returns. *Journal of Financial Economics, 105,* 457–472.

Fama, E. F., & French, K. R. (2015a). A five-factor asset pricing model. *Journal of Financial Economics, 116,* 1–22.

Fama, E. F., & French, K. R. (2015b). *Dissecting anomalies with a five factor model.* Fama-Miller Working Paper. SSRN. Retrieved from http://ssrn.com/abstract = 2503174. doi:10.2139/ssrn.2503174

Fama, E. F., & MacBeth, J. D. (1973). Risk, return and equilibrium: Empirical tests. *Journal of Political Economy, 81,* 607–636.

Ferson, W. E., & Harvey, C. R. (1999). Conditioning variables and the cross section of stock returns. *Journal of Finance, 54,* 1325–1360.

Galariotis, E. C., Holmes, P., Kallinterakis, V., & Ma, X. S. (2014). Market states, expectations, sentiment and momentum: How naïve are investors? *International Review of Financial Analysis, 32,* 1–12.

Geczy, C., & Samonov, M. (2013). *212 years of price momentum (The world's longest backtest: 1801–2012).* SSRN. Retrieved from http://ssrn.com/abstract = 2292544. doi:10.2139/ssrn.2292544

Griffin, J. M., Ji, X., & Martin, J. S. (2003). Momentum investing and business cycle risk: Evidence from pole to pole. *Journal of Finance, 58,* 2515–2547.

Grinblatt, M., & Moskowitz, T. J. (2004). Predicting stock price movements from past returns: The role of consistency and tax-loss selling. *Journal of Financial Economics, 71,* 541–579.

Harvey, C. R., Liu, Y., & Zhu, H. (2014). *....and the cross-section of stock returns.* Working Paper. SSRN. Retrieved from http://ssrn.com/abstract = 2249314. doi:10.2139/ssrn.2249314

Harvey, C. R., & Siddique, A. (2000). Conditional skewness in asset pricing tests. *Journal of Finance, 55,* 1263–1295.

Hendricks, D., Patel, J., & Zeckhauser, R. J. (1993). Hot hands in mutual funds: Short-run persistence of relative performance, 1974–1988. *Journal of Finance, 48,* 93–130.

Hong, H., Lim, T., & Stein, J. C. (2000). Bad news travels slowly: Size, analyst coverage, and the profitability of momentum strategies. *Journal of Finance, 55,* 265–295.

Hong, H., & Stein, J. C. (1999). A unified theory of underreaction, momentum trading, and overreaction in asset markets. *The Journal of Finance, 54,* 2143–2184.

Hung, C.-H. (2008a). Return predictability of higher-moment CAPM market models. *Journal of Business Finance & Accounting, 35,* 998–1022.

Hung, C.-H. (2008b). *Momentum, size and value factors versus systematic co-moments in stock returns.* SSRN. Retrieved from http://ssrn.com/abstract = 965765. doi:10.2139/ssrn.965765

Jagannathan, R., & Wang, Y. (2007). Lazy investors, discretionary consumption, and the cross-section of stock returns. *Journal of Finance, 62,* 1623–1661.

Jegadeesh, N., & Titman, S. (1993). Returns to buying winners and selling losers: Implications for stock market efficiency. *Journal of Finance, 48,* 65–91.

Johnson, T. C. (2002). Rational momentum effects. *Journal of Finance, 57,* 585–608.

Kang, J., Kim, T. S., Lee, C., & Min, B.-K. (2011). Macroeconomic risk and the cross-section of stock returns. *Journal of Banking & Finance, 35,* 3158–3173.

Kogan, L. (2004). Asset prices and real investment. *Journal of Financial Economics, 73,* 411–431.

Leahy, J., & Whited, T. M. (1996). The effect of uncertainty on investment: Some stylized facts. Journal of Money, Credit and Banking, *28,* 64–83.

Lettau, M., & Ludvigson, S. (2001). Consumption, aggregate wealth, and expected stock returns. *Journal of Finance, 61*, 815–849.

Lewellen, J. (2002). Momentum and autocorrelation in stock returns. *The Review of Financial Studies, 15*, 533–563.

Liew, J., & Vassalou, M. (2000). Can book-to-market, size and momentum be risk factors that predict economic growth? *Journal of Financial Economics, 57*, 221–245.

Liu, L. X., & Zhang, L. (2008). Momentum profits, factor pricing, and macroeconomic risk. *Review of Financial Studies, 21*, 2417–2448.

Moskowitz, T. J., & Grinblatt, M. (1999). Do industries explain momentum? *Journal of Finance, 54*, 1249–1290.

Novy-Marx, R. (2012). Is momentum really momentum? *Journal of Financial Economics, 103*, 429–453.

Pettengill, G. N., Sundaram, S., & Mathur, I. (1995). The conditional relation between beta and returns. *The Journal of Financial and Quantitative Analysis, 30*, 101–116.

Sagi, J. S., & Seasholes, M. S. (2007). Firm-specific attributes and the cross-section of momentum. *Journal of Financial Economics, 84*, 389–434.

Savov, A. (2011). Asset pricing with garbage. *Journal of Finance, 66*, 177–201.

Stattman, D. (1980). Book values and stock returns. *The Chicago MBA: A Journal of Selected Papers, 4*, 25–45.

Stivers, C. T., & Sun, L. (2010). Cross-sectional return dispersion and time-variation in value and momentum premia. *Journal of Financial and Quantitative Analysis, 45*, 987–1014.

Vassalou, M. (2003). News related to future GDP growth as a risk factor in equity returns. *Journal of Financial Economics, 68*, 47–73.

Zheng, L. (1999). Is money smart? A study of mutual fund investors' fund selection ability. *Journal of Finance, 54*, 901–933.

# IPO ADVERTISING: A POSSIBLE CAUSE OF SHORT-TERM OVERVALUATION

Konpanas Dumrongwong

## ABSTRACT

*This research investigated the market conditions caused by IPO advertising by examining the impact of IPO advertising, based on the US stock market from 1986 to 2009. The relationship between advertising intensity in the IPO year and the degree of IPO underpricing was examined. It was found that an increase in advertising intensity around an IPO event increases the initial returns. Simultaneously, however, advertising intensity around an IPO event also increases the degree of overvaluation, which raises the question as to whether advertising serves primarily as a mechanism to convey a firm's true value to investors. The theoretical valuation of IPO and the relation between IPO advertising and the degree of stock overvaluation are discussed. Based on the Peasnell's (1982) residual-income valuation framework (henceforth RIV), IPO advertising was proved to cause stock price to be more overvalued in the secondary market: a positive relationship was found between advertising and the degree of stock overvaluation relative to its theoretical value. Accordingly, an alternative hypothesis, that advertising inflates the*

The Spread of Financial Sophistication Through Emerging Markets Worldwide
Research in Finance, Volume 32, 145–163
ISSN: 0196-3821/doi:10.1108/S0196-382120160000032006

*short-run stock price, was proposed. The results of this study are consistent with the view of Purnanandam and Swaminathan (2004), namely that the stock price of newly listed firms can be overvalued.*

**Keywords:** Asset pricing; IPO; information and market efficiency; event studies; financial forecasting

**JEL classifications:** G12; G14; G17; G24

# INTRODUCTION

Research into IPO advertising is in its infancy; as yet, little has been written about it. Chemmanur and Yan (2009) document that that IPO firms maximise their advertising in the IPO year. Still, the true reason for the practice of maximising advertising intensity in the IPO year remains unclear. Existing literature suggests that advertising is either a mechanism that conveys the true value of a firm to investors (Chemmanur & Yan, 2009) or it causes media bias and thus inflates stock prices (Gurun & Butler, 2012).

According to Chemmanur and Yan (2009), advertising around an IPO event helps to reduce the degree of information asymmetry. If this theory is correct, then one would expect higher advertising intensity to reduce the degree of underpricing due to the increased amount of information provided. However, the empirical evidences, which are reported in this chapter, do not support the aforementioned prediction. Rather the new evidences suggest that advertising causes higher degree of stock overvaluation.

Gurun and Butler (2012) have reported that positive media bias strongly relates to a firm's equity values. They also identify advertising expenditures as a possible cause of media bias. In the light of this contribution, an alternative explanation, namely that IPO advertising causes short-term stock overvaluation, was investigated: the link between advertising and the degree of stock overvaluation is discussed in this chapter.

To the extent that advertising intensity can drive the stock price of newly listed firms to diverge from their fundamental value in the early days post IPO, it is particularly important to investigate the actual intrinsic value of these IPO firms before stating any conclusion about their true value. In this regard, this chapter has directly assessed an alternative empirical value estimated when stock price itself is a noisy measure of intrinsic value. The valuation methodology used in this study (Ohlson, 1995, RIV model) allows for the convergence of stock prices and value over time, rather than relying on an assumed assumption of static equality.

## METHODOLOGY AND DATA

### *Ohlson (1995) Model*

Peasnell (1982) and Ohlson (1995) demonstrated that the intrinsic value defined in equation could be rewritten as the reported book value, plus an infinite sum of discounted future residual income, given that a firm's earnings and book value are forecast in a manner consistent with 'clean surplus' accounting. (Clean surplus accounting requires that all gains and losses affecting book value of equity are included in earnings.) Therefore, the net change in book value from one period to the next is equal to earnings minus total dividends. In this framework, the value of a firm ($\hat{V}$) can be calculated as the summation of two main components: (1) the current amount of capital invested in the company ($B_t$: current book value of equity) and (2) the present value of all future residual income (the infinite sum of future residual income). Eq. (1), which represents the residual-income valuation of a firm's value, is thus:

$$\hat{V}_t = B_t + \sum_{i=1}^{\infty} \frac{E_t[\mathrm{NI}_{t+i} - (r*B_{t+i-1})]}{(1+r)^i} = B_t + \sum_{i=1}^{\infty} \frac{E_t[(\mathrm{ROE}_{t+i} - r)B_{t+i-1}]}{(1+r)^i} \quad (1)$$

For practical implementation, an explicit forecast period must be specified in order to calculate. That is, the forecast period needs to be specified in order to transform the above infinite-form valuation function (Eq. (1)) as a finite-form valuation. Consequently, Eq. (1) can be rewritten as:

$$\hat{V}_t = B_t + \frac{(\mathrm{FROE}_{t+1} - r)B_t]}{(1+r)^i} + \frac{(\mathrm{FROE}_{t+2} - r)B_{t+1}]}{(1+r)^2} + \mathrm{TV} \quad (2)$$

where $\mathrm{TV} = \sum_{i=3}^{T-1} \frac{(\mathrm{FROE}_{t+i} - r)B_{t+i-1}}{(1+r)^i} + \frac{(\mathrm{FROE}_{t+i} - r)B_{t+T-1}}{k(1+r)^{T-1}}$

The model was that future returns on equity (ROE) linearly converge from the ROE level at the end of second year to the level of target industry ROEs within seven years. Accordingly, from the third year onwards (inclusive), FROEs were forecast using a linear interpolation to the industry median ROE (discussed below). The terminal values (TV) were calculated in such a way that earnings from year nine to perpetuity were calculated by the industry median ROE (firm's ROE in perpetuity), multiplied by the clean surplus forecasted opening book value for year nine. Accordingly, the analysis forecast 10 intervals ($T = 10$) future residual incomes including the terminal value. Ofcourse it is possible to calculate value using longer intervals, but it was found that the valuation results from longer intervals were very similar and did not affect the hypothesis testing. This finding, in fact, is not surprising because Gebhardt, Lee, and Swaminathan (2001) sensitised the RIV model and found that the results for varying $T = 6$ to $T = 21$ were very similar. Accordingly, $T = 10$ was substituted (as discussed) in Eq. (2), and the RIV model can be written as:

$$\hat{V}_t = B_t + \frac{(\text{FROE}_{t+1} - r)B_t]}{(1 + r)^i} + \frac{(\text{FROE}_{t+2} - r)B_{t+1}]}{(1 + r)^2}$$
$$+ \sum_{i=3}^{9} \frac{(\text{FROE}_{t+i} - r)B_{t+i-1}}{(1 + r)^i} + \frac{(\text{FROE}_{t+i} - r)B_{t+9}}{k(1 + r)^9} \qquad (3)$$

where $B_t$ = current book value of equity per share from the last fiscal year immediately after IPO event from Compustat, $r$ = the cost of equity (discussed below), $\text{FROE}_{t+i}$ = forecasted ROE for period $t + i$. For the first two years, these variables were computed as $\text{FEPS}_{t+i}/B_{t+i-1}$, where $\text{FEPS}_{t+i}$ is the consensus analyst's forecasted EPS from I/B/E/S for year $t+i$ and $B_{t+i-1}$ is the book value per share for year $t + i - 1$. Beyond the second year, FROE was forecast using a linear interpolation to the industry median ROE.

$B_{t+i}$ = Forecasted book value of equity per share using clean surplus relation, this is computed as $B_{t+i} = B_{t+i-1} + \text{FEPS}_{t+i} - \text{FDPS}_{t+i}$, where $\text{FDPS}_{t+i}$ is the forecasted dividend per share for year $t + i$, estimated using the current dividend payout ratio ($k$). That is, $\text{FDPS}_{t+i} = \text{FEPS}_{t+i} * k$.

Lee, Myers, and Swaminathan's (1999) approach of residual-income valuation model (RIV) was utilised to examine the theoretical value of stock. This was for two main reasons: firstly, this approach provides superior ability to explain cross-sectional variation of US stock prices – close to 70 per cent of cross-sectional variation of US stock prices can be explained by this model, and secondly, this approach avoids the use of ex post realisation of earnings and relies solely on publicly available information such as consensus analysts' earnings forecasts.

## Cost of Equity

Cost of equity was calculated using the CAPM framework. This variable was computed by grouping the sample into 49 industries following Fama and French (1997). Then, for each IPO in the sample, three pieces of data were collected, namely 10 years historical monthly market risk premium data, monthly risk-free rate, and monthly industry returns from the Fama-French data library. The observation period was January 1976 to December 2009, as all the IPO samples were issued during the period. All data were observed 120 months (10 years) before the IPO month, excluding the month of the IPO event. This process yielded the required data to be used to compute equity's beta at time of IPO $(\beta_{it})$. Since 10-years equity return prior to IPO was not observable, industry beta were employed as a proxy of equity beta $(\beta_{it})$. For each IPO, the CAPM equation was regressed using the monthly data to estimate the industry beta $(\beta_{it})$. The beta of each IPO issued at time $t$ was computed by solving the following regression equation: $(R_{it} - R_{ft}) = \beta_{it}(\text{Market risk premium}_t) + c_i$, ignoring the error term $c_i$. This process yielded 10 years historical rolling betas observations of each IPO in the sample.

The beta was then used to calculate the firm's cost of capital. The cost of capital $(r_i)$ was then estimated using CAPM framework as:

$$r_{it} = R_{ft} + \beta_{it} * \left[ E(R_{mt}) - R_{ft} \right] \qquad (4)$$

where $R_{ft}$ = average risk-free rate, $[E(R_m) - R_{ft}]$ = market risk premium. A 10-year forward-looking T-bond rate was used as a proxy for ex ante expectations of a risk-free rate $(R_{ft})$ at the time of IPO. This variable was observed from the US department of the Treasury. The market risk premium was estimated to be 4.2 per cent because the US historical premium for the 1928–2013 time period is averaged at 4.2 per cent, if computed as the difference in compounded returns on US stocks and on the 10-year US treasury bond.

Other means of estimating cost of equity could have been utilised (e.g., Fama-French 3-factor model method). However, Frankel and Lee (1998) argued that the choice of cost of equity capital $(r)$ had little effect on their cross-sectional analysis. Likewise, it was found that the choice of cost of equity capital estimated did not affect the hypothesis testing.

Fama-French 3-factor model yields different cost of capital estimates to those computed by CAPM. However, on average, the firm value estimates suggest overvaluation regardless of how the cost of capital is computed (either CAPM or FF 3-factor model). This result is consistent with prior research as Frankel and Lee (1998).

In theory, cost of capital should be firm-specific, reflecting the premium demanded by equity investors to invest in a firm or project of comparable risk. In practice, however, there is little consensus on how this discount rate should be determined. Earlier research was followed (Frankel & Lee, 1998, among others) and thus a firm's cost of capital was estimated by using the industry cost of capital.

## Industry ROE

To compute a target industry return on equity (ROE), all stocks were grouped into the same 49 industry classifications, as stated by Fama and French (1997). The returns on equity of all firms in the same industry within the past 10 years were collected from Compustat. The ROE was computed as net income divided by total book value of total equity. The Compustat data set was then classified into 49 industries using SIC code as matching method. The industry return on equity was calculated using all firms in the same industry for the past 10 years. Specifically, the industry target ROE was the median of past ROEs from all firms in the same industry.

To ensure that the estimate of industry ROE was not biased by low value estimates, the target industry ROE were winsorised at a risk-free rate $(R_t)$, on the basis of a realistic assumption that a firm's rate of return (ROE) cannot indefinitely stay below the risk-free rate. The upper bound of industry ROE could be winsorised, however, the sample did not contain many implausible target ROE values. In particular, the model was sensitised using industry ROE winsorised at 30 per cent and no significant change in the valuation results was found.

## Price-to-Valuation Ratio (P/V)

The theoretical valuation of each firm in the sample was calculated using Eq. (3) as stated above. Stock price at the time of earning forecasts were obtained from CRSP. Where stock price at earning announcement was the closing price (or closing average bid-ask if closing prices were not available) of a firm on the announcement day of earning forecasts obtained from I/B/E/S, the date of earning forecasts was observed from

I/B/E/S database. All I/B/E/S forecasts were observed from detail history file instead of summary history file, in order to observe the correct announcement date for each observation.

Price-to-theoretical-valuation ratio was calculated by dividing the observed stock price at earning announcement $(P_t)$ by its valuation. The model was sensitised using initial-price-to-valuation ratio $(P_0/V_t)$ and three months-price-to-valuation ratio $(P_{3m}/V_t)$ to vary the price observed in the early days following IPO event. Finally, to prevent possible bias caused by outliers when calculating $P/V$ ratio, extreme observations were excluded from the sample, specifically, those implausible $P/V$ ratios such as the $P/V$ ratio of more than $30\times$ as well as those valuations that were less than zero (negative valuation). The trimming procedure was done to ensure that the $P/V$ ratio samples were not biased by outliers and implausible values. To ensure that the choice of method used to eliminate outliers did not affect the hypothesis testing, the analysis was also sensitised using 3 per cent winsorisation, and it was found that the $P/V$ ratio and regression results were very similar.

*Industry-Adjusted Advertising Intensity*

A firm's advertising intensity was computed as the cost of advertising, media, and promotional expenses obtained from Compustat item #45 divided by total sales revenue in the same fiscal year. Advertising intensity was scaled with its sales revenue to control for a firm's size and sales volume. In addition, a firm's size measurement (total market capitalisation) was also included in the regression model to control for size effect. Eq. (5) represents the advertising intensity:

$$\text{Advertising intensity } (\text{Ad}_i) = \frac{\text{Advertising expense}}{\text{Sales revenue}} \quad (5)$$

To the extent that certain industries may naturally exhibit higher (or lower) average advertising intensity than others, the advertising intensity calculation was adjusted by computing a firm's advertising intensity relative to its matching peers based on industry matching. The expected value of industry-wide advertising intensity was calculated by the mean advertising intensity from all firms in the same industry using Fama-French's

49 industry grouping as grouping criteria. Accordingly industry-adjusted advertising intensity, for each firm was calculated as follows:

$$\text{Ad}_{\text{industry\_adjusted}} = \frac{\left(\text{Ad}_i - \text{Ad}_{\text{industry}}\right)}{\text{Ad}_{\text{industry}}} \tag{6}$$

## Industry Portfolios

The universe for industry portfolio was constructed from all trading firms that had their advertising expenditure for the period of 1986−2009 available on the Compustat annual database. A firm's industry was identified using the Standard Industrial Classification (SIC) code and the code was used as a basis to assign each IPO into different industry portfolios. The industry portfolios were constructed following French's 49 industry classification observable from French's website. This process identified 49 industry classes. The industry's average advertising intensity was defined as the average advertising intensity of all firms in each portfolio.

## Regression Model

The literature on IPO established that certain issue-specific characteristics are related to the initial return of IPOs. Prior-IPO underpricing research identified several determinants of IPO price in the early days post-IPO. For example, firm size (or equivalent issue size), underwriter's reputation, VC-backed dummy, certain markets in which IPOs are listed (NASDAQ) and pre-IPO market demand for stock (offer price revision). To the extent that price-to-valuation (P/V) ratio contains stock price information (as nominator) and the sample in this study consisted of IPOs, it was important to include these control variables in the RHS of the regression analysis. Accordingly, to examine a clean relation between advertising intensity and stock valuation, the following control variables were included.

Offer *price_revision* was used as the proxy for the pre-market demand for IPO. This variable was defined as the difference between the highest and midprice of the original filing, divided by the midpoint of the filing price ((offer price − midprice)/midprice). Offer price and midprice were observed from SDC platinum. *NASDAQ* dummy variable equal to 1 if the firm was listed in NASDAQ, and 0 otherwise. Total market capitalisation was the proxy for firm size, this variable was computed as first-day closing price (or closing average bid-ask, whichever was available from CRSP) multiplied by its total number of share outstanding. Market capitalisation was expressed as natural logarithm, ln(*market_cap*). The *VC-backed* dummy equals 1 if the firm was a VC-backed IPO and 0 otherwise. This variable was observed from SDC platinum. Underwriter reputation (*reputation*) was measured by the rank score of Carter and Manaster ranking. The ranking score was allocated to each underwriter following Carter and Manaster (1990) and Carter, Dark, and Singh (1998) methodologies. The underwriter prestige rankings are on a 0–9 scale, and are based on the pecking order seen in 'tombstone' advertisements. The Carter-Manaster ranking was matched to the IPO sample using company name as matching criteria. All stock price, number of shares outstanding and stock market data (including the *NASDAQ* dummy) were observed from CRSP. Industry-adjusted advertising intensity was computed by Eq. (6). Finally the following cross-sectional regression was estimated:

$$P_i/V_{it} = \alpha + \beta_1 \cdot advertising + \beta_2 \cdot reputation + \beta_3 \cdot \ln(market\_cap)$$
$$+ \beta_4 \cdot price\_revision + \beta_5 \cdot VC\_backed + \beta_6 \cdot NASDAQ \qquad (7)$$

where

$P_i$ = market closing price per share of firm's *i*, equal to first-day closing price observed from CRSP (other variants of $P/V$ ratio are also reported, discussed in Results and Discussion section)

$V_{it}$ = theoretical value per share of firm *i*, computed by Peasnell (1982) RIV as stated by Eq. (3).

*Sample Selection of IPOs*

The offering data of the IPOs of ordinary common shares were observed as well as the book value of equity (after the offer) during the period from January 1986 to December 2009. The data source was Thomson Financial Securities Data Company (SDC Platinum) new issues database. To ensure that the results were not disproportionately affected by extremely small firms, the analyses restricted the sample to firms with an offer price of at least $5. Finally, from these samples unit IPOs, closed-end funds, real estate investment trusts (REITs), and American Depositary Receipts

(ADRs) were excluded. In summary, the IPO data collected from SDC Platinum had to satisfy at least the three following criteria:

1. Stock price data must be available on the Centre for Research in Security Prices (CRSP) database.
2. The IPO should issue ordinary common shares and should not be investment trust offerings, Close end funds or ADRs (these financial instruments have different characteristics from common stock IPOs).
3. The IPO should have a value of $5 or more (those with smaller price per share have poor market liquidity; earlier research into IPOs has usually excluded those with a value of less than $5).

Lee et al.'s (1999) approach of Ohlson−Peasnell RIV model required that one-year-ahead analysts' forecasts and two-year-ahead analysts' forecasts must be simultaneously available from I/B/E/S. In addition, since the firms needed to be valued in the early days after IPO, it was required that each forecast observation had to be announced no later than three months post IPO. Accordingly, those observations with missing analysts' earnings forecasts (either missing one-year-ahead and/or missing two-years-ahead earnings forecasts) were dismissed. Similarly, firms that were not covered by CRSP (those firms with missing first-day closing price) were also excluded. Finally, the three data sets (CRSP, I/B/E/S and Compustat) were merged and missing values (price, analyst forecasts and advertising expenditures) were eliminated. The final sample consisted of 501 IPO observations that satisfied all of the above criteria.

*Heckman (1979) Selection Model Probit Regression Model*

Simpson (2008) has suggested that there are fundamental differences between firms that reported their advertising expense before 1994 and firms that reported their advertising expense after that date. Before 1994, the Securities and Exchange Commission (SEC) required industrial and commercial firms to supply information regarding advertising expense. The SEC's Financial Reporting Release No. 44 (FRR44) from 1994 eliminated the requirement to furnish this schedule. Since advertising expense was one of the items previously referenced by this release, FRR44 effectively made separate disclosure of advertising outlays optional. According to Simpson (2008), firms disclosed their advertising expense voluntarily when they earned the valuation benefit, and chose not to disclose their advertising when they earned no valuation benefit. Since the sample we examined was naturally limited to those firms that reported their advertising expenditures, our sample represents a portion of the full IPO sample (approximately 22 per cent of the IPOs sample reported their advertising expenditures). In order to address the concern that the sample selection might have affected our results, we ran the Heckman (1979) selection model to correct for the sample selection bias.

The dummy variable for the advertising disclosure (*Disclosure*) was constructed: Disclosure equals 1 if the firms disclose their advertising expenditure and 0 otherwise. Following Chemmanur and Yan (2011) we estimated the selection equation using a probit regression with *Disclosure* as the dependent variable. In discussing prior knowledge about the possible determinants of advertising disclosure, the literature on industrial organisation suggests that sales are an important consideration in corporate advertising decisions; therefore, we included sales in our analysis. The following variables are the plausible determinants of advertising disclosure: sales, firm size, book-to-market ratio and profitability (defined as the EBITDA scales by book value of assets), according to Chemmanur and Yan (2011). This led us to include these variables in Eq. (8). Following Chemmanur and Yan (2011), we calculated $Sale_t$ as the log value of sales revenue in year $t$. $Size_t$ is the log of market capitalisation in year $t$. $Prft_t$ is operating income before interest, tax, depreciation and amortisation (EBITDA) in year $t$ scaled by the book value of assets in year $t$. $BM_t$ is the ratio of the book value to the market value of equity. $NASDAQ$, is a dummy variable, equals 1 if the firms are trading in NASDAQ and 0 otherwise. After each variable was constructed, we ran the following probit regression:

$$Disclosure_i = \alpha + \beta_1 \cdot Prft_t + \beta_2 \cdot Sales_t + \beta_3 \cdot Size_t + \beta_4 \cdot BM_t + \beta_5 \cdot NASDAQ \quad (8)$$

Column 1 of Table 4 showed that Profitability, Sales and NASDAQ dummy are determinants of advertising disclosure. Accordingly, we adjusted our probit regression to include only the significant variables. Thus, the final probit regression can be expressed as:

$$Disclosure_i = \alpha + \beta_1 \cdot Prft_t + \beta_2 \cdot Sales_t + \beta_3 \cdot Size_t + \beta_4 \cdot BM_t + \beta_5 \cdot NASDAQ \quad (9)$$

We ran regression Eq. (9) to see if all RHS variables explain the decision to disclose advertising. The regression results of Eq. (9) are reported in column 2 of Table 4.

*Response Equation*

In order to address the concern that sample selection may bias the inference about the association between advertising and price-to-valuation ratio, the relationship was investigated further using the Heckman selection model. The results of Heckman two-step regression are reported in Table 5.

# RESULTS AND DISCUSSION

Table 1 shows the summary statistics. The average price-to-value $(P/V)$ ratio, at a mean of 1.81, showed clear evidence of stock overvaluation in the early days post-IPO. This result is robust, no matter whether stock price was observed immediately after trading, at the time of earnings announcement (sometime between naught to three months following IPO, vary by each IPO) or at three months following the IPO event. The average price-to-valuation ratios observed at these periods were 1.75, 1.81 and 1.80, respectively. All of the mentioned average $P/V$ ratios were statistically different from unity (discussed below).

Theoretically, if firm stocks are appropriately priced, the price-to-valuation ratio should be close to unity: by definition, the price-to-valuation ratio of greater (smaller) than one suggests stock overvaluation (undervaluation). Accordingly, a conventional $t$-test was employed to test for equality of mean $(P/V)$ on the null hypothesis that mean price-to-valuation ratio $(P_t/V_t)$ is equal to 1, against an alternative hypothesis that mean price-to-valuation ratio is not equal to 1. The test method was also sensitised by employing a non-parametric Wilcoxon signed-rank test to test for the equality of median. The hypotheses for non-parametric test were:

*Table 1.* Summary Statistics.

| Variables | Mean | Median |
|---|---|---|
| Valuation at earning announcements $(V_t)$, in dollars | 16.52 | 13.21 |
| Initial price $(P_0)$ | 17.43 | 15.80 |
| Price at earning announcements $(P_t)$ | 17.98 | 16.50 |
| Price 3 months post-IPO $(P_{3m})$ | 18.48 | 15.95 |
| Initial price-to-valuation ratio $(P_0/V_t)$ | 1.75 | 1.17 |
| Price-to-valuation ratio $(P_t/V_t)$ | 1.81 | 1.17 |
| 3 months-price-to-valuation ratio $(P_{3m}/V_t)$ | 1.80 | 1.19 |

$H_0$: The median price-to-valuation ratio ($P_t/V_t$) is 1.

$H_a$: The median price-to-valuation ratio is not equal to 1.

Both hypotheses were stated in such a way to test for the existence of stock valuation. Table 2 reports the results.

Table 2 shows that the IPO sample had an average $P/V$ ratio of significantly greater than one. Both test statistics were highly significant and both $p$-values were approximately zero (0.00). Thus, the null hypothesis, that the sample average $P_t/V_t$ ratio = 1, was rejected, and the alternative hypothesis, that the sample average $P_t/V_t$ ratio is not equal to 1, was accepted. To summarise, Table 1 shows that sample average $P_t/V_t$ ratio was 1.81, and Table 2 shows that the average price-to-valuation ratio is statistically different from unity ($t$-stat 7.40). Thus it can be inferred with 99 per cent confidence ($p$-value 0.00) that, on average, the sample of IPOs was overvalued. This result was consistent, whether a parametric $t$-test or a non-parametric Wilcoxon signed-rank test was employed. Please note that the above tests are two-tailed tests, thus the test statistics from one-tailed test will yield the same inference. Overall, both tests suggest that IPOs are generally overvalued in the early days post-IPO. It did not matter at what point observations were made during the first three months after an IPO event. All variants of computed $P/V$ ratio consistently suggested the same results, namely that stock is overvalued in the early days following IPO. The results yielded from the price observed from the first day of trading ($P_0$) and the

***Table 2.*** Test Statistics of Price-to-valuation Ratio.

| Test and Hypothesis | $t$-Stat. | $p$-Value |
|---|---|---|
| $t$-test for the equality of mean<br>$H_0$: mean $P_t/V_t$ ratio = 1 | 7.40 | 0.00 |
| Wilcoxon signed-rank test for the equality of median<br>$H_0$: median $P_t/V_t$ ratio = 1 | 8.21 | 0.00 |
| $t$-test for the equality of mean<br>$H_0$: mean $P_0/V_t$ ratio = 1 | 7.32 | 0.00 |
| Wilcoxon signed-rank test for the equality of median<br>$H_0$: median $P_0/V_t$ ratio = 1 | 8.15 | 0.00 |
| $t$-test for the equality of mean<br>$H_0$: mean $P_{3m}/V_t$ ratio = 1 | 7.79 | 0.00 |
| Wilcoxon signed-rank test for the equality of median<br>$H_0$: median $P_{3m}/V_t$ ratio = 1 | 8.07 | 0.00 |

results observed from stock price at three months following IPO event ($P_{3m}$) consistently suggested the overvaluation of stock.

Table 3 shows that advertising intensity is a significant determinant of the degree of stock overvaluation. There is a strong and positive relation between advertising intensity and price-to-valuation ratio of newly listed firms. Regardless of the point at which the stock price was observed within the first three months ($P_0/V$, $P_t/V$, and $P_{3m}/V$), the results consistently suggest that an increase in industry-adjusted advertising intensity increases the price-to-valuation ratio ($p$-value 0.05, 0.00 and 0.00, respectively). Thus, it can be inferred, with 95 per cent confidence ($p$-value 0.05), that the degree of overvaluation is driven significantly by industry-adjusted advertising intensity. Evidently, firms can maximise their share price in the secondary market by spending more on advertising around the IPO event. These results are inconsistent with the Chemmanur et al.'s (2008) inference that advertising should reduce the degree of information asymmetry. Rather the results are consistent with the view of Purnanandam and Swaminathan (2004), namely that the stock price of newly listed firms can be overvalued.

There are two other determinants that explain the price-to-valuation ratio: the offer price revision and VC-backed dummy. The coefficient of

*Table 3.*   Regression Results.

| | Dependent Variable | | | | | | | | | VIF |
|---|---|---|---|---|---|---|---|---|---|---|
| | $P_0/V_t$ | | | $P_t/V_t$ | | | $P_{3m}/V_t$ | | | |
| | Coeff. | $t$-Stat. | $p$-Val. | Coeff. | $t$-Stat. | $p$-Val. | Coeff. | $t$-Stat. | $p$-Val. | |
| Industry-adjusted advertising intensity | 0.26 | 1.93 | 0.05 | 0.69 | 5.13 | 0.00 | 0.57 | 4.50 | 0.00 | 1.00 |
| Underwriter reputation | 0.09 | 1.03 | 0.30 | 0.15 | 1.61 | 0.11 | 0.13 | 1.45 | 0.15 | 1.27 |
| ln(Market capitalisation) | 0.15 | 1.61 | 0.11 | 0.09 | 0.90 | 0.37 | 0.07 | 0.79 | 0.43 | 1.55 |
| Price revision | 2.67 | 4.90 | 0.00 | 2.90 | 5.08 | 0.00 | 2.70 | 5.01 | 0.00 | 1.25 |
| VC-backed dummy | 0.70 | 3.19 | 0.00 | 0.81 | 3.55 | 0.00 | 0.81 | 3.75 | 0.00 | 1.21 |
| NASDAQ dummy | 0.26 | 1.01 | 0.31 | 0.38 | 1.40 | 0.16 | 0.40 | 1.54 | 0.12 | 1.31 |
| Intercept | −0.05 | −0.07 | 0.95 | −0.16 | −0.20 | 0.84 | 0.01 | 0.01 | 0.99 | |
| *F statistics* | | 12.18 | | | 16.67 | | | 15.54 | | |
| *R-squared* | | 0.14 | | | 0.19 | | | 0.18 | | |

offer price revision is positive (Table 3: $\beta_4$ ranging from 2.67 to 2.9), and statistically significant at 1 per cent significance level. This result suggests that pre-market demand for stock is a significant determinant of price-to-valuation ratio. Similarly, the coefficient of VC-backed dummy ($\beta_5$) was positive and statistically significant at 1 per cent significance level ($p$-value 0.00). This result is consistent with common intuition that investors tend to value VC-backed IPOs more highly in the early market. All test statistics reported were corrected for heteroskedasticity using the methodology of White (1980).

Table 4 reports the probit regression results. Column 1 reports the results from the whole sample. The IPO universe includes all IPOs issued during 1986–2009, regardless of whether or not firms report their advertising. It can be seen from the table that Profitability, Sales and NASDAQ dummy are determinants of advertising disclosure. The coefficient of profitability ($\beta_1$) was found to be negative and statistically significant at 5 per cent significance level ($p$-value 0.04). This result, which suggests that firms with higher profitability are less likely to report advertising to Compustat, is consistent with Chemmanur and Yan (2011). The coefficient of sales ($\beta_2$) and the coefficient of NASDAQ dummy ($\beta_5$) were also found to be significant. The coefficient of sales ($\beta_2$) was positive and statistically significant at 1 per cent significance level ($p$-value 0.00). The coefficient of NASDAQ

***Table 4.*** Probit Regression Results.

| | Dependent Variable: Advertising Disclosure (*Disclosure*) | | | | | | | |
|---|---|---|---|---|---|---|---|---|
| | Column (1) | | | | Column (2) | | | |
| | Coeff. | *t*-Stat. | *p*-Value | VIF | Coeff. | *t*-Stat. | *p*-Value | VIF |
| Profitability (*Prft*) | −0.08 | −2.07 | 0.04 | 1.43 | −0.06 | −1.85 | 0.06 | 1.26 |
| Sales (*Sales*) | 0.02 | 3.01 | 0.00 | 2.12 | 0.02 | 3.97 | 0.00 | 1.56 |
| Firm size (*Size*) | 0.01 | 1.28 | 0.20 | 1.54 | − | − | − | − |
| Book-to-market ratio (*BM*) | 0.00 | −0.93 | 0.35 | 1.00 | − | − | − | − |
| NASDAQ dummy (*NASDAQ*) | 0.14 | 6.62 | 0.00 | 1.28 | 1.34 | 6.43 | 0.00 | 1.26 |
| Intercept | 0.11 | 2.66 | 0.01 | | 0.16 | 4.97 | 0.00 | |
| *F statistics* | | 11.87 | | | | 14.58 | | |
| *R-squared* | | 0.012 | | | | 0.011 | | |
| *Observations* | | | | 6,541 | | | | |

dummy ($\beta_5$) was positive and statistically significant at 1 per cent significance level (p-value 0.00). These results suggest that firms with higher sales
and firms in NASDAQ stock market are more likely to disclose their advertising to Compustat.

Altogether, the results suggest that profitability, sales revenue and
NASDAQ dummy are relevant to a firm's decision to disclose advertising
to Compustat. Therefore, Eq. (9) was used as the selection equation in
Heckman's selection model.

Table 5 confirms our initial finding that advertising intensity is a significant determinant of the degree of stock overvaluation. There is a positive
relationship between advertising intensity and price-to-valuation ratio of
newly listed firms. The coefficient of advertising intensity ($\beta_1$) is positive
and statistically significant at 1 per cent significance level for all variant of
price-to-valuation ratios studied (p-value 0.00). Thus, we can infer with
99 per cent confidence that the advertising intensity related positively to
price-to-valuation ratio. There are two other determinants that explain the
price-to-valuation ratio: the offer price revision and VC-backed dummy.
The coefficient of offer price revision is positive ($\beta_4$ ranging from 2.91

*Table 5.*   Heckman Two-Step Regression Results.

| | Dependent Variable | | | | | | | | | |
|---|---|---|---|---|---|---|---|---|---|---|
| | $P_0/V_t$ | | | $P_t/V_t$ | | | $P_{3m}/V_t$ | | | VIF |
| | Coeff. | t-Stat. | p-Val. | Coeff. | t-Stat. | p-Val. | Coeff. | t-Stat. | p-Val. | |
| Industry-adjusted advertising intensity | 2.58 | 3.13 | 0.00 | 3.02 | 4.31 | 0.00 | 3.09 | 3.45 | 0.00 | 1.02 |
| Underwriter reputation | 0.09 | 1.03 | 0.30 | 0.13 | 1.24 | 0.22 | 0.10 | 1.09 | 0.28 | 1.31 |
| In (Market capitalisation) | 0.15 | 1.53 | 0.13 | 0.12 | 1.05 | 0.29 | 0.09 | 0.94 | 0.35 | 1.58 |
| Price revision | 2.91 | 4.45 | 0.00 | 3.21 | 4.91 | 0.00 | 2.95 | 5.20 | 0.00 | 1.27 |
| VC-backed Dummy | 0.78 | 3.13 | 0.00 | 0.93 | 3.25 | 0.00 | 0.81 | 3.37 | 0.00 | 1.20 |
| NASDAQ dummy | 0.29 | 1.01 | 0.31 | 0.41 | 1.26 | 0.20 | 0.45 | 1.54 | 0.12 | 1.15 |
| Intercept | −0.29 | −0.35 | 0.73 | −0.50 | −0.61 | 0.54 | −0.41 | −0.49 | 0.62 | |
| *Estimation method* | | | | Heckman Two-Step | | | | | | |
| *Observations* | | | | *6541* | | | | | | |

to 3.21), and statistically significant at 1 per cent significance level ($p$-value 0.00). This result suggests that the IPO pre-market demand is a determinant of price-to-valuation ratio. Similarly, the coefficient of VC-backed dummy ($\beta_5$) was positive and statistically significant at 1 per cent significance level ($p$-value 0.00). This result suggests that investors tend to value VC-backed IPOs more highly in the early days post-IPO.

Overall, the results from the Heckman selection model are consistent with those results presented earlier from our advertising-reported sample: that advertising, offer price revision and VC-backed dummy related positively to price-to-valuation ratio. Therefore, we can infer that the observed relation between advertising and price-to-valuation ratio is unlikely to be biased by the sample selection.

# CONCLUSION

This research provided an investigation of the stock overvaluation caused by advertising around an IPO event. Evidence was presented that firms that intensify their advertising in the IPO year (relative to their industry peers) earn higher stock price appreciation in the secondary market. The direct valuation of IPOs, using residual-income valuation framework, revealed that the positive initial returns in the early days post-IPO were not caused by systematic underpricing. Rather, the results suggest that the observed positive initial returns were the direct results of stock overvaluation (measurable by its price-to-theoretical value ratio), which is systematically caused by advertising around an IPO event.

It has been well documented that the extent of initial returns earned from holding IPO stocks in the short run is significantly positive. This research has contributed to the IPO underpricing literature by documenting a possible explanation for IPO underpricing: that advertising around an IPO event drives the stock price to be more overvalued in the secondary market. Interestingly, other forms of good news such as sale side analysts' recommendations are strictly prohibited during the early days after IPO, while the extent of advertising activities around the IPO event is completely unregulated. The results showed that industry-adjusted advertising intensity directly affects the price-to-valuation ratio in the early days after IPO event. This raises a serious question about the necessity to regulate IPO advertising in order to prevent stock misevaluation in the secondary market.

162 KONPANAS DUMRONGWONG

Unlike the sale side analysts' forecasts, which are prohibited during the quiet period, advertising activities are not subject to the same legal prohibition. The current US legal regimes, such as the Blue Sky Law and the 1933 Securities Act, partially regulate the promotion of new issues by underwriters; these are designed to 'to assure the availability of adequate reliable information about securities which are offered to the public'. However, such statements are inadequate to prevent the misuse of advertising (as a mechanism to manipulate stock prices). This warrants the need for future amendment of the relevant market regulations in order to regulate the activities of advertising around the IPO event. Future regulations should prevent advertising from generating media bias while still allowing the dissemination of adequate and reliable information about the securities being offered to the public.

# REFERENCES

Carter, R. B., Dark, F. H., & Singh, A. K. (1998). Underwriter reputation, initial returns, and the long-run performance of IPO stocks. *Journal of Finance, 53*, 285–311.
Carter, R. B., & Manaster, M. (1990). Initial public offerings and underwriter reputation. *Journal of Finance, 45*, 1045–1068.
Chemmanur, T., & Yan, A. (2009). Product market advertising and new security issues. *Journal of Financial Economics, 92*, 40–65.
Chemmanur, T., & Yan, A. (2011). Advertising, investor recognition, and stock returns. In AFA 2011 Denver Meetings Paper.
Fama, E. F., & French, K. R. (1997). Industry costs of equity. *Journal of Financial Economics, 43*, 153–193.
Frankel, R., & Lee, C. M. C. (1998). Accounting valuation, market expectation, and cross-sectional stock returns. *Journal of Accounting and Economics, 25*, 283–319.
Gebhardt, W. R., Lee, C. M. C., & Swaminathan, B. (2001). Toward an implied cost of capital. *Journal of Accounting Research, 39*, 135–176.
Gurun, U. G., & Butler, A. W. (2012). Don't believe the hype: Local media slant, local advertising, and firm value. *Journal of Finance, 67*(2), 561–598.
Heckman, J. J. (1979). Sample selection bias as a specification error. *Econometrica: Journal of the Econometric Society, 47*, 153–161.
Lee, C., Myers, J., & Swaminathan, B. (1999). What is the intrinsic value of the Dow. *Journal of Finance, 54*, 1693–1741.
Ohlson, J. A. (1995). Earnings, book values, and dividends in equity valuation. *Contemporary Accounting Research, 11*(2), 661–678.
Peasnell, K. V. (1982). Some formal connections between economic values and yields and accounting numbers. *Journal of Business Finance and Accounting, 13*, 361–381.

Purnanandam, A. K., & Swaminathan, B. (2004). Are IPOs really underpriced? *Review of Financial Studies, 17*, 811–848.

Simpson, A. (2008). Voluntary disclosure of advertising expenditures. *Journal of Accounting, Auditing and Finance, 23*, 403–436.

White, H. (1980). A heteroskedasticity-consistent covariance matrix estimator and a direct test for heteroskedasticity. *Econometrica: Journal of the Econometric Society, 48*, 817–838.

# A COMPARATIVE STUDY OF THE INFLUENCE OF DERIVATIVES ON BANK STABILITY IN EMERGING AND RECENTLY DEVELOPED COUNTRIES: EVIDENCE FROM THE LAST FINANCIAL CRISIS

Mohamed Rochdi Keffala

## ABSTRACT

*The major objective of this study is to inspect the differences in the effect of derivatives on the stability between banks from emerging countries and those from recently developed countries.*

*According to the repercussions of the recent financial crisis, we divide the whole period into normal period "the pre-crisis period," 2003–2006, and turbulent period "the crisis & post-crisis period," 2007–2011. We use the Generalized Methods of Moments (GMM) estimator technique developed by Blundell and Bond (1998) to estimate our regressions.*

The Spread of Financial Sophistication Through Emerging Markets Worldwide
Research in Finance, Volume 32, 165–183
Copyright © 2016 by Emerald Group Publishing Limited
ISSN: 0196-3821/doi:10.1108/S0196-382120160000032007

*Our main conclusions show that, in general, using derivatives by banks from emerging countries deteriorates their stability especially during the turbulent period, whereas, using derivatives do not weaken the stability of banks from recently developed countries. We deduce that banks from emerging countries are more destabilized by using derivatives than banks from recently developed countries.*

**Keywords:** Derivatives; emerging countries; crisis; BSI

**JEL classifications:** G01; G21

# INTRODUCTION

The last financial crisis that started in the United States at the end of 2007 had many repercussions on financial institutions around the world and in particular in emerging countries (see Farhi & Borghi, 2009). Indeed, banks from emerging countries have suffered from the consequences of this crisis due to the fragility of their financial systems. Therefore, the causes of financial systems fragility in emerging countries are investigated by many studies (Akyuz & Boratav, 2003; Bai, Christopher, & Leger, 2012; Cavallaro, Maggi, & Mulino et al., 2011; Fu, Lin, & Molyneux, 2014; Komulainen & Lukkarila, 2003; Nilsen & Rovelli, 2001; Sensoy, Ozturk, & Hacihasanoglu, 2014). For this reason, we decide to focus on banks from emerging countries in order to investigate whether using derivatives affects their stability.

On the other hand, we remark that countries like Poland and Singapore which were defined as emerging countries are considered recently as developed countries. Therefore, we are motivated in this study to examine the issue in banks from these countries and to compare them with banks from emerging countries.

According to our reference paper Chiaramonte, Poli, and Oriani (2015), we separate two periods: the ordinary period which defines "the pre-crisis period (from 2003 to 2007)," and the troubled period which represents "the crisis & the post-crisis period (from 2008 to 2011)."

We choose Generalized Method of Moments (GMM) estimator, as proposed by Blundell and Bond (1998), to conduct our empirical analysis because of its relevance. The dependent variable is defined by the $z$-score which is common accounting measure of bank stability used in many papers (Beck, Jonghe & Schepens, 2011; Beck & Laeven, 2006; Chiaramonte et al., 2015; Demirguc-Kunt & Huizinga, 2010). The independent variables are divided into two categories: the variables of interest defined by derivative instruments (forwards, futures, options, and swaps), and the control variables represented by both bank-specific factors and country-specific variables.

The main purpose of this study is to compare the influence of derivatives on bank stability between emerging countries and recently developed countries.

In that case, we address the following research question: what are the differences in the effects of derivatives use on the stability of banks from emerging countries and those from recently developed countries?

This research question is investigated both in the pre-crisis period and in the crisis & post-crisis period in order to analyze whether the influence of derivatives on bank stability changes from stable to unstable period.

The contributions of this study to the literature are numerous. First, this chapter fulfills the lack of papers in inspecting the impact of derivatives on bank stability. Second, it is the first to compare banks from emerging countries to those from recently developed countries when examining this topic. Third, this chapter is the pioneer to estimate this issue with Generalized Methods of Moments estimator technique. Finally, this study provides empirical results related to the role played by derivatives during the recent financial crisis in emerging countries and recently developed countries.

The outcomes of this chapter can be summarized as follows. In comparison to banks from recently developed countries, banks from emerging countries are more destabilized by using derivatives.

This chapter is structured as follows: in the section "Statistics about Derivatives," statistics about the evolution of derivatives in emerging countries and in recently developed countries are presented. In the section "Literature Review," we summarize the related literature. In the section "Methodology," we present the methodology used. In the section "Results Analysis," we analyze and discuss the results obtained; and in the section "Conclusion," we summarize and conclude.

## STATISTICS ABOUT DERIVATIVES

During the last decade, we remark notably the evolution of derivatives usage either in emerging countries or in recently developed countries. Indeed, in this section, we present some statistics which confirm this growth.

The volume of options and futures traded in National Stock Exchange of India augmented from 39,110,566 in 2005 to 525,299,023 in 2013.

Equally, in JSE South Africa and in the same period, this volume increased notably moving from 14,947,523 to 254,514,098.

In Shanghai Futures Exchange, this volume increased from 40,079,750 to 365,329,379 in 2012.

In Korea Futures Exchange, the volume of options and futures traded jumped from 678,045,824 in 2003 to 1,835,617,727 in 2012.

In the same period, this volume augmented from 1,854,413 to 156,731,912 in Taiwan Futures Exchange. Fig. 1 below shows the evolution of options and futures volume in both Taiwan Futures Exchange and Shanghai Futures Exchange.

From these statistics, we deduce evidently the development of derivatives markets in emerging and recently developed countries. For this reason, we are motivated to inspect the impact of these instruments on the stability of banks from countries above-mentioned.

## LITERATURE REVIEW

Many papers have discussed the fragility and the instability of banks in emerging countries. In fact, as it is said by Nilsen and Rovelli (2001),

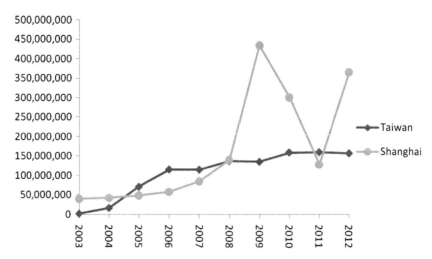

*Fig. 1.* The Evolution of Options and Futures Volume in Taiwan Futures Exchange and in Shanghai Futures Exchange.

emerging market economies have been affected by a long series of financial crises, starting with Chile in 1982, then Mexico in 1994—1995, followed by Southeast Asia in 1997 (Indonesia, Korea, Malaysia, Philippines, and Thailand), Russia in 1998, and Brazil in 1999.

Each crisis had its own particular characteristics and determinants. However, they also shared common factors: each demonstrated the potential for sharp changes in investor sentiment, often triggered by a combination of unsustainable external imbalance, overvalued exchange rate, unsustainable fiscal policy, poorly monitored bank loans, unwise investments, and especially financial fragility.

Farhi and Borghi (2009) show that companies from key emerging markets such as Brazil, China, South Korea, India, and Mexico posted heavy losses as a result of the financial crisis of 2008.

Fu et al. (2014) use information on 14 Asia-Pacific economies from 2003 to 2010 to investigate the influence of bank competition, concentration, regulation and national institutions on individual bank fragility as measured by the probability of bankruptcy and the bank's $z$-score. They argue that a larger value of the bank-level $z$-score means less overall bank risk and higher bank stability.

Cavallaro et al. (2011) address the issue of financial instability in Argentina which plunged into a severe recession that led to a financial crisis and the abandonment of the currency-board arrangement.

Akyuz and Boratav (2003) reveal financial fragility in Turkey results from irresponsible policies and lack of fiscal discipline. They argue that the Turkish banking system was extremely fragile, as it had been deregulated and granted deposit insurance without effective supervision.

On the other hand, other authors argue in their studies that financial innovations as derivatives can affect negatively firm stability. Indeed, Klemkosky (2013) explains that the causes of a financial crisis are many and varied such as shadow banking system, overconfidence, underestimating of risks, and financial innovations use. He concludes that financial innovation is good; however, since the recent financial crisis, there has been some doubt regarding whether all financial innovations are good for the system. Additionally, Buffet (2002) has called derivatives "financial weapons of mass destruction." Moreover, Gatopoulos and Loubergé (2013) investigate the determinants of firms' use of foreign currency derivatives in Latin American countries exposed to currency crises. They claim that derivative markets have been effective tools for firms in these countries, at least in the post-crisis era. In the study of Coutinho, Sheng, and Coutinho (2012), a sample with 47 nonfinancial Bovespa Listed Brazilian companies from 2004 and 2010 was used to test the hypothesis that use of derivatives as a risk management policy tool reduces companies' cost of capital. In contrast to other countries, the results of this study rejected this hypothesis, showing that in Brazil there is a positive relationship between using these tools and cost of capital. Furthermore, according to Rossi (2009), companies based in emerging markets suffer more from derivatives market volatility than companies based in more developed economies.

For these reasons, emerging country companies have started to increasingly invest in a conservative risk policy, by using derivative instruments correctly and with greater transparency in their earnings releases to the market. For example, Kim and Sung (2005) investigated determinants and the hedging instruments used by Korean firms after 1997-Asian Crisis.

Schiozer, Oliveira, & Saito (2010) found evidences that Brazilian firms use derivatives for hedging purpose.

The results of the paper of Ghysels and Seon (2005) indicate that futures markets and trading by foreign investors played a key role during the Korean stock market turbulence in 1997.

Compared to these studies, there are few empirical papers that have investigated the issue on banks. In the rest of this section, we present these studies.

As studies on developed countries, studies on emerging countries have investigated the impact of derivatives on bank stability.

As example of studies on developed countries we can find the study of Wagner (2007) who finds a positive relationship between derivatives and the opacity of US large banks.

However, papers on emerging countries studying this issue are not so frequent.

The empirical literature on the role played by derivatives within the banking stability puzzle is still limited, mostly because of the marginal importance of such banks in many emerging countries in comparison with developed countries.

As written by Capelle-Blancard (2010), the recent literature on the dangers of derivatives is more concerned by systemic risks. Several studies suggest that the sophistication of the products and the concentration of risks are potential sources of instability because of the increasing uncertainty, the repeated occurrence of extreme losses, and finally the greater possibility of global crisis.

Li and Marinc (2014) find that the use of financial derivatives is positively and significantly related to BHCs' systematic risk exposures. Higher use of interest rate derivatives, exchange rate derivatives, and credit derivatives corresponds to greater systematic interest rate risk, exchange rate risk, and credit risk. The positive relationship between derivatives and risks persists for derivatives for trading as well as for derivatives for hedging.

Gatopoulos and Loubergé (2013) argue that derivative markets have been effective tools for firms in emerging countries, at least in the post-crisis era.

Mayordomo, Rodriguez-Moreno, and Peña (2014) find that banks' aggregate holdings of five classes of derivatives do not exhibit a significant effect on the bank's contribution to systemic risk. On the contrary, the banks' holdings of certain specific types of derivatives such as foreign exchange and credit derivatives increase the banks' contributions to systemic risk whereas holdings of interest rate derivatives decrease it. Nevertheless, the proportion of non-performing loans over total loans and the leverage ratio have much stronger impact on systemic risk than derivatives holdings. Therefore, the derivatives' impact plays a second fiddle in comparison with traditional banking activities related to the former two items.

According to Farhi and Borghi (2009), the negative effects of derivatives use on bank stability may be intensified in countries with more volatile currency markets, such as Brazil, Mexico, China, India, and South Korea – emerging markets.

The main purpose of their research was to study the influence of the use of currency derivatives on bank stability, based on data collected from financial publicly traded companies issued from emerging countries.

After this deep review of literature, we remark that there are few empirical papers that have examined the effect of derivatives use on bank stability. Thus, the main contribution of this chapter is to fulfill this gap in the literature.

As regards the results of the literature, we stipulate as main hypothesis that using derivatives depreciates bank stability.

# METHODOLOGY

## *Data*

We use accounting data which are available in the websites of retained banks during the period 2003–2011. We employ, additionally, economic data in order to define country variables which are collected from World Bank database.

*Period*

According to our reference paper, Chiaramonte et al. (2015), we identify two periods: the pre-crisis period which is from 2003 to 2006, and the crisis and post-crisis which is from 2007 to 2011.

Moreover, this choice is also motivated by the aim to show the differences in the issue in the normal period and in the turbulent period.

*Sample*

The sample is composed of banks from both emerging countries and also recently developed countries.

There are 66 banks from emerging countries and 63 banks from recently developed countries.

Emerging countries are defined according to the list of countries announced by the United Nations Office in 2010. Countries having Human Development Index less than 0.784 are classified as emerging countries and countries having index more than this are considered as developed countries. On the other hand, during the last decade, countries like Czech Republic and Singapore were considered as emerging countries but nowadays they are called developed countries according to the United Nations Office. For this reason, we are motivated in this work to include banks from these countries in order to compare them with banks from emerging countries. In our current work, we call these countries "recently developed countries" In the following, the Table 1 classifies the sample banks as issued from emerging countries or recently developed countries.

*Generalized Methods of Moments*

Referred to the study of Chiaramonte et al. (2015), we utilize the Generalized Methods of Moments (GMM) estimator technique. This choice is motivated by the fact that GMM are known as robust tests since their relevance in estimating regressions. In addition, GMM is proposed by Blundell and Bond (1998) and built on the works of Arellano and Bover (1995), Farhi and Borghi (2009), and Li and Marinc (2014). The consistency of the system GMM estimator depends both on the assumptions that the error term is not auto-correlated as well as on the validity of the instruments used. Two specification tests are reported. The first is the Hansen test of over-identifying restrictions, which examines the validity of

***Table 1.*** Classification of Banks by Countries from Emerging Countries or Recently Developed Countries.

| Banks | Emerging Countries | Banks | Recently Developed Countries |
|---|---|---|---|
| Banco de Chile | Chile | Ahli United Bank B.S.C.<br>United Gulf Bank | Bahrain |
| Raiffeinsen Bank | Bulgaria | Bank of Cyprus<br>Hellenic Cyprus Bank | Cyprus |
| Zagrebacka Banka<br>Privrednabanka zagreb<br>Erste & Steiermarkische | Croatia | Komerční banka<br>Raiffeinsenban | Czech Republic |
| Halyk Bank | Kazakhstan | Swedbank | Estonia |
| Trasta Komercbanka Bank<br>Norvik Banka<br>Baltic International Bank<br>DNB Nord Banka<br>AS SEB banka Latvijas<br>Parex Banka Bank<br>Aizkraukles Banka<br>Rietumu Banka | Latvia | Bank of East Asia<br>Chong Hing Bank<br>DAH SING Bank<br>Fubon Bank<br>Hang Seng Bank<br>Wing Hang Bank | Hong Kong |
| Šialiu Bankas<br>DNB Nord Banka<br>Swedbank | Lithuania | FIBI Bank<br>Bank Hapoalim | Israel |
| TransCreditBank<br>GazpromBank | Russia | Bank BPH S.A.<br>Bank Pekao S.A.<br>PKO Bank Polski<br>Bank Zachodni WBK<br>BRE Bank<br>Kredyt Bank S.A.<br>Nordea Bank Polska S.A. | Poland |
| AK Bank<br>Seker<br>Anadolubank Anonim Sirketi<br>Garanti Bank | Turkey | Commercial Bank of Qatar<br>Qatar National Bank | Qatar |
| Gulf Bank<br>Burgan Bank | Kuwait | DBS Bank<br>United Overseas Bank | Singapore |
| Arab National Bank | Bahrain | Dexia banka Slovensko<br>a.s Výročná správa<br>Tatra banka | Slovakia |
| OCBC Bank | Malaysia | Abanka Vipa d.d. Slovenska | Slovenia |
| Philippine National Bank | Philippine | Industrial Bank of Korea<br>Korea Exchange Bank | Korea |
| United Bank Limited | Pakistan | Hua Nan Commercial Bank<br>Mega International<br>Commercial Bank<br>Taiwan Business Bank | Taiwan |

**Table 1.** (*Continued*)

| Banks | Emerging Countries | Banks | Recently Developed Countries |
|---|---|---|---|
| KTB Bank Bank of Ayudhya Bangkok Thailand Kasikorn Thailand | Thailand | National Bank of Abu Dhabi | United Arab Emirates |
| Capital Bank Jordan Ahli Bank Jordan Kuweit Bank | Jordan | | |
| Muskat Bank | Oman | | |
| BLOM Bank | Lebanon | | |
| Sasfin ABSA Capitec bank | South Africa | | |

the instruments by analyzing the sample analogue of the moment conditions used in the estimation procedure. The second test examines the hypothesis of no autocorrelation in the error term. The presence of first-order autocorrelation in the differenced residuals does not imply that the estimates are inconsistent. However, the presence of second-order autocorrelation implies that the estimates are inconsistent. Specifically, we use the two-step system GMM estimator (or linear dynamic panel-data) with Windmeijer corrected standard errors, including lagged differences. In fact, all explanatory variables are lagged with one-year period to solve the potential endogeneity problem.

*Variables Description*

The current work uses as dependent variable a popular accounting measure of bank stability: the $z$-score (see Ayadi, Llewellyn, Schmidt, Arbak, & de Groen, 2010; Beck et al., 2011; Beck & Laeven, 2006; Boyd & Runkle, 1993; Chiaramonte et al., 2015; Fu et al. 2014; Garcia-Marco & Roblez-Fernandez, 2008; Groeneveld & de Vries, 2010; Hesse & Cihák, 2007; Ivičić, Kunovac, & Ljubaj, 2008; Laeven & Levine, 2009; Maechler, Srobona, & Worrell, 2005; Mercieca, Schaeck, & Wolfe, 2007).

In fact, in their study Fu et al. (2014) define bank fragility by the probability of bankruptcy and the bank's $z$-score. They argue that a larger value of bank-level $z$-score means less overall bank risk and so higher bank stability.

The $z$-score reflects the number of standard deviations by which returns would have to fall from the mean in order to wipe out bank equity. Higher values of $z$-score are indicative of lower probability of insolvency risk and greater bank stability. Since the $z$-score is highly skewed, we use the natural logarithm of the $z$-score, so-called ln_$z$, which is normally distributed (see Ivičić et al., 2008; Laeven & Levine, 2009; Liu, Molyneux, & Wilson,, 2010). The formula of $z$-score is as follows:

$$z\text{-score} = [ROA + EQTA]/stdROA$$

From the first panel regression it emerges that average bank stability, measured by natural logarithm of $z$-score. This dependent variable is explained by variables of interests and control variables which are all one-period lagged.

Variables of interests are defined by the derivative instruments (forwards, futures, options, and swaps). The control variables are both bank-specific factors and country-specific variables. Variables attached to banks are: bank size, the credit risk, the efficiency measure, the income diversification, bank lending behavior, capital adequacy, and on-balance-sheet interest risk.

The macroeconomic variables are: the annual percent change of Gross Domestic Product, the inflation, the degree of concentration (CR3 and CR5), and the bank market concentration determined by the normalized Herfindahl−Hirschman Index.

The independent variables used in our present piece are engaged in previous studies such as Komulainen and Lukkarila (2003) who utilize inflation and GDP as control variables.

Finally, we think that it is not necessary to include country dummies since all banks are from emerging countries so they seem to have almost the same specificities.

## The Model

The model seeks to empirically test the relationship between, on the one hand, stability measure, and on the other hand, derivative instruments and control variables.

The research model is as follows:

$$\begin{aligned}
Stability\ measure_{i,t} = {} & \gamma_0 + \gamma_1 FWD_{i,t} + \gamma_2 SWP_{i,t} + \gamma_3 OPT_{i,t} + \gamma_4 FUT_{i,t} \\
& + \gamma_5 LOAN_{i,t} + \gamma_6 CAD_{i,t} + \gamma_7 LIQ_{i,t} + \gamma_8 CRISK_{i,t} \\
& + \gamma_9 SIZE_{i,t} + \gamma_7 NIM_{i,t} + \gamma_{10} NONIM_{i,t} + \gamma_{15} EFF_{i,t} \\
& + \gamma_{13} GDP_{i,t} + \gamma_{14} INFLATION_{i,t} + u_i + e_{i,t}
\end{aligned}$$

As in many papers mentioned above, the stability is measured by Log $z$-score. $(u_i + e_{i,t})$ is the composite error term. $u_i$ is the random error in which heterogeneity is specifically to a cross-sectional unit – in this case, bank; and $e_{i,t}$ is the random error in which heterogeneity is specifically to a particular observation. Independent variables are described in Table 2.

CR3 is a country-level structural indicator of bank concentration, measured by the concentration of assets held by the three largest banks in each country, with higher value indicating greater market concentration.

*Table 2.* Explanatory Variables Definitions.

| Variable | | Measure | Notation | Expected Sign |
|---|---|---|---|---|
| Variables of interest | Forwards | The notional amount of forwards divided by the total assets | FWD | − |
| | Swaps | The notional amount of swaps divided by the total assets | SWP | − |
| | Options | The notional amount of options divided by the total assets | OPT | − |
| | Futures | The notional amount of futures divided by the total assets | FUT | − |
| Bank-specific variables | Size | Natural log of total assets | SIZE | +/− |
| | Bank lending behavior | The ratio of gross loan divided by total assets | LOAN | − |
| | Capital adequacy | Defined by the ratio of risky assets (loans) to equity | CAD | +/− |
| | Liquidity | Defined by the ratio of liquid assets to total assets | LIQ | + |
| | Credit risk | The ratio of loan loss reserve divided by gross loan | CRISK | − |
| | Income diversification | Net interest income | NIM | +/− |
| | On-balance-sheet interest rate risk | Non-interest income | NONIM | − |
| | Efficiency | The ratio of total operating expenses divided by total operating incomes | EFF | +/− |
| Country-specific variables | Gross domestic product | Annual percent change of GDP | PCGDP | +/− |
| | Inflation | Inflation rate | INF | +/− |

CR5 is a country-level structural indicator of bank concentration, measured by the concentration of assets held by the five largest banks in each country, with higher value indicating greater market concentration. In order to measure each country's degree of banking system concentration, we determined the normalized Herfindahl–Hirschman Index (norm_HHI) where HHI is the sum of squared market shares (in term of total assets) of all banks in the country.

As a general rule, a normalized HHI Index below 0.10 signals low concentration, while above 0.18 signals high concentration, whereas an index between 0.10 and 0.18 shows that the industry is moderately concentrated.

# RESULTS ANALYSIS

## *Presentation of Results*

The results are presented in Tables 3 and 4.

The regression findings on banks from emerging countries show differences between derivative instruments during each period test. Indeed, the relationship between forwards and stability measure is negative in the pre-crisis period and becomes positive during the crisis & the post-crisis period. In the opposite, the influence of swaps on stability measure is positive in the pre-crisis episode and turns into negative during the crisis & the post-crisis epoch, but this effect remains positive in the whole period.

However, the impact of options on stability measure is negative only in pre-crisis episode. Equally, the effect of futures on stability measure is negative but only in the whole period.

As regards control variables, the ratio of risky assets (LOAN) has positive influence on stability measure during the pre-cris and also the crisis & post-crisis periods. In contrast, the relationship between capital adequacy and bank stability is negative during all periods. Finally, gross domestic product affects positively the stability measure during the crisis & post-crisis and also in the whole periods.

On the other hand, in the case of banks from recently developed countries, the regressions results show the significance only for the relationship between options and stability measure. In fact, the effect of options on bank stability is significantly positive only during the whole period.

**Table 3.**  Two-Step System GMM Estimator: The Case of Banks from Emerging Countries.

| | Pre-Crisis Period | Crisis & Post-Crisis Period | Whole Period |
|---|---|---|---|
| FWD (−1) | −0.5850062*** | 0.285652** | 0.0017102 |
| | 0.2042648 | 0.1232232 | 0.0964101 |
| SWP (−1) | 0.4400622* | −0.3559456* | 0.0381461* |
| | 0.2285965 | 0.2115074 | 0.0226887 |
| OPT (−1) | −1.035055 | −0.076447** | −0.0059155 |
| | 2.87223 | 0.0320715 | 0.0428379 |
| FUT (−1) | −0.0093527 | −1.110565 | −0.0730782*** |
| | 0.890406 | 0.7840606 | 0.0270619 |
| SIZE (−1) | 5.011874*** | 0.4221781 | −0.0422067 |
| | 0.6182663 | 0.4058543 | 0.0811979 |
| LOAN (−1) | 13.26754*** | 0.9358887*** | 0.3505004 |
| | 2.520358 | 0.2968691 | 0.3429746 |
| CAD (−1) | −0.5000665*** | −0.0854053*** | −0.06957*** |
| | 0.1779837 | 0.0150018 | 0.0089933 |
| LIQ (−1) | −0.8544894 | −0.5360488 | −0.9304475** |
| | 0.6957863 | 0.6766704 | 0.3658422 |
| CRISK (−1) | 6.23054 | 1.002004 | −2.386512 |
| | 3.832758 | 3.200659 | 2.232526 |
| NIM (−1) | 4.719944 | n/a | 4.582903** |
| | 8.71274 | | 2.199609 |
| NONIM (−1) | 4.295793 | −2.227381 | −0.8027046 |
| | 11.28709 | 5.150628 | 3.519121 |
| EFF (−1) | −0.2682075 | −0.0656392 | −0.0506061 |
| | 0.2353647 | 0.0544524 | 0.0679234 |
| GDP (−1) | −0.0514015 | 0.0330651** | 0.0286401*** |
| | 0.0772295 | 0.0138819 | 0.0089507 |
| INFLATION (−1) | 0.0789082** | 0.0229803 | 0.0111777 |
| | 0.0337042 | 0.0223943 | 0.0153052 |
| Number of observations | 132 | 198 | 330 |
| Sargan test | 0.0127 | 0.0520 | 0.4189 |
| AR(2) | 0.0000 | 0.0000 | 0.0000 |

Italic values denote the significant coefficients.
Values between parentheses denote standard deviations.
*** denotes coefficient statistically different from zero (1% level, two-tail test), **5% level, *10% level.

Regarding the control variables, capital adequacy ratio has negative influence in stability measure during the crisis & post-crisis period and also in the whole period. Similarly, and during these two periods, the effect of credit risk on bank stability is negative. In opposition, the relationship between efficiency measure and bank stability is positive during all periods. Finally, the gross domestic product affects positively the stability of banks but only in the whole period.

**Table 4.** Two-Step System GMM Estimator: The Case of Banks from Recently Developed Countries.

| | Pre-Crisis Period | Crisis & Post-Crisis Period | Whole Period |
|---|---|---|---|
| FWD (−1) | *0.1111618* | *0.1895767* | *0.1611246* |
| | *0.3964681* | *0.6601706* | *0.1224054* |
| SWP (−1) | −*0.0375258* | −*0.1472884* | −*0.0423539* |
| | *0.1880472* | *0.3626569* | *0.0653179* |
| OPT (−1) | *0.8424367* | −*0.3134258* | *0.3880154*** |
| | *0.9973037* | *0.5401875* | *0.1867252* |
| FUT (−1) | −*2.249099* | −*0.0160163* | *0.1775711* |
| | *2.783288* | *0.983819* | *0.2531672* |
| SIZE (−1) | −0.5151918 | −0.0660622 | −*0.4580942**** |
| | 0.4183631 | 0.4455808 | 0.0832505 |
| LOAN (−1) | 2.214473 | 0.6123035 | 0.4667483 |
| | 1.365024 | 1.272298 | 0.558398 |
| CAD (−1) | −0.054044 | −*0.1444569**** | −*0.0560241*** |
| | 0.1227649 | 0.0537997 | 0.0236482 |
| LIQ (−1) | 0.0737041 | 5.453953 | 0.2891943 |
| | 1.856096 | 3.615888 | 0.7309862 |
| CRISK (−1) | −10.24245 | −*2.020651*** | −*1.626356*** |
| | 10.81673 | 1.01312 | 0.7713039 |
| NIM (−1) | −65.44778 | 15.11 | 12.10292 |
| | 61.43407 | 21.38387 | 8.994912 |
| NONIM (−1) | −5.632391 | 1.724435 | −0.6734852 |
| | 5.803888 | 2.43056 | 1.126224 |
| EFF (−1) | *1.972163** | *0.9086902*** | *0.5921288**** |
| | 1.102308 | 0.4594416 | 0.1808785 |
| GDP (−1) | 0.0772622 | −0.0068757 | *0.0165765**** |
| | 0.0808249 | 0.0157758 | 0.0063953 |
| INFLATION (−1) | −0.0230512 | 0.0152008 | −0.006928 |
| | 0.1166989 | 0.0174825 | 0.0101484 |
| Number of observations | 126 | 189 | 441 |
| Sargan test | 0.000 | 0.5326 | 0.5238 |
| AR(2) | 0.000 | 0.0011 | 0.0000 |

Italic values denote the significant coefficients.
Values between parentheses denote standard deviations.
*** denotes coefficient statistically different from zero (1% level, two-tail test), **5% level, *10% level.

*Comments on Results*

From the regression findings, we can say that using options by banks from emerging countries, during the crisis and the post-crisis period, affects negatively the stability of banks. Indeed, we deduce that using options during the turbulent period aggravates the instability of banks. Thus, options can be considered as disruptive derivatives.

In contrast, in the case of banks from recently developed countries, the relationship between options use and stability is significantly positive in the whole period. Therefore, using options do not destabilize banks. Hence, contrary to banks from emerging countries, banks from recently developed countries should continue to use options commonly.

For this reason, we recommend banks from emerging countries to regulate more their use of options by providing more regulations and control.

As regards futures, using this instrument by banks from emerging countries affects their stability negatively in the whole period. However, this relationship is not significant in the case of banks from recently developed countries. Consequently, we advise banks from emerging countries more control when they use futures.

As for futures, the impact of swaps and forwards on stability in the case of banks from recently developed countries is not significant. Nevertheless, noteworthy results are obtained in the case of banks from emerging countries. In fact, using swaps in the pre-crisis period and in the whole period affects positively the stability; however, this effect becomes negative during the crisis and the post-crisis era. Thus, using swaps in the unstable episode is not recommended for banks from emerging countries. In the opposite, using forwards affects negatively the stability in the pre-crisis epoch but this impact becomes positive during the turbulent time. Therefore, using forwards by banks from emerging countries is recommended especially during the chaotic period.

As regards control variables, we remark that capital adequacy affects negatively the stability of both banks from emerging countries and banks from recently developed countries. Hence, there is evidence as the negative impact of capital adequacy on bank stability. Therefore, we suggest banks either from emerging countries or from recently developed countries to manage well their capital adequacy ratio in order to avoid its negative effect on stability.

Nevertheless, efficiency has positive effect on stability of banks from recently developed countries; however, it does not have significant effect in the case of banks from emerging countries. Thus, efficiency of banks from recently developed countries plays a favorable role in strengthening their stability.

On the other hand, credit risk has a negative impact on stability of banks from recently developed countries; however, it does not have a significant effect in the case of banks from emerging countries. For this reason, we deduce that banks from recently developed countries manage worse their risky assets than banks in emerging countries. As a consequence, we recommend banks from recently developed countries to enhance their management of loans by making more control.

In sum, banks from emerging countries have suffered during the last crisis by using derivatives especially options, futures, and swaps. In contrast, the use of derivatives by banks from recently developed does not deteriorate their stability.

## CONCLUSION

The major purpose of this work is to compare the effect of derivatives use on bank stability in emerging countries to that in recently developed countries.

A widespread accounting measure of bank stability, the $z$-score is employed as proxy of bank stability and so defines the explanatory variable. The four derivative instruments (forwards, futures, options, and swaps) represent the variables of interest while control variables are split into bank-specific factors and country-specific factors.

To estimate regressions, that is, to test empirically the relationship between bank stability measure and the explanatory variables, we use Generalized Methods of Moments model as proposed by Blundell and Bond (1998) because of its convenient results. All the variables are one-period lagged to solve the endogeneity problem.

Based on the paper of Chiaramonte et al. (2015) and referring to the consequences of the last financial crisis we choose as period sample the period between 2003 and 2011 because we are motivated to separate between the pre-crisis period and the crisis and the post-crisis to investigate our issue.

This chapter contributes mostly to the literature essentially in three ways, first, it is the first to investigate the effect of derivatives on bank stability either in emerging countries or in recently developed countries, second, it is the pioneer to explore whether derivatives affect bank stability during the normal and the turbulent periods, third, it is the first to compare this issue between banks from emerging countries and those from recently developed countries, finally, it is the pioneer to be based on Generalized Methods of Moments to estimate the current issue.

Our major conclusions prove that using derivatives destabilizes banks from emerging countries while banks from recently developed countries do not weaken their stability by using derivatives.

Noteworthy recommendations are revealed from this study: for banks
from emerging countries we advise them for more regulation when they use
options and futures, however banks from recently developed countries
should continue to use options ordinary.
Finally, further studies should compare banks from emerging countries
to those from developed countries when investigating this issue.

# REFERENCES

Akyuz, Y., & Boratav, K. (2003). The making of the Turkish financial crisis. *World Development, 31*, 1549–1566.
Arellano, M., & Bover, O. (1995). Another look at the instrumental variable estimation of error-components models. *Journal of Econometrics, 68*, 29–51.
Ayadi, R., Llewellyn, D., Schmidt, R. H., Arbak, E., & de Groen, W. P. (2010). *Investigating diversity in the banking sector in Europe: Key developments, performance and role of cooperative banks*. Brussels: Centre for European Policy Studies Banking and Finance, no. 28.
Bai, Y., Christopher, J. G., & Leger, L. (2012). Industry and country factors in emerging market returns: Did the Asian crisis make a difference? *Emerging Markets Review, 13*, 559–580.
Beck, T., De Jonghe, O., & Schepens, G. (2011). *Bank competition and stability: Cross country heterogeneity*. European Banking Center discussion paper, no. 019.
Beck, T., & Laeven, L. (2006). *Resolution of failed banks by deposit insurers: Cross-country evidence*. World Bank eLibrary, Policy Research Working papers, Mai 2006.
Blundell, R., & Bond, S. (1998). Initial conditions and moment restrictions in dynamic panel data models. *Journal of Econometrics, 87*, 115–143.
Boyd, J., & Runkle, D. E. (1993). Size and performance of banking firms. *Journal of Monetary Economics, 31*, 47–67.
Buffet, W. (2002). Warren Buffet on derivatives. Center for Economic and Policy Research. Federal Reserve Board Chairman Ben Bernanke's greatest hits.
Cavallaro, E., Maggi, B., & Mulino, M. (2011). The macrodynamics of financial fragility within a hard peg arrangement. *Economic Modelling, 28*, 2164–2173.
Capelle-Blancard, G. (2010). Are derivatives dangerous? A literature survey. *International Economics, 123*, 67–90.
Chiaramonte, L., Poli, F., & Oriani, M. (2015). Are cooperative banks a lever for promoting bank stability? Evidence from the recent financial crisis in OECD countries. *European Financial Management, 21*(3), 491–523.
Coutinho, J. R. R., Sheng, H. H., & Coutinho, M. I. L. (2012). The use of Fx derivatives and the cost of capital: Evidence of Brazilian companies. *Emerging Markets Review, 13*, 411–423.
Demirguc-Kunt, A., & Huizinga, H. (2010). Bank activity and funding strategies: The impact on risk and returns. *Journal of Financial Economics, 98*(3), 626–650.
Farhi, M., & Borghi, R. (2009). Operations with financial derivatives of corporations from emerging economies. *Advanced Studies, 23*(66), 169–188.

Fu, X., Lin, Y., & Molyneux, P. (2014). Bank competition and financial stability in Asia Pacific. *Journal of Banking & Finance, 38,* 64–77.

Garcia-Marco, T., & Roblez-Fernandez, M. (2008). Risk-taking behavior and ownership in the banking industry: The Spanish evidence. *Journal of Economics and Business, 60,* 332–354.

Gatopoulos, G., & Loubergé, H. (2013). Combined use of foreign debt and currency derivatives under the threat of currency crises: The case of Latin American firms. *Journal of International Money and Finance, 35,* 54–75.

Ghysels, E., & Seon, J. (2005). The Asian financial crisis: The role of derivative securities trading and foreign investors in Korea. *Journal of International Money and Finance, 24,* 607–630.

Groeneveld, H., & de Vries, B. (2010). European cooperative banks: First lessons of the subprime crisis. *International Journal of Cooperative Management, 4,* 8–21.

Hesse, H., & Cihak, M. (2007). *Cooperative banks and financial stability.* IMF Working paper no. 2.

Ivičić, L., Kunovac, D., & Ljubaj, I. (2008). *Measuring bank insolvency risk in CEE countries.* Croatian National Bank Working paper.

Kim, W., & Sung, T. (2005). What makes firms manage FX risk? *Emerging Markets Review, 6,* 263–288.

Klemkosky, R. C. (2013). Financial system fragility. *Business Horizons, 56,* 675–683.

Komulainen, T., & Lukkarila, J. (2003). What drives financial crises in emerging markets? *Emerging Markets Review, 4,* 248–272.

Laeven, L., & Levine, R. (2009). Bank governance, regulation and risk taking. *Journal of Financial Economics, 93,* 259–275.

Li, S., & Marinc, M. (2014). The use of financial derivatives and risks of U.S. bank holding companies. *International Review of Financial Analysis, 35,* 1–47.

Liu, H., Molyneux, P., & Wilson, J. (2010). Competition and stability in European banking: A regional analysis, Preliminary Draft.

Maechler, A., Srobona, M., & Worrell, D. (2005, October 6–7). Exploring financial risks and vulnerabilities in new and potential EU member states. Paper presented at the Second Annual DG ECFIN Research Conference on Financial Stability and the Convergence Process in Europe.

Mayordomo, S., Rodriguez-Moreno, M., & Peña, J. I. (2014). Derivatives holdings and systemic risk in the U.S. banking sector. *Journal of Banking & Finance, 45,* 84–104.

Mercieca, S., Schaeck, K., & Wolfe, S. (2007). Small European banks: Benefits from diversification? *Journal of Banking and Finance, 31,* 1975–1998.

Nilsen, J., & Rovelli, R. (2001). Investor risk aversion and financial fragility in emerging economies. *Journal of International Financial Markets, Institutions and Money, 11,* 443–474.

Rossi, J. L. (2009). Corporate financial policies and the exchange rate regime: Evidence from Brazil. *Emerging Markets Review, 10,* 279–295.

Schiozer, R., Oliveira, R. F., & Saito, R. (2010). Why do banks go public? Evidence from 2005–2007 wave of Brazilian bank IPOs. *Banks and Bank Systems, 5*(2), 96–107.

Sensoy, A., Ozturk, K., & Hacihasanoglu, E. (2014). Constructing a financial fragility index for emerging countries. *Finance Research Letters, 11*(4), 319–470.

Wagner, W. (2007). Financial development and the opacity of banks. *Economics Letters, 97,* 6–10.

# IS THERE A RELATIONSHIP BETWEEN THE LIQUIDITY OF CLOSED-END FUNDS' PORTFOLIOS, FUND OWNERSHIP BY SMALLER INVESTORS, AND THE LIQUIDITY OF THE FUNDS' SHARES?

Charles P. Cullinan, Xiaochuan Zheng and
Elena Precourt

## ABSTRACT

*We assess whether smaller investors are more likely to hold shares of closed-end funds that invest more heavily in illiquid securities. We also examine the relationship between the liquidity of the securities held in the portfolios of closed-end mutual funds (portfolio liquidity) and the liquidity of the closed-end funds' shares (fund-share liquidity). Using a sample of 1,619 fund-years from 2010 to 2012, we find that smaller investors are more likely than institutional investors to own closed-end*

The Spread of Financial Sophistication Through Emerging Markets Worldwide
Research in Finance, Volume 32, 185–205
Copyright © 2016 by Emerald Group Publishing Limited
All rights of reproduction in any form reserved
ISSN: 0196-3821/doi:10.1108/S0196-382120160000032008

*funds. We also find that the liquidity of closed-end funds' portfolios is positively associated with the liquidity of the funds' shares. Our findings are consistent with the "liquidity benefits" notion that closed-end funds are a means for smaller investors to invest in less liquid securities. In addition, our findings are consistent with the "valuation skepticism" notion which indicates that, due to the difficulty of objectively valuing illiquid securities, different perceptions of the value of illiquid securities held in funds' portfolios may result in greater fund-share liquidity.*

**Keywords:** Closed-end funds; portfolio liquidity; fund-share liquidity

**JEL Classifications:** G11; G12; G23; M41

# INTRODUCTION

The liquidity of the securities held in a closed-end fund's portfolio (portfolio liquidity) may be related to the types of investors holding the fund's shares and to the liquidity of the shares of the closed-end mutual fund (fund-share liquidity). If a fund's portfolio holds a larger percentage of illiquid securities, smaller investors may view the fund as a useful means to gain access to illiquid segments of the securities markets (the "liquidity benefits" idea), and smaller investors may therefore be more likely to own the fund's shares. Portfolio liquidity could also relate to fund-share liquidity when the fund invests in less liquid securities because the valuation processes for the illiquid securities could result in different perceptions about the appropriate valuation of the securities, and such differing valuation perceptions may yield higher liquidity of fund shares ("the lack of valuation consensus" notion).

There is a fairly rich literature on the liquidity of traded stocks. However, the literature on the liquidity of the shares of closed-end mutual funds is less well developed (e.g., Barnhart & Rosenstein, 2010). There is also a relatively small body of literature on the liquidity of the securities held in the portfolios of closed-end funds (e.g., Cullinan & Zheng, 2014; Elton, Gruber, Blake, & Shacher, 2010). We draw upon this limited literature to develop and analyze the possible relationships between the liquidity of the securities held in the fund's portfolio, the ownership of the fund by smaller investors, and the liquidity of the shares of the closed-end fund itself.

One possible implication of fund portfolio liquidity is based on Cherkes, Sagi, and Stanton's (2009) theory of closed-end funds as an effective means for investors (especially smaller investors) to gain access to illiquid segments of the market through the relatively liquid shares of closed-end funds. Because smaller investors may be less likely to invest in illiquid securities directly due to large transaction costs, they may view the shares of closed-end funds holding illiquid securities more favorably (i.e., the funds holding illiquid securities provide liquidity benefits), resulting in more of the fund's shares being held by smaller investors.

The relationship between the liquidity of the securities in the fund's portfolio and the liquidity of the fund shares may be based on the credibility of the valuations of the securities in the fund's portfolio. Cullinan and Zheng (2014) suggest that fund management's reported valuations for illiquid securities are more subjective than their valuations of more actively traded securities. As a result, the market may develop different perceptions about what the securities in the fund's portfolio are really worth (i.e., there is a lack of consensus among market participants). A lack of investor consensus is associated with higher liquidity (e.g., Beaver, 1968; Cho & Kwon, 2014). If this lack of consensus about the appropriate valuation exists for the illiquid investments in the closed-end funds' portfolios, the fund's shares may be more liquid when the fund's portfolio contains a larger percentage of illiquid securities.

We examine the fund portfolio liquidity, smaller investor ownership, and fund-share liquidity relationships for 1,619 closed-end fund-years for the period from 2010 to 2012. There are two main empirical findings of our study: (1) funds with more illiquid securities have more shares held by smaller (i.e., non-institutional) investors; and (2) fund shares are more liquid when the funds have a larger portion of their portfolio invested in illiquid securities. Our results for the fund portfolio/smaller investor relationship are consistent with the "liquidity benefits" theory (proposed by Cherkes et al., 2009) that investors (particularly smaller investors) view closed-end funds as a useful means of gaining access to less liquid segments of the financial markets. The results of the fund portfolio/fund-share liquidity relationship are consistent with the "lack of valuation consensus" theory (drawn from Cho & Kwon, 2014; Cullinan & Zheng, 2014) that the differing perceptions of the appropriate valuation for the illiquid investments in the closed-end funds' portfolios lead to more liquid fund shares.

Our study makes a number of contributions to the literature. First, we propose two theories for the possible relationship between the liquidity of a closed-end fund's portfolio, holdings by smaller investors, and the liquidity of the fund's shares. We also empirically examine these competing theories.

In addition, we are among the first in the literature to develop and use recently mandated accounting disclosure to measure the liquidity of a closed-end fund's portfolio of securities.

The remainder of this chapter is structured as follows: The section "Theories and Hypothesis Development" provides background on the literature related to mutual funds and formulates hypotheses based on the extant research. In the section "Research Method" we develop the research methodology. The "Results" section provides descriptive statistics and regression results. The final section summarizes and concludes the chapter.

## THEORIES AND HYPOTHESIS DEVELOPMENT

### Liquidity Benefits and Liquidity of Fund Shares

The existence of closed-end mutual funds has been viewed as a "puzzle" in the literature (e.g., Lee, Schleifer, & Thaler, 1991), especially because these funds often trade at a discount relative to the per-fund-share value of the portfolio (called the "net asset value" or NAV). A closed-end fund has a limited number of shares that are traded among investors, rather than shares which are issued and redeemed by the fund itself (as occurs with open-end mutual funds). Because the fund has no need to redeem the shares, the fund can invest in less liquid securities without the concern that portfolio securities may need to be sold (possibly on less favorable terms) to meet fund redemption requirements. In effect, the closed-end fund's shares may be actively traded (and highly liquid), while the fund's portfolio is relatively illiquid. Cherkes et al. (2009) assert that the structure of closed-end mutual funds permits investors (especially smaller investors) to gain access to illiquid segments of the markets and offers lower transactions costs than if they invested in the illiquid securities directly.

Cullinan and Zheng (2014) provide some evidence for Cherkes et al.'s (2009) conclusion that the closed-end fund structure is desirable to investors who seek access to illiquid securities. They find that for funds trading at a premium, the premium is higher when the funds invest in less liquid types of securities, which they attribute to the liquidity benefits proposed by Cherkes et al. (2009). However, for funds trading at a discount, Cullinan and Zheng (2014) find that the discount is greater when the funds invest in less liquid shares, which they attribute to the lower credibility of the valuations of the less liquid securities.

Existing research finds that smaller (i.e., non-institutional) investors tend to hold large portions of the shares of closed-end funds (e.g., Lee et al., 1991; Weiss, 1989). However, we are not aware of any research that has examined whether smaller investors' ownership is related to the types of securities held in the fund's portfolio, specifically illiquid securities. Smaller investors' preference for closed-end funds holding illiquid securities relates to the high costs of trading these securities directly, which is "particularly severe for the small investors" (Cherkes et al., 2009, p. 10). We therefore expect that closed-end funds with more illiquid portfolios are more likely to be held by smaller investors rather than by institutional investors. As the liquidity benefits notion (Cherkes et al., 2009) suggests, these smaller investors may view the closed-end fund as a cost-effective means of investing in illiquid securities. This discussion leads to the first hypothesis of our study as follows:

**H1.** There is a positive relationship between the percentage of the fund's portfolio invested in illiquid securities and the percentage of the fund's shares held by smaller (i.e., non-institutional) investors.

Smaller investors tend to hold smaller blocks of shares than institutional investors. Fund-share illiquidity is based on the effect that the sale of a given number of shares may have on the share price, and is related to average trading volume of the shares. If smaller investors hold more fund shares, average trading volume may be lower due to the smaller blocks of shares held[1] which may make the shares of fund held by smaller investors less liquid than shares of fund held by institutional investors, who are more likely to buy and sell larger blocks of shares.[2] Based on these ideas we posit hypothesis two as follows:

**H2.** Closed-end funds held by larger percentages of smaller investors have less liquid fund shares.

Hypotheses 1 and 2 suggest an indirect path between portfolio liquidity and fund-share liquidity running through the ownership by smaller investors. This indirect path from fund portfolio liquidity to fund-share liquidity is depicted in Fig. 1.

*Lack of Valuation Consensus and Illiquidity of Fund Shares*

Research has noted that the fund's measurement of the fair value of illiquid securities is more difficult and/or subjective (e.g., Cullinan & Zheng, 2014; Lee et al., 1991) than of actively traded investments. The difficulty of valuing illiquid securities could lead to a lack of consensus about the fund's

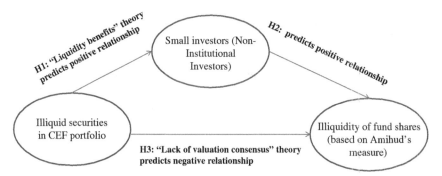

*Fig. 1.*  Theoretical Relationships between Portfolio Liquidity, Type of Investors,
and Fund-Share Illiquidity.

Net Asset Value (NAV) and fund mis-valuation, either unintentionally
(due to the difficulty of valuation of underlying securities) or intentionally
(due to the opportunity to intentionally mis-value inherent in the subjectivity of the valuation process). The subjective valuation of the fund's illiquid
securities could lead to differences of opinion about the market value of the
fund's shares,[3] and hence the price to be paid for the shares. Different perceptions of the appropriate price for the fund shares lead to higher liquidity
(e.g., Bamber, Barron, & Stevens, 2011; Bamber, Barron, & Stober, 1997;
Beaver, 1968; Cho & Kwon, 2014).

  If the potential buyers and sellers of fund shares both agree on the
appropriate valuations, the potential buyer would only be willing to pay
what the current owners thinks the security is worth, making the trade
less likely to occur when there is consensus among the investors. If investors have different perceptions of the appropriate value of fund securities,
an investor who thinks the security may be overvalued is more likely to
sell and an investor who thinks the security is undervalued may be more
inclined to buy the security. If the valuations of illiquid securities are
more subjective, this subjectivity would lead to differing investor perceptions, resulting in the higher fund-share liquidity. We will refer to this
notion as the "lack of valuation consensus" theory. Thus, we propose our
third hypothesis as follows:

**H3.** There is a positive relationship between the percentage of the fund's
portfolio invested in illiquid securities and the liquidity of fund shares.

Because the lack of valuation consensus on illiquid fund portfolio is applicable to both smaller investors and institutional investors, the impact of the lack of valuation on the fund-share liquidity is less likely to be related to whether the funds' investors are smaller or institutional investors. We therefore depict this relationship as a direct path from portfolio liquidity and fund-share liquidity in Fig. 1.

# RESEARCH METHOD

## Sample

We obtained data on all of the closed-end mutual funds in the Morningstar Direct database for fiscal year ends during 2010–2012. Morningstar contains 1,894 closed-end fund-years for this period. We downloaded the annual reports for these funds to hand-collect data on the portfolio liquidity and other variables. We also obtained data from Morningstar Direct database for some other variables, and matched the data in our hand-collected/Morningstar datasets with the Mergent Horizon database, which contains data on funds' institutional shareholdings.[4] Due to missing data, our sample is reduced to 1,657 closed-end fund-years.

## Variable Measurements

### Dependent Variables

To test H1, we use the percentage of shares held by non-institutional investors ($\%NON\_INSTITUTIONAL\_HOLDINGS_{i,t}$) as the dependent variable to test H1. Because the data we obtained are the percentages of closed-end fund shares held by institutional investors, we subtract these percentages from 100% to determine the percentages of shares held by non-institutional investors. We measured this variable for the quarter closest to the fund's fiscal year end.

To test H2 and H3, we use Amihud's (2002) measure of illiquidity ($SHAREILLIQUIDITY_{i,t}$). We utilize Morningstar Direct and CRSP to obtain share trading data. The Amihud (2002) illiquidity measure is the daily ratio of absolute stock return to its dollar volume (we use the square-root transformation to reduce skewness):

$$SHAREILLIQUIDITY_{i,y} = \frac{\sum\limits_{t=1}^{D_{i,y}} \sqrt{\frac{|r_{i,t}|}{DVOL_{i,t}}}}{D_{i,y}}$$

where $r_{i,t}$ is daily fund share $i$ returns, $DVOL_{i,t}$ is daily fund share $i$ dollar trading volume, and $D_{i,y}$ is the number of days with available illiquidity ratio for fund $i$ in a year $y$. The ratio is a measure of the price impact that describes the daily price response associated with one dollar of trading volume.[5]

*Main Independent Variable*

In our models of the percentage of shares held by non-institutional investors, and of fund-share illiquidity, we include a measure of the percentage of securities in the fund's portfolio that are illiquid. This variable, *%PORTFOLIOILLIQUID*, is measured as the percentage of the fund's assets valued using Level 2 or Level 3 valuation inputs, which we hand-collect from the fund's annual report. In the United States, Accounting Standards Codification (ASC) 820 requires companies (including closed-end funds) to disclose the nature of valuation inputs used to calculate the fair value of assets, called Levels 1, 2, and 3 valuation inputs. Level 1 valuation inputs are directly observable inputs, which are market prices of actively traded securities. Level 2 inputs are indirectly observable valuation inputs. These Level 2 inputs are used when the security in question is not actively traded, but there are other market-determined criteria that can be used to estimate the value of the security, such as yield curves on bonds. Finally, Level 3 valuation inputs are unobservable (i.e., estimated by management), such as the amounts and variability of future cash flows and appropriate discount rates.

Level 1-valued assets are actively traded securities, and so are highly liquid. Level 2-valued assets may be traded, but not often enough to provide a clean market measure of the valuation at a certain point in time, indicating that Level 2 assets are less liquid than those valued using Level 1 inputs. Level 3 assets are the least liquid type of assets because there are no market measures available to assess their valuations, suggesting that the securities are rarely traded. Therefore, the percentage of Levels 2 and 3 valued securities (*%PORTFOLIOILLIQUID*) measures the percentage of illiquid securities held in the fund's portfolio.[6]

## *Analysis Techniques and Control Variables*

To test our hypotheses, we run the following OLS regression models:

$$
\begin{aligned}
\%NON\_INSTITUTIONAL\_HOLDINGS_{i,t} = {} & \beta_0 + \beta_1 \%PORTFOLIOILLIQUID_{i,t} \\
& + \beta_2 SIZE_{i,t} + \beta_3 NYSE_{i,t} \\
& + \beta_4 RETURN_{i,t} + \beta_5 LEVERAGE_{i,t} \\
& + \beta_6 PRICE_{i,t} + \beta_7 DIVIDEND_{i,t} \\
& + \beta_8 AGE_{i,t} + \beta_9 EXPENSE_{i,t} \\
& + \beta_{10} PREMIUM/DISCOUNT_{i,t} \\
& + \text{year indicator variables} + \varepsilon_i
\end{aligned}
$$

$$(1)$$

$$
\begin{aligned}
SHAREILLIQUIDITY_{i,t} = {} & \beta_0 + \beta_1 \%NON\_INSTITUTIONAL\_HOLDINGS_{i,t} \\
& + \beta_2 \%PORTFOLIOILLIQUID_{i,t} + \beta_3 SIZE_{i,t} \\
& + \beta_4 NYSE_{i,t} + \beta_5 RETURN_{i,t} + \beta_6 LEVERAGE_{i,t} \\
& + \beta_7 PRICE_{i,t} + \beta_8 DIVIDEND_{i,t} + \beta_9 AGE_{i,t} \\
& + \beta_{10} EXPENSE_{i,t} + \beta_{11} PREMIUM/DISCOUNT_{i,t} \\
& + \text{year indicator variables} + \varepsilon_i
\end{aligned}
$$

$$(2)$$

Model (1) tests H1, model (2) tests H2 and H3.

In both models, we use the following fund characteristics as control variables. These variables are commonly used in prior studies of closed-end funds:[7,8]

*SIZE* is measured as a natural log of a fund's total assets at the end of year. We use the log transformation of *SIZE* in our regression models due to the skewed distribution of the variable. Large funds usually have higher trading volumes (Pontiff, 1996). Size may also be associated with non-institutional shareholdings (e.g., Ackert & Athanassakos, 2003; Below, Stansell, & Coffin, 2000).[9]

*NYSE* is a variable indicating whether the fund's shares are traded on the New York Stock Exchange (coded 1) or elsewhere (coded 0). Previous research indicates that the exchange on which the shares are traded relates to both fund-share liquidity (e.g., Tang, 2012) and institutional share ownership (e.g., Below et al., 2000).

*RETURN* is measured as a fund's three-year compound return (%). On the one hand, high returns reflect positive investor sentiment (Gemmill & Thomas, 2002); on the other hand, high returns are associated with a concern of "reversion of the mean" in the funds' future portfolio performance (Chay & Trzcinka, 1999). Thus, a high *RETURN* value might result in different perceptions about the fund's value leading to higher liquidity. In our model of non-institutional ownership, smaller investors may be more likely to employ a buy-and-hold strategy that is less sensitive to *RETURN*.

*LEVERAGE* is measured as the fund's total liabilities divided by total assets at the end of the fiscal year. Tang (2012) finds that leverage is negatively related to market liquidity of fund shares. *LEVERAGE* may also be associated with non-institutional shareholdings, as smaller investors are less likely than institutional investors to employ a leveraging strategy in their own portfolios, seeking this strategy in the closed-end fund setting.

*PRICE* is the fund's average daily market price over the year. Funds with lower share prices are traded less frequently as they are more likely to be held by smaller investors, who access these funds with smaller investments (Minnick & Raman, 2013).

*DIVIDEND* is the fund's yearly dividend yield. Pontiff (1996) provides evidence that higher dividend yields can reduce arbitrage costs. Higher dividends may also make the fund more attractive to smaller investors.

*AGE* is the fund's age (logged due to its skewed distribution). Because new funds are usually issued when a particular sector is in a "hot period" (Gemmill & Thomas, 2002), their shares may trade more frequently than the shares of older funds. Newer funds may also be less likely to attract smaller shareholders because they are not well-known.

*EXPENSE* is the fund's yearly gross expense ratio. Kumar and Noronha (1992) find that investors tend to avoid funds with high expense ratio. As such, funds with higher expense ratios may have higher fund-share illiquidity, and are perhaps less attractive and affordable to smaller investors than less expensive funds.

*PREMIUM/DISCOUNT* is the fund's mean 12 month premium (positive) or discount (negative). Datar (2001) suggests that there is a positive (negative) association between the premium (discount) and the liquidity of fund's shares. Non-institutional investors are less likely to buy funds traded at a discount.

# RESULTS

## Descriptive Statistics and Correlation Analysis

Descriptive statistics for our sample are presented in Table 1. Non-institutional shareholders own 88.4% of the mean fund's shares. Amihud's

***Table 1.*** Descriptive Statistics.

Number of observations = 1,619

| Variable | Mean | Std. Dev. | Median | Minimum | Maximum |
|---|---|---|---|---|---|
| SHAREILLIQUIDITY | 0.160 | 0.242 | 0.111 | 0.021 | 5.622 |
| %NON_INSTITUTIONAL_HOLDINGS | 88.486 | 11.054 | 92.119 | 32.900 | 99.996 |
| %PORTFOLIOILLIQUID | 74.476 | 38.618 | 98.744 | 0 | 100 |
| %Level2 | 72.427 | 39.149 | 97.647 | 0 | 100 |
| %Level3 | 2.049 | 8.731 | 0 | 0 | 100 |
| SIZE (in millions) | $470.677 | $510.707 | $292.089 | $4.128 | $4,497.796 |
| NYSE | 0.774 | 0.419 | 1.000 | 0.000 | 1.000 |
| RETURN (%) | 35.204 | 33.525 | 32.846 | −74.117 | 233.642 |
| LEVERAGE (%) | 23.215 | 15.531 | 28.560 | 0 | 53.495 |
| PRICE | $13.895 | $5.477 | $14.010 | $2.145 | $57.560 |
| DIVIDEND (%) | 5.671 | 2.877 | 5.998 | 0 | 19.316 |
| AGE | 14.280 | 10.460 | 11.000 | 1.000 | 85.000 |
| EXPENSE (%) | 1.577 | 0.698 | 1.480 | 0 | 9.700 |
| PREMIUM/DISCOUNT (%) | −1.591 | 15.227 | −2.408 | −32.467 | 66.850 |
| YEAR2011 | 0.342 | 0.475 | 0.000 | 0.000 | 1.000 |
| YEAR2012 | 0.333 | 0.471 | 0.000 | 0.000 | 1.000 |

*Notes: Variable definitions*:
*SHAREILLIQUIDITY* is the Amihud (2002) measure of closed-end fund shares' illiquidity.
*%NON_INSTITUTIONAL_HOLDINGS* is the percentage of shares held by non-institutions investors.
*%PORTFOLIOILLIQUID* is the percentage of fair value of less liquid assets.
*%LEVEL2* is the percentage of fair value of level 2 assets.
*%LEVEL3* is the percentage of fair value of level 3 assets.
*SIZE* is the fund's total assets.
*NYSE* is a dummy variable which is coded as one if the fund is listed in NYSE, and zero otherwise.
*RETURN* is the fund's three-year compounded market return.
*LEVERAGE* is measured as the total liabilities divided by total assets.
*PRICE* is the fund's average daily market price over a year.
*DIVIDEND* is the fund's yearly dividend yield.
*AGE* is the fund's age.
*EXPENSE* is the fund's yearly gross expense ratio.
*PREMIUM/DISCOUNT* is the fund's average monthly premium (positive) or discount (negative) over a year.
*YEAR2011* is a dummy variable which is coded one for year 2011 observations, and zero otherwise.
*YEAR2012* is a dummy variable which is coded one for year 2012 observations, and zero otherwise.

196                                          CHARLES P. CULLINAN ET AL.

illiquidity measure has a mean of 0.16, which is lower than illiquidity of
0.27 in Agarwal (2007),[10] who examines 4,578 firms listed on NYSE and
AMEX over the period 1980–2005. Amihud (2002) analyzes the effect of
illiquidity on stock returns for NYSE-traded securities in the years
1963–1997 (a total of 408 months) and reports mean of annual illiquidity
means of 0.337. For comparison purposes we recalculate our illiquidity
measure without taking a square-root of absolute returns divided by the
daily trading volume and find illiquidity mean to equal to 0.12, which is
lower than Amihud's average of 0.337. These differences in illiquidity measures could be explained by characteristics of the securities included in the
samples (closed-end fund securities versus all NYSE- and/or AMEX-traded
securities) and the time periods under review (2010–2012 vs. mid to late
1900s), when the capital markets have experienced changes in trading behaviors and capabilities. The mean closed-end fund holds 74.5% of its
assets in illiquid securities.[11] Total assets held by the average fund are
about $470 million with the largest fund holding over $4.4 billion in assets.
Over 77% of the funds are traded on the New York Stock Exchange.[12]
Three-year market returns ranged from a 74.1% loss to a gain of 233.6%,
with a mean three-year return of 35.2%. The average debt to asset ratio is
23.2% and the mean fund share is priced at $13.89, with a range from
$2.14 to $57.56. The average dividend yield is 5.7% and the average
expense ratio is 1.575. The funds trade at a mean discount of 1.59% of
their NAV.

Table 2 presents a Pearson correlation matrix among the variables. As predicted in H1, there is positive correlation between %PORTFOLIOILLIQUID
and NON_INSTITUTIONAL_HOLDINGS. As predicted in H2, there is a
positive correlation between %NON_INSTITUTIONAL_HOLDINGS and
SHAREILLIQUIDITY. The correlation between %PORTFOLIOILLIQUID
and SHAREILLIQUIDITY is negative, but statistically insignificant. Many
other variables are also associated with each other, supporting our use of
regression methods to analyze our hypotheses.

*Regression Analyses*

Table 3 presents results of model (1) with the percentage of shares held
by smaller investors (NON_INSTITUTIONAL_HOLDINGS) as a dependent variable. The overall model is significant at <0.0001 ($F = 79.74$),
and the adjusted $R^2$ is 36.33%, indicating that the model has reasonable
explanatory power. As predicted by H1, there is a positive relationship

**Table 2.** Pearson Correlations.

| | SHARE ILLIQUIDITY | %NON_INSTITUTIONAL_HOLDINGS | %PORTFOLIOILLIQUID | SIZE | NYSE | RETURN | LEVERAGE | PRICE | DIVIDEND | AGE | EXPENSE | PREMIUM/DISCOUNT | YEAR2011 |
|---|---|---|---|---|---|---|---|---|---|---|---|---|---|
| %NON_INSTITUTIONAL_HOLDINGS | 0.120*** | 1 | | | | | | | | | | | |
| %PORTFOLIOILLIQUID | -0.019 | 0.436*** | 1 | | | | | | | | | | |
| SIZE | -0.550*** | -0.123*** | -0.132*** | 1 | | | | | | | | | |
| NYSE | -0.324*** | -0.196*** | -0.129*** | 0.375*** | 1 | | | | | | | | |
| RETURN | -0.127*** | 0.002 | 0.048* | 0.135*** | 0.038 | 1 | | | | | | | |
| LEVERAGE | -0.018 | 0.424*** | 0.483*** | 0.069** | -0.179*** | 0.134*** | 1 | | | | | | |
| PRICE | -0.129*** | -0.270*** | -0.196*** | 0.137*** | 0.02186 | -0.00848 | -0.099*** | 1 | | | | | |
| DIVIDEND | -0.156*** | 0.396*** | 0.491*** | 0.139*** | 0.02338 | 0.262*** | 0.485*** | -0.296*** | 1 | | | | |
| AGE | 0.112*** | -0.02476 | 0.096*** | -0.02353 | 0.03866 | 0.101*** | 0.00159 | -0.112*** | -0.091*** | 1 | | | |
| EXPENSE | 0.291*** | -0.058** | -0.132*** | -0.125*** | -0.184*** | 0.072*** | 0.299*** | 0.014 | 0.02361 | -0.161*** | 1 | | |
| PREMIUM/DISCOUNT | -0.024 | 0.236*** | 0.190*** | 0.03883 | 0.00754 | 0.091*** | 0.211*** | -0.068** | 0.292*** | -0.02416 | 0.01179 | 1 | |
| YEAR2011 | 0.022 | -0.00818 | 0.00744 | -0.02199 | -0.00424 | 0.589*** | 0.01879 | -0.01238 | 0.048* | -0.01057 | -0.00684 | -0.049** | 1 |
| YEAR2012 | -0.045* | 0.025 | 0.003 | 0.050** | 0.018 | -0.00735 | -0.011 | 0.068** | -0.063** | 0.063** | 0.078*** | 0.03427 | -0.509*** |

Notes. All variables are defined in Table 1. SIZE and AGE are logged.
*, **, and *** indicates significance at the 0.10, 0.05, and 0.01 levels, respectively. Sample size = 1,619.

198                                                 CHARLES P. CULLINAN ET AL.

*Table 3.*   The Association between the Liquidity of a Fund's Portfolio and
the Percentage of Shares Held by Non-Institutional Investors.

Dependent variable = *%NON_INSTITUTIONAL_HOLDINGS*

| Variable | Coeff. Est. | *t*-Stat. | *p*-Value |
|---|---|---|---|
| *INTERCEPT* | 104.20 | 29.67 | 0.0000*** |
| *%PORTFOLIOILLIQUID* | 0.03 | 3.03 | 0.0024*** |
| *SIZE* | −1.06 | −4.59 | 0.0000*** |
| *NYSE* | −3.33 | −6.14 | 0.0000*** |
| *RETURN* | −0.03 | −2.63 | 0.0087*** |
| *LEVERAGE* | 0.24 | 10.93 | 0.0000*** |
| *PRICE* | −0.30 | −4.09 | 0.0000*** |
| *DIVIDEND* | 0.64 | 5.10 | 0.0000*** |
| *AGE* | −0.72 | −2.00 | 0.0452** |
| *EXPENSE* | −3.14 | −5.33 | 0.0000*** |
| *PREMIUM/DISCOUNT* | 0.08 | 1.71 | 0.0869* |
| *YEAR2011* | 1.65 | 2.02 | 0.0438** |
| *YEAR2012* | 1.28 | 1.97 | 0.0494** |
| Observations | 1,657 | | |
| Adjusted $R^2$ | 0.3633 | | |
| *F*-stat. | 79.74 | | |
| Prob. > *F*-stat. | <.0001 | | |

*Notes*: All variables are as defined in Table 1. *SIZE* and *AGE* are logged in the models. All *t*-statistics are based on robust standard errors.
*, **, *** indicates significance at the 0.10, 0.05, and 0.01 levels, respectively.

between the percentage of illiquid securities held by the fund
*(%PORTFOLIOILLIQUID)* and the percentage of shares held by smaller
investors. Consistent with the liquidity benefits notion, these results indicate
that smaller investors are more likely to invest in closed-end funds that contain more illiquid securities. Regarding the control variables, non-institutional
investors own a smaller percentage (than institutional investors) of larger and
older funds, funds traded on the NYSE, funds with better market returns,
higher prices, and higher expense ratios. Smaller investors are likely to own a
larger percentage of funds with higher leverage, higher dividends, and larger
premium/smaller discount.

Table 4 presents the results of our model (2), which tests the hypotheses
related to the effect of non-institutional ownership (H2) and portfolio
liquidity (H3) on the liquidity of fund shares.[13] The dependent variable is
Amihud's illiquidity ratio. The models' $R^2$ is 42%, suggesting that the
model has reasonable explanatory power.

**Table 4.** The Association between the Liquidity of a Fund's Portfolio and Fund-Share Liquidity.

| Dependent variable = *SHAREILLIQUIDITY* | | | |
|---|---|---|---|
| Variable | Coeff. Est. | *t*-Stat. | *p*-Value |
| *INTERCEPT* | 1.02725 | 11.3100 | 0.0000*** |
| *%PORTFOLIOILLIQUID* | −0.04252 | −2.5600 | 0.0107** |
| *%NON_INSTITUTIONAL_HOLDINGS* | 0.32052 | 5.7400 | 0.0000*** |
| *SIZE* | −0.09881 | −18.8200 | 0.0000*** |
| *NYSE* | −0.06292 | −5.1100 | 0.0000*** |
| *RETURN* | −0.09525 | −4.5100 | 0.0000*** |
| *LEVERAGE* | −0.00133 | −3.0800 | 0.0021*** |
| *PRICE* | −0.00244 | −2.6000 | 0.0095** |
| *DIVIDEND* | −0.54904 | −2.2700 | 0.0231** |
| *AGE* | 0.05477 | 8.1500 | 0.0000*** |
| *EXPENSE* | 0.09707 | 12.4600 | 0.0000*** |
| *PREMIUM/DISCOUNT* | 0.00037 | 1.1300 | 0.2568 |
| *YEAR2011* | 0.04775 | 2.9300 | 0.0034** |
| *YEAR2012* | −0.00703 | −0.5400 | 0.5893 |
| Observations | 1,619 | | |
| Adjusted $R^2$ | 0.4173 | | |
| *F*-Stat. | 90.14 | | |
| Prob. > *F*-stat. | <.0001 | | |

*Notes*: All variables are as defined in Table 1. *SIZE* and *AGE* are logged in the models. All *t*-statistics are based on robust standard errors.
*, **, *** indicates significance at the 0.10, 0.05, and 0.01 levels, respectively.

The *%NON_INSTITUTIONAL_HOLDINGS* variable is positively related to Amihud's illiquidity ratio. This result supports H2 and indicates that smaller investor ownership is associated with less liquid fund shares. Because smaller investors tend to trade smaller blocks of fund shares, the shares may be less liquid (i.e., the price is more sensitive to trading). A one standard deviation increase in *%NON_INSTITUTIONAL_HOLDINGS* leads to a 32% increase in fund-share illiquidity. The coefficient estimate on the variable *%PORTFOLIOILLIQUID* is negative (−0.043) and statistically significant at a 5% level when controlling for other firm- and investor-related characteristics. This result supports hypothesis H3 and suggests that funds with higher percentages of illiquid securities held in the funds' portfolio have fund shares with higher (lower) fund-share (il)liquidity. A one standard deviation increase in *%PORTFOLIOILLIQUID* results in a 4.3% decline in Amihud's illiquidity ratio. Because model (2) simultaneously controls for both non-institutional shareholdings (%*NON_INSTITUTIONAL_ HOLDINGS*) and liquidity of fund's portfolio (%*PORTFOLIOILLIQUID*), the findings suggest that the linkage between portfolio liquidity and fund-share liquidity is not solely through the non-institutional holding. With regard to the control variables, Table 4 shows that smaller and older NYSE-traded fund securities with lower returns, leverage, price, and dividends, and greater expenses have higher illiquidity.

In order to examine the overall effects of fund portfolio liquidity on fund-share liquidity, we also run a regression of model (2) with %*NON_INSTITUTIONAL_HOLDINGS* excluded. We find that there is an overall negative relationship between fund portfolio liquidity and fund-share liquidity (%*PORTFOLIOILLIQUID* has a coefficient of −0.03268 with $p$-value of 0.0507, untabulated), indicating that the indirect path and the direct path (as shown in Fig. 1) partially offset each other and the direct path is dominant.

*Sensitivity Analysis*

Panels A and B of Table 5 present the results of sensitivity testing in which we separate the illiquid securities into those valued using level 2 and 3 valuation inputs. Results from Panel A indicate that smaller investors own more fund shares when the funds invest in level 2 securities (e.g., municipal bonds), but fewer shares when the fund invests more heavily in level 3 securities (e.g., derivatives), with which smaller investors may be less comfortable. In Panel B, we report that both level 2- and 3-valued assets significantly and negatively relate to fund-share liquidity, with level 3 assets contributing more to this relationship than level 2 assets.

*Limitations*

Our study is subject to a number of limitations. For example, the existing literature does not provide widely agreed upon models that examine relationships between non-institutional holdings or portfolio liquidity and fund-share liquidity. While our models control for other variables in addition to portfolio liquidity and non-institutional holdings, our results may have been different if other control variables were included (i.e., there is a potential for omitted variable bias). Also, the "lack of valuation consensus" theory is based on the existing research that focuses on trading

**Table 5.** Sensitivity Analysis – Segregates Less Liquid Assets into Those Valued using Level 2 and Those Valued using Level 3 Valuation Inputs.

*Panel A: Dependent variable = %NON_INSTITUTIONAL_HOLDINGS*

| Variable | Coeff. Est. | *t*-Stat. | *p*-Value |
|---|---|---|---|
| INTERCEPT | 103.89 | 30.20 | 0.0000*** |
| % LEVEL2 | 0.03 | 3.44 | 0.0006*** |
| % LEVEL3 | −0.08 | −2.04 | 0.0413** |
| SIZE | −1.12 | −4.89 | 0.0000*** |
| NYSE | −3.08 | −5.47 | 0.0000*** |
| RETURN | −0.03 | −2.89 | 0.0039*** |
| LEVERAGE | 0.22 | 10.44 | 0.0000*** |
| PRICE | −0.30 | −4.08 | 0.0000*** |
| DIVIDEND | 0.70 | 5.66 | 0.0000*** |
| AGE | −0.65 | −1.80 | 0.0724* |
| EXPENSE | −2.64 | −4.66 | 0.0000*** |
| PREMIUM/DISCOUNT | 0.08 | 1.71 | 0.0876* |
| YEAR2011 | 1.80 | 2.21 | 0.0270** |
| YEAR2012 | 1.33 | 2.06 | 0.0391** |
| Observations | 1,657 | | |
| Adjusted $R^2$ | 0.3695 | | |
| *F*-stat. | 75.66 | | |
| Prob. > *F*-stat. | <.0001 | | |

*Panel B: Dependent variable = SHAREILLIQUIDITY*

| Variable | Coeff. Est. | *t*-Stat. | *p*-Value |
|---|---|---|---|
| INTERCEPT | 1.04321 | 11.4900 | 0.0000*** |
| % LEVEL2 | −0.03709 | −2.2200 | 0.0267** |
| % LEVEL3 | −0.19799 | −3.3300 | 0.0009*** |
| %NON_INSTITUTIONAL_HOLDINGS | 0.30113 | 5.3600 | 0.0000*** |
| SIZE | −0.10004 | −19.0200 | 0.0000*** |
| NYSE | −0.05941 | −4.8000 | 0.0000*** |
| RETURN | −0.1013 | −4.7800 | 0.0000*** |
| LEVERAGE | −0.00153 | −3.5100 | 0.0005*** |
| PRICE | −0.00249 | −2.6500 | 0.0081** |
| DIVIDEND | −0.42607 | −1.7400 | 0.0824* |
| AGE | 0.05556 | 8.2800 | 0.0000*** |
| EXPENSE | 0.10377 | 12.7200 | 0.0000*** |
| PREMIUM/DISCOUNT | 0.000375 | 1.1500 | 0.2497 |
| YEAR2011 | 0.05085 | 3.1200 | 0.0018*** |
| YEAR2012 | −0.00579 | −0.4500 | 0.656 |
| Observations | 1,619 | | |
| Adjusted $R^2$ | 0.4196 | | |
| *F*-stat. | 84.56 | | |
| Prob. > *F*-stat. | <.0001 | | |

*Notes*: All variables are as defined in Table 1. *SIZE* and *AGE* are logged in the models. All *t*-statistics are based on robust standard errors.
*, **, *** indicates significance at the 0.10, 0.05, and 0.01 levels, respectively.

volume and share liquidity *changes* in response to new information (such as an earnings release) being disclosed to the market. In this chapter, we examine fund-share illiquidity cross-sectionally, rather than in response to the releases of new information such as funds' NAVs, which is done at least once a week. The traditional view that fund liquidity is driven by a lack of consensus about the appropriate price may be less applicable in a cross-sectional analysis as the lack of consensus could fade over time (e.g., Beaver, 1968).

## SUMMARY AND CONCLUSIONS

The liquidity of the shares of closed-end mutual funds has been the subject of only very limited research. In this study, we examine whether there is a relationship between the liquidity of the securities in a closed-end fund's portfolio (portfolio liquidity), smaller investor ownership, and the liquidity of the fund's shares (fund-share liquidity).

Investors may view the closed-end fund structure as a means of investing in illiquid securities with lower transaction costs than if they had invested in the illiquid securities directly. This concern with reducing transaction costs may be particularly important for smaller investors, who may enjoy the liquidity benefits of being able to invest in illiquid securities through relatively liquid closed-end fund shares. For illiquid securities in a fund's portfolio, there may be a lack of consensus among market participants about the appropriate valuations of the illiquid securities because such valuations are more subjective. These differences in opinions could then lead to more liquid fund shares (Bamber et al., 1997; Cho & Kwon, 2014) as investors seek to capitalize on the profit-making opportunities such differences of opinion can present. Thus, funds with more illiquid securities in their portfolio would be associated with more liquid fund shares.

We gather data on the liquidity of closed-end funds' investment portfolios from 2010 to 2012, as recent accounting disclosure changes have facilitated the measurement of fund portfolio liquidity. We also gather data on fund-share liquidity, and non-institutional ownership of closed-end funds for this period. We find that smaller (i.e., non-institutional) investors own a larger percentage of closed-end fund shares when the fund invests more heavily in illiquid securities, consistent with liquidity benefits being valuable to smaller investors. We also find that funds' investment portfolios are related to the fund-share liquidity. Specifically, funds more heavily invested in illiquid securities have more liquid fund shares, potentially due to lack of consensus on the valuation of the illiquid investments in the funds' portfolios. Overall, our results suggest that closed-end funds' investment portfolios are related to share ownership by smaller investors and to the liquidity of the funds' shares. Our findings support the notion that closed-ends may be a useful means for smaller investors to invest in illiquid securities and that closed-end funds with a larger percentage of their portfolios invested in illiquid securities have more liquid fund shares, even when controlling for presence of smaller shareholders, who are more likely to buy and sell smaller blocks of shares.

# NOTES

1. Smaller investors owning closed-end fund shares may also be more likely to pursue a buy-and-hold strategy and trade less frequently.
2. Note that lower share liquidity when shares are held by smaller investors may still be consistent with the liquidity benefits notion of closed-end funds being a relatively liquid means for investors to gain access to illiquid securities. The liquidity benefits theory posits that closed-end fund shares are more liquid than *investing in the illiquid securities directly*. Our study examines whether fund-share liquidity differs *among funds* with differing types of shareholders and different portfolio characteristics.
3. Cho and Kwon (2014, p. 9) refer to the lack of certainty about share value as investors' "differential interpretation of information."
4. The Mergent Database does not have access through its interface to historical data on institutional ownership. However, Mergent retains this information in its database, and we were able to obtain a customized report of this data.
5. Note that Amihud's measure is of fund-share *il*liquidity. As such, a negative relationship between portfolio liquidity and Amihud's illiquidity measure would be consistent with the positive relationship predicted between portfolio liquidity and fund-share liquidity posited in H3. In the literature and hypotheses development, we believe that discussing fund-share liquidity (rather than illiquidity) is more clear.
6. Note that this measure is equivalent to the percentage of "good-faith-valued" securities as defined by the Investment Company Act of 1940.
7. Other control variables considered were the fund's beta, which was excluded due to collinearity concerns, and the percentage of fund's assets held in cash, which was excluded due to a large number of fund-years for which this data was not available, which would have resulted in a material reduction of our sample size.
8. We include these same control variables in our model of the percentage of shares held by non-institutional investors. Given the paucity of literature on factors associated with institutional (or non-institutional shareholdings) of closed-end fund shares, the model of closed-end fund non-institutional ownership is rather ad hoc, as are the explanations of the possible relationships between the variables and non-institutional shareholdings.

9. Alternative size measures examined in our models include the fund's market cap and number of shares outstanding. Our results were not materially affected by the inclusion of these size measures as alternatives to the total assets size measure. We could not include these other size variables and the total asset size measure due to correlations among these variables causing collinearity concerns in our models.

10. Consistent with Agarwal (2007), we measure illiquidity as the square-root of absolute returns over daily volume to reduce the data skewness.

11. For comparison purposes, we took a random sample of 50 *open-ended* mutual funds from 2011 and hand-collected data on the percentage of illiquid securities held by these funds. For the *open-ended* funds, the mean percentage of illiquid securities was 30.35%, which is significantly lower than the 72.4% of illiquid securities held by the mean *closed-end* fund in 2011 ($t = 7.22$, $p < 0.0001$)). These results are consistent with Cherkes et al.'s (2009) theory that closed-end funds' raison d'etre is to invest in illiquid securities.

12. Most of the remaining funds (20.9%) are traded on AMEX.

13. The data necessary to compute Amihud's illiquidity measure were not available for 38 fund-years, reducing our sample size for the *SHAREILLIQUIDITY* analyses to 1,619 fund-years.

# ACKNOWLEDGMENT

The authors gratefully acknowledge helpful comments received from participants at the Eastern Finance Association Annual meeting.

# REFERENCES

Ackert, L., & Athanassakos, G. (2003). A simultaneous equations analysis of analysts' forecast bias, analyst following, and institutional ownership. *Journal of Business Finance and Accounting*, 30(7–8), 1017–1042. doi:10.1111/1468-5957.05452

Agarwal, P. (2007). *Institutional ownership and stock liquidity*. Working Paper. Cornell University, November 13, 2007. SSRN: 1029395. doi:10.2139/ssrn.1029395

Amihud, Y. (2002). Illiquidity and stock returns: Cross-section and time-series effects. *Journal of Financial Markets*, 5(1), 31–56. doi:10.1016/s1386-4181(01)00024-6

Bamber, L. S., Barron, O. E., & Stevens, D. E. (2011). Trading volume around earnings announcements and other financial reports: Theory, research design, empirical evidence, and directions for future research. *Contemporary Accounting Research*, 28(2), 431–471. doi:10.2139/ssrn.1473439

Bamber, L. S., Barron, O. E., & Stober, T. L. (1997). Trading volume and different aspects of disagreements coincident with earnings announcements. *The Accounting Review*, 72(4), 575–597.

Barnhart, S. W., & Rosenstein, S. (2010). Exchange traded fund introductions and closed-end fund discounts and volume. *The Financial Review*, 45, 973–994. doi:10.1111/j.1540-6288.2010.00281.x

Beaver, W. H. (1968). The information content of annual earnings announcements. *Journal of Accounting Research, 6*(Suppl.), 67−92. doi:10.2307/2490070

Below, S., Stansell, S., & Coffin, M. (2000). The determinants of REIT institutional ownership: Tests of the CAPM. *The Journal of Real Estate Finance and Economics, 21*(3), 263−278. doi:10.1023/a:1012003803494

Chay, J. B., & Trzcinka, C. A. (1999). Managerial performance and the cross-sectional pricing of closed-end funds. *Journal of Financial Economics, 52*, 379−408. doi:10.1016/s0304-405x(99)00013-6

Cherkes, M., Sagi, J., & Stanton, R. (2009). A liquidity theory of closed end funds. *The Review of Financial Studies, 22*(10), 258−297. doi:10.1093/rfs/hhn028

Cho, M., & Kwon, Q. Y. (2014). Trading volume and investor disagreement around management disclosure forecasts. *Journal of Accounting, Auditing & Finance, 29*(1), 3−30. doi:10.1177/0148558x13516977

Cullinan, C. P., & Zheng, X. (2014). Valuation scepticism, liquidity benefits and closed-end fund premiums/discounts: Evidence from fair value disclosures. *Accounting & Finance, 54*(3), 729−751. doi:10.1111/acfi.12023

Datar, V. (2001). Impact of liquidity on premia/discounts in closed-end funds. *The Quarterly Review of Economics and Finance, 41*, 119−135. doi:10.1016/s1062-9769(00)00065-x

Elton, E. J., Gruber, M. J., Blake, C. R., & Shacher, O. (2010). *Why do closed-end bond funds exist? An additional explanation for the growth in domestic closed-end bond funds.* Working Paper, New York University, June 14, 2010. doi:10.2139/ssrn.1591157

Gemmill, G., & Thomas, D. C. (2002). Noise trading, costly arbitrage, and asset prices: Evidence from closed-end funds. *The Journal of Finance, 57*, 2571−2594. doi:10.1111/1540-6261.00506

Kumar, R., & Noronha, G. M. (1992). A re-examination of the relationship between closed end fund discounts and expenses. *Journal of Financial Research, 15*, 139−147. doi:10.1111/j.1475-6803.1992.tb00794.x

Lee, C. M., Schleifer, C. A., & Thaler, R. H. (1991). Investor sentiment and the closed-end fund puzzle. *The Journal of Finance, 46*(1), 75−110. doi:10.1111/j.1540-6261.1991.tb03746.x

Minnick, K., & Raman, K. (2013). Why are stock splits declining? *Financial Management, 43*(1), 26−60. doi:10.1111/fima.12024

Pontiff, J. (1996). Costly arbitrage: Evidence from closed-end funds. *Quarterly Journal of Economics, 111*, 1135−1151. doi:10.2307/2946710

Tang, Y. (2012). Leverage and Liquidity: Evidence from the closed-end fund industry. SSRN No. 1729296. doi:10.2139/ssrn.1729296

Weiss, K. (1989). The post-offering price performance of closed-end funds. *Financial Management, 18*(3), 57−67. doi:10.2307/3665649

# DOES DEMOGRAPHIC CHANGE IMPACT HONG KONG ECONOMIC GROWTH?

Ping-fu (Brian) Lai and Wai Lun (Patrick) Cheung

## ABSTRACT

*This chapter introduces demographic variables in empirical regression to help find whether demographic changes have an impact on economic growth. There is evidence from estimated values in this chapter to suggest that there is no impact that demographic changes in Hong Kong is affecting the economic growth. The population growth has purely a transition impact where the fertility rate was low in early 2000 up to 2015 as the size of the dependency ratio increases. Besides testing demographic variables the government emphasises better education for all people of ages for prosperous growth but in fact has a negative response on educational investment on the growth of the economy. A well-educated country individual does not suggest a higher productivity in economy growth. An important implication is that there has been no single variable as yet that has seriously impacted the economy growth, but there will be changes in the coming years and has to be attended in result to avoid a diminishing economy.*

**Keywords:** Demographic; economy; stock; Hong Kong

The Spread of Financial Sophistication Through Emerging Markets Worldwide
Research in Finance, Volume 32, 207–241
Copyright © 2016 by Emerald Group Publishing Limited
All rights of reproduction in any form reserved
ISSN: 0196-3821/doi:10.1108/S0196-382120160000032009

# INTRODUCTION

Hong Kong's population is aging rapidly. Since the 1970s the population has demonstrated trends towards aging. Especially, fertility rate has dropped to 0.9 in 2004 as compared to 3.5 in the 1970s, which is below the replacement rate of 2.1, simultaneously the life expectancy rate has remained high. In combination of low fertility rate and rising aging there has been a gradual decline in the population and it has been enough to affect the economic growth over the last decade. From the shift of the age structure in the population there arises a greater share of the elderly, while Hong Kong's dependency ratio is 1,000:160, which is nearly 16%, which is low in the Asia Pacific region and is expected to rise by twofolds in 2030 (World Development indicators, World Bank) and the population is expected to peak in 2060.

This chapter discusses whether demographic changes have an impact on the economic growth. As the analysis is based on open small economy sharing many of the characteristics expressed in the IMF's global macroeconomic simulation models, but conventional economic models usually ignore demographics variables, in this chapter it has extended the use of social variables such as fertility, investment in human are some of the highlighted variables that might shift the balance of being optimum to a disequilibrium state in the economy. This simulated model extends the use of these variables to incorporate them in demographics and life cycle dynamics (Faruqee, 2002). The chapter concludes there is no explicit evidence that the change in demographics has impacted the economy but concludes the total population and rise of fertility rate of Hong Kong will impact the economy growth. This is in line with the findings of inverse and adverse relationships between population size over GDP.

# LITERATURE REVIEW

The aging of the world's population poses major challenges to economic growth, and its nature means that we cannot use historical data for guidance on how this demographic change will unfold or on how best it can be managed. Recent literature of empirical modelling incorporates demographic variables as part of their economic growth model. Demographic changes affect economic growth, as Malthusian catastrophe (Malthus, 1798) states the power of population is so superior that the subsistence level of population growth outpaced the agricultural growth of the planet.

## Demography Transition

The timing and pace of the demographic change led to an enormous divergent trend in population age and growth structure in Asia (Bloom & Williamson, 1997). As demonstrated the ratio of working age population versus non-working age population has been increasing since 1975. According to UN projections the ratio of working age to non-working age population will peak in 2010 (Csis), followed by a decline in transition. This reflects an increase of elderly dependency ratio for the region as the age distribution works through population. Economic models of economic growth are plentiful in the academic society. Some discussions highlight the importance of improved productivity within all industries and the need for skill set shifts, such as reallocation of low productivity agricultural industry to more productive industries and service sectors. Others, focus on the contribution of growth in technological progress, governance and institutions and human capital, larger scale macroeconomics and trade policies to defer random shocks in the economy. Still some oppose to suggest that run from human capital accumulation to technical progress influences economic growth. Tyers and Shi (2007) introduce demographic variables such as population size, age, sex and skill differences into an empirical dynamic equilibrium model of the economy with exogenous determined age structure of labour force participation, consumption and savings that lead to GDP growth rate. Their work point towards an accelerated aging population via lower fertility being inclined to enhance real per capita income growth in an economy with young population and slows with older populations and low labour force participation rate among the elderly.

## Food and Population

First regardless of Malthus (1798) on the outlook of world economic pessimist view, his theory of population growth is that of linear growth, while growth in food production is based on calculated progression, and ultimately the size of population will outgrow the food supply. From an economic standpoint, there is an increase in labour input as population grows, while food production is capital equipment of land resource, short term there can be increase or decrease. In a condition where land is a fixed quantity and with the growth of labour input and output, the law of diminishing returns will lead to labour since the marginal production is reduced because of population growth effect. Unless, effectively controlling the growth of population the fate of mankind will be destined for famine. Fougere and Merette (2000) stated that decline in infertility rate, increase of life expectancy, and growth in labour force population (LPR), the projection for senior population is expected to grow by two times in 2050 in OECD countries. Importantly, the structural change will affect the overall economy and influence countries' fiscal policies, as Fougere and Merette (2000) tested their extended inter-temporal model (in Canada, France, Italy, Japan, Switzerland, United Kingdom and United States) to prove this aging population impact on economic growth. The difference model is constructed on 15 overlapping generations each having generations differing between 4 years, selected scope 16–75 years of age, integrated into the endogenous growth model, producing the human capital, physical capital, accumulation capital and maximisation of consumption life state.

Basically, a majority of young age people invest as human capital, while the middle age people invest as substantive capital. As a result, aging population will create more generations to invest in more human capitals in future. This model can be used to simulate future economy growth parameterised with human form factor.

## Economic and Human Input

Bloom and Williamson (1997) explained the dynamics of Asian population that economic growth rate averages between 1.4% and 1.9% over the decade years 1965–1990, but assessed the labour and capital inputs' contribution on relative terms averages 1/3 and 2/3, respectively, the aging population will age as economic growth decreases (Shimasawa & Hosoyama, 2004) as the decline in fertility rate and increase in life expectancy in many regions in the world is experiencing a demographic transition. Although population aging usually takes time, Asian countries have been facing a rapid fertility decline for the past decade. To study the impact of these population structures, the chapter uses an overlapping generation model (OLG) and uses infant costs to suggest an important economic indicator, and not only cost of old age but also low birth rate in terms of cost is part of the construct in this model, in an attempt to evaluate Asian economy drivers (China, Japan, Korea, Singapore, Taiwan). As the OLG model has become more useful, Tamirisa and Fernadez-Ansola (2006) conducted a simulation test on a small open economy using this model to study the overall impact of population aging on the economy. The model designed for Czechoslovakian Republic and compared with other advanced European countries their findings that population aging can be associated with work force reduction will slow down economic growth, thereby lowering living standards.

Chen, Li, and Yin (2004) empirically analysed using horizontal data of the form panel data checking economic growth-related variables that would measure its elastic analysis on the impact of economic growth. Using data observation method, Chen (2001) explains about aging population, pointed out that this population will cause the society to absorb fewer new knowledge or speed of new ideas and invariably innovation technology ability will also drop. As the negativity develops the national income uses unproductiveness of the society, for example old age caring, medical service, thereby bringing reduces in production investment. A study by Wang (2006) on population and economic growth used endogenous growth models that include production labour time invested but has abbreviated the capital and work externalities. A journal by Wen (2007) also conducted data observation in which data survey points out that in Taiwan and OECD population the wave of baby boom was caused by the impact of the population structure. The journal points out that the overall economic view of declining birth rate, population decline, aging population and long-term sustainable economic growth will eventually reduce. The size of baby boomer increased rapidly after WWII to create the elderly nowadays outputting a total demand, causing the aggregate demand to shift on the left and falling prices, as the shrinking domestic market because the baby boom generation the population tend to save more stimulating private consumption to fall in the same population as the industries began to oversupply. Deflation is very serious as it will cause the population to negative growth stage and as time moves a large population of retired workers causes labour supply to decline, aggregate supply curve will shift to the left causing a fall in output, prices of stagflation and hence further economic downturn.

A painful pressure put on economic policies and societies caused by rising elderly share is not inevitable. Increased life expectancy has been strongly related with increased per capita income (Preston, 1975). Changes in health profiles are important when becoming older. When population is advancing into their retirement age healthier than previous generations the attention for sustainable health care will be less intense and continue to contribute to the economy (Kulish, Smith, & Kent, 2006). Should elderly population is not healthy than earlier population the expected burden on health costs are set to rise holding down economic developments and requiring additional treatment by the government policies for this age group.

*Life Expectancy and Fertility*

The demographic changes in greater life expectancy, lower fertility rate and higher education levels are some of the trends commonly to occur during the demographic transition of economies. They are trends recognised as major differences between a well-developed country and countries beginning to be developing countries and viewed as causes or effects of changes in total economic activity, after all humans are countries' capital asset. Increases in life expectancy can be staggering when the economy develops. Fogel (1994) studied that between 1850 and 1950 life expectancy at birth in the United States rose by 75% from 40 to 68 years of age. By 1995 the trend was 100% as the average life time was 76 years. Similar changes have been identified in other countries as documented by Easterlin (1996). Furthermore, Mirowsk and Ross (1998) suggest that these changes were indicative of higher levels of education and human capital accumulation, which help by raising the standards of living and development of economic growth and encouraging a healthy lifestyle. Personal and educational growth improves the effective agency that includes education for knowledge development, skills and abilities that are better equipped to create a way of living that is favourable to their welfare not brought by economic status.

At the same time as longevity is happening there will be shifts in fertility trends phenomenon revealing a fall in birth rates and a growing propensity for births to occur later than sooner in life. The decline in fertility rate is probably the most well-known fact of demographic transition as proposed by Coale and Watkins (1996), as Hotz, McElroy, and Sanders (2005) surveyed the variation of fertility decisions has gone backwards. For example over the past 30 years for those early marriages the chance of a first child is in mid-20s or earlier; this has fallen and the chance of having a child at 35 years of age has been rising. Likewise, the decline in mortality substituted by a decline in fertility is never what the society had expected. The study of human capital accumulation is significant in a positive versus negative relationship between the number of first-birth timing and the length of time required for education (Mathews, 1992). There exists a rising class of dynamic equilibrium models at a theoretical level. Barro and Becker (1989) study a seminal analysis of fertility growth and choice, treating both conditions, the timing of births and life time span as given isolated from human capital accumulation. Blackburn and Cipriani (1998) extended the framework with the inclusion of endogenous mortality rate and human capital accumulation, whereas Ehrlich and Lui (1991) developed a similar model as exogenous for life times with human capital accumulation using fertility choice but not with the timing. A detailed explanation has been provided by Sanderson and Scherbov (2008) based on the remaining life expectancy of the concept of 'prospective age' since people become more healthier and more active in their generations compared to their counterparts several decades ago. The decisions about retirement take place differently on a personal environment. Sanderson and Scherbov (2008) point out that using prospective age in studying the effects of an aging population instead of chronological age is a better way to implement a population-based concept of old age that would consider improvements in health and life expectancy. The new indicators they define as 'old age' as above has a remaining life expectancy of 15 years or less. Their results show the set of countries that are classified as oldest depends crucially on the old age dependency ratio that is used based on expected remaining life expectancy. For example Japan either in 2005 or 2045 does not appear in the list of 10 oldest countries when the criterion is prospective dependency ratio. Taking changes in life expectancy into consideration has actuarial implications for policy pension schemes. If there are concerns the neutral response would be to lower the retirement age.

It's important to realise that individual aging contributes to population aging with. The phenomenon of demographic transition has portrayed attention for economists (Bos & von Weizsacker, 1989), as they have discussed in their empirical findings the impact and effect of demographic changes on national savings, investment and economic growth. There are two separate sets of study areas, first set is concerned with indicators on the effect of population dependency rates on aggregate savings Leff (1969) and the second finds a negative relationship of the old age dependency rate on the aggregate savings rate supported by Edwards (1996). Contradictorily, Adams (1971), Gupta (1971) and Ram (1982, 1984), signifies that the dependency effect of old age on savings may be insignificant or even positively related. This debate has focused only on one important relationship, namely savings and age. They have ignored an important aspect of the study, which is the savings and expected life span relationship. In contrast, the other study paid little attention to dependency ratio on savings and instead concentrates on the effect of longevity on investment.

In contrast to the studies on aggregate saving rates, the other set of the related studies has paid little attention to dependency rates and has instead focused on the effect of longevity in investment and economic growth regressions (Barro & Sala-i-Martin, 1995). Such a positive effect of longevity on growth is interpreted as an indicator of growth enhancing factor, such as good work habits and good high level of skills are maintained. It has offered a different representation by giving longevity a more direct role in life cycle optimisation. By understanding to remove a group of working labour and adding them to the dependent population will change the level of economic growth rate of output per capita and level.

*Education and Economic Growth*

In China, moral education was the major focus in traditional Chinese education. The imperial college was founded in the Zhou Dynasty (11th century BC to 221 BC) to teach children of the royal families moral education as the education curriculum was a collection of virtue of cultural content. The United Nations Education, Scientific and Culture Organisation's (UNESCO) institute of statistics described that many countries maintain stable public spending expenditure. Governments of the world invest in education in PPP$ 2.46 trillion in 2004 equivalent to $1.97 trillion. The figure represents 4.4% of global Gross Domestic Product in PPP$. PPS (purchasing power parities) is equal (near equal) rates of conversion to eliminate price differential among countries; furthermore, the same sum of money when converted into US$ at PPP rates will have the same purchasing power in purchasing a basket of goods and services in all countries. As a comparison, governments in North America and Western Europe invested 5.6% of GDP in education, followed by Arab states 4.9%, Africa 4.5%, Latin America, Caribbean and Central and Eastern Europe averaged 4.4% and 4.2%, respectively. By far the lowest of all regions found in Central Asia, East Asia and Pacific averaged 2.8% of GDP.

Despite these figures the economic benefits to invest in education to improve economic growth rates are very large. In previous longevity (Barro & Sala-i-Martin, 1995), it has a positive effect between relationships of longevity on growth. As societies become more educated, which translates into higher economic growth rates, and more competitive in the region, the immediate effect is that it allows the government to alleviate poverty. A large number of scholars, Benhabib and Spiegel (1994), Gemmell (1996), have attempted to address a positive association between educational quantity and economic growth. As Mankiw, Romer, and Weil (1992), Barro (1991), Levine and Renelt (1992) measure using educational schooling enrolment ratios, Hanushek and Woessmann's (2007) and Krueger and

Lindahl's (2001) study composed the average years of schooling. Durlauf and Johnson (1995) and Romer (1990) used adult literacy rate and education spending Baldacci, Guin-Siu, and Mello (2003). However, not all scholars and economists acknowledge this relationship and to the point some finds a weak association between quantity education and economic growth. Bils and Klenow (2000) and Pritchett (2001) find no evidence at all between schooling years and economic growth. Barro (1995), Hanushek and Kimko (2000) and Hanushek and Woessmann (2007) studied the relationship between schooling quality and economic growth. Based on their research, the work by Kimko, Hanushek and Kim, and Hanushek and Woessmann developed a measure of labour force cognitive skill quality such as mathematics and science such that these topics have a strong association and influence on economic growth. Barro (1999) discovers that educational quality has a positive relationship between educational quality and economic growth based on international comparable examinations student test scores.

*Evidence on Enrolment, Growth*

Becker (1964), Schultz (1961), and Romer (1990) recognised human capital as the engine of all economic growth. Several attempts have been tried by scholars to explain why human capital is important; Nelson (2005), Benhabib and Spiegel (1994) and Cobb Douglas, find two valuable separations, namely the accumulation and assimilation theories. The first hypothesis has a direct impact of human capital on labour productivity as an unequivocal factor of production realised in effective labour. This approach directs to the forecast that only new investment in human capital helps in economic growth. In contrast, the second hypothesis considers the level of human as capital and total factor productivity growth or technological change. The emphasis on relationship between human capital and disconnected knowledge has signified in technology.

Dowrick (2003) states that the stock of human capital accumulation can produce the effect of economic growth. It has emerged that a technical progress can be recognised as a process of a new product development, thereby suggesting an understanding of the role of knowledge and skills involved in the process of technology growth. This draws the link where human capital is in education of innovation and sustainable growth (Aghion & Howitt, 1998; Romer, 1990). The second insight is where the human capital is in 'absorptive capacity' (Falvey, Foster, & Greenaway, 2007; Wolff, 2001) since it allows workers to understand to incorporate new technology. Nelson and Phelps (1966) assessed education as the catalyst in distributing new technologies. Their assessment assumed that further the economy is away from technology the stronger is the desire to exploit externalities; the larger the human capital the greater is the capacity to learn and adopt new technology.

Benhabib and Spiegel (1994) generalised a model of human capital that tries to explain technology and innovation diffusion. It is built on the knowledge that human capital is complementary to technology, rather competing. They explain the different stages of economic development activity, for example a nation closer to the technology frontier has high human capital that could support innovation, while countries away from it have less focus on technology diffusion.

Nelson-Phelps' hypothesis aims that the imitation of new foreign technology is beneficial provided that educated labour can follow and understand new technological developments. More importantly, less use of innovation economies could overtake technology leader by relying on human form of capital.

Interest in the rate of return in education has always intrigued developments in economic research in the 1990s (Mincer, 1974). Mincer studies the theoretical and empirical aspects of human capital earnings function. The formulation of log linear 'earnings education' has a strong correlation relationship. As such his findings suggest that each additional year of education appears to raise earnings approximately by 10% in the United States, although investment rate of return to education is treated no different to other investment proxies as they vary over time and across other countries. There is little evidence to suggest that omitted variables such as inherent ability which might be correlated with earnings and education to create an OLS simple wage equation by Mincer to explicitly overstate the return to education variable. It is conclusive (Griliches, 1977) that most of the modern hypothesis finds that the upward 'ability bias' and downward bias is about the same order of magnitude caused by measurement of error in education attainment.

Mincer's model implies that the average level of schooling should be the main determinant of income growth. The empirical macro growth literature specifies that growth is a function of the initial education level. Should the education changes over time, for example in previous literature of exogenous skills bias technological changes the macro view models are unidentified.

# METHODOLOGY

The empirical study was carried out to research based on Bloom and Williamson (1998) as a basic structure to analyse the ageing population affecting the economic growth of Hong Kong SAR. The secondary data used as the main source and collected through HKSAR Census and Statistics Department (C&SD) would provide the latest figures of various official statistics on population and demographics structures. This research chapter uses Hong Kong as the target place from time period 2000 to 2010 record years to conduct the effects of demographic changes on economic growth. The rationale behind the model design is considered when only one place is targeted. When there is only one place involved it would be approachable to use time series as the foundation for basic analysis. Many literature reviews concluded that a cross-sectional data analysis approach is applicable for studying larger capacity such as Asia or OECD countries in comparison for which a lot of data are required for such analysis. Many studies form an argument whether the right approach is to carry cross-sectional data, time series or panel data analysis. The weakness of cross-sectional data is that they cannot explain the movement of time series and therefore suffer from explaining the observation of the actual situation of a single country. Hence, this research for Hong Kong as a single country ordinary least squares (OLS).

*Secondary External Sources*

The data source of this study is provisioned by HKSAR C&CSD. External sources also included research papers, journals, IMF, UNESCO, Greenwhich University Databases and OECD databases through education access as supplementary data collection, and statistical textbooks are used for framework methodology guidance. The data source is organised specifically for designated models. Data is collected going as far back as 10 years and sectioned into classes such as total population, total population of labour force in years 2000–2010; the availability of these data supported the research models and are conclusive in the analysis.

*The Model Hypothesis*

The null hypothesis denotes no effect of the independent variables, as stated 'The Demographic transition change has no direct impact to the Hong Kong

GDP growth', where the opposite would be that 'The Demographic changes has direct impact to the Hong Kong GDP growth'.

$H_0$ = *The demographic change has direct impact to the Hong Kong GDP growth.*
$H_1$ = *The demographic change has no direct impact to the Hong Kong GDP growth.*

## RESEARCH ANALYSIS

This research uses the annual record from 2000 to 2010 for a total of 10 years, the variables defined as the value of individual GDP, the growth rate of population, the working aging group rate, the expected life time and human capital and total fertility rate. First, the demographic factors lead to the model design. The main focus of the research, according to Bloom and Williamson (1997), uses data from Asian population growth and decline rate; in this case the demographic factors are related to HK SAR.

*Earlier Model Work*

The research paper is largely based on Bloom and Williamson's (1998) model as the basic structure is to analyse the demographic impact affecting economic growth of Hong Kong.

The Solow-Swan model is used to construct capital, accumulation, population growth, productivity and technological as exogenous variables that explain the long-run economic growth. Although this chapter does not simulate long run models, it is worthy to examine the originality of development. The neoclassical growth model has been expressed by Cobb and Douglas (1928) model:

$$Y = L^{1-\alpha}K^{\beta} \tag{1}$$

where $Y$ = Total production GDP (the monetary value of all goods produced in a year); $L$ = Labour input for worked year; and $K$ = Capital Input, human for year.

$\alpha$ and $\beta$ are output elasticity of labour and capital, respectively. Dividing each sides with Labour ($L$) becomes:

$$\frac{Y}{L} = \frac{(Y)^2}{(L)} = K^\alpha \tag{2}$$

which it is defined with time value as $T1$ in the beginning and $T2$ at the end. $G_y$ represents the average growth and $Y$ represents the individual productivity at slow growth model.

$$G_y = \frac{1}{(T2 - T1)} LN \left[ \frac{Y \ T2}{(Y \ T1)} \right] = \Delta LN \left[ \frac{Y*}{(Y \ T1)} \right] \tag{3}$$

Bloom and Williamson later worked on the long-term slow growth model situation where every unit of productivity can be affected by economic activities.

$$Y* = X\beta \tag{4}$$

Bloom and Williamson defined the aging population effect and working population $Y$ as individual effect which explains $Y\%$ as individual per capita income, $Y$ as total productivity, $N$ as total population and $L$ the working population.

$$Y\% = \frac{Y}{N} = \frac{L}{N}\frac{Y}{L} = \frac{L}{N}y \tag{5}$$

Using Eq. (6) we derive individual product growth rate interpreted form,

$$G_y = G_{\text{workers}} + G_{\text{population}} + G_y \tag{6}$$

We extend the use of Bloom and Williamson model when we include three more endogenous variables.

Model as: $G_y$
$$= \delta_0 + \delta_1 T_{\text{population}} + \delta_2 G_{\text{workers},t} + \delta_3 e_{\text{life},s} + \delta_4 K_{\text{human},s} + \delta_5 \text{Total}_{\text{fertility rate}} + \varepsilon_t \tag{7}$$

*Symbols of Model*

1. *Working age population = G(workers)*
2. *Gross Domestic Product = G*
3. *Total population = TP(Population)*
4. *Expected life time = E(Life)*
5. *Total fertility Rate = F(Fertility)*
6. *Human capital = K(Human)*

*Framing the Model*

This research chapter considers Hong Kong SAR actual data set for economic growth, using the expected life time, working population, total fertility rate, education investment and population growth to the effect of GDP under slow growth model as the assumption. The Model devised using OLS corresponds to the economic growth, namely GDP. As all the variables have been collected for use we build the model as follows:

1. $G_y = \dfrac{\text{GDP}_t^{2000} - \text{GDP}_{t-1}^{2000}}{\text{GDP}_{t-1}^{2000}}$

2. $G_{\text{worker}} = \dfrac{(\text{age } 15-64 \text{ working total population})_t - (\text{age } 15-64 \text{ working total population})_{t-1}}{(\text{age } 15-64 \text{ working total population})_{t-1}} \times 100$

3. $T_{\text{population}} = \dfrac{(\text{total population})_t - (\text{total population})_{t-1}}{(\text{total population})_{t-1}} \times 100$

4. $E_{\text{life}} = \text{Ln} \dfrac{(\text{Male Life Time})_t + (\text{Female Life Time})_t}{2}$

5. $\text{Total}_{\text{fertility rate}} = \dfrac{\sum (\text{age specific fertility rates})(\text{age interval})}{1,000}$

6. $K_{\text{human}} = \ln \dfrac{\text{Education Expenditure}}{\text{GDP}} \times 100$

This chapter studies period between 2000 and 2010, 10 years in total.

Model as: $G_y = \delta_0 + \delta_1 T_{\text{population}} + \delta_2 G_{\text{worker } s,t} + \delta_3 e_{\text{life},s} + \delta_3 K_{\text{human},s}$
$+ \delta_4 \text{Total}_{\text{fertility rate}} + \varepsilon_t$

Expectation where: $G_{\text{worker}} \delta_0 > 0$, $T_{\text{population}} \delta_1 < 0$, $E_{\text{life}} \delta_2 > 0$, $K_{\text{Human}} \delta_3 > 0$, $K_{\text{fertility}} \delta_4 \gtrless 0$

The variables are in simplified form of multiple regression equation. Mathematical representation as:

$$Y = \alpha + \delta_1 A_1 + \delta_2 A_2 + \delta_3 A_3 + \delta_4 A_4 + \delta_5 A_5$$

where $Y$ is the main dependent value representing the GDP of Hong Kong; $A$ (Alpha) is the constant or commonly known as intercept of $x$, $y$ crosses;

$A_1$ — States as the first independent variable which explains the variance of $Y$, representing working population of Hong Kong within modelling years. $\delta_1$ is used as the nominated representation of the slope beta coefficient for $A_1$;

$A_2$ — States as the second independent variable which explains the variance of $Y$, representing total population of Hong Kong within modelling years. $\delta_2$ is used as the nominated representation of the slope beta coefficient for $A_2$;

$A_3$ — states as the third independent variable which explains the variance of $Y$, representing expected life time of Hong Kong within modelling years. $\delta_3$ is used as the nominated representation of the slope beta coefficient for $A_3$;

$A_4$ — states as the third independent variable which explains the variance of $Y$, representing human capital of Hong Kong within modelling years. $\delta_4$ is used as the nominated representation of the slope beta coefficient for $A_4$;

$A_5$ — states as the forth independent variable which explains the variance of $Y$, representing total fertility rate of Hong Kong within modelling years. $\delta_5$ is used as the nominated representation of the slope beta coefficient for $A_5$;

$\varepsilon_t$ — standard error as part of the equation.

## EMPIRICAL FINDINGS AND ANALYSIS

*Independent Test*

Before we go further with our multiple regression equation it would be good to identify whether these independent variables have cointegration relationships with our dependent variables. Sometimes there are spurious regression problems — GDP and total population have unit roots and error epsilon has a unit root. However, in some cases these are cancelled and epsilon does not have unit root problems, and spurious regressions is no longer an issue. A cointegration of variables will have some equilibrium relationships between them and since cointegration exists they hold other important economic information. We test using Engle and Granger (1987) and Dickey-Fuller (1981) test for unit root testing and cointegration tests on time series. Gretl, a statistical software, has been used to find the results of these tests (Table 1).

***Table 1.***   Unit Root Outputs Reformatted Output.

| | |
|---|---|
| Step 1: Testing for a unit root in GDP | Asymptotic *p*-value 0.7052 |
| Step 2: Testing for a unit root in TotalPop | Asymptotic *p*-value 0.06194 |
| Step 3: Testing for a unit root in Gworker | Asymptotic *p*-value 0.3086 |
| Step 4: Testing for a unit root in Elife | Asymptotic *p*-value 0.9617 |
| Step 5: Testing for a unit root in Khuman | Asymptotic *p*-value 0.7324 |
| Step 6: Testing for a unit root in TotalFertility | Asymptotic *p*-value 0.9612 |

*Note*: 95% $p = 0.05$ − for full outputs refer Table 2 Gretl Tests unit and regress tab.

Defining a hypothesis tests for unit root are,

$$H_0 = p < 0.05$$
$$H_1 = p > 0.05$$

Defining a hypothesis tests for cointegration are,

$\mathbf{H_0}$ = *The time series is not cointegrated and residuals are non-stationary form*
$\mathbf{H_1}$ = *The time series is cointegrated and residuals are stationary form*

*Model Assessment*

*Correlation between Variables*
On first sight the correlation holds the linear relationship between each variable, particularly assessing GDP variable against other variables. Early statistics implies that linearity between GDP and total population has the strongest positive relationship of 51.7% (Table 3), whereas, Khuman has the highest negative relationship implying −58%, which represents that an increase in human capital investment does not always positively produce more GDP output. It would be an inclusion of public spending and private spending on human capital accumulation which doesn't always suffice a return on investment. According to the output the regression model has concluded an intercept point. The formula now becomes:

$$Y = -13.994 + (-0.001)A_1 + (0.079)A_2 + (3.420)A_3 + (-0.674)\,A_4 + (-0.007)A_5$$

We start by asking whether it is significantly true when a demographic transition change will affect the economy growth of Hong Kong since the population debate that affects the economy has been wrongly couched. The model results are examined using $R^2$, $T$-value, one-way Anova $p$-values

***Table 2.*   Cointegrating Regression.**

| Dependent Variable: GDP | | | | |
| --- | --- | --- | --- | --- |
| | Coefficient | Std. error | *t*-Ratio | *p*-Value |
| Const | −1.21324 | 12.9353 | −0.09379 | 0.9289 |
| TotalPop | 0.00142597 | 0.00105491 | 1.352 | 0.02344 |
| Gworker | 0.000156158 | 0.000335867 | 0.4649 | 0.04615 |
| Elife | 0.320783 | 2.96609 | 0.1082 | 0.03181 |
| khuman | −0.191981 | 0.216918 | −0.8850 | 0.04167 |
| TotalFertility | 0.000619774 | 0.00240822 | 0.2574 | 0.01072 |
| Sum-squared resid | 0.005157 | S.E. of regression | | 0.032117 |
| $R^2$ | 0.723880 | Adjusted $R^2$ | | 0.447759 |

***Table 3.*   Correlation Coefficient.**

| | Gworker | Total Population | Elife | Khuman | Total Fertility | GDP |
| --- | --- | --- | --- | --- | --- | --- |
| Gworker | 1 | | | | | |
| Total Population | 0.1016 | 1 | | | | |
| Elife | −0.33213 | 0.250585593 | 1 | | | |
| Khuman | 0.134662 | −0.438218632 | −0.77356 | 1 | | |
| Total Fertility | −0.35714 | 0.431399752 | 0.886306 | −0.898921 | | |
| GDP | −0.07176 | 0.517236138 | 0.326288 | −0.5803 | 0.352954037 | 1 |

and *F*-value. By observing that the standard error is 0.0311 is small, which is an estimate of standard deviation from the sample size. The output of $R^2$ denotes the correlation coefficient of the proportion of variability in the data set, simple put, the variation dependent of *Y* output can be explained by the variation of independent variable *X*, such that the 1.0 (100%) indicates a line of perfect fit to the sample data. Since the output is 0.7775 as 77.75% Table 4 which is valid and close to a perfect fit expectation.

*Findings*

Using our regression model equation;
   Regression 1#

GDP = −13.994 + (−0.001)Gworker + (0.079)Total population
   + (3.420) Elife + (−0.674) Khuman + (−0.007) Total Fertility

The value of intercept alpha = −13.42 has no relevance in the model.

***Table 4.***    Summary Results of Multiple Regression.

*Regression Statistics*

| | |
|---|---|
| Multiple *R* | 0.8817 |
| *R*$^2$ | 0.7775 |
| AdjustedSquare | 0.5549 |
| Standard Error | 0.0311 |
| Observations | 11 |

*Anova*

| | df | SS | MS | F |
|---|---|---|---|---|
| Regression | 5 | 0.017 | 0.003 | 13.494 |
| Residual | 5 | 0.005 | 0.001 | |
| Total | 10 | 0.022 | | |

| | Coefficients | Standard Error | *t*-Stat. | *p-value* |
|---|---|---|---|---|
| Intercept | −13.994 | 12.610 | −1.110 | 0.118 |
| Gworker | −0.001 | 0.000 | −1.769 | 0.137 |
| Total Population | 0.079 | 0.035 | 2.240 | 0.050 |
| Elife | 3.420 | 2.888 | 1.184 | 0.290 |
| Khuman | −0.674 | 0.211 | −3.200 | 0.024 |
| Total Fertility | −0.007 | 0.002 | 2.688 | 0.043 |

*Working Age Population (Gworker) and Longevity (Elife)*

In the model the two independent variables Gworker (0.137) and Elife (0.290) explains that there is no significant relevance to Gross Domestic Product. Their *p*-value is relatively large that there is no evidence to conclude these two variables have a positive correlation and a linear relationship with GDP for the given years. The working age population is banded between 15 and 64 years of age; the main age group of 25–44 has significantly a larger working population (Table 2). A majority of this population are middle class citizens where contributions have been high but benefits have been low. Government policies' decision to shift the retirement age above 64 years of age provides little evidence for growth in GDP where pension expenditure is variably between 3% and 5% between years 2000 and 2010 as shown in Table 3. Longevity, where the death rate has decreased and life time increased, the expected life time is averaged at 80 years of age. It is proved that longer life has no direct impact on the growth of an economy. Although the dependency ratio is large, approximately 15%, this is offset by a relatively small longevity population in Hong Kong.

Hong Kong has reached over 7.1 million people. The total population has grown fast over the last decade due to the introduction of legislation allowing mainland families to immigrate as citizen of Hong Kong, thereby contributing to the increase. There is evidence that total population level has a linear relationship with GDP growth level, as *t*-statistics has a value of 2.240 and a *p*-value of 0.050. The coefficient of 0.079 specifies one or more year of total population, 0.079% negative impact on the level of GDP rate, holding all variables at constant (Table 4). The higher the rate of total population the GDP rate decreases. Using *t*-statistics of $-3.2$ and a *p*-value of 0.024, highly suggest that human capital, as investment capital, and GDP growth is linearly related. The beta coefficient of $-0.64$ explains that for each additional investment on human capital, that is education, training, surprising computations resulted that the more investment programmes on humans the less will be the GDP growth in the economy (Table 4). If more capital is spent, whether private or public, then it has a negative relationship towards GDP growth. The *t*-statistics (2.688) and *p*-value (0.043) have a linear relationship between total fertility rate and GDP growth rate. A beta coefficient of $-0.007$ for each unit of total fertility increases will deflate the GDP growth decreasing by 0.007% subject to all other variables at constant. The higher the rate of fertility the less will be the GDP growth (Table 4).

# FURTHER FINDINGS

*Further Findings*

The basic model of all dependent and independent variables is captioned (Table 5).

$$\text{Model as: } G_y = \delta_0 + \delta_1 T_{population} + \delta_2 G_{worker\,s,t} + \delta_3 e_{life,\,s} + \delta_4 K_{human,s} + \delta_5 + \varepsilon_t$$
$$Y = \alpha + \delta_1 A_1 + \delta_2 A_2 + \delta_3 A_3 + \delta_4 A_4 + \delta_5 A_5 + \varepsilon_t$$

Our design of the model justifies the inclusion of interaction variables in the multiple regression analysis whether the change of GDP-dependent variable as one of the independent variables causes a change in the GDP (Stock & Watson, 2003). The pessimist camp believes that rapid population growth is

*Table 5.* Correlation Total Population and GDP.

|  | GDP | Total Population |
|---|---|---|
| GDP | 1 | |
| Total Population | 0.950486395 | 1 |

worse off than before because it will overwhelm any lead response by capital accumulation investment and technology innovation (Ehrlich, 1968). However, optimists contradict that allowing rapid growth in population will effectively bring economies of scale that captures and promotes institutional and technology innovation (Kuznets, 1967) (Table 6).

Regression 2#

Model as: $G_y = \delta_0 + \delta_1 T_{\text{population}}$ as mathematical form $Y = \alpha\delta_1 A_1$

A very significant test that shows the relationship of correlation test between GDP and total population supports the pessimist's camp. It does not explicitly show what impact it has on GDP; however, it does explain the strength and a positive linear relationship between the two variables (0.95). With each unit of total population there correlates a single unit of GDP (Table 7). Anova finds Total Population is highly correlated to GDP as p-value is small 0.0009 and F-value is 84.19. The model of best fit $R^2$ is 0.95 means that the model is highly valid as close to 1. It does suggest that over the years Hong Kong have been either been affected by an increase of population as there are more immigrants affecting GDP, and Hong Kong itself is a highly open economy that is affected by externalities but the growth in the population have always increased. Even at time when SARs

*Table 6.*   Anova Test Total Population and GDP.

| Anova | | | | | |
|---|---|---|---|---|---|
| | df | SS | MS | F | Significance F |
| Regression | 1 | 3.08571E + 11 | 3.09E + 11 | 84.19122865 | 7.28782E − 06 |
| Residual | 9 | 32986129725 | 3.67E + 09 | | |
| Total | 10 | 3.41558E + 11 | | | |
| | | Coefficients | Standard Error | t-Stat. | p-Value |
| Intercept | | −3865610.322 | 579486.0757 | −6.67076 | 9.15398E − 05 |
| Total Population | | 1050.424803 | 114.480507 | 9.175578 | 7.28782E − 06 |

95% Interval.

*Table 7.*   R tests Total Population and GDP.

| Regression Statistics | |
|---|---|
| Multiple R | 0.950486395 |
| $R^2$ | 0.903424387 |

virus was inflicting Hong Kong in 2003, GDP recovered and grew along with population. The rapid growth in population diluted the GDP output since the population has grown faster than expected over the last 10 years when Hong Kong was handed over to China. We further take population growth into consideration its longevity and fertility as the demographic component effects GDP growth (Barlow, 1994; Brander & Drowick, 1994; Kelley & Schmidt, 1995). These measures of fertility rates, specifically after birth rate, are significantly and negatively related with economic growth, whereas the longevity is statistically insignificant. In so far, the decomposition of these two variables has different implications of populations, thereby affecting the economic growth. The growth regression is more appealing than adding ad hoc birth rates, death rates long life rates. By adding controlled growth rates of the total population to an economic active population allows the population to affect GDP economic growth by its overall controlled age structure, fertility and longevity. Thus, regression 3# model is derived (Table 8).
Regression 3#

Model as: $G_y = \delta_0 + \delta_1 T_{population} + \delta_3 e_{life,s} + \delta_5 Total_{fertility\ rate} + \varepsilon_t$
$Y = \alpha + \delta_1 A_1 + \delta_3 A_3 + \delta_5 A_5$

Test where

$H_0$: $\beta_1 = \beta_2 = 0$
$H_1$: $\beta_1$ and $\beta_2$ not both zero and $\alpha = 0.05$

Evidently, the regression critical $p$-value test is small, 0.000016, or close to zero and $F$-test value of 67.07 suggests that there is a linear relationship between all independent variables used in the model considered together with $Y$. Although, there is some form of linear relationship, it is not perfect linear as the one calculated in regression 2#. It does conclude that the $F$-test hypothesis general term would be

$H_0$: $\beta_1 = \beta_2 = \cdots = \beta_k = 0$ *(there is no linear relationship)*.
$H_1$: *at least one $\beta_i \neq 0$ (at least one independent variable affects $Y$)*.

**Table 8.**   Correlation Tests Total Population, Elife, Fertility and GDP.

|  | GDP | Total Population | MALE + FEMALE | Fertility |
|---|---|---|---|---|
| GDP | 1 |  |  |  |
| Total Population | 0.950486395 | 1 |  |  |
| MALE + FEMALE | 0.885050145 | 0.958475236 | 1 |  |
| Fertility | 0.98263829 | 0.960345252 | 0.887415776 | 1 |

If $p$-value is less than $\alpha = .05$, we reject the $H_0$ hypothesis and accept $H_1$.

In $T$-test we test whether the individual variables are significant.

$H_0$: $\beta_i = 0$ (there is no linear relationship)

$H_1$: $\beta_i \neq 0$ (a linear relationship does exist between $X_i$ and $Y$).

We find that while using total population, longevity (male and female, Elife) and fertility contribute to a higher goodness of fit shown as $R^2$ 98% more than total population from model regression 2#, but the finding is when total population and Elife are less significant to the model since, total population is 0.02, 0.97 and Elife is 0.207, 0.841; this could be the validity that multicollinearity is existing in the model. The fertility rate proved as a factor that affects the GDP significantly, where $t$-stat is 3.3 and a low $p$-value of 0.011, and rejects the null hypothesis since there is one or more variables affecting the model.

In combination with the three independent variables the multiple regression model is derived as

$$Y = -629,407 + 13.1A_1 + 7,984A_3 + 1,185A_5$$

For every 100 new births, elderly remains constant and total population would be factored with 100. The result would be the effect on GDP as $498,455 per 100 new births or the government has to spend an additional of $498,455 to maintain the fertility rate.

Cole and Hoover (1958) finds the elderly population longevity life extension affects not only elderly dependency rate but also on GDP. In fact, to maintain 100 newly dependent elderly would produce change on GDP by $181,560. The maintenance is much less than treating 100 new births in the economy. Although, aging population is inevitable this does not mean there is no work output as they can be transformed to other minor roles (Kulish et al., 2006). The society can adjust to such population aging which extends their role to participating in business. The elderly are healthier than in the past; they can work longer in terms of years that benefits the society on taxable income for government and places less emphasis on public resources. Private and government scheme businesses play an important factor in encouraging older workers as part of working scheme, in turn younger apprentices can benefit from such workers' experience and commitment. Such schemes that are in place in Hong Kong as pay to performance-based compensation that allows businesses to still find it worthwhile to maintain this population on the payroll. The economic variables in the multiple regressions include those of inputs and outputs contributed to the economy. The Khuman, the indicator that measures the education investment through schooling, training raises the country's level of literacy and helps to increase the capital accumulation (Jones, 2001). This is factored by the government expenditure on education in Hong Kong for the 10 years period. The Khuman is a spending variable or an investment to the GDP, as it decreases or increases how this is affected to the capital accumulation or vice versa. One of the variables that contribute to the GDP is Gworkers working population between 15 and 64 years old. What matters is a change in the working population age structure that might significantly have an impact on economic growth. A normal life perspective is when people's life is based on the needs and contributions over the different stages of life cycle. The consumption to production is high for youth cohorts and low for working population. A country with a large dependency of young and elderly cohorts will likely slow the economy growth than a large working age population (Bloom, Canning, & Fink, 2011).

Regression 4#

Model as: $G_y = \delta_0 + \delta_2 G_{\text{worker s},t} + \delta_4 K_{\text{human},s} + \varepsilon_t$

$Y = \alpha + \delta_2 A_2 + \delta_4 A_4 + \varepsilon_t$

$H_0$: $\beta_1 = \beta_2 = \cdots = \beta_k = 0$ *(there is no linear relationship)*
$H_1$: *at least one* $\beta_i \neq 0$ *(at least one independent variable affects Y)*.

We take the model to find the effects on GDP with no demographics variables at first stage.

Total working population is significant in contributing to GDP 0.67, and Total Education as expenditure is insignificant to GDP 0.31 (Table 9). The working population rate has been growing at 1.2% over the last 10 years, slowly contributing to the GDP. The phenomenon is that ages between 15 and 24 years group has been gradually on the decline suggesting that 24−44 age group has a much higher proportion of working age group, thus, next age group 44−64 is on the growth which is explained in the previous model regression 3# that longevity (Elife) has less burden on public resource. Simply because the working group 15−24 has been on the decline soon it can be realised that when ready for work they belong to 24−44 age band and working life extends further to 64 or higher ages. The model has a goodness of fit $R^2$ 0.567123074 which is not significant as the previous demographics type tests. The Total Education expenditure is not significant to affect the GDP as much as we expect; over the last 10 years education spending has been increasing 1.12% which is on relative terms of Total Working population growth. As for $F$-tests 5.24 greater $F$-critical 0.035 it proves the regression between has some effect but not absolutely indicative (Tables 10–13).

The multiple regressions of independent variables and GDP on substituted representation are derived as

$$Y = -1,913,751 + 513A_2 + 39.47A_4$$

To cancel out a zero GDP effect the government has to spend $1 on education from 3,726.192 working people which accounts for 0.001% of the total working population in 2010. Over the last 10 years the government has spent more expenditure on secondary education rather than on tertiary or training programmes. It is not conclusive whether good education for all brings higher GDP; however, education as expenditure has minimal impact on the overall budget expenditure based on year-on-year comparisons. A rationale behind a neutralist or revolutionist view when high population

**Table 9.** Anova Tests Total Population, Elife, Fertility and GDP.

*Anova*

|  | df | SS | MS | F | Significance F |
|---|---|---|---|---|---|
| Regression | 3 | 3.30075E + 11 | 1.10025E + 11 | 67.07373 | 1.60056E-05 |
| Residual | 7 | 11482514573 | 1640359225 |  |  |
| Total | 10 | 3.41558E + 11 |  |  |  |

|  | Coefficients | Standard Error | t-Stat. | p-value |
|---|---|---|---|---|
| Intercept | −629407.0835 | 4523825.514 | −0.1391316 | 0.893264 |
| Total Population | 13.17868744 | 488.1974514 | 0.026994585 | 0.979218 |
| Elife | 7984.636036 | 38501.5987 | 0.207384532 | 0.841614 |
| Fertility | 11185.60335 | 3315.419212 | 3.373812672 | 0.011858 |

**Table 10.** R tests Total Population, Elife, Fertility and GDP.

*Regression Statistics*

| Multiple $R$ | 0.983047254 |
|---|---|
| $R^2$ | 0.966381904 |

**Table 11.** Correlation GDP, Total Working Population and Total Education Expenditure.

|  | GDP | Total Working | Total Education |
|---|---|---|---|
| GDP | 1 | | |
| Total Working | 0.679897768 | 1 | |
| Total Education | 0.311710799 | −0.01774151 | 1 |

**Table 12.** Anova Tests GDP, Total Working Population and Total Education Expenditure.

*Anova*

|  | df | SS | MS | F | Significance F |
|---|---|---|---|---|---|
| Regression | 2 | 1.93705E + 11 | 96852584034 | 5.240502 | 0.035112176 |
| Residual | 8 | 1.47852E + 11 | 18481547846 | | |
| Total | 10 | 3.41558E + 11 | | | |

|  | Coefficients | Standard Error | t-Stat. | p-value |
|---|---|---|---|---|
| Intercept | −1913751.092 | 1304327.171 | −1.467232405 | 0.180492 |
| TOTAL Working | 513.5935906 | 174.2716031 | 2.947087084 | 0.018508 |
| Total Education | 39.47209369 | 28.35424675 | 1.392105177 | 0.201368 |

**Table 13.** R Tests GDP, Total Working Population and Total Education Expenditure.

Regression Statistics

| Multiple R | 0.753075742 |
|---|---|
| $R^2$ | 0.567123074 |

growth rates in developing countries from the middle of the 20th century have had little effect on economic growth (Kuznets, 1967; Kelly, 1998). Nevertheless, recent consensus is that as more demographics data become available rapid population growth will significantly affect the impact on economic growth. Recent decline in fertility rate in Hong Kong has reduced the dependency ratio which creates a faster economic growth through higher saving ratios and investment levels on various public-funded projects (Bloom & Canning, 2001).

Regression 5# factor total population growth and fertility growth impact on GDP outcome (Tables 14–16).

***Table 14.*** Correlation Tests Total Population, Fertility and GDP.

|  | GDP | Fertility | Total Population |
|---|---|---|---|
| GDP | 1 |  |  |
| Fertility | 0.982638 | 1 |  |
| Total Population | 0.950486 | 0.960345 | 1 |

***Table 15.*** Anova Tests GDP, Total Population and Fertility and GDP.

*Anova*

|  | df | SS | MS | F | Significance F |
|---|---|---|---|---|---|
| Regression | 2 | 3.30004E + 11 | 1.65002E + 11 | 114.257 | 1.30898E − 06 |
| Residual | 8 | 11,553,063,708 | 1,444,132,963 |  |  |
| Total | 10 | 3.41558E + 11 |  |  |  |

|  | Coefficients | Standard Error | *t*-Stat | *p-value* |
|---|---|---|---|---|
| Intercept | 274627.5395 | 1134588.427 | 0.242050362 | 0.814831 |
| Fertility | 10899.79317 | 2829.304542 | 3.852463744 | 0.004861 |
| Total Population | 96.87632046 | 257.7370336 | 0.375872722 | 0.716783 |

***Table 16.*** R Tests Total Population and Fertility and GDP.

Regression Statistics

| Multiple $R$ | 0.982942192 |
|---|---|
| $R^2$ | 0.966175353 |

Model as: $G_y = \delta_0 + \delta_1 T_{\text{population}} + \delta_5 \text{Total}_{\text{fertility rate}} + \varepsilon_t$
$Y = \alpha + \delta_1 A_1 + \delta_5 A_5 + \varepsilon_t$

$H_0$: $\beta_1 = \beta_2 = \cdots = \beta_k = 0$ *(there is no linear relationship)*
$H_1$: *at least one $\beta_i \neq 0$ (at least one independent variable affects Y).*

First, the validity of the model is almost at $R^2$ at 0.98%, almost 1, as 1 being the highest. It states that from earlier regression 3# model longevity (Elife) value has no contribution to the model or much effect to GDP terms. Using total population itself has a significant impact on GDP of the form GDP per capita, and total fertility rate has significance on GDP and both are highly positive correlated to GDP. On this basis the model rejects the null hypothesis where there exists more than one independent variable affecting the GDP. Although the correlation exists for total population it is less significant in terms of *t*-tests value of 0.3785, *F*-value 0.716. Although, total fertility has a higher significance on the overall model, $t$-test 3.852 and $F$-value 0.00486, it does prove that fertility rate has been slow and decreasing in early years; over the last five years it has steadily climbed back to 1.2 child birth per family which is still below as compared to UNESCO's average of 2.0 per family (UNESCO, 2010). We take the model in the form of mathematical replacements:

$$\text{derived as } Y = 274,627 + 96.87A_1 + 10,899A_5$$

Qualitative results where total population is increasing at a rate of 1 people and fertility rate is 1, a ratio 1:1 produce would affect 285,624 units of GDP output. This is conclusive since the fertility rate has more impact to the GDP should the ratio is 10:1. The effects of population aging on economic growth are increasingly negative (Peng, 2006; Golley & Tyers, 2006). If there is a low fertility rate, the labour working population is forced to decline and will decelerate the economic growth ambitions. There should be an optimum level of fertility rate and labour force level that would help mitigate the growing aging population concerns and in course of economic growth. However, the draw back as per capita income will deteriorate since the rapid growth in the total population is caused by higher fertility regimes (Peng, 2005). To increase fertility rate to offset a rapid growth on aging population requires time to reach a balance of transition, there should be a concentration of resource where the working population and fertility growth rate allows a window to reduce the dependency ratio that would slow down the economy growth.

The regression 6# model as:

$$\text{Model as: } G_y = \delta_0 + \delta_2 G_{\text{worker s},t} + \delta_5 \text{Total}_{\text{fertility rate}} + \varepsilon_t$$
$$Y = \alpha + \delta_2 A_2 + \delta_5 A_5 + \varepsilon_t$$

$H_0$: $\beta_1 = \beta_2 = \cdots = \beta_k = 0$ *(there is no linear relationship)*
$H_1$: *at least one* $\beta_i \neq 0$ *(at least one independent variable affects Y)*.

We take our two highest correlated variables total fertility and working population (Table 17–19).

The test results on correlation for both indicators have a strong correlation to GDP which is no different to previous regression results, total fertility 0.98, 0.67 total working population. The fertility rate has an extremely high influence on GDP as $F$-tests 11.55 and $p$-value 0 both reject the null hypothesis Also, significantly, the total working population does affect the outcome of GDP in this case, the null hypothesis is rejected. The overall significance is

**Table 17.**   Correlation Tests Total Fertility, Working Population
and GDP.

|  | GDP | Fertility | Total Working |
|---|---|---|---|
| GDP | 1 | | |
| Fertility | 0.98263829 | 1 | |
| Total Working | 0.679897768 | 0.64234 | 1 |

**Table 18.**   Anova Tests Total Fertility, Working Population and GDP.

*Anova*

|  | df | SS | MS | F | Significance F |
|---|---|---|---|---|---|
| Regression | 2 | 3.3118E + 11 | 1.6559E + 11 | 127.6537 | 8.52133E − 07 |
| Residual | 8 | 10,377,451,048 | 1,297,181,381 | | |
| Total | 10 | 3.41558E + 11 | | | |

|  | Coefficients | Standard Error | t-Stat. | p-value |
|---|---|---|---|---|
| Intercept | 527700.2 | 174490.8538 | 3.024228455 | 0.016453 |
| Fertility 000 | 11.274.87 | 975.4917221 | 11.55814447 | 2.85E-06 |
| Total Working | 62.11625 | 60.23136359 | 1.031294181 | 0.033257 |

**Table 19.**   Anova Tests Total Fertility, Working Population and GDP.

| Regression Statistics | |
|---|---|
| Multiple R | 0.984691 |
| $R^2$ | 0.969617 |

where the $F$-value 127.63 is greater than $F$-critical value 0 in terms of both the total working population and fertility is correlated and significant that affects GDP.

In the form of mathematical expression,

$$Y = 527700.2 + 62.11A_2 + 11274A_5 + \varepsilon_t$$

The regression equation indicates for every increase in 100 people in working population will bring 1,127,400 unit increases to GDP and working population at 1,000 would bring 62,110 unit increases to GDP. On relative terms where 1:10 effect on every growth on fertility would require a 10% rate of increase in working population. As modelled using regression 6# fertility and total population have highest impact from the set of independent variables. It typically refers that population growth and stages of demographic transitions do matter and affect GDP growth as positives or negative correlation. To repeat the source of these two independent matters, as child mortality declines due to changes in hygiene, food resource and medical improvements and promotes baby boom both raise dependency ratios in general. Although elderly population is living longer raising the retired dependency ratio, immigration policies in Hong Kong allow working age population to expand by choosing young ready skilled adults who can be induced in current working population, offsetting any burden to government expenditure. Improving the working capacity of working population has no impact on the age structure in general. As total population has the effect of positively or negatively affecting the GDP especially on GDP per capita, in general assumption when population increases the GDP will increase balancing the effect of input and output relationship. When total population increases and GDP remains constant, the dilution effects on input and output is misbalanced which require further contributions of policy changes. The consensus of fertility rate has raised some concerns in the overall expenditure requirement on social implementations such as schools, hospitals and public housing. A phenomenon finding is that the general consensus towards fertility is becoming of late, the later it gets the size of working population from 15 to 24, 25 to 44, 45 to 64 are increasingly been forced to go beyond their retirement age. The effect of low fertility rate forces the dependency ratio further into the aging bracket. As majority of marriages are late and giving births become more late breaks down the consumption and savings level that was in 25−44 age group could well fall into the 45−64 age group, affecting the overall of GDP. The trend line in working population for 15−24 has been on the decrease; this group has minimal effect on the GDP, the working population largely extends to 25−44 that has higher working population ratio and 45−64 has to go beyond the retirement age effect which brings less dependency on government expenditure and continues to earn, save and consume.

# DISCUSSION, CONCLUSION, FUTURE RESEARCH AND OUTLOOK

Many reports find a typical profile pattern when earnings rise as young individuals enter into the labour market force. As they progress in gaining more experience, they peak in middle age and then decline as they move into retirement, a humped shape curve. In the supply side age earnings reflect changes in productivity and labour supply for an individual's working life. Changes aggregate labour supply in relative productivity and individual labour supply (Wen, 2007) from changes in age structure. The demand side individuals are assumed to adjust their savings and consumption based on their life cycle income. Young population are net borrowers of their income; mature agents save more when at peak of their income in anticipation of retirement. The elderly have also been viewed to save but assets are reduced given the uncertainty of health cost and life span.

*Population Pessimism*

In most part of the 20th century, the demography focused on rapid explosion in population increases caused by lower mortality rate, helped further by continuing increase of high fertility rate. The predicted negatives by Malthus to Ehrlich of high population growth rates and high population densities seem not to have alarmed neutralists or optimists. For example population they predicted between years 1960 and 1990 doubled from 3 to 6 billion people. The population discussion has been focused on the size of the numbers, neglecting the importance of age structure changes. In combination with population growth increase caused by high fertility, falling mortality is likely to bring different economic consequences because working population does not tend to stay in the same time line. We examined those structural movements in working age when family gets smaller and smaller and fertility becomes of late, the accounting effects, in particular, impacting on spending, saving and welfare anomalies. Caution is taken when this type of structural change has a long-term or short-term effect as these effects can cause explosions of behavioural changes.

*Conclusions*

It is clear that Hong Kong population over 7.1 million people in 2010 (Census Statistics Government) there are pressures on the government to react to this increase. Not only that it has an effect on housing alone but also the general GDP level is also affected whether it is a positive or negative relationship. As the demographic transition is working towards a higher level and labour participation rate expected to double in 2030 to 32% (3:10 ratio) and the fertility rate has steadied over the last five years there are no ideal offsets between the two populations. One of the reason that demographic variables have not entirely affected Hong Kong is that the working population accounts for more than half of the population with a majority of working age between 25 and 44 where savings, spending is at peak in mid-30s and the balance of saving, investing and spending has been equally well sustained. The government will have to draw public finances that would combat the demographic changes of working population. The rising health care, income tax allowances for dependant working population, thus lower government income, government expenditure sets to increase as aging population increasing, are some of the challenges that lie ahead for the government to tackle. However, just in time the labour force support ratio is set to peak in 2015; this leaves an opportunity to incorporate counter measures before they become too late. These are some highlights of various policies that were reported by the task force on population study.

## Future Research Direction

The model of multiple linear regression can certainly be improved by introducing more economic variables, such as savings and investment. The advances in the model used could be re-used to extend to other countries to make valuable comparisons with Hong Kong. Interesting observation should discover the type of policies used by the government such that these policies are highly correlated to demographics variables that can be used to make better forecasts in future econometrics modelling.

## REFERENCES

Adams, N. A. (1971). Dependency rates and saving rates: Comments. *American Economic Review, 61*(June), 472–475.

Aghion, P., & Howitt, P. (1998). *Endogenous growth theory*. Cambridge, MA: MIT Press.

Baldacci, E., Guin-Siu, M. T., & Mello, L. D. (2003). More on the effectiveness of public spending on health care and education: A covariance structure model. *Journal of International Development, 15*(6), 709–725.

Barlow, R. (1994). Population growth and economics: Some more correlation. *Population and Development Review, 20*(1), 153–165.

Barro, J. (1991). Economic growth in a cross section of countries. *The Quarterly Journal of Economics, 106*(2), 407–443.

Barro, J. (1995). *Inflation and economic growth*. NBER Working paper no. 5326, National Bureau of Economic Research, Inc.

Barro, J. (1999). *Inflation and economic growth*. NBER Working paper no. 7038, National Bureau of Economic Research, Inc.

Barro, R., & Becker, G. (1989). Fertility choice in a model of economic growth. *Econometrica, 57*(2), 481–501.

Barro, R., & Sala-i-Martin, X. (1995). *Economic growth*. New York, NY: McGraw-Hill.

Becker, G. (1964). *Human capital* (2nd ed.). New York, NY: Columbia University Press. 1975 and 3rd 1994.

Benhabib, J., & Spiegel, M. (1994). The role of human capital in economic development evidence from aggregate cross-country data. *Journal of Monetary Economics, 34*, 143–173.

Bils, M., & Klenow, P. (2000). Does schooling cause growth? *American Economic Review, 90*(5), 1160–1183.

Blackburn, K., & Cipriani, G. P. (1998). Endogenous fertility, mortality and growth. *Journal of Population Economics, 11*, 517–534.

Bloom, D. E., & Canning, D. (2001). Cumulative causality, economic growth, and the demographic transition. In N. Birdsall, A. C. Kelley, & S. W. Sinding (Eds.), *Population matters: Demographic change, economic growth, and poverty in the developing world*. Oxford: Oxford University Press.

Bloom, D., Canning, D., & Fink, G. (2011). *Implications of population aging for economic growth*. NBER Working paper no.16705, National Bureau of Economic Research, Inc.

Bloom, D., & Williamson, J. (1997). Demographic transition and economics miracles in emerging Asia. *World Bank Economics Review, 12*(3), 419–455.

Bloom, D., & Williamson, J. (1998). *Demographic transitions and economics miracles in emerging asia*. NBER Working paper no.6268, National Bureau of Economic Research, Inc.

Bos, D., & von Weizsacker, R. K. (1989). Economic consequences of an aging population. *European Economic Review, 33*, 345–354.

Brander, J. A., & Drowick, S. (1994). The role of fertility and population in economic growth empirical results from aggregate cross national data. *Journal of Population, Springer, 7*(1), 1–25.

Chen, C. (2001). Aging and life satisfaction. *Social indicators Research, 54*, 57–79.

Chen, Y., Li, Y., & Yin, J. (2004). High saving rate, high investment rate and Chinese economic growth during labour transition. *Economic Research Journal, 12*(2), 18–45.

Coale, A., & Watkins, S. (Eds.). (1996). The decline of fertility in Europe. *Population and Development Review, 12*(2), 323–340.

Cobb, C. W., & Paul, H. D. (1928). A theory of production. *The American Economic Review, 18*(1), 139–165.

Cole, A. J., & Hoover, E. (1958). *Population growth and economic development in low income countries*. Princeton, NJ: Princeton University Press. Center for Strategic International Studies Csis, UN, 2011.

Dickey, D. A., & Fuller, W. A. (1981). Likelihood ratio statistics for autoregressive time series with a unit root. *Econometrica, 49*, 1057–1072.

Dowrick, S. (2003). *Ideas and education: Level or growth effects?* NBER Working Paper No. 9709 NBER, Cambridge.

Durlauf, S., & Johnson, P. (1995). Multiple regimes and cross-country growth behaviour. *Journal of Applied Econometrics, 10*, 365–384.

Easterlin, R. (1996). A conversation with Richard Easterlin. *Journal of Population Economics, 10*, 119–136.

Edwards, S. (1996). Why are Latin America's savings rates so low? An international comparative analysis. *Journal of Development Economics, 51,* 5–44.

Ehrlich, P. (1968). *The population bomb.* Rivercity, MA: Rivercity Press. 01337.

Ehrlich, I., & Lui, F. T. (1991). Intergenerational trade, longevity and economic growth. *Journal of Political Economy, 99,* 1029–1059.

Engle, R., & Granger, W. (1987). Co-integration and error correction: Representation, estimation and testing. *Econometrica, 55*(2), 251–276.

Falvey, R. E., Foster, N., & Greenaway, D. (2007). Relative backwardness, absorptive capacity and knowledge spillovers. *Economics Letters, 97,* 230–234.

Faruqee, H. (2002). *Population aging and its macroeconomic implications: A framework for analysis.* IMF Working Paper No. 02/16. International Monetary Fund, Washington.

Fogel, R. W. (1994). "Economic growth, population theory, and physiology": "The bearing of long-term processes on the making of economic policy". *American Economic Review, 84,* 369–395.

Fougere, M., & Merette, M. (2000). Population aging, intergenerational equity and growth: An analysis with an endogenous growth overlapping generations model. In G. Harisson, S. Jensen, L. Pedersen, & T. Rutherford (Eds.), *Using dynamic general equilibrium models for policy analysis.* Amsterdam: North Holland.

Gemmell, N. (1996). Evaluating the impacts of human capital stocks and accumulation on economic growth: Some new evidence. *Oxford Bulletin of Economics and Statistics, 58*(1), 9–28.

Golley, J., & Tyers, R. (2006). *China's growth to 2030: Demographic change and the labour supply constraint.* Working Paper No.467, College of Business and Economics, Australia National University, Canberra.

Griliches, Z. (1977). Estimating the returns to schooling: Some econometric problems. *Econometrica, 45*(1), 1–22.

Gupta, K. L. (1971). Dependency rates and saving rates: Comment. *American Economic Review, 61,* 469–471.

Hanushek, E., & Kimko, D. (2000). Schooling, labor-force quality, and the growth of nations. *The American Economic Review, 90*(5), 1184–1208.

Hanushek, A., & Woessmann, L. (2007). The role of education quality for economic growth. Policy Research Working Paper No. 4122, World Bank, Washington, D.C.

Hotz, J., McElroy, S. W., & Sanders, S. G. (2005). Teenage childbearing and its life cycle consequences: Exploiting a natural experiment. *Journal of Human Resources., 40,* 683–715.

Jones, P. (2001). Are educated workers really more productive. *Journal of Development Economics, 64,* 57–79.

Kelly, J. (1998). *Rethinking industrial relations: Mobilization, collectivism and long waves.* London: Routledge.

Kelley, C., & Schmidt, R. M. (1995). "Economic and demographic change: A synthesis of models", findings, and perspectives. Duke Economics Working Paper No. 99–01.

Krueger, A., & Lindahl, M. (2001). Education for growth: Why and for whom? *Journal of Economic Literature, American Economic Association, 39*(4), 1101–1136.

Kulish, M., Smith, K., & Kent, C. (2006). *Ageing, retirement and savings: A general equilibrium analysis.* Reserve Bank of Australia Research Discussion Paper No. 2006-06.

Kuznets, S. (1967). Population and economic growth. *Proceedings of the American Philosophical Society, 111*(3), 170–193.

Leff, N. l. H. (1969). Dependency rates and saving rates. *American Economic Review*, *59*, 886–895.

Levine, R., & Renelt, D. (1992). A sensitivity analysis of cross-country growth regressions. *American Economic Review*, *82*, 942–963.

Malthus, T. R. (1798). An essay on the principle of population. J. Johnson, London.

Mankiw, G., Romer, D., & Weil, D. N. (1992). Health capital and cross-country variation in income per capita in the Mankiw-Romer-Weil model. *Economics Letters*, *48*(1), 99–106.

Mathews, T. J. (1992). Birth and Fertility Rates by Educational Attainment: United States. *Monthly Vital Statistics Report*, *45*(10), 2–20.

Mincer, J. A. (1974). Introduction to "schooling, experience, and earnings". *Schooling, experience, and earnings* (pp. 1–4). National Bureau of Economic Research, Inc.

Mirowsk, J., & Ross, C. E. (1998). Education, personal control, lifestyle and health – A human capital hypothesis. *Research on Ageing*, *20*, 415–449.

Nelson, T. (2005). Ageism: Prejudice against our feared future self. *Journal of Social Issues*, *61*(2), 207–221.

Nelson, R., & Phelps, E. (1966). Investment in humans, technological diffusion, and economic growth. *American Economic Review*, *56*(1–2), 65–75.

Peng, X. J. (2005). *Population ageing, economic growth and population policy option in China – A dynamic general equilibrium analysis*. Ph.D. thesis, Monash University.

Peng, X. J. (2006). Macroeconomic consequences of population ageing in China – A computable general equilibrium analysis. *Journal of Population Research*, *30*(4), 12–22. (in Chinese).

Preston, S. H. (1975). The changing relation between mortality and level of economic development. *Population Studies*, *29*(2), 231–248.

Pritchett, L. (2001). Where has all the education gone? How to explain the surprising finding that more education has not led to faster economic growth? The *World Bank Economic Review*, *15*(3) 367–391.

Ram, R. (1982). "Dependency rates and aggregate savings": A new international cross-section study. *American Economic Review*, *72*, 537–544.

Ram, R. (1984). Dependency rates and savings: Reply. *American Economic Review*, *74*, 234–237.

Romer, P. (1990). *Endogenous technological change*. NBER Working paper no. 3210, National Bureau of Economic Research, Inc.

Sanderson, W., & Scherbov, S. (2008). Rethinking Age and Aging. *Population Bulletin, The Population Reference Bureau*, *63*(4).

Schultz, T. (1961). Investment in human capital. *American Economic Review*, *51*, 1–17.

Shimasawa, M., & Hosoyama, H. (2004). *"Economic implications of an aging population": The case of five aisan economies*. ESRI Discussion Paper Paper Series No. 117.

Stock, J. H., & Watson, M. W. (2003). *Introduction to econometrics* (pp. 217–230). Upper Saddle River, NJ: Pearson Education, Inc.

Tamirisa, N. T., & Fernadez-Ansola, H. (2006). *Macroeconomic effects and policy challenges of population aging*, 2006 International Monetary Fund.

Tyers, R., & Shi, Q. (2007). Global demographic change, policy responses and their economic implications. *The World Economy*, *30*(4), 537–566.

UNESCO. (2010). *The impact of the global financial and economic crisis on the education sector. No. 1: The impact of the crisis on public expenditure on education: Findings from the UNESCO Quick Survey*. UNESCO, Education Sector, Paris.

Wang, X. (2006). Does Financial Repression Inhibit Economic Growth Empirical Examination of China's Reform Experience. China Centre for Economic Research Working Paper, Peking University China.

Wen, Z. (2007). The "demographic changes on the overall Economic and financial market", 2007 Strait Cross-Strait and East Asia Finance and Business Seminar Thesis.

Wolff, E. N. (2001). The role of education in the postwar productivity convergence among OECD countries. *Industrial and Corporate Change, 10*(3), 735–759.

# DOES OPTIMIZING THE CASH CONVERSION CYCLE AMELIORATE FIRM'S PERFORMANCE? UNRAVELING THE RELATIONSHIP IN THE INDIAN CORPORATE LANDSCAPE

Nityanand Tripathi and Naseem Ahamed

## ABSTRACT

*This chapter examines the impact of working capital management (WCM now onwards) which is measured by cash conversion cycle (CCC now onwards) on the financial performance of firms in the Indian context. The period of study is from the year 2000 to 2014, that is, for a span of 15 years for 4,687 companies listed on the National Stock Exchange. This chapter uses regression model to analyze panel data. Data for 4,687 listed companies have been analyzed for a period of 15 years. For some companies with data availability issues, the period of inclusion is less than 15 years. This chapter is limited to a sample of Indian firms; further research could examine the generalizability of these*

The Spread of Financial Sophistication Through Emerging Markets Worldwide
Research in Finance, Volume 32, 243–255
ISSN: 0196-3821/doi:10.1108/S0196-382120160000032010

*findings to other countries. Some previous studies have been undertaken on this topic, but the dataset used for this chapter is comprehensive enough to delineate the WCM and performance dynamics in the Indian context. Improved working capital policy could improve firm profitability by reducing the firm's CCC, thereby creating additional firm value. In addition, the results can be used for other purposes, including monitoring of firms by auditors, debt holders, and other stakeholders. This chapter contributes to the literature by extending the extant literature in an emerging market context. To the authors' knowledge, this is the first empirical study to address this issue in the Indian context based on a large dataset covering more than 4000 companies.*

**Keywords:** Cash conversion cycle; working capital management; firm profitability

## INTRODUCTION

Working capital management falls under the gambit short-term investment and financing decisions, unlike capital expenditure (popularly known as CapEx) which involves a substantial amount of capital. WCM can also be easily distinguished from the CapEx decisions by its virtue of frequency and reversibility. Singh and Kumar (2013) state that considerable amount of research has been dedicated to long-term investment and financing decisions over the past four decades leading to both theoretical- and application-based developments. The field of short-term investments and finance, that is, WCM in contrast, fallen short in terms of attention deserved. Analyzing the trend of research articles published on the stream of WCM year on year reveals that post-2008 following the global financial crisis, the research work on WCM picked up. The importance of WCM research has also been highlighted in the study by Padachi (2006), which states that WCM is often high in proportion to the total assets employed, so it becomes imperative to utilize it effectively. Most of the research in extant literature has unanimously agreed that improved working capital policy could improve firm profitability by reducing the firm's CCC, thereby creating additional firm value. In addition, the results can be used for other purposes, including monitoring of firms by auditors, debt holders, and other stakeholders. Increased competition in recent decades has directed attention to the rationalization of short-term investments, giving working capital management a crucial role in firm profitability (Falope & Ajilore, 2009; Appuhami, 2008; Jose, Lancaster, & Stevens, 1996; Lazaridis & Tryfonidis, 2006; Shin & Soenen, 1998). Furthermore, various problems related to working capital management have been regarded as significant reasons for small- and medium-sized enterprise (SME) failure (Cielen, Peeters, & Vanhoof, 2004). Working capital management, which involves managing cash, inventory, accounts receivable, and account payable, etc., affects a firm's short-term financial performance. Several previous studies have measured the impact of working capital on firm profitability (e.g., Garcia-Teruel & Martinez-Solano, 2007; Padachi, 2006). According to Ebben and Johnson (2011), working capital management has increasingly been measured by cash conversion cycle (CCC). Most previous studies of CCC have investigated its impact on profitability in large countries (e.g., Jose et al., 1996; Shin & Soenen, 1998).

This chapter analyses the impact of CCC (a proxy for WCM) on performance in terms of profitability in Indian firms. The results confirm the inverse relationship between CCC length and profitability. Firm size (proxied by Sales) is significantly and positively related to profitability, firm age does not exhibit any relation to profitability. This chapter contributes to the financial management literature in at least two ways. First, it uses a unique method to analyze a large sample of firms. Second, it confirms previous findings regarding the relationship between CCC and firm profitability in a previously unstudied context.

The next section describes the conceptual framework and summarizes previous research briefly in the area. The section "Literature Review" elaborates on the variable selection, research hypotheses, sample and data, and model specification. The section "Results" reports the results of the empirical analyses, and the final section presents the concluding discussion.

## CONCEPTUAL FRAMEWORK

Numerous transactions take place in a company which is short term in nature that leads to cash inflow and outflow on a routine basis. WCM fundamentally is related with all these transactions that include current assets and current liabilities. Current assets include inventory or stocks that comprises all forms of stock, that is, raw materials, work in progress as well as finished goods, debtors, trade credit, cash in hand and miscellaneous short-term securities. On the other hand, current liabilities comprise bank overdrafts, short-term loans if any, creditors, outstanding tax, dividend obligations, interest to be serviced, etc. These payments and incomes take place continuously and WCM attempt to match the current assets to the current liabilities. The CCC has been repeatedly used in the extant literature as a measure for working capital management. This chapter is not different from the earlier ones in that regard. The concept behind CCC is that it takes a firm certain amount of time in completing one full business operating cycle that encompasses everything from procurement of raw materials to completion of final product and receiving payment for the product. This entire cycle completion takes various numbers of days depending upon various factors like the sector in which a company is operating, the credit policy of the company, size of the firm, etc. CCC has been calculated using the following formula:

CCC = Number of days of inventories + Number of days accounts receivable
− Number of days accounts payable

The following model illustrates how this study has been modeled to test the impact of WCM on firm performance.

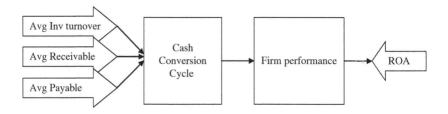

The longer the CCC results in more money getting locked in for a longer period leading to channelizing money from other sources, thus disturbing the frail balance of short-term and long-term money requirements. Reducing the CCC way too much on the other hand could lead the company to lose customers and business. Hence, companies should maintain a balance in formulating their CCC policy. Shin and Soenen (1998) found significant impact on efficient cash cycle conversion management on profitability and liquidity of companies.

## LITERATURE REVIEW

Working capital management has not received the same degree of attention from the research community as long-term sources/avenues of finance and investment did for a long time. However, the insurgence of a global market meltdown by the end of 2008, made researchers to look into this dimension as well as an important one that may have an influence on the overall health of the company. Singh and Kumar (2013) did an extensive literature review survey that included important articles in this field from the year 1980 to 2012. Using a sample of 126 articles out of 527 screened initially, they concluded that the majority of the papers were empirical in nature that attempted to study the relationship between WCM and firm's profitability. Given the recent surge in the number of articles post-2008 crisis, WCM research could be considered as a stream of recent origin in the new world financial order setting. This does not discount the relevance or importance of a handful of studies prior to 2008, but it emphasizes that to be turning point in WCM research. Important articles include studies by Yazdanfar and Ohman (2014) where they undertake the study on small and medium Swedish manufacturing firms and conclude the existence of a negative relation between the CCC and firm profitability. Their study focused on four important sectors of Swedish economy.

Other significant contribution has been by Shin and Soenen (1998), who analyzed more than 50,000 companies based in the United States over a period of 20 years to conclude the existence of a strong negative relation between CCC and profitability. In the European context, Deloof (2003) studied more than a thousand Belgian firms for five years arriving at the same conclusion as that of the previous studies mentioned. Lazaridis and Tryfonidis (2006) analyzed the Greek firms, Garcia-Teruel and Martinez-Solano (2007) conducted similar study on a large scale in the Spanish corporate environment taking almost 9,000 companies for a period of seven years.

In the African corporate landscape, Mathuva (2010) studied the relationship between WCM and profitability in Kenyan firms for a period of 15 years reaching the same conclusion as that of the earlier research.

The literature however is not vehemently unanimous in its conclusion as there are other studies which found a positive relationship between working capital management and firm's profitability. Some of the notable works are that of Lyroudi and Lazaridis (2000), who examined the relationship in the European context and found a positive relationship between CCC and ROA. Among other research indicating the existence of a positive relationship between CCC or WCM and performance are that study of Gill, Biger, and Mathur (2010) in the context of US manufacturing companies. Sharma and Kumar (2011) analyzed 263 nonfinancial firms in India for a period of nine years to establish a positive relationship between CCC and profitability. Abuzayed (2012) is one of the latest studies in the string of studies on the WCM substantiating positive relationship between CCC and performance of the firm.

Although there is an overwhelming amount of research suggesting a negative relationship between WCM and firm performance, there is no dearth of studies suggesting otherwise. Hence, one can safely conclude that there is a mixed bag of results which warrants further exploration into the subject. As mentioned earlier that the study undertaken by Sharma and Kumar (2011) established a positive relation between WCM and firm performance, we set out to delve deep into this relationship by increasing the sample size almost 20-fold and increasing the period of study from 9 years to 15 years. This chapter would provide additional insights into the study for the Indian context.

### Hypotheses Postulated

In order to explore the relationship between working capital management and firms' performance, the study picks up proxy variables as relevant indicators of dependent and independent variables. The dependent variable that is the indicator of firm performance would be Return on Assets. The primary independent variable is the CCC. In addition to these, a battery of control variables are employed which include size of firm (proxied by ln Sales), leverage condition of the firm (proxied by debt-to-equity ratio), ownership of firm (dummy variable) which gets the value 1 if the ownership is private and 0 otherwise, age if the firm.

In line with the majority of previous studies, we hypothesize:

**H1a.** CCC negatively influences ROA.

**H1b.** Firm size positively influences ROA

**H1c.** Firm age positively influences ROA

Next set of hypothesis has to do with the CCC per se. CCC in and of itself depends on several factors. We attempt to test whether age, ownership of the firm impacts the total operating cycle (CCC) forms the base for next set of hypotheses.

**H2a.** Firm ownership negatively influences CCC.

**H2b.** Firm age negatively influences CCC.

Last set of hypothesis tests out the impact of change in the WCM on the change in the performance of the firm.

**H3a.** ΔCCC negatively influences ΔROA.

*Data and Methodology*

The data for this chapter come from a "Prowess" database managed by Centre for Monitoring Indian Economy (CMIE). CMIE contains firm level data for approximately 27,000 firms in India under listed and unlisted category. Out of the total, approximately 5,000 firms are listed on various national and regional exchanges. Depending upon the availability of data for the listed firms, we have gathered 4,687 for analysis for this chapter for a period ranging from 2000 to 2014. A descriptive statistics of the data is tabulated in Table 1.

***Table 1.*** Summary Statistic.

| Variable | No. | Mean | Standard Deviation | Coefficient Variation | $Q1$ | $Q2$ | $Q3$ |
|---|---|---|---|---|---|---|---|
| ROA (return on assets) | 23,571 | 0.0315 | 0.192 | 608.62 | 0.00 | 0.03 | 0.06 |
| ln(CCC) | 20,248 | 4.548 | 1.319 | 29.019 | 3.86 | 4.58 | 5.26 |
| ln(Sales) | 23,205 | 6.811 | 2.18 | 32.00 | 5.54 | 6.88 | 8.22 |
| Debt ratio | 23,659 | 3.268 | 52.53 | 1606.99 | 0.45 | 0.97 | 1.88 |
| Pvt*ln(CCC) | 20,248 | 2.78 | 2.48 | 89.13 | 0.00 | 3.60 | 4.86 |
| Age | 23,659 | 37.54 | 20.19 | 53.77 | 24 | 30 | 43 |

*Notes*: ROA indicates Pat/total assets. ln(CCC) denotes the natural logarithm of cash conversion cycle. ln(Sales) represents the natural logarithm total sales of the company. Debt ratio denotes total debt/total assets. Pvt*ln(CCC) stand for interaction between private ownership and the natural logarithm of cash conversion cycle. Pvt is a dummy that is assigned 1 when the ownership of firm is private (Indian or Foreign) and 0 otherwise. Age denotes age of the firm.

This chapter uses a panel regression analysis to analyze the impact of CCC on performance of firm measured by ROA. The model used for this chapter is as follows:

$$\text{ROA}_{i,t} = \alpha + \beta_1 \ln \text{CCC}_{i,t} + \beta_2 \ln \text{Sales}_{i,t} + \beta_3 D/E_{i,t} + \beta_4 \text{Pvt}*\ln \text{CCC}_{i,t} + \beta_5 \text{Age}_{i,t} + \varepsilon_{i,t}$$

The equation for impact of ownership and age on working capital management is as follows:

$$\ln \text{CCC}_{i,t} = \alpha + \beta_1 \ln \text{Sales}_{i,t} + \beta_3 D/E_{i,t} + \beta_4 \text{Pvt}*\ln \text{CCC}_{i,t} + \beta_5 \text{Age}_{i,t} + \varepsilon_{i,t}$$

In both the equations, $\alpha$ is the intercept or constant, $\text{ROA}_{i,t}$ is the profitability percentage of $i$th firm in $t$th time, $\ln \text{CCC}_{i,t}$ is the CCC (the natural logarithm of number of days), $\ln \text{Sales}_{i,t}$ indicates the size of the firm measured by their sales volume, $\text{Age}_{i,t}$ indicates the age of the firm, $\text{Pvt}*\ln \text{CCC}_{i,t}$ is the interaction term of ownership variable with the CCC and $\varepsilon_{i,t}$ is the error term.

# RESULTS

# CONCLUSION AND DISCUSSION

The study analyses the impact of CCC on the performance of firms in the Indian context. Based on the results exhibited in Tables 2–9, one can safely conclude that CCC does have a negative impact on profitability, that is, more efficient CCC leads to higher profitability and vice versa. This chapter validates the previous literature speaking of the relation between working capital management and firm performance in the same vein. Managers should pay heed to the results in the sense that short-term liquidity is imperative for the well-being of their company and ignoring it could lead to pernicious impact. An efficient CCC would help keep the entire production cycle function without any stifle and the proceeds can be effectively channeled to the required areas. Internal finance sources are cheaper than the external ones so it is important that a company effectively manages it and free up additional internal fund for investment into various ventures.

**Table 2.** Pearson Correlation Coefficients.

|  | ROA | ln(CCC) | ln(Sales) | Debt Ratio | Pvt*ln(CCC) | Age |
|---|---|---|---|---|---|---|
| ROA | 1.00000 | | | | | |
| ln(CCC) | −0.05181 | 1.00000 | | | | |
|  | (<.0001)*** | | | | | |
| ln(Sales) | 0.09114 | −0.29049 | 1.00000 | | | |
|  | (<.0001)*** | (<.0001)*** | | | | |
| Debt ratio | −0.01734 | −0.00359 | −0.00401 | 1.00000 | | |
|  | 0.0078 | 0.6091 | 0.5409 | | | |
| Pvt*ln(CCC) | −0.04058 | 0.38193 | −0.51098 | 0.00107 | 1.00000 | |
|  | (<.0001)*** | (<.0001)*** | (<.0001)*** | 0.8791 | | |
| Age | 0.01665 | −0.04633 | 0.17774 | −0.00514 | −0.25041 | 1.00000 |
|  | 0.0106 | (<.0001)*** | (<.0001)*** | 0.4295 | (<.0001)*** | |

*Notes*: ROA denotes Pat/total assets. ln(CCC) denotes the natural logarithm of cash conversion cycle. ln(Sales) denotes the natural logarithm total sales of the company. Debt Ratio denotes total debt/total assets. Pvt*ln(CCC) denotes interaction between private ownership and the natural logarithm of cash conversion cycle. Pvt is a dummy that is assigned 1 when the ownership of firm is private (Indian or Foreign) and 0 otherwise. Age denotes age of the firm. In each cell, the coefficient is reported in the upper part and the *p*-value in parentheses is reported in the lower part. *** represents the significance level of 1%.

**Table 3.** Regression Model: ROA (Return on Assets).

| | |
|---|---|
| Intercept | −0.00751 |
| | (0.2842) |
| ln(CCC) | −0.00366 |
| | (<0.0001)*** |
| ln(Sales) | 0.00763 |
| | (<0.0001)*** |
| Debt ratio | −0.00005968 |
| | (0.0019)** |
| Pvt*ln(CCC) | 0.00131 |
| | (0.0131)** |
| Age | 0.00000876 |
| | (0.8735) |
| No. | 20,248 |
| Adjusted $R^2$ | 0.0103 |

*Notes*: The hypothesis is tested via the following model:

$$ROA = \beta_1 + \beta_2 \ln(CCC) + \beta_3 \ln(Sales) + \beta_4 \text{ Debt ratio} + \beta_5 \text{ Pvt} * \ln(CCC) + \beta_6 \text{ Age} + \varepsilon$$

where ROA denotes Pat/total assets. ln(CCC) denotes the natural logarithm of cash conversion cycle. ln(Sales) denotes the natural logarithm total sales of the company. Debt Ratio denotes total debt/total assets. Pvt*ln(CCC) denotes interaction between private ownership and the natural logarithm of cash conversion cycle. Pvt is a dummy that is assigned 1 when the ownership of firm is private (Indian or Foreign) and 0 otherwise. Age denotes age of the firm. In each cell, the coefficient is reported in the upper part and the *p*-value in parentheses is reported in the lower part. ***, **, and * represent the significance level of 1%, 5%, and 10%, respectively.

**Table 4.** Summary Statistic.

| Variable | No. | Mean | Standard Deviation | Coefficient Variation | Q1 | Q2 | Q3 |
|---|---|---|---|---|---|---|---|
| ln CCC | 20,809 | 4.55 | 1.35 | 29.78 | 3.86 | 4.60 | 5.26 |
| ln(Sales) | 23,205 | 6.811 | 2.18 | 32.00 | 5.54 | 6.88 | 8.22 |
| ln NWC | 21,274 | 5.53 | 2.01 | 36.31 | 4.26 | 5.52 | 6.82 |
| Debt ratio | 23,659 | 3.268 | 52.53 | 1606.99 | 0.45 | 0.97 | 1.88 |
| Pvt*ln CCC | 20,248 | 2.78 | 2.48 | 89.13 | 0.00 | 3.60 | 4.86 |
| Age | 23,659 | 37.54 | 20.19 | 53.77 | 24 | 30 | 43 |

*Notes*: ln CCC denotes the natural logarithm of cash conversion cycle. ln(Sales) denotes the natural logarithm of total sales of the company. ln(NWC) denotes the natural logarithm of net working capital (NWC = debtors + inventory − creditors). Debt ratio denotes total debt/total assets. Pvt*ln(CCC) denotes interaction between private ownership and the natural logarithm of cash conversion cycle. Pvt is a dummy that is assigned 1 when the ownership of firm is private (Indian or Foreign) and 0 otherwise. Age denotes age of the firm.

**Table 5.** Pearson Correlation Coefficients.

| | ln CCC | ln(Sales) | ln NWC | Debt Ratio | Ownership | Pvt*ln (CCC) | Age |
|---|---|---|---|---|---|---|---|
| ln CCC | 1.00000 | | | | | | |
| ln(Sales) | −0.28819 (<.0001)*** | 1.00000 | | | | | |
| ln NWC | −0.01110 0.1181 | 0.83996 (<.0001)*** | 1.00000 | | | | |
| Debt ratio | −0.00145 0.8344 | −0.00401 0.5409 | −0.00119 0.8621 | 1.00000 | | | |
| Ownership | 0.05322 (<.0001)*** | −0.45107 (<.0001)*** | −0.40480 (<.0001)*** | 0.00168 0.7965 | 1.00000 | | |
| Pvt*ln (CCC) | 0.38193 (<.0001)*** | −0.51098 (<.0001)*** | −0.37838 (<.0001)*** | 0.00107 0.8791 | 0.90908 (<.0001)*** | 1.00000 | |
| Age | −0.04675 (<.0001)*** | 0.17774 (<.0001)*** | 0.14303 (<.0001)*** | −0.00514 0.4295 | −0.22951 (<.0001)*** | −0.25041 (<.0001)*** | 1.00000 |

*Notes*: ln CCC denotes the natural logarithm of cash conversion cycle. ln(Sales) denotes the natural logarithm of total sales of the company. ln(NWC) denotes the natural logarithm of net working capital (NWC = debtors + inventory − creditors). Debt ratio denotes total debt/total assets. Ownership is a dummy that is assigned 1 when the ownership of firm is private (Indian or Foreign) and 0 otherwise. Pvt*ln(CCC) denotes interaction between private ownership and the natural logarithm of cash conversion cycle. Pvt is a dummy that is assigned 1 when the ownership of firm is private (Indian or Foreign) and 0 otherwise. Age denotes age of the firm. In each cell, the coefficient is reported in the upper part and the *p*-value in parentheses is reported in the lower part. *** represents the significance level of 1%.

**Table 6.** Regression Model: ln CCC (The natural logarithm of Cash Conversion Cycle).

| | |
|---|---|
| Intercept | 5.41164 |
| | (<.0001)*** |
| ln(Sales) | −0.38578 |
| | (<.0001)*** |
| ln NWC | 0.32095 |
| | (<.0001)*** |
| Debt ratio | −0.00000502 |
| | (0.9569) |
| Ownership | −3.87952 |
| | (<.0001)*** |
| Pvt*ln CCC | 0.83743 |
| | (<.0001)*** |
| Age | 0.00127 |
| | (<.0001)*** |
| No. | 19,594 |
| Adjusted $R^2$ | 0.6628 |

*Notes*: The Hypothesis is tested via the following model:

$$\ln CCC = \alpha_1 + \alpha_2 \ln(Sales) + \alpha_3 \ln(NWC) + \alpha_4 \text{ Debt ratio} + \alpha_5 \text{ Ownership} + \alpha_6 \text{ Pvt*ln CCC} + \alpha_7 \text{ Age} + \varepsilon$$

where ln CCC denotes the natural logarithm of cash conversion cycle. ln(Sales) denotes the natural logarithm of total sales of the company. ln(NWC) denotes the natural logarithm of net working capital (NWC = debtors + inventory − creditors). Debt ratio denotes total debt/total assets. Ownership is a dummy that is assigned 1 when the ownership of firm is private (Indian or Foreign) and 0 otherwise. Pvt*ln(CCC) denotes interaction between private ownership and the natural logarithm of cash conversion cycle. Pvt is a dummy that is assigned 1 when the ownership of firm is private (Indian or Foreign) and 0 otherwise. Age denotes age of the firm. In each cell, the coefficient is reported in the upper part and the *p*-value in parentheses is reported in the lower part. ***, **, and * represent the significance level of 1%, 5%, and 10%, respectively.

**Table 7.** Summary Statistic.

| Variable | No. | Mean | Standard Deviation | Coefficient Variation | Q1 | Q2 | Q3 |
|---|---|---|---|---|---|---|---|
| lnΔPAT | 10,909 | 3.42 | 2.36 | 69.22 | 1.80 | 3.41 | 5.03 |
| lnΔNWC | 11,569 | 4.53 | 2.36 | 52.08 | 2.98 | 4.51 | 6.09 |
| ln(Sales) | 23,205 | 6.811 | 2.18 | 32.00 | 5.54 | 6.88 | 8.22 |
| Debt ratio | 23,659 | 3.268 | 52.53 | 1606.99 | 0.45 | 0.97 | 1.88 |
| Pvt*lnΔNWC | 11,569 | 2.32 | 2.51 | 108.21 | 0.00 | 1.91 | 4.31 |
| Age | 23,659 | 37.54 | 20.19 | 53.77 | 24 | 30 | 43 |

*Notes*: lnΔPAT denotes the natural logarithm of change in profit after tax. ln(ΔNWC) denotes the natural logarithm of change in net working capital (NWC = debtors + inventory − creditors). ln(Sales) denotes the natural logarithm of total sales of the company. Debt ratio denotes total debt/total assets. Pvt*lnΔNWC denotes interaction between private ownership and the natural logarithm of change in net working capital. Pvt is a dummy that is assigned 1 when the ownership of firm is private (Indian or Foreign) and 0 otherwise. Age denotes age of the firm.

*Table 8.* Pearson Correlation Coefficients.

| | lnΔPAT | lnΔNWC | ln(Sales) | Debt ratio | Age | Pvt*lnΔNWC |
|---|---|---|---|---|---|---|
| lnΔPAT | 1.00000 | | | | | |
| lnΔNWC | 0.70117 | 1.00000 | | | | |
| | (<.0001)*** | | | | | |
| ln(Sales) | 0.69191 | 0.76624 | 1.00000 | | | |
| | (<.0001)*** | (<.0001)*** | | | | |
| Debt ratio | 0.01625 | 0.00304 | −0.00401 | 1.00000 | | |
| | 0.0897 | 0.7437 | 0.5409 | | | |
| Age | 0.13546 | 0.09748 | 0.17774 | −0.00514 | 1.00000 | |
| | (<.0001)*** | (<.0001)*** | (<.0001)*** | 0.4295 | | |
| Pvt*lnΔNWC | −0.02811 | 0.20524 | −0.00961 | 0.00495 | −0.19053 | 1.00000 |
| | (0.0219)** | (<.0001)*** | 0.3028 | 0.5943 | (<.0001)*** | |

*Notes:* lnΔPAT denotes the natural logarithm of change in profit after tax. ln(ΔNWC) denotes the natural logarithm of change in net working capital (NWC = debtors + inventory − creditors). ln (Sales) denotes the natural logarithm of total sales of the company. Debt ratio denotes total debt/ total assets. Pvt*lnΔNWC denotes interaction between private ownership and the natural logarithm of change in net working capital. Pvt is a dummy that is assigned 1 when the ownership of firm is private (Indian or Foreign) and 0 otherwise. Age denotes age of the firm. In each cell, the coefficient is reported in the upper part and the *p*-value in parentheses is reported in the lower part. *** and ** represent the significance level of 1% and 5%, respectively.

*Table 9.* Regression Model: lnΔPAT (The natural logarithm of change in profit after tax).

| | |
|---|---|
| Intercept | −1.74962 |
| | (<.0001)*** |
| lnΔNWC | 0.36332 |
| | (<.0001)*** |
| ln(Sales) | 0.51477 |
| | (<.0001)*** |
| Debt ratio | 0.00064796 |
| | (0.0058)* |
| Pvt*lnΔNWC | −0.07730 |
| | (<.0001)*** |
| Age | 0.00174 |
| | (0.0590) |
| No. | 6620 |
| Adjusted $R^2$ | 0.5929 |

*Notes:* The Hypothesis is tested via the following model:

$$\ln\Delta PAT = \alpha_1 + \alpha_2 \ln(\Delta NWC) + \alpha_3 \ln(Sales) + \alpha_4 \text{ Debt ratio} + \alpha_5 \text{ Pvt*}\ln\Delta NWC + \alpha_6 \text{ Age} + \varepsilon$$

where lnΔPAT denotes the natural logarithm of change in profit after tax. ln(ΔNWC) denotes the natural logarithm of change in net working capital (NWC = debtors + inventory − creditors). ln(Sales) denotes the natural logarithm of total sales of the company. Debt ratio denotes total debt/total assets. Pvt*lnΔNWC denotes interaction between private ownership and the natural logarithm of change in net working capital. Pvt is a dummy that is assigned 1 when the ownership of firm is private (Indian or Foreign) and 0 otherwise. Age denotes age of the firm. In each cell, the coefficient is reported in the upper part and the *p*-value in parentheses is reported in the lower part. ***, **, and * represent the significance level of 1%, 5%, and 10%, respectively.

# REFERENCES

Abuzayed, B. (2012). Working capital management and firms' performance in emerging markets: The case of Jordan. *International Journal of Managerial Finance, 8*(2), 155–179.

Appuhami, B. R. (2008). The impact of firms' capital expenditure on working capital management: An empirical study across industries in Thailand. *International Management Review, 4*(1), 11–24.

Cielen, A., Peeters, L., & Vanhoof, K. (2004). Bankruptcy prediction using a data envelopment analysis. *European Journal of Operational Research, 154*(2), 526–532.

Deloof, M. (2003). Does working capital management affect profitability of Belgian firms? *Journal of Business Finance & Accounting, 30*(3/4), 573–588.

Ebben, J. J., & Johnson, A. C. (2011). Cash conversion cycle management in small firms: Relationships with liquidity, invested capital, and firm performance. *Journal of Small Business & Entrepreneurship, 24*(3), 381–396.

Falope, O. I., & Ajilore, O. T. (2009). Working capital management and corporate profitability: Evidence from panel data analysis of selected quoted companies in Nigeria. *Research Journal of Business Management, 3*(3), 74–84.

Garcia-Teruel, J., & Martinez-Solano, P. (2007). Effects of working capital management on SME profitability. *International Journal of Managerial Finance, 3*(2), 164–177.

Gill, A., Biger, N., & Mathur, N. (2010). The relationship between working capital management and profitability: Evidence from the United States. *Business and Economics Journal, 10*(1), 1–9.

Jose, M. L., Lancaster, C., & Stevens, J. L. (1996). Corporate returns and cash conversion cycles. *Journal of Economics and finance, 20*(1), 33–46.

Lazaridis, I., & Tryfonidis, D. (2006). Relationship between working capital management and profitability of listed companies in the Athens stock exchange. *Journal of Financial Management and Analysis, 19*(1), 26–35.

Lyroudi, K., & Lazaridis, Y. (2000). The cash conversion cycle and liquidity analysis of the food industry in Greece. Paper presented at EFMA 2000, Athens, June.

Mathuva, D. (2010). The influence of working capital management components on corporate profitability: A survey on Kenyan listed firms. *Research Journal of Business Management, 4*(1), 1–11.

Padachi, K. (2006). Trends in working capital management and its impact on form's performance: An analysis on Mauritian small manufacturing firms. *International Review of Business Research Papers, 2*(2), 45–58.

Sharma, A. K., & Kumar, S. (2011). Effect of working capital management on firm profitability: Empirical evidence from India. *Global Business Review, 12*(1), 159–173.

Shin, H. H., & Soenen, L. (1998). Efficiency of working capital management and corporate profitability. *Financial Practice & Education, 8*(2), 39–45.

Singh, H. P., & Kumar, S. (2013). Working capital management: A literature review and research agenda. *Qualitative Research in Financial Markets, 6*(2), 173–197.

Yazdanfar, D., & Ohman, P. (2014). The impact of cash conversion cycle on firm profitability: An empirical study based on Swedish data. *International Journal of Managerial Finance, 10*(4), 442–452.

# BUDGET INVESTMENTS IN RUSSIA: NOT INVESTMENT BUT TRANSFORMATION OF PUBLIC PROPERTY ☆

Dmitry L. Komyagin

## ABSTRACT

*This chapter is devoted to budget investments in the Russian Federation, which nowadays have a double meaning. This fact often causes confusion and misunderstandings in the implementation of investment activities.*

*Traditional Russian understanding of investment corresponds to the concept of capital expenditures or investments in fixed assets. As a result of budget investments, according to the budget legislation, the cost of public property necessarily increases. Such investments are budget expenditures*

---

☆This chapter covers the budget investments, which can be understood both as a type of budget expenses and as a procedure of transformation of budget funds to public property. At the same time, budget and public property are parts of the state (municipal) treasury. This chapter raises an issue of no account taken of future benefits when exercising budget investments.

---

The Spread of Financial Sophistication Through Emerging Markets Worldwide
Research in Finance, Volume 32, 257–267
Copyright © 2016 by Emerald Group Publishing Limited
All rights of reproduction in any form reserved
ISSN: 0196-3821/doi:10.1108/S0196-382120160000032011

*for the creation (or purchase) of new capital assets. In this case, the budget investments are like a synonym for capital expenditures.*

*A new approach to the concept of cost of investments is linked to perception and rethinking of the concept of investment prevailing in the countries of Western Europe and North America. Under this approach, investments are understood as a commercial activity of the foreign investors, which consist of investing their funds in an unlimited range of objects of entrepreneurial activity in the territory of Russia. This approach is also embodied by the legislation of the Russian Federation.*

*However, in the second (not traditional for Russia) meaning, investment are carried out at the budget execution. These are, for example, assets of sovereign wealth funds of the Russian Federation, which are called the Reserve Fund and National Welfare Fund. These funds are formed by part of the revenues associated with oil production in the case of it exceeding its cost base per barrel, and the free assets of these funds are located in certain foreign currencies and securities.*

**Keywords:** Budget; investments; budget expenses; public and municipal property; state and municipal treasury

According to the Russian legislation, budget investments refer to a type of budget expense allotted on the grounds of economic substance of a debit transaction.[1]

The legislation and doctrinal sources refer to different definitions for investment.[2] In the large sense of the word, investment is understood as all types of assets (funds) are put into economic activity with a view to obtaining an income.[3] One should distinguish the notions of investment and investment activity, which means the act of transformation of investment resources in investments.[4]

In economics, investment can be considered as a conscious renunciation to increase the current consumption in favor of a relatively large income in the future (or future saving of expenses), which will ensure larger total consumption.[5] In other words, investment is "a part of income for this period, which was not used for consumption."[6]

The sources of investments can be, first, savings and also borrowing and a variety of assets measurable in monetary terms. In connection with such a broad approach to investments, there is a notion of investing that is the act of putting the above-mentioned assets into objects of investments.[7] There are many definitions of investment[8] but all of them have the semantic meaning of the notion, which derives from Latin "invest" – to put something and what is more to put something with the expectation of obtaining a future worthwhile result. However, the other interpretations of this term are possible: from English "in vest" or (in most translations) from English "investments."[9]

The last meaning (investments) is historically the first for the Russian reality. O. A. Akopyan notes that before 1991 "when the domestic investment legislation began its forming, the notion of 'investment' was subordinated to the notion of 'capital investment.'"[10] Initially, "investment," "capital investments," and "fixed assets" were used in legal and economic literature, and regulatory normative acts as very close in meaning, as different sides of the same event.

Today "capital investment" can be considered as a form of investment activities when an object of investment is fixed assets. In international relations, the cross-border investment is a special event and an object of special regulation.[11] This state of affairs is fixed in the domestic legislation. The RSFSR law dated June 26, 1991 No. 1488-I "On Investment Activity in RSFSR"[12] was actually transformed into two laws, which determine two different approaches to the notion of investment. The Federal Law dated February 25, 1999 No. 39-FZ "On Investment Activity in the Russian Federation in the Form of Capital Investments"[13] refers, as appears from its title, to the investment in the form of *capital investment* that is fixed asset investment. The Federal Law dated July 9, 1999 No. 160-FZ "On Foreign Investments in the Russian Federation"[14] regulates the commercial activity of foreign investors, which consists in putting money into *unlimited number of objects of entrepreneurial activity* in the territory of the Russian Federation.

The last approach to investments is determined in the other regulatory legal acts. For example, the Federal Law dated November 28, 2011 No. 335-FZ "On Investment Partnership"[15] and the Federal Law dated November 29, 2001 No. 156-FZ "On Investment Funds"[16] clearly determine securities as a possible object of investment, including for foreign issuers. Such investment cannot be determined as capital investment.

Consequently, the notion of investment is diverse, and depends on in which form of investments there are (only expenses, that is money or any other property and non-property assets) and what object the investment activity is directed for (for capital investment or acquisition of unlimited number of assets).

The budget legal relations reflect both above-mentioned approaches to investment. First, certain budget expenses for capital investment are directly determined as budget investments. Second, budget funds can be invested in different assets. In that case, we have dealings with sovereign funds, which are the Reserve Fund and the National Welfare Fund (Articles 96.9–96.11 of the Budget Code of the Russian Federation). These funds are formed owing to a part of budget income; their funds are placed in foreign currency and financial assets. Placement of sovereign funds is made in order to save it and to obtain an income that is, in actual fact, a type of investment, which is provided, for example, by the Federal Law "On Investment Funds." The Federal Treasury carries out the similar activity while managing the rest of money on a single budget account (BCRF Article 166.1). This activity, however, is not determined as investment, and the act of putting temporarily available budget funds into financial assets is not determined as investments.

Then we consider in detail the contents of budget investments according to the budget legislation based on the legal definition. Budget investments distinctly differ from other investments, first, in a source and a form of investments, and, second, in an object of investment. Most training courses do not even consider budget investments as a type of investments.[17] In such training courses, the notion of investment is essentially related to management of multiple assets acquired in the equity and financial derivatives markets. The specifics of budget investments become clear after analysis of their definitions.

The Budget Code of the Russian Federation (hereinafter referred to as BCRF) determines that the budget investments are budget funds allotted to create or to increase, owing to budget funds, the cost of public (municipal) property (BCRF Article 6). Thus, an object of budget investments practically always is fixed assets,[18] and money allotted from the budget stands as investment. At the same time, the legislator does not hint that the target of budget investments is a future benefit (income, profit, or saving). This (absent of future benefit) distinguishes fundamentally the notion of budget investments from the economic notion of investment in commerce.

The legal notion of budget investments refers to that its target direction is *public (municipal) property cost increase*. In other words, increment of a property part of the treasury is carried owing to decrease of its monetary part (budget). We can say, in general, that under the definition, budget investment is one of procedures of treasury transformation.

The notion of property and monetary parts of the treasure shall be considered in detail. According to clause 4 of Article 214 and clause 4 of

Article 215 of the Civil Code of the Russian Federation (hereinafter referred to as CCRF), the state (municipal) treasury consists of funds of appropriate budget and other public (municipal) property not secured to public enterprises and institutions. This implies that the state (municipal) treasury can be divided into two parts: either budget and undistributed property, or monetary and nonmonetary parts.

The truth is that nonmonetary part of the treasure consists of all public property (i.e., property referred to public or municipal property). The notion of "undistributed property" introduced to the Civil Code of the Russian Federation has rather practical task to separate registered and distributed public property from other public property. The Civil Code of the Russian Federation only regulates certain legal relations regarding a legal status of participants of civil commerce.[19] At the same time, the relations, developed with regard to public assets or public property, are not always characterized by equality, autonomy of will and property autonomy of their participants.

Beyond the civil law, the relations are regulated by land, forest, water, environmental, budget, public material reserve, mineral resources, precious metals and precious stones, wildlife, fishery and water biological resources, cultivated biological resources, continental shelf, cultural heritage objects legislation, etc. The above-mentioned list of public relations connected with the treasury is not secret as technical development and other global processes offer new objects to be putted into circulation. Thus, after adoption of the United Nations Framework Convention on Climate Change 1992,[20] the greenhouse gas and precursor quotas appeared. The development of biotechnologies raises an issue of preservation and protection of gene pool of not only agricultural cultures but also a human (nation). Success in research and use of outer space can eventually raise an issue on ownership of space bodies.[21] Development of the private law necessitated the evaluation of good name and reputation.[22]

The term *"undistributed property"* used in the Civil Code of the Russian Federation can have different meanings. Actually, "undistributed" implies a certain state as the same property can transfer from undistributed property to distributed property (and vice versa when it is possible). Division of public property for undistributed and other (distributed) is very conditional, and does not meet the requirement of legal certainty as there is its transient state, and it is difficult to establish a border, beyond which a thing acquiring a particular status ceases to be undistributed or distributed, or withdraws the treasury. It is not clear, whether withdrawal from the treasury means its automatic exclusion from public property.

Thus, the treasury consists of the following parts: undistributed public property, distributed (or registered) public property,[23] and budget of appropriate public and legal unit. In other words, *the treasury is public property and budget funds.*[24]

The analysis of notion and treasury structure has become necessary to make clear a role of budget investments in treasury transformation.

The budget investment is a type of budget expenses, whereby the transfer of budget investments decreases the monetary part of the treasury. At the same time, based on its determination, the budget investments finish by increasing nonmonetary part of the treasury that is public property (it is mentioned above that there is of no importance whether the property is distributed or not). Consequently, the budget investment is a procedure of internal treasury transformation, while a proportion of its monetary and nonmonetary parts changes.[25]

To cover in detail the content of budget investments it is expedient to examine in brief their classification and registration according to the budget legislation.

First, as it is mentioned above, the budget investments are budget expenses that are "money paid out of budget" according to BCRF Article 6. Real estate investments and long-term investments refer to capital expenses. According to the Budget Code of the Russian Federation (Articles 21, 79), subgroups "Budget Investments" and "Budget Investments in Other Legal Entities" are included in group "Capital Investments in Object of Public (Municipal) Property" of the Unified Classification of Budget Expenses in the Budget System of the Russian Federation. In addition, there are investments at the expense of the Investment Fund of the Russian Federation made in the framework of public-private partnership (BCRF Articles 69, 69[1], 79, 80).

Budget investments in objects of public or municipal property according to the list of codes of the budget expenses classification are capital investment in real estate objects of public (municipal) property (code of expense group 400)[26] of the following types:

- budget investments in acquiring real estate objects of federal property in the state defense order (type of expenses 410);
- budget investments in acquiring real estate objects of public (municipal) property (type of expenses 412);
- budget investments in capital construction objects in the state defense order (type of expenses 413);

- budget investments in capital constructions objects of public (municipal) property (type of expenses 414); and
- budget investments according to the concession agreements (type of expenses 415).

That is to say that depending on object, we can distinguish budget investments into public (municipal) property aimed to increase the existing objects of the public (municipal) property and budget investments aimed to create (to acquire) new objects. In this and in another case, the budget investments are specially considered in the sphere of state defense order.[27]

The newly acquired (created) objects at the expense of budget investments can be transferred based on operational management or economic control of the public (municipal) institutions and unitary enterprises or included in general undistributed treasury.

The budget investments from the federal budget are allotted for more than RUB 1.5 billion rubles to the federal foreign institutions and unitary enterprises regardless of the cost, which are decided upon in the form of normative legal acts of the Government of the Russian Federation. A decision concerning other budget investments is made in the form of legal acts of the principal administrators of budget funds (BCRF Article 79).

In budget accounting, budget investments are distinguished as follows: budget investments planned to be submitted to the legal entities are approved as a separate *appendix to a law (decision) on budget*, which specifies the recipients, volumes, and targets of allotted budget (BCRF Article 80). Capital budget investment (other budget investments are not provided by the legislation) allotted from the federal budget are included into *the federal target investment program* (BCRF Article 179.1), which is also an appendix to the Federal Law on federal budget.

There is a clear specific feature for all budget investments including for those, which are targeted to legal entities not being public (municipal) institutions or unitary enterprises. This lies in the fact that provision of investment entails *public cost increase* or *creation of public or municipal property right* by equivalent part of authorized (share) capitals of legal entities, which are recipients of budget investments.

This feature of budget investments calls into doubt the legitimacy of their referring to the budget expenses. It is obvious that payments from the budget in the form of investments shall be accompanied by the receipt (increase) of non-financial assets.[28] Thus, in terms of the government finance statistics (GFS), the budget investments are not net expenses.[29]

The result of budget execution, in terms of the GFS, will be expressed in net assets (NA), which are the sum of changes in non-financial assets (NFA) and financial assets (FA) minus changes in liabilities (L).[30] These data should be included in the balance of budget execution, which is a part of budget reports for the budgets in the budget system of the Russian Federation (BCRF Article 264.1).

However, the balance of budget execution is not a principal document of budget reports. A final report of budget execution, which is approved by a competent authority, includes data on expenses, incomes, and sources of budget deficit financing (BCRF Article 264.1). According to the current rules of budget accounting and reporting, the NFA including those obtained owing to budget investments remain beyond a budget balance and do not affect a final report of its execution, which is a result of cash flow of funds. This situation leaves unanswered the inevitable question: *how adequate is public property increase made by budget investments (expenses)?*

The goal of investment result measurement is not easy. If we remember that the main economic criterion of investment is a future income or saving, then we need to introduce this result in reports. That is, the result of budget investments should be no increase of public property (nonmonetary part of the treasury) but *a future benefit.*[31] The current legislation does not establish a mechanism that would allow seeing the future benefits from budget investments.

## NOTES

1. For more details about classification of budget expenses, see Komyagin (2014).

2. RSFSR Law dated June 26, 1991 No. 1488-I "On Investment Activity in RSFSR" (*Journal of the RSFSR Supreme Soviet* 1991. No 29. Article 1005) determines investments as money, target bank deposits, interests, shares and other securities, technologies, machineries, equipment, credits, any other property or property rights, intellectual values invested in objects of entrepreneurial and other activities to obtain a profit (income) and to achieve a positive social effect. The Federal Law dated February 25, 1999 No. 39-FZ "On Investment Activity in the Russian Federation carried in the Form of Capital Investments" (RF Code of Laws. 1999. No. 9. Article 1096) determines investments as money, securities, other property including property rights, other rights having monetary value invested in objects of entrepreneurial and (or) other activity to obtain a profit (income) and (or) to achieve other worthwhile effect. One more definition: investments are expenses for

creation, expansion, reconstruction, and technical rearmament of fixed and working capital. See: Vakhrin (2002); Gushchin and Ovchinnikov (2009).

3. See Sharpe, Alexander, and Bailey (1998) and Gushchin and Ovchinnikov (2009) Op. cit.

4. See Gilmanov (2007).

5. Kovalev, Ivanov, and Lyalin (2014).

6. This definition formulated by J. Keynes (see Bogatyrev, 1992).

7. Askinadzi and Maksimova (2014).

8. The review of approaches to the notion of investment is given in Investments. Kovalev et al. (2014).

9. Tselovalnikova (2013).

10. Akopyan (2010).

11. Convention on the Settlement of Investment Disputes Between States and Nationals of Other States. Concluded in Washington on March 18, 1965. Access from ConsultantPlus.

12. Bulletin of the RSFSR Supreme Soviet. 1991. No. 29. Article 1005.

13. RF Code of Laws. 1999. No. 9. Article 1096.

14. RF Code of Laws. 1999. No. 28. Article 3493.

15. RF Code of Laws. 2011. No. 49 (Section 1) Article 7013.

16. RF Code of Laws. 2001. No. 49. Article 4562.

17. See, for example, Bodie, Marcus, and Kane (2013); Sharpe, Alexander, and Bailey (2014); Maksimova V. F. Op. cit.

18. The notion of capital is widely interpreted; capital investment herein refers to the act of investing in fixed assets.

19. CCRF Article 2.

20. RF Code of Laws No. 46, Article 5204. 1996.

21. It is necessary to note that today outer space is a territory of common use, which is open for free research by all states. Activity in space is referred in clause I, Article 71 of the Constitution of the Russian Federation, Law of the Russian Federation dated August 20, 1993 No. 5663-1 in vigor "On Space Activity," a number of international agreements are adopted with regard to principles governing the activities of states in the exploration and use of outer space, and international liability for damage caused by space objects, and activities of states on the Moon and other celestial bodies, etc.

22. It is referred, inter alia, to evaluation of intangible assets (goodwill), which is made according to the International Financial Reporting Standards enacted by the Order of the Ministry of Finance of Russia dated November 25, 2011 No. 160н, and to commercial use of the name of Russia and the Russian Federation and their derivatives, which use is regulated today by the decree of the Government of the Russian Federation dated February 3, 2010 No. 52 "On Approval of the Rules of inclusion in a trade name of a legal entity of the official name "Russian Federation" or "Russia" and their derivate, formerly regulated by the Law of the Russian Federation dated April 2, 1993 No. 4737-1 "On Fees for Use of the Names "Russia" and "Russian Federation" and derived words and phrases."

23. The draft of the federal law No. 47538-6 "On Amendments to Section One, Two, Three, Four of the Civil Code of the Russian Federation, and to Certain Legislative Acts of the Russian Federation" (version adopted by the State Duma at

the first reading on April 27, 2012) has referred to an article, according to which the public property secured to institutions and enterprises is a distributed treasury (this version has not been adopted).

24. More details see Komyagin (2014, Chapter 1).

25. The notion of "internal transformation" of the treasury arises in comparison of budget investments with other procedures, which represent "internal transformation." This is privatization (decrease in nonmonetary part of the treasury), nationalization (increase in the treasury). In reference to such large legal procedures as budget process and purchasing for public needs, they represent an internal transformation of the treasury exactly in case of exercise of budget investments.

26. Instruction for procedure of use of budget classification approved by the Order of Ministry of Finance of the Russian Federation dated July 1, 2013 No. 65н.

27. See also Article 12 of the Federal Law dated December 29, 2012 No. 275-FZ "On State Defense Order."

28. Code 300, according to the classification of operations of public management sector (BCRF Article 23.1).

29. IMF Government Finance Statistics Manual (2001).

30. That is, NA = NFA changes + NA changes − O changes.

31. In this context, the teleological criterion for investment differentiation proposed by O. A. Akopyan is justified: see Konyukhova (2010).

# ACKNOWLEDGMENT

This chapter (research Grant No. 15-01-0030) was supported by the National Research University − Higher School of Economics' Academic Fund Program in 2015−2016.

# REFERENCES

Akopyan, O. A. (2010). Capital investments legislation. *Russian Law Journal, 2*, 13−22.
Askinadzi, V. M., & Maksimova, V. F. (2014). *Investment* (321 pp.). Moscow: Urait.
Bodie, Z., Marcus, A. J., & Kane, A. (2013). *Investments*. McGraw-Hill Education.
Bogatyrev, A. G. (1992). *Investment law* (p. 8). Mascow: Eksmo.
Gilmanov, E. M. (2007). Investment activity of the state in budget expenses of the Russian Federation. *Financial Law, 10*, 64.
Gushchin, V. V., & Ovchinnikov, A. A. (2009). *Investment law* (p. 153). Moscow: Velby.
IMF Government Finance Statistics Manual. (2001). Washington. Retrieved from http://www.imf.org/external/pubs/ft/gfs/manual/rus/pdf/allr.pdf
Komyagin, D. L. (Ed.). (2014). Treasury and Budget. *Science* [Казна и бюджет / под ред. Д. Л. Комягина − М.: Наука] (pp. 203−218).
Konyukhova, T. V. (2010). Legal regulation of budget investments. *Russian Law Journal, 10*, 114−119.

Kovalev, V. V., Ivanov, V. V., & Lyalin, V. A. (Eds.). (2014a). *Investments. Textbook for Bachelors* (p. 9). Moscow: Dashkov and company.

Kovalev, V. V., Ivanov, V. V., & Lyalin, V. A. (Eds.). (2014b). *Textbook for bachelors* (pp. 20–22). Moscow: Dashkov and company.

Sharpe, W. F., Alexander, G. D., & Bailey, D. V. (1998). *Investments.*

Sharpe, W. F., Alexander, G. J., & Bailey, J. V. (2014). *Investments* (225 pp.). Moscow.

Tselovalnikova, I. Y. (2013). Legal regulation of investment activity: Monograph – M. Access from ConsultantPlus Information and Legal System.

Vakhrin, P. I. (2002). Investments. In Gushchin, V. V. & Ovchinnikov, A. A. (Eds.), *Investment Law* (p. 153). Moscow: Infra-M.

# SPECULATIVE BUBBLE ON THE MOROCCAN REAL ESTATE MARKET: IDENTIFICATION AND CYCLES

Firano Zakaria

## ABSTRACT

*This chapter presents several approaches for identifying and dating the speculative bubble on real estate market. Using the real estate price index (IPAI), statistical and structural approaches were combined in order to detect the existence of a bubble on the Moroccan real estate market. The results obtained affirm that the Moroccan real estate market experienced a speculative bubble during the period 2006–2008 explained mainly by the boom of credit during the same period. The use of the Markov switching model affirmed that the speculative bubble on Morocco is cyclic and consequently corroborates the critic formulated by Evans (1991) concerning the traditional approaches for the detection of financial bubbles. Thus, the analysis of the series of the bubble, extracted using the Kalman filter, affirms the existence of two regimes, namely an explosive regime and a normal regime. The first regime describes the periods of explosion of*

The Spread of Financial Sophistication Through Emerging Markets Worldwide
Research in Finance, Volume 32, 269–309
ISSN: 0196-3821/doi:10.1108/S0196-382120160000032012

*the bubble and lasts for about 9 quarters, while the second, lasting for 14 quarters, describes the periods of return to the average cycle.*

**Keywords:** Real estate bubble; market efficiency; financial stability; pricing; equilibrium

**JEL classifications:** G12; E44

# INTRODUCTION

For a long time the theory of efficiency was able to formulate relevant explanations with regard to the pricing of rates on financial markets. Indeed, the works by Bachelier (1900), Samuelson (1965), Fama, Fisher, Jensen, and Roll (1969), and Fama (1970) affirmed that prices often follow a random path, and any prediction of their future trajectories is impossible.

By adopting these doctrines, prices remain influenced only by exogenous factors in the market and which are of a fundamental nature. The efficiency paradigm stipulates that prices at a given moment incorporate all economic and financial information (public and private) likely to determine their future trends. From this point of view, the prices and the fundamental values coincide, and any skid of the intrinsic securities of prices is corrected by mechanisms of arbitration, speculation, and hedging.

The close relationship between prices and fundamental value constitutes the basic postulate of market efficiency theory, and it is very critical to take into consideration toward this relation of dependence (co-integration) calling into question several fundamental aspects (rationality, transitivity, and atomicity) of the market pricing of the capital.

However, the market evolutions and the regular supervening of the financial and real crises called into question the assumption of market efficiency. Financial asset prices often have the attitude to deviate compared to the fundamental value under the negotiable instrument of several endogenous factors in the market. Keynes (1936) was the first to recognize that the actors of the markets tend to have a behavior instead of adopting a rational attitude (the example of mode competition).

Admittedly, capital markets have known several speculative bubbles which have brought prices back to euphoric levels; however, the whole of the economic theories continue to believe in the relevance of the assumption of efficiency and in the objectivity of the fundamental value. Although the prices are disconnected compared to the fundamental value, the markets tend to correct and bring back the prices to their rational level.

In the same way, the actors on the capital market, by giving more interest and weight to variables other than those which are fundamental, contribute to the formation of a difference between the financial price and their fundamental values, thereby contributing to the birth of a speculative bubble.

The theory of speculative bubbles was developed in response to criticisms formulated against the paradigm of efficiency. Indeed, in the capital market, there can be a multiplicity of equilibrium and it is not that a single equilibrium describes the fundamental value. Thus, the definition of the prices on the markets includes, in addition to the fundamental value, another component related to the anticipation of the future prices.

In theory, there exist several forms of speculative bubbles of which most important are those of rational, intrinsic, and irrational. The first family is known as rational, since it continues to adhere to the assumption of rational anticipation, according to which, the solution of the differential equation of the prices (Euler equation) admits a solution more general than that of the fundamental value (in the presence of the assumption of transitivity). The second intrinsic family of bubble is founded on the assumption that the movements of euphoria result from the anticipations of future prices based on fundamental and exogenous indicators in the market. On the other hand, the irrational bubbles are founded on the possibility of rejecting the rationality and the objectivity of the fundamental value.

Real estate markets are frequently affected by speculative bubbles following the example of financial markets. The real estates are the subject of purchase and sale by taking account of anticipations of the agents. For this reason, the price determination on the market of the real estate is the fundamental question which also worries the actors of the market as the public authorities because of the impact of this market on economic development and financial stability. The fall of prices on real estate markets has fatal consequences on the economy and, in particular, on the value of the balance sheets of various economic agents. Indeed, the fall of the real asset prices generates a fall of financial asset prices in the whole of markets, with a deceleration of growth and a loss of confidence resulting in a significant decrease returned to the sectors in connection with the real sector.

The international financial crisis showed that the models of economic growth deteriorated with the real estate sector tending to suffer from a great brittleness because of the strong correlation, which can exist between the price level on the real estate market and the economic growth prospects.

In this direction and because of the importance of the real estate sector in Morocco, this study is interested in the analysis of the trend of real estate price and the checking the assumption, according to which, there can be a speculative bubble on the real estate market in Morocco. For this reason, this chapter proposes to use several approaches to detect speculative bubbles by using the real price indexes and rents.

The rest of this chapter is organized in the following way: the next section presents a literature review of the notion of speculative bubbles. Then, a presentation of empirical work is considered. The fourth and the fifth sections evaluate, according to two approaches, structural and nonstructural, the presence of speculative bubbles. Finally, the last section analyzes the cycle of speculative bubbles in order to detect the phases of explosion and deflation of the bubbles on the Moroccan real estate market.

## LITERATURE REVIEW

The theory of speculative bubbles was often referred to in academic debates concerning the market pricing of capital and, in particular, financial markets and real estate markets. A broad consensus was established on the fact that the prices often tend to deviate compared to their fundamental value, giving more reason for the existence of speculative bubbles. The modern theory of finance rejects this assumption of existence of skid of the prices of their fundamental value, by stating clearly that financial markets are efficient and that the given price is an arbitrated price.[1]

The efficiency theory was built on the fact that the prices are always efficient and their formation is purely exogenous. For this purpose, the fluctuations of asset prices are given through the developments of a fundamental macroeconomic. Thus, on the econometric plan, the difference between the price and the fundamental value in a financial credit must be a white noise whose expectation is null. In practice, the majority of empirical work on the efficiency of the market remain unable to validate with relevance the assumption of efficiency (strong, weak, and semi strong) letting it to prevail that the prices can be disconnected compared to the fundamental aggregates.

Although the market efficiency remains in the paradigm dominating in modern finance, several works were concerned with the formation of the speculative bubbles in order to describe, obviously, the development of the asset prices. Famous stock exchange crash landings also propelled this research orientation, one quotes as example: crash in prices of tulip mania between 1631 and 1634 in the Netherlands, Mississippi bubble[2] (1719–1720), the deflation of the prices during the crisis of 1929, the collapse of bubble Internet in 2001, and the crash in 2008 (subprime).

These episodes of financial crises, initiated by the appearance of speculative bubbles, gave rise to several economic and financial theories capable to formulate answers concerning the causes of birth of the financial euphorias. The most important contributions on the matter are those of Fisher (1932), Keynes (1936), Kindleberger (1978), and Minsky (1957). These authors advance that the business cycle is at the origin of the formation of the speculative bubbles and they are the strategies of innovation and massive debt which support the emergence of speculative bubbles. To the contrary, other authors allotted this formation of the bubbles to the intrinsic behaviors, and sometimes irrational, of the economic and financial agents and with the nature even of the structure institutional, which coordinate the activities of financing of the economy (see Davis, 1997).

The speculative bubbles, creation of the facts and realities of the markets, were defined according to several disciplinary approaches. For the historian Kindleberger (1978) the bubbles are upward movements constant of the asset prices, while the economists consider that the bubbles refer to the asset prices which exceed the fundamental value since the investors always believe that they can resell their assets at higher prices (Barlevy, 2007; Brunnermeier, 2009; Diba & Grossman, 1988; West, 1987). On the same register, Garber (2000, p. 4) definite a speculative bubble as being the party of the curve of the prices which cannot be explained by the fundamental ones of the economy.

The bubbles thus come from an economic reality, and an official report in relation to the indetermination of the solutions in the models of rational anticipation whose usual form in the case of the asset prices is the Euler equation. Indeed, this equation indicates that the price of today is relative so that we will be able to obtain in the future in terms of output and also in terms of appreciation (resulting from the resale prices). The indetermination of this solution is related to the existence of resale price which can accept several securities (solution) and which also depends on other future prices. Therefore, there exists an infinity of solutions for the Euler equation in the event of imposition of a condition of transversality, according to which the price at the infinite horizon tends toward 0.

The abolition of the condition of transversality makes it possible to include another solution to the Euler equation. Indeed, the inclusion of a possibility of resale of the assets necessarily implies that the price can deviate from its fundamental value, according to the following design:

$$P_t = \delta(E_t P_{t+1} + ED_{t+1}) \text{ ``Equation Euler''} \qquad (1)$$

where $\delta = 1/(1 + x)$ and $x$ is the discount rate.

If we adopt the fundamental design of the evaluation of the asset prices with rational anticipations (Muth, 1961), and by accepting the condition of transversality,[3] then the fundamental value is regarded as being the single solution to the problem of valorization of the asset prices:

$$P_t^* = \sum_{i=1}^{n} \delta^i \text{ED}_{t+i} \tag{2}$$

where $P_t^*$ is the fundamental value.

In practice, the prices tend to deviate compared to their intrinsic value, letting us to predict the existence of a component other than that of fundamental. This party of the prices is often called the speculative bubble. While referring with the basic Euler equation which determines the price of a financial credit, we can easily conclude that the price of assets on date $- T -$ depends on two components, which arise from two types of anticipations rational, namely a component relating to the amount of the outputs and which is closely related to the fundamental and economic factors. This first component is exogenous compared to the market and is influenced by no feature of the market. In addition, the second component is in relation to the prices of exit or resale on a later date, that is, relating to anticipations of the future prices by the various investors. It is indeed about an endogenous component in the market. For this reason, another component intervenes in the price determination to know the speculative bubble $B_t$. In this direction we can write that

$$P_t = \sum_{i=1}^{n} \delta^i \text{ED}_{t+i} + B_t \tag{3}$$

On the basis of this analysis the fundamental value constitutes only one specific solution to the Euler equation; the second party of the solution is resulting from the suppression of the assumption of transversality and makes it possible to converge toward a more general solution. This additional solution should lead to the emergence or the acceptance of a speculative bubble. However, for the reason that this solution is in conformity with the assumption of rational anticipation and that it is also accepted and allowed by the whole of the economic agents, it is necessary that this solution is rational and independent of the endogenous behaviors of the market. On the theoretical plan and for the reason that the difference between the price and the fundamental value is rational (rational bubble),

it is necessary that Eq. (3), that is to say a single and sufficient solution to the Euler Eq. (1).
We accept that

$$E_t P_{t+1} = E_t \left[ \delta E_{t+1} D_{t+2} + \delta^2 E_{t+2} D_{t+3} + \cdots + B_{t+1} \right] \qquad (4)$$

If we use the iterative expectation law, we can write the following form:

$$E_t P_{t+1} = \delta E_t D_{t+2} + \delta^2 E_t D_{t+3} + \cdots + E_t B_{t+1} \qquad (5)$$

While replacing $E_t P_{t+1}$ in the Euler equation, then we obtain

$$\delta(E_t P_{t+1} + ED_{t+1}) = \delta ED_{t+1} + \delta^2 E_t D_{t+2} + \delta^3 E_t D_{t+3} + \cdots + \delta E_t B_{t+1} \qquad (6)$$

Then

$$P_t = \delta(E_t P_{t+1} + ED_{t+1}) = P_t^* + \delta E_t B_{t+1} \qquad (7)$$

According to this formulation, it arises that the solution with speculative bubble (rational) is a solution to the Euler equation and represents a more general solution in absence of condition of transversality. The deviation in the prices compared to their fundamental value is thus rational and always adheres to the assumptions of rational anticipation and objectivity of the economic model.[4] However, for the reason that the solution with the component is single, it is necessary that the equation above is in equivalence with the formula of Euler (1). For this purpose, it is necessary that the bubble follows a martingale process, according to which the prediction of the future value of this martingale is its present value. On this register we propose the following definition of rational bubble:

$$E_t B_{t+1} = \frac{B_t}{\delta} = (1 + x)B_t \qquad (8)$$

According to this formulation, the solution of the Euler equation is single and includes, in addition to, the basic components (dividends or rents) and other components related to the future trajectories of the prices. From this point of view, the investors are not only satisfied any more to only formulate anticipations on the future outputs but also on the future prices; they thus contribute to increase the bubble in a rational way while being based on self-fulfilling prophecy[5] of future price. By adopting anticipations on the trajectory of the prices, the participants on the market continue to accept a fair game which supports informational efficiency. In other words, the prices include anticipations of the outputs and the future prices; therefore, the probability of generating important gains is almost impossible.

It should also be noted that the fact of considering that $(1 + x)$ is higher than 1 makes it possible to consider that the bubble is always ascending and consequently, we draw aside the possibility of having negative speculative bubbles indicating the possibility of having negative prices $\lim_{n \to \infty} E(B_{t+n}) = +\infty$ and thus it is noted that $B_t > 0$.[6]

The first generation of rational bubble models only accept their explosive characters and do not integrate the possibility of their deflation (deterministic bubbles). However, Blanchard (1979) and Blanchard and Watson (1982) develop this definition of rational bubble by admitting that the bubbles can burst according to a given probability. Indeed, he proposes to integrate a probability of crash landing into the level of the definition of the process martingale generator of the bubble, by adopting the following equation:

$$
\begin{cases}
B_{t+1} = B_t \left( \dfrac{1 + x}{\pi} \right) & \text{with probability } \pi \\[2ex]
B_{t+1} = 0 \, (1 - \pi)
\end{cases}
\tag{9}
$$

Under the probability $\pi$ the bubble continues its bullish tendency, while in some case reverses the bubble to burst so that the asset price is equalized with its fundamental value. According to this definition the speculative bubble is to characterize by a sustained high growth during the periods of rise of the prices, while in case of inversion of the prices the bubble becomes null. Thus, the bubbles can appear and disappear during the formation process of the prices. In this direction, the prices can only increase under the negotiable instrument of the bubbles, but in the event of their absence they are equalized with the fundamental value.

However, the nature of the bubbles on the markets of the capital is different from the model of Blanchard and Watson (1982). Indeed, the bubbles can be periodic with several regimes whose value can't be zero. During the first phase the bubble is constituted and continuous to grow until it reaches a certain threshold, to enter the second phase during which it increases, at faster intervals, where it deflates to be stabilized on an average level equal to the discount rate $x$ (see Evans, 1991).

# EMPIRICAL STUDIES

Empirical work concerning the speculative bubbles started to submerge with large scales for setting up of analytical operative paragraphs able to distinguish the fundamental developments from the prices of those in relation to the formation from the speculative bubbles. Several empirical approaches were developed of which most important will be thereafter detailed.

The tests of the variance are the oldest tests as regards detection of the speculative bubbles. This approach was initiated by Shiller (1979, 1981) and is based on the fact that the financial asset price must be always in agreement with the fundamental value explained by the current value of the sum of the outputs. For this purpose, these tests were conceived to manage to check the assumption of informational efficiency; however, their use was enlarged to make it possible to detect the speculative bubbles. The principal idea of the method is to examine the relation which can exist between the development of the variance of the prices and the variance of the outputs of assets (approximation of the fundamental value). According to Shiller (1981) the generated error of the difference between the price and the fundamental value must not be correlated with the fundamental value and must be also equal to 0. In this direction, the volatility of the prices must entirely result from the volatility of the value intrinsic to the economy or lower. The volatility of the prices, more important than that of the fundamental value, can induce the existence of factors other than those of fundamental intervening in the market pricing.

On the level empirical, and seeing the difficulty in defining the fundamental price, Shiller (1981) considered that the price trend is an approximation of the fundamental value and that discount rate is constant. The results obtained by the author on the series of SP500 of 1871−1979 affirm that the prices are equipped with volatility largely higher than that of the dividends, then one can confirm the existence of speculative bubbles. LeRoy and Porter (1981) developed a similar approach by using the profitability of the assets and they managed to corroborate the results already forwarded by Shiller (1981).

The approach of West (1987) is different from that of Shiller (1981), in the direction where it is based on the checking of two assumptions to know: $H0$, according to which the courses of action are fixed by a model adhering to the assumption of efficiency of the markets, while $H1$ indicates that the prices, in addition to the basic component, are composed of a speculative bubble. The step of the author is thus based on the comparison of two types of models. The test thus suggested rests on three stages: the first consists of estimating the fundamental value by using the hoped securities of the returns on assets (dividends) by using an estimate using instrumental variables. In the second place, the author uses an estimate ARIMA to describe the generating process of the dividends (or rents). Lastly, the last model describes the relation between the real prices and the outputs. Resulting from these three stages, a test of comparison of the coefficients obtained is used to compare the results obtained.

The results obtained on market indexes SP500 (1871–1980) and the index Dow-Jones (1928–1978) made it possible to reject the null assumption of absence of bubble. Dezhbakhsh and Demirguc-Kunt (1990) uses the same step as recommended by West (1987) on very small samples and manages to conclude that it is difficult to affirm the conclusion of West (existence of bubbles) on similar samples.

For Diba and Grossman (1988) detection, speculative bubbles, is carried out by means of the analysis of the stationary properties of the asset prices and their principal fundamental ones; it is indeed a question of examining the assumption of co-integration of the two series. Thus, if the series of the dividends are not stationary and are integrated of order 1, the price on the market must also be integrated of the same order, under the assumption of speculative inexistence of bubbles. In practice, the two authors used the test of Bhargava and the method of Engel-Granger to affirm or cancel the existence of speculative bubbles.[7]

Evans (1991) stresses in his work that the bubbles are supposed to appear and disappear throughout the formation process of the prices within the markets of the capital. Into this direction, it rejects the relevance of the tests of roots unit and also of co-integration in the detection of the periodic speculative bubbles of nature. The simulations used by the author affirm that when the bubbles appear on the markets, the stock exchange exchange rates do not seem to be more explosive than the dividends within the meaning of the unit tests of roots, which lets predict the weakness of these tests and leaves the problems of largely open detection of the bubbles.

Froot and Obstfeld (1991) forward a fundamental distinction between the rational bubbles and the intrinsic bubbles. The first results from the developments of exogenic macroeconomic factors, while the intrinsic bubbles are endogenous sources (factors related to the firms). The model that they forward is based on a nonlinear relation between the fundamental ones and the asset prices. This nonlinearity is the reason according to which a change of fundamental has an impact increased on the asset price, giving rise to speculative bubbles.

Donaldson and Kamstra (1996) built a nonlinear model ARMA-ARCH-ANN[8] to provide for growth rates of the dividends, thereby allowing to obtain an approximation of the fundamental value. By approaching the fundamental value simulated with the real prices, they could not reject the assumption of existence of bubble.

Koustas and Serletis (2005) used a fractional modeling using the average autoregression models mobile fractional integrated (ARFIMA) to test the presence of bubbles. The results obtained using the traditional procedure of the tests of roots unit and that of fractional integration made it possible to reject the assumption of absence of bubbles on the studied markets.

Work of Wu (1995, 1997) forwards a step more innovating as regards detection of the speculative bubbles. The basic principle of the step suggested is to consider that the rational bubbles are a deviation compared to the fundamental value. On the basis of the formula of Campbell and Shiller (1988), the author proposes to express the variation of the real prices according to the sum of two components, namely variation of the dividends and variation of the rational bubbles. By taking account of the fact that the bubbles are inobservable components of the price, the author proposes the use of filters of Kalman in order to quantify its development.

Van Norden and Vigfusson (1996, 1998) proposed to use the tests of regime change in Markovian model (Markov switching model) in order to detect the phases of explosion and deflation of the speculative bubbles according to the definition suggested by Kindleberger (1978). Indeed, they define two probable states, to check, first to be relative to a significant rise of the prices and the second indicates a deflation of the bubble and a return to the fundamental value.

Nael Al-Anaswah and Bernd Wilfling (2011) use a model of space state with chain of Markov to test the presence of bubbles. For this purpose, they used a model describing the current value of the financial assets and which is estimated via the filter of Kalman. Thereafter, the two authors think of two regimes by using the chain of Markov in order to detect the regimes (bull and bear) controlling the development of the speculative bubbles.

Phillips, Shi, and Yu (2011) propose a generalization of the test ADF (sup-ADF), which makes it possible to detect the bubbles on the markets of the capital. The implementation on index SP500 showed clearly that between the periods 1871 and 2010, several bubbles were identified. Yiu, Yu, and Jin (2013) forward an implementation of the method suggested by Phillips, Shi and Yu (2011) on the real estate market of Hong Kong. Their results confirm the presence of several positive bubbles on this market of which most important is that of 1997.

The examination of work on the speculative bubbles lets predict several approaches of detection of the speculative bubbles. The approach suggested in this chapter rests on two methods of identification of the bubbles on the Moroccan real estate market. The first method is based on direct and univariés tests in order to collect the statistical properties of the series of price and to deduce the presence from it or not from a bubble. This approach uses the unit tests of roots, stationarity and co-integration. The second method suggested rests on the structural use of model (Campbell & Shiller, 1988) defining the prices in two large components: a fundamental party and another relative to a bubble.

While taking as a starting point the work by Chung and Lee (1998), we choose to approximate the real asset price through the price index of the real assets (IPAI) available. The incomes generated by the detention of the real assets are the rents which the tenant in the event of use of the real estate pours and consequently, they are regarded as being the fundamental factors. In the absence of such statistics, allowing to describe the yield, we privilege the use of proxy rents by knowing the index of the rent which belongs to the components of consumer price index (IPC). For this purpose, the whole of the tests and the models which will be used to check the presence of bubbles on the Moroccan real estate market will be carried out by using these two indicators.

## STATISTICAL APPROACHES

The statistical tests were the first to be used to be able to cancel or affirm the existence of speculative bubble on the markets of the capital. These tests base on a fundamental idea, according to which, the two generating processes of the prices and the dividends must be co-integrated, in the event of absence of speculative bubble. Diba and Grossman (1988) were the first to implement this type of approach by suggesting the use of the tests of unit roots and the co-integration tests, in particular, augmented Dickey Fuller (ADF) test, the tests of Granger and Engel, and the test of Bhargava. Other recent approaches proposed to adopt new tests of unit roots allowing of stage the limits of the traditional tests. Indeed, the latter adopted the assumption of existence of deterministic bubbles answering the definition of Blanchard (1979) and Blanchard and Watson (1982), without having to claim that the bubbles can be characterized by several regimes. Thus, other statistics, taking account of the criticism of Evans (1991), were used; it acts in particular of those of Busetti and Taylor (2004) and of Phillips, Wu, and Yu (2011, 2012).

## First-Generation Tests

Diba and Grossman (1988) proposed to identify the speculative bubbles by using three statistical tests by knowing ADF test, the test of co-integration, and the test of Bhargava. In theory, they used the definition of the rational bubbles to describe the unobservable party of the asset prices, which is anything else only the difference between the real price and the fundamental value. The linear regression described according to the definition of the rational bubbles, between the prices and the fundamental ones (dividends or rent) makes it possible to identify yes or not one is in the presence of bubble. In other words, if the prices and the dividends (or rents) are co-integrated in the same order implies that the variation of the prices is largely faded with the variations of the intrinsic elements to the economy.

The procedure of test is based on the use of several statistics making it possible to validate the null assumption of nonexistence of bubble by indicating that the asset prices and the outputs are integrated in the same order. Indeed, if the prices and the outputs are not stationary in level and are in first difference, in this respect the assumption of nonexistence of bubble is checked.

The first test used is based on the statistics of the test of ADF which makes it possible to check the existence or not of unit root in the series in question (Table 1).

It arises according to the analysis of the statistics ADF in which the prices and the outputs are stationary of difference, while the series is in level post heterogeneous results. Indeed, the series of the prices is not stationary in level; on the other hand, the series of the outputs (rent) are stationary. On the basis of these results, it proves that for the first test the prices seem to be not co-integrated with the series of the outputs. For this purpose, the variations of the real asset prices cannot arrive from a volatility of the fundamental ones.

Diba and Grossman (1988) also propose to use the test of Bhargava (1986) to test the nature of the relation between the asset prices and the outputs which result from this. Indeed, if the prices are completely explained by the fundamental ones, from this point of view, the residues of the linear relation between the prices and the rents should be stationary. For this purpose, the test of Bhargava makes it possible to check this assumption directly (Table 2).

According to the statistical table of Wulf, Lee, and Schmidt (1994) and knowing that the number of observation is between 50 and 100 then $-1.56$

282                                                        FIRANO ZAKARIA

**Table 1.** Test ADF on the Series of the Prices and the Outputs.

| Series | ADF Probability | Lag Used in ADF |
|---|---|---|
| Log of outputs (LD) | 0.0006 | 9 |
| Log of the real asset prices (LP) | 0.9507 | 9 |
| D (LD) | 0.0006 | 9 |
| D (LP) | 0.0000 | 9 |

**Table 2.** Bhargava Test.

| Series | Bhargava Stat | Observation Number |
|---|---|---|
| LP-LD | −1.56 | 51 |

**Table 3.** Johansen Test.

| Assumption | Eigen Values | Statistical Test | Critical Value to 5% | Critical Probability |
|---|---|---|---|---|
| None | 0.20 | 13.65 | 15.49 | 0.09 |
| At most 1 | 0.05 | 2.78 | 3.84 | 0.09 |

The test of the trace indicates that the series is not co-integrated with the threshold of 5%.

**Table 4.** Granger Test.

| | Z-Statistic | Critical Probability |
|---|---|---|
| Log real prices | −7.147741 | 0.5323 |
| Log rent | −6.648238 | 0.5748 |

is largely higher than the critical points than 1%, −18.3, and −19.3. In this respect one can conclude that the linear combination between the real asset prices and the price of the rent is not stationary; it acts on a stationary series of difference.

To confirm this first intuition, we call upon a third test, suggested by the authors, of co-integration between the two variables. The tests of Johansen and Granger-Engel were used to check the existence of this relation (Tables 3 and 4).

According to the two tests of co-integration, it arises that the two series of the prices and the outputs are not co-integrated with the threshold of 5%, then it is difficult to reject the assumption of existence of bubble. Indeed, the long-term independence of the real asset prices compared with the index of the rent confirms that other components contribute to the explanation of the trend of prices on the Moroccan real estate market.

According to these results, one can note that the residue of the linear combination between the two aggregates, real asset prices, and the index of the rent, are not stationary, which lets us to predict the existence of a persistent gap on the level of the price index of the real assets which cannot be explained on the basis of the fundamental ones.

The approaches suggested by Diba and Grossman (1988) rest on tests of unit roots on the series of the asset prices and the series of the dividends (rents) to check the correspondence between the two variables and to affirm or cancel the existence of speculative bubble. This methodology rests indeed on the adoption of a step of co-integration. However, the criticism of Evans (1991) called in question, this approach is based on the tests of unit roots usually (in particular co-integration tests). Indeed, it has been proven that these tests do not make it possible to collect the case where the bubbles are formed and deflated on several occasions. Consecutive collapses of the bubbles complicate the possibility of detecting the existence of bubbles on the various markets of capital in an effective way.

## Second-Generation Tests

The tests of unit roots and the tests of co-integration thus do not make it possible to provide such a convincing analysis of the existence of speculative bubble on the markets of the capital. Indeed, these tests can be skewed if it is necessary to note that the series is characterized by a regime change according to which, it can vary between a stationary state in an explosive state. The speculative bubbles appear and disappear according to an unknown frequency, which gets a quasi-cyclic character whose usual tests of unit roots and co-integration are adapted.

Thus, in answer to the criticism of Evans (1991), other tests were developed in order to arrive at a better checking of the presence of speculative bubbles. Among these approaches, those proposed by Busetti and Taylor (2004), Phillips and Yu (2009) and Phillips, Wu, and Yu (2011, 2012), "PWY" seemed to be more relevant.

Busetti and Taylor (BT, 2004) propose statistics to test the assumption according to which a series is stationary compared to an alternative assumption which suggests that the series passes from a stationary regime to an integrate regime. The test is based on the calculation of the following statistics:

$$\text{sup-BT}(\tau_0) = \sup_{\tau \in [0, 1 - \tau_0]} \text{BT}_\tau \tag{10}$$

where

$$\mathrm{BT}_\tau = \frac{1}{s_0^2(T - \tau T)^2} \sum_{t=[\tau T]+1}^{T} (y_T - y_{t-1})^2 \tag{11}$$

And $s_0^2$ is an estimate of the variance over all the temporal period of the series there and $\tau$ is under interval chooses to work out the test.

The BT test (2004) provided results more or less similar to those obtained using the statistical tests previously used. Thus, one can reject with the threshold of 5% the assumption of stationary state of the series of the price index real estate to the detriment of the alternative assumption, according to which, the real asset prices forward to a stationary state in an explosive state (Table 5).

Phillips and Yu (2009) and PWY (2011, 2012) use a sup-ADF (SADF) according to which the usual ADF test is retorted on small fragments of the series in a sequential way, on several occasions, by prolonging each time the samples are used (windows). Then, and on the basis of the value superior exit of various simulations, a statistical test of inference is worked out to make it possible to check the existence or not of explosive behavior, thereby testifying the presence of bubble. They manage to confirm the power of their test compared to the other traditional tests like unit roots and co-integration[9] as regards checking of the presence of speculative bubbles.

Moreover, PWY (2012) proposes an improvement of their test to manage to detect several speculative bubbles by generalizing procedure SADF. Indeed, their new test makes it possible to provide a more suitable framework of analysis of the explosive behavior of the long series and to provide a more relevant appreciation of the various speculative bubbles which can emerge over one more or less-long period.

The new test suggested by PWY (2012) is called GSADF "generalization of sup-ADF." Based on the same principle as that of the SADF,

*Table 5.*  BT Test (2004).

| | |
|---|---|
| Log of price index of the real assets | 1.4858 |
| *Critical value* | |
| 90% | 0.5057 |
| 95% | 1.0153 |
| 99% | 5.9401 |

*Note*: The breaking values were obtained using simulation (5,000 iterations) on a sample of 51 observations and with an interval $\tau_0 = 0.1$.

the GSADF is conceived to be an overall and a more flexible device, as regards fixing of the initial points and in the determination of the windows to be tested. Thus these two tests make it possible to collect any explosive behavior in the series of the prices and to ensure a better amendment of the test the number of observation used (Fig. 1).

Statistical test SADF is based on the sequence of test ADF that is usually used to detect the existence of unit roots. If it is supposed that the sample of regression (ADF) starts from one moment $\tau_1$ and finishes at one final moment $\tau_2$, with $\tau_2 = \tau_1 + \tau w$, where $\tau w$ is the fraction of the sample used at the time of regression. In this case the number of observations used in the regression is $Tw = T^*\tau w$. The test is thus based on the repetition of test ADF on several temporal breaches $\tau w$ which starts starting from the starting point $\tau_1$ up to the point to arrive at $\tau_2$. Thus $\tau w$ is selected enters $\tau_0$ and 1 and $\tau_0$ is given in such a way that the estimate of test ADF is effective. These new statistics of ADF repeated are commonly called SADF and indicated as:

$$SADF = \sup\nolimits_{\tau w \in [\tau 0,1]} ADF_{\tau w} \qquad (12)$$

What one can write in the following asymptotic form:

$$SADF = \sup\nolimits_{\tau w \in [\tau 0,\,1]} \left\{ \frac{\tau w \left[ \int_0^{\tau w} W dW - 1/2\tau w \right] - \int_0^{\tau w} W dW(\tau w)}{\tau w^{1/2} \left[ \int_0^{\tau w} W^2 dr - \left[ \int W(\tau) d\tau \right]^2 \right]^{1/2}} \right\} \qquad (13)$$

under the assumption that $W$ is a stationary process (Fig. 2).

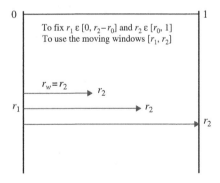

*Fig. 1.* SADF Test.

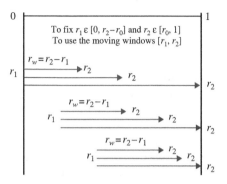

*Fig. 2.* GSADF Test.

Test GSADF is based on reproduction of test ADF on a sequence of small samples even broader than that deployed in test SADF. Indeed, the fact of changing the starting point of the test "$\tau 1$" is made so that it is there several windows on which one can carry out test ADF. From this point of view the GSADF is defined in the following form:

$$\text{GSADF}(r_0) = \sup_{\substack{r_2 \in [r0, 1] \\ r_1 \in [0, r_2 - r_0]}} \{\text{ADF}\} \qquad (14)$$

Another fundamental contribution of the authors is to set up tests of detection of the dates of formation of bubbles, by using recursive tests with SADF statistics. More precisely, the strategy consists of comparing statistics resulting from one canvassed recursive of statistics of SADF and GSADF (BSADF, BGSADF) with the breaking values of SADF, which makes it possible to detect the dates of formation of the bubbles or the start dates of the explosion of the variable.

Tests SADF and GSADF can be used to detect the existence of the speculative bubbles on the level of the series of the prices through replication on several, under sample of the series of test ADF in answer to the criticism formulated by Evans (1991). Authors PWY (2011, 2012) set up statistical tables which describe the breaking values of the two tests.

By implementing the two tests to the series of the prices and the rents, the results obtained are forwarded in Table 6.

The analysis of the results obtained affirm that the series of the real asset prices is explosive. Indeed, test GSADF is higher than the breaking values with the threshold of 1%, 5%, and 10%, which implies that the series east can be characterized by the existence of a speculative bubble.

***Table 6.*** SADF and GSADF Tests.

|  | SADF Test | GSADF Test |
|---|---|---|
| Log of real asset prices | 0.7058 | 2.6392 |
| Log of index of the rents | −1.2689 | 0.1204 |
| *Critical value* |  |  |
| 90% | 2.7879782 | 1.1915780 |
| 95% | 3.4615806 | 1.5360598 |
| 99% | 3.5906605 | 2.1555409 |

*Notes*: The whole of the tests were carried out on a sample of 51 observations with an interval $r_0 = 0.4$; the breaking values were obtained on the basis of 5,000 Monte Carlo simulation.

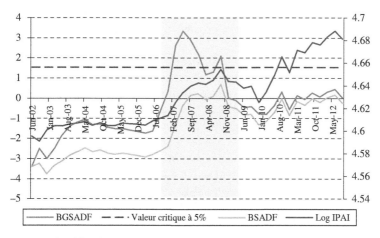

*Fig. 3.* Identification of the Boost Period of the Real Estate Prices Index.

In addition, with regard to the series of rent index, it arises according to the two tests that the H0 assumption cannot be rejected and consequently, the series indicates the presence of an explosive behavior making it possible to explain the explosion of the series of the real prices.

Using recursive test BGSADF developed by PWY (2012) we can provide an estimate of the date of formation of this bubble in Morocco. This is presented in Fig. 3.

According to the development of recursive test BGSADF we note that the value of the test largely exceeds the breaking value of test GSADF (1.53). Thus, we can affirm that there was a formation of bubble during the period going from December 2006 to March 2009.

288 FIRANO ZAKARIA

**Table 7.** Zivot and ADF Tests.

|  | Zivot–Andrews | Test of sup-DCF |
|---|---|---|
| Log of real asset prices | −4.64 (0.06) | 2.3486 (0.00) |
| *Critical value* |  |  |
| 90% | −5.57 | 1.5762 |
| 95% | −5.08 | 1.9327 |
| 99% | −4.82 | 2.2685 |

These results can be confirmed using the tests of change regime which makes it possible to detect the points of change of the tendencies of the time series. In this direction, one uses the test of Zivot–Andrews and the statistics of the Chow type implemented to test ADF (sup-DFC). The results to which one led make it possible to affirm the results of tests SADF and GSADF (Table 7).

By comparing the two tests with their breaking values, the assumption of absence of speculative bubbles is difficult to reject. In this direction, we can affirm that there is a deviation in the prices compared to their fundamental value. These last two tests also confirm that the explosion of the series of the asset prices intervened as from 2006 to corroborate the results of the preceding tests.

The use of the statistical tests of the first and the second generation affirms that the series of the real estate's price index is explosive and seems to be independent, and not cointegrate, of the developments of the rents. This conclusion can check the assumption according to which the trend of prices indicates the presence of a speculative bubble.

# STRUCTURAL APPROACH

The concept of speculative bubble is strictly related to the developments of the asset prices on the various financial markets. The asset prices are often higher than the fundamental value, thereby describing the presence of another source of pricing of the rates. Keynes (1933) mentioned this question of skid of the prices of fundamental while taking as a starting point its famous example about the contest of mode. In the facts, the speakers in the markets are not solely interested in the economic sizes in order to provide for the trajectories of the prices, but they also stick to anticipations car-directors of the other speakers as for the future trend of the asset prices.

The examination of the statistical properties of the series of the real asset prices and the series of the rents confirmed the presence of an explosive nature in the first series, thereby representing the formation of a speculative bubble lasting for the period 2006–2008. However, the statistical tests are limited only to the econometric properties of the analyzed series, without taking account of an economic design and a definition more structural of the speculative bubbles. For this purpose, other economic approaches (structural) were suggested in order to check the assumption of existence of bubble on the capital market in a relevant way.

### West Model

The central idea of West (1987) model is to test the assumption according to which the price is equal to the fundamental value, against the assumption that the price, in addition to the fundamental value, includes another component, which is the speculative bubble.

Let us note that:

$$S_t = P_t^f + B_t \text{ où } S_t = P_t^f \tag{15}$$

In the case of the West model, we note that the bubble $B_t$ is defined according to the model of Blanchard and Watson (1982) and that the discount factor is unknown and should be estimated. It also supposes that the dividends follow an autoregression process (AR $(P = 1)$).

$$D_t = \theta D_{t-1} + \varepsilon_t \text{ avec : } |\theta| < 0 \tag{16}$$

It is also known that according to the assumption of rational anticipation that, $\sum_{i=1}^{\infty} b^i D_{t+i} = \gamma D_t$ then we can write that $\gamma = b\theta/(1 - b\theta)$. If the asset price is equal to the fundamental value, then in this case:

$$S_t = P_t^f = \gamma D_t \tag{17}$$

According to this design, the West model thus proposes to estimate three Eqs. (1), (5), and (6). Eqs. (16) and (17) can be estimated with ordinary least square (OLS), while the first equation has a character of forward looking, which requires the adoption of an estimate with instrumental variables or by using the generalized method of moments (GMM).

In order to check the existence of bubble in the series of the asset prices, it is necessary to compare the two estimates, direct and indirect, of $\gamma$. In the event of divergence of the two estimators confirms that there exist other factors that those fundamental making it possible to explain the trend of prices.

The series used are relating to the price index of the assets and the index of the rents. The latter is an approximation of the real returns on assets. The step of West consists of initially estimating the process of the dividends using model ARIMA. For this purpose, a stepwise approach was used to obtain the optimal delays. The model obtained is the following:

$$\log(D_t) = 0.96^{(0.00)}\log(D_{t-1}) + 0.14^{(0.00)} \tag{18}$$

For the two other equations the estimate was carried out using the instrumental variables and the results obtained are presented in Table 8.

According to the estimates the discount factor is equal to 0.5, which is the rate required by the holders of the real asset neighbor the 50%. In other words, the purchasers of the real assets wait for an yield equal to 50% for each real assets, which is a more or less important rate. Concerning the factor $\gamma$ it was estimated using the instrumental variables and the value obtained is equal to 1.0007.

According to the specification of West (1987), we can determine $\gamma$ according to the following relation: $\gamma = b\theta/(1 - b\theta)$. The use of a test of Wald to compare the two estimates of $\gamma$ allows to obtain the following results (Table 9).

On the basis of result of the test of Wald, the coefficient $\gamma$ seems to be different for the two types of estimates. So we can affirm that the fundamental value do not determine only the formation of the asset prices. For this purpose, we can affirm that there exists a speculative bubble in the formation process of the real asset prices. Although the West model

**Table 8.**   Estimation of Eqs. (16) and (17).

|          | Coefficients | $t$-Statistic | Critical Probability |
|----------|--------------|---------------|----------------------|
| $b$      | 0.501667     | 2942.179      | 0.0000               |
| $\gamma$ | 1.007637     | 1638.173      | 0.0000               |

**Table 9.**   Wald Test $\hat{\gamma} = \frac{\hat{b}\hat{\theta}}{1-\hat{b}\hat{\theta}} = \gamma$.

| Statistical Test | Value    | Probability |
|------------------|----------|-------------|
| Chi-square       | 23.98319 | 0.0000      |

(1987) makes it possible to validate in a structural way the existence or not of a speculative bubble, it remains unable to quantify the development of it from where the recourse to innovating approaches adopting the Kalman filter.

### *Kalman Filer Approach*

A new approach presented by several authors is based on the use of the Kalman filter. Indeed, since the bubbles are unobservable components in the asset prices, Wu (1995) arrived at setting up a methodology to extract the bubble from the series of the asset prices.

On the basis of work Campbell and Shiller (1988) could develop the Euler equation under the assumption of constancy of the yields using Taylor development. A new linear representation of the prices can be considered:

$$P_t = c + \alpha P_{t+1} + (1 - \alpha)D_{t+1} - x_{t+1} \tag{19}$$

The analysis of this relevant relation emphasizes that the price of a financial credit is according to the outputs, which it can get following its detention and also on a future price level anticipated. Thus, the model of Campbell and Shiller (1988) makes it possible to obtain a general solution for the equilibrium prices of assets.

By retaining that the fundamental value of the financial assets is equal to:

$$P_t^f = \frac{(c - x)}{(1 - \alpha)} + (1 - \alpha) \sum_{i=0}^{n} \alpha^i E(D_{t+i}) \tag{20}$$

with
$$c = -\ln(\alpha) - (1 - \alpha)\left(\ln\left(\frac{1}{1+D/P}\right)\right) \text{ and } \alpha = \frac{1}{1+D/P}$$

On the basis of this definition of fundamental value, Campbell and Shiller (1988) propose to define the variation of the asset prices as being the variation of the two following components:

$$\Delta P_t = \Delta P_t^f + \Delta B_t \tag{21}$$

where $\Delta P_t^f$ is the variation of the fundamental value and $\Delta B_t$ is the variation of the speculative bubble.

In this case, the fluctuations in prices are described according to the following formulation:

$$\Delta P_t = (1 - \alpha) \sum_{i=0}^{n} \alpha^i E\left(D_{t+i} - D_{t+i-1}\right) + \Delta B_t \qquad (22)$$

According to work of Wu (1995, 1997), the first party of the equation above can be in relation to the developments of the hopes of output of the dividends and is approximated according to a process ARIMA ($H$, 1, 0) with drift. The author thus proposes to forward the variation of the dividends according to the following form:

$$\Delta d_t = u_t + \sum_{i=0}^{n} \delta_i \Delta d_{t-i} + \varepsilon_t \qquad (23)$$

with, $\varepsilon \to N\left(0, \sigma^2\right)$ and $u_t$ is the drift.

The resolution of the basic Euler equation is conditioned by the determination of the conditionally anticipated outputs, which is also not obvious. This problem known under the connotation "multiplicity equilibrium" was mentioned right now by a large number of theorists. Indeed, the existence of variables anticipated in the fundamental equilibrium equation complicates the possibility of estimating a value of balance of it, since there exists a possible infinity of solution.[10] In order to circumvent this constraint, Wu (1995) proposes to approach the securities anticipated in the equation of Campbell and Shiller (1988) by their last achievements and their securities. It is thus be noted that:

$$Y = AY_{t-1} + \eta \qquad (24)$$

where

$$y = \begin{pmatrix} \Delta d_t \\ \Delta d_{t-1} \\ . \\ . \\ . \\ \Delta d_{t-n} \end{pmatrix}, \eta = \begin{pmatrix} \varepsilon \\ 0 \\ . \\ . \\ . \\ 0 \end{pmatrix} \text{ et } A = \begin{bmatrix} \delta_1 & \cdots & \delta_n \\ \vdots & \ddots & \vdots \\ 0 & \cdots & 0 \end{bmatrix}$$

If it is considered that $g = (1, 0, 0, \ldots, 0)$, we can thus write that:

$$\Delta d_t = gY_t \tag{25}$$

In this direction, we can rewrite the value of the expected dividends in the following form:[11]

$$E_t(\Delta D_{t+i}) = gE_t Y_{t+i} = gA^i Y_t \tag{26}$$

If it is noted that $E_t(D_{t+i}) = E\left(D_t + \sum_{j=1}^{i} D_{t+j}\right)$ then:

$$E_t(D_{t+i}) = D_t + g\sum_{j=1}^{i} A^j Y_t \tag{27}$$

While replacing in the equation describing the variation of the prices, we thus obtain that:

$$\Delta P_t = (1-\alpha)\sum_{i=0}^{n} \alpha^i \left[ D_t + g\sum_{j=1}^{i} A^j Y_t - D_{t-1} - \sum_{j=1}^{i} gA^j Y_{t-1} \right] + \Delta B_t \tag{28}$$

In this direction we can finally write that:

$$\Delta P_t = \Delta D_t + \Delta Y_t + \Delta B_t \tag{29}$$

This relation thus makes it possible to collect the variations of the prices and explained by the means of the variations of the dividends and the variations of the bubbles. Wu (1995, 1997) proposes to model the variations of the prices by having recourse to the Kalman filter. The choice of this approach is based on impossibility to quantify the component $B_t$ since it remains unobservable while belonging to the curve of the prices.

The Kalman filter is a filter which makes it possible to estimate unobservable components using other measurable variables. If it is considered that "there" is an observable variable that depends on another unobservable variable "$X$" of which the variance $\sigma_x^2$ is unknown according to the following formulation:

$$\begin{cases} y = c(1) + c(2)x + \varepsilon \\ x_{t+1} = c(3) + c(4)x + \vartheta \end{cases} \tag{30}$$

where $C(.)$ are the parameters to be estimated, $\varepsilon(0, \nu_1)$ and $\vartheta(0, \nu_2)$ are the errors of the models. The first equation of the system is appointed the equation of measure, while the second is often the qualified equation of state or transition. The simulation of the unobservable variable passes by three fundamental stages.

The first stage consists of providing for the value of $X$ at the moment $(T-1)$ and its variance $\sigma_x^2$ while basing itself on the following presentation:

$$\begin{cases} x_{t|t-1} = c(3) + c(4)x_{t-1} \\ \sigma_{t|t-1}^2 = c(7) + c(4)^2 \sigma_{t|t-1}^2 \end{cases} \tag{31}$$

In the second stage and at the moment "$T$" we have information on the variable observed "there," then we can provide an estimate of $\varepsilon$.

$$\varepsilon = y - c(1) - c(2)x_{t|t-1} \tag{32}$$

The variance of the error is written in the form:

$$\nu 1 = c(2)^2 * \sigma_{t|t-1^2} \tag{33}$$

To estimate the securities of $X$ and variance we thus have recourse to the securities of $\varepsilon$ and of $\nu_1$. For this purpose, we can write that:

$$x_t = x_{t|t-1} + \frac{c(2) * \sigma_{t|t-1}^2 * \varepsilon}{\nu_1} \tag{34}$$

$$\sigma_t^2 = \sigma_{t|t-1}^2 + \frac{c(2)^2 * \sigma_{t|t-1}^2}{\nu_1} \tag{35}$$

They is two blue estimators consist and without skews, which minimize the conditional variance.

In the last stage, we use the method of maximum likelihood in order to estimate the parameters $C(.)$. The function of probability used is:

$$L = \frac{1}{2}\sum_t \log(v_1) - \frac{1}{2}\sum_t \frac{\varepsilon}{v_1} \tag{36}$$

The use of Kalman filter should make it possible to extract the component bubble, unobservable, of the series of the real asset prices, by taking account of the developments of the fundamental value. From this point of view, we consider the equation proposed by Wu (1995):

$$\Delta P_t = \Delta D_t + \Delta Y_t + \Delta B_t \tag{37}$$

where $\Delta P_t$ is the variation of the price index of the real assets; $\Delta D_t$ is the variation of the index of the rents (approximation of the real returns on assets); and $\Delta B_t$ is the variation of the speculative bubble.

In order to apply this approach, it is necessary to identify two equations of measure and two equations of transition or state:

The equations of measure, integrating the observable variables $P$ and $D$, are

$$\Delta P_t = \Delta D_t + \Delta Y_t + \Delta B_t \tag{38}$$

$$\Delta d_t = u_t + \sum_{i=0}^{n} \delta_i \Delta d_{t-i} + \varepsilon_t \tag{39}$$

The equations of transition are

$$Y = A Y_{t-1} + \eta \tag{40}$$

$$\Delta B_t = \gamma \Delta B_{t-1} + \mu \tag{41}$$

The estimates using[12] the maximum of probability are carried out over one period going from 2000 to 2012 in quarterly frequency. The variation of the price index of the assets can be negative, which also lets us to predict the possibility of having negative variations in the component bubble (Cagan, 1956). The series observed difference is first stationary and do not reveal any regime change (see preceding section).

The estimate of the equation by Wu (1995) using the Kalman filter provided the results according to Table 10.

The estimates gave more or less satisfactory results. Indeed, the two parameters $C(1)$ and $C(2)$, relating to the formation processes of the rents as $C(3)$ post consistent estimates.

Knowing that $C(3)$ represents the coefficient connecting the variation of the bubble compared to its last:

$$\Delta B_t = 0.699 * \Delta B_{t-1} \tag{42}$$

we can consider that:

$$B_t = 0.699 * \Delta B_{t-1} + B_{t-1} \tag{43}$$

where

$$B_t = 0.699 * B_{t-1} + B_{t-1} - B_{t-2} \tag{44}$$

$$B_t = 1.699 * B_{t-1} - B_{t-2} \tag{45}$$

If it is noted that the speculative bubble is characterized by a continuity in the belief in the rise and that the economic agents integrate this perception car director, then

$$B_t > B_{t-1} > B_{t-3} \cdots > B_{t-n}$$

**Table 10.** Kalman Filter Estimation.

| Coefficients | Value |
|---|---|
| $C(1)$ | 0.136075 (0.00) |
| $C(2)$ | 0.430003 (0.00) |
| $C(3)$ | 0.699998 (0.00) |
| State variables | |
| $\Delta D_t$ | 0.164742 (0.00) |
| $\Delta Y_t$ | 0.066667 (0.00) |
| $\Delta B_t$ | −0.736229 (0.00) |
| Log $L$ | −1676067 |

Note: Estimated using the maximum probability of 50,000 iterations.

which implies that the speculative bubble tends to increase during the periods of rise of the prices; however, in the event of deflation, it tends to drop to fall under an average regime.

Graphically, it appears that the fundamental party, which must, normally, mainly explain the pricing of the rates on the real estate market, seems to have a less important impact. By opposition, the component bubble largely explains the extreme movements of the real asset prices (Fig. 4).

It proves that the development of the price index of the real assets is impacted by the development of the rents in Morocco. Indeed, the component bubble explains best the developments and the variations of the real asset prices. ANOVA analysis makes it possible to confirm this official report (Table 11).

The test of the variance affirms that the volatility of the real index is resulting mainly from the component bubble and that the development of the rent in Morocco contributes marginally to the variations of the real prices.

The evolution of speculative bubble during 2000 and 2012 fact of arising several significant rises during two periods 2006–2008 and 2010–2012. Indeed the speculative bubble during the period 2009–2010 knew the east, can be explained by the negotiable instruments of the international financial crisis and its transmission with the Moroccan economy (Fig. 5).

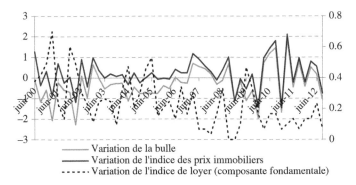

——— Variation de la bulle
——— Variation de l'indice des prix immobiliers
------ Variation de l'indice de loyer (composante fondamentale)

*Fig. 4.* Presentation of the Basic Components and Speculative of the Real Prices.

***Table 11.*** Source of the Variations of the Real Price Index.

|  | Bubble | Rent Index (Fundamental Component) |
| --- | --- | --- |
| ANOVA test | 9.32 (0.00) | 0.193 (0.66) |

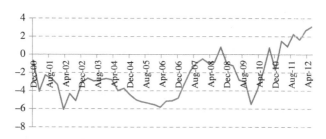

*Fig. 5.*  Development of the Bubble on the Moroccan Real Estate Market between
2000 and 2012.

Indeed, according to the formulation of Blanchard and Watson (1982),
we can note that the bubble on the Moroccan real estate market is
following form:

$$\begin{cases} B_{t+1} = B_t \left( \dfrac{1 + 0.5}{\pi} \right) + \mu_t & \text{with probability } \pi \\ B_{t+1} = \mu_t, \ (1 - \pi) \end{cases} \qquad (46)$$

where $\mu$ is the average tendency of long run and discount rate (capitalization) is of 50%. This bubble determined using the model of Wu (1995) is
also characterized by an important degree of persistence according to the
results obtained using the exhibitor of Hurst.

The exhibitor of Hurst "*H*" is a tool that allows to measure the persistence of a financial series while referring to the calculation of statistics $R/S$
"Arranges over standard deviation." The latter is defined as being wide
sums partial of the gaps of a time series to its average divided by its écar-
type. The standard formalization of the $R/S$ is the following one:

$$\frac{R}{S} = \frac{\text{MAX} \sum_{i=1}^{n} \left( X_i - \overline{X} \right) - \text{MIN} \sum_{i=1}^{n} \left( X_i - \overline{X} \right)}{\sqrt{\sum_{i=1}^{n} \left( X_i - \overline{X} \right)^2 / n}}$$

The majority of the studies (Peters, 1994) concluded that statistics $R/S$ can
be written in the following form:

$$\frac{R}{S} \cong n^h$$

where $N$ is the number of observation and $H$ the exhibitor of Hurst. When we
are in the presence of a random functioning (not persistence) $H$ is equal to 0.5.

We can obtain $H$ by having recourse to log the linear presentation of statistics $R/S$:

$$\log(R/S) = h * \log(n) + \log(a)$$

- If $H = 0.5$: independent system or a random walk;
- If $0.5 < H < 1$: a strong persistence;
- If $H < 0.5$: anti-persistent.

The result of the regression logarithmic curve of statistics $R/S$ on the logarithm of time, in the case of the series of the bubble, is the following:

$$\log(R/S) = 0.92^{(0.00)} * \log(N) - 0.37^{(0.00)} \qquad (47)$$

The exhibitor of Hurst is of 0.92 what locates it in the interval (0.5, 1) to indicate a strong persistence in the series of the bubble: If the series records a rise during the previous period, there are great chances that it maintains this pace. Thus, the bubble on the Moroccan real estate market is equipped with a long, capable memory to confirm the spreading out of temporal of the latter. The events which occur at one moment given, for example, the explosion of the bubble, tend to affect the future trend of the series.[13]

# SPECULATIVE BUBBLES CYCLES

The cycle of the speculative bubbles has a seminal importance for the monetary and financial regulation policies. Indeed, the determination of the moments when the prices start to post deformations compared to the fundamental value makes it possible for the authorities to manage to reduce the volatility of the prices and set up the policies able to rationalize the market pricing and, in particular, that of the real estate.

Several work suggested using the Markov switching model to test the phases of boost and bust of the bubbles. The characteristic of this model lies in their capacity to describe in an empirical way the phase's hawser and depression of the asset prices. Indeed, the criticism formulated by Evans (1991) on the cyclic nature of the bubbles constituted a catalyst for this type of work which tries to identify the regimes of the speculative bubbles.

According to the methodology of Rock (2001) and Kim, Leybourne, and Newbold (2002) the duration of bubble cycle is detected by the use of the Markov switching model with changes, which makes it possible to approximate the probability of supervening of the various regimes involved.

The model is characterized by their capacity to detect heterogeneous states of the world. In continuation of this paragraph, one proposes a short description of these models; however, for more details, it is necessary to see work of Hamilton (1994), Kim and Nelson (1999), and Vayanos and Wang (2003).The simple following process is considered:

$$y_t = \mu_{s_t} + \varepsilon_t \tag{48}$$

where $s_t$ is the state by which the stochastic process passes during its existence, $\varepsilon_t$ is the Gaussian white noise, and $\mu$ makes it possible to detect the transition between the various states from the endogenous variable.

In this case, it should be noted that it depends on the states of the world of "there" we obtain securities different as well with regard to the expectation $\mu$ as from the moments of the residues of the equation.

If it is supposed that the world knows only two states, 1 and 2, for this purpose, the system can arise following system:

$$y_{1t} = \mu_{s_1} + \varepsilon_{1t} \quad : \text{first state}$$
$$y_{2t} = \mu_{s_2} + \varepsilon_{2t} \quad : \text{second state}$$

where $\varepsilon_{1t} \sim \left(0, \sigma_1^2\right)$ and $\varepsilon_{2t} \sim \left(0, \sigma_2^2\right)$

This formulation induces clearly that the two processes $y_1$ and $y_2$ are different. When we are in the presence of state 1 then there is the hope of $y1$ and $\mu_{s_1}$, while there is an expectation of $\mu_{s_2}$ with the emergence of state 2.

The variances of the residues, forwarded in each process, describe predictive uncertainties of the model in each state of the system. In other words, the variances of the residues of the models, describe volatilities of each state of the system, for example, for a state 1 we could have a volatility more increased compared to that noted on the level of the second state.

The characteristic of the models with Markovian change is their capacity to collect the transitions from a state given to another. Simply, the proposal of the Markov switching model is to consider that the presence of a state 1 is related to the presence or on a realization of an exogenous variable $(X)$, and the transition toward another state is provided for in the event of absence of this variable. Thus, if we are in a deterministic situation we note that:

$$y_t = D\left(\mu_{s_1} + \varepsilon_{1t}\right) + (1 - D)\left(\mu_{s_2} + \varepsilon_{2t}\right) \tag{49}$$

$D$ is equal to unity in the event of presence of the variable $x > 0$ and zero differently.

In the case of the models of Markov, the regime change is stochastic. This means that there is a possibility of forwarding a regime to another. However, the dynamics of the process of change is regarded as being known and being generated via a matrix of transition. The latter controls the probabilities of change of a state to another and forwards the following form:

$$P = \begin{pmatrix} p_{11} & \cdots & p_{1k} \\ \vdots & \ddots & \vdots \\ p_{k1} & \cdots & p_{kk} \end{pmatrix}$$

In the matrix of transition, the probability $(p_{ij})$ makes it possible to approximate the chances to forward a state to another. For the case where we see forwarding of a state 1 to a state 2 then the probability of transition would be $p_{21}$, while the probability of persisting in state 1 is qualified as $p_{11}$. Within the forwarded framework, the probabilities of transition are regarded as being stationary, which is not always the case. In the presence of probability varying in time, another type of models is used, knowing the variable models with parameter in time with Markov model.

The estimate is carried out according to two steps in fact: the Bayesian approach or the method of maximum likelihood. However, the second approach is largely used with the detriment of the first. For a regime in two states in the form $y_{1t} = \mu_{s_1} + \varepsilon_{1t}$, in this case, the function of maximum likelihood is given by:

$$\ln L = \sum_{t=1}^{T} \ln \left( \frac{1}{\sqrt{2\pi\sigma^2}} \exp\left(-\frac{y-\mu}{2\sigma^2}\right) \right)$$

If the states of the world are well defined, it is enough to maximize likelihood to have the parameters $\mu$ and $\sigma^2$ for each state of the system, however, and what relates to the model of Markov these states are unknown. For this purpose, it is necessary to amend the function of probability to take account of the absence of an exact knowledge of the state of the system in question. It is noted that

$$\ln L = \sum_{t=1}^{T} \ln \sum_{j=1}^{2} \left( f(y_t | S_t = j, \varphi) \Pr(S_t = j) \right)$$

In order to maximize the function of probabilities, it is necessary to know the probabilities of transition, from where the recourse to the filter of Hamilton makes it possible to initialize the probabilities of transition and to determine them according to an iterative process (see Hamilton, 2005).

For the case of the Moroccan real estate market, the results obtained in the preceding section confirm the presence of a speculative bubble. Indeed, the prices indicate the presence of a component other than that of fundamental, whose quantification was carried out using the Kalman filter.

In this section and by using the model of Markov, it is proposed to measure the date of the bubbles by specifying their birth date and also their date of deflation. It should thus make it possible to detect the phases of ascending and descending of prices.

By adopting the formulation of Blanchard and Watson (1982), we consider that the process of bubble is controlled by two types of phases: a first ascending phase and a second depression.

$$
\begin{cases}
B_{t+1} = B_t \left( \dfrac{1+r}{\pi} \right) + \mu_t \\[2em]
B_{t+1} = \mu_t, (1 - \pi)
\end{cases}
$$

where $r$ is the rate of capitalization and $\pi$ is the probability of birth of the bubble.

In this case and by using the model of Markovian regime change we can estimate both states of the bubbles according to the following formulation:

$$
\begin{cases}
B_{1t} = \mu_{s_1} + \varepsilon_{1t}, \; \pi \\
B_{2t} = \mu_{s_2} + \varepsilon_{2t}, (\pi - 1)
\end{cases}
$$

The first state is relative to a speculative bubble hawser, during which the prices tend to increase, while the second state describes the phase depression or the bubble with the tendency to burst itself under the negotiable instruments of the fall of the prices.

The model with change with Markovian regimes used makes it possible to approximate two types of states. The estimates using the maximum likelihood made it possible to lead to the following results (Table 12).

According to the results obtained we are in the presence of two types of bubble on the Moroccan real estate market: first positive whose average of the rise is of 0.04 and the second phase of fall of the prices whose hope is equal to −3.9. Moreover and according to the analysis of the variance (volatility) of the two states, it arises that the phase of fall of the prices is less volatile than this rise. This can be explained by the fact that when the market is with a tendency to be more bull, volatility increases in answer to the increased request of the purchasers of good against the phase depression which is often interpreted in the same manner by the unit of the agents and where there is weakened volatility.

Most interesting facts in terms of analysis using the model with Markovian regime change, is the production of the matrix of probability of transition from one regime to another "*D*." The results obtained affirm that when we are in the presence of the first state (*E*1) we have a 93% probability of persisting there and a 6% of chance to forward toward a regime bull. In this direction and normal situation there is a 6% of speculative probability of seeing a bubble being born. However, when we are in the second state of rise of the prices we have a chance of only 89% that the bubble persists, while a 11% of chance is in favor of a return to the first state (Fig. 6).

***Table 12.*** Identification of the Markov Regimes.

| States | Mean | Variance |
|---|---|---|
| Boost (*E*2) | 0.047453 (0.09) | 2.118854 (0.00) |
| Bust (*E*1) | −3.903149 (0.00) | 1.290944 (0.01) |

*Note*: Log *L*:−89.6689, the estimates were carried out by supposing the normal distribution.

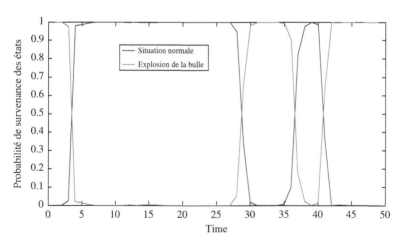

*Fig. 6.* Probabilities of Transition from a Normal State in an Explosive State of the Real Estate Bubble between 2000 and 2012.

304                                                    FIRANO ZAKARIA

$$\text{Matrix of transtion probabilities} = \begin{bmatrix} 0.93 & 0.11 \\ 0.07 & 0.89 \end{bmatrix}$$

The analysis of the development of the probability of supervening of an explosion of a bubble indicates that the frequency of formation of bubble is very limited. Indeed, it is noted that there exist only two periods which are affected by a rather important explosion of the prices, that is, the two jumps of the curve in worms to cross the threshold of 100%. Most important to note is that this situation of euphoria persists only for a more or less short period being neighborly the six and nine quarters. Thus, the analysis of the duration of the two regimes resulting from the Markovian model emphasizes the results presented in Table 13.

The explosion of the bubble during the periods 2006 and 2008 coincides with the beginning of the boom of the credit in Morocco. Indeed, in this period the growth rate of the credit in Morocco was of two digits testifying to a broad expansion in the distribution of the loan to the economy and, in particular, the real estate market.

The analysis of the correlation between the bank credits and the real estate bubble emphasizes a significant rate of correlation between the two series, as we can note in Table 14.

As the graphical comparison between the series of the bubble and the development of the bank credits and the real estate credits confirm that there is a certain relation of dependence between the decision of granting of credit and the explosion of the bubble on the Moroccan real estate market. We note in Fig. 7 since the boom of the appropriations which Morocco during the period 2006–2008 knew coincides largely with the explosion of the bubble over the same period. Indeed, the analysis of the correlation

*Table 13.* Duration of Bubbles Cycles.

| States | Expected Duration |
| --- | --- |
| Boost (*E2*) | 9.11 quarters |
| Bust (*E1*) | 14.55 quarters |

*Table 14.* Correlation between the Development of the Bank Credits and the Real Estate Bubble.

| Lag | 0 | 1 | 2 | 3 |
| --- | --- | --- | --- | --- |
| Correlation | 38.13% | 46.72% | 52.71% | 44.32% |

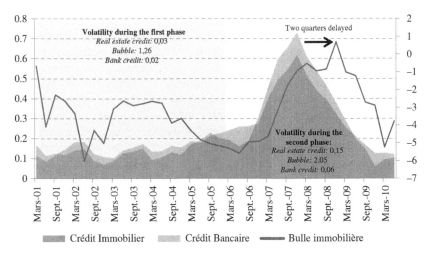

*Fig. 7.* Development of the Bank Credits, the Real Estate Credits, and the Real Estate Bubble between 2001 and 2010.

indicates that the rise of the real prices intervened two quarters after the beginning of the boom of the credit. This confirms that the increase in appropriations is among the principal determinants of the bubble which was formed over the period 2006–2008.

# CONCLUSION

The objective of this chapter is to present several steps suitable for checking the existence of speculative bubble on the Moroccan real estate market. In absence of a series of the real asset prices, the price index of the real assets was used to deduce the existence from it or not from a speculative bubble. Two approaches were recommended, namely a statistical approach and a structural approach. The first methodology uses the statistical tests suggested in the theoretical and empirical literature and which rests on the identification of the explosive character of the series of the prices and the fundamental value. In addition, the structural approach is based on the theoretical definition of the bubble and a test of estimate of the various forms of the Euler identity.

The results obtained confirmed that the real asset prices deviate significantly from the fundamental value, whose explanatory capacity is less important. For this purpose, a speculative bubble characterized the development of the real asset prices during the period 2006—2008. In addition, the analysis of the dating of the bubble on the real estate market lets predict the existence of two regimes which control the formation of the speculative bubble. The first state describes one period of rise of the prices, an explosion of the bubble, and a second state relative to a return at the normal or average state. According to these results obtained using the Markovian regimes we can affirm that the criticism of Evans (1991) on the cyclic nature of the financial bubbles is confirmed. Indeed, on the level of the Moroccan real estate market the explosion of the bubble lasts about 9 quarters and the normal cycle is of 14 quarters lifespan. At the end of each cycle begins another and so on.

The formation of the speculative bubble on the Moroccan real estate market is largely faded with the developments that the credit market in Morocco recorded. Indeed, the boom of the credit market during the period 2006—2008 contributed to the explosion of the real estate bubble during the same period with a two quarters shift. This is known as the easing of the conditions of granting of credit during this phase to feed positively the beliefs of the economic agents intervening on the real estate market, until managing to form a certain consensus on the continuity of the rise of the real prices, thereby giving rise to a bubble on the market. This myopia anticipation characterized the market throughout one 2 year to return to a normal situation, after the transmission of the crisis to the Moroccan economy. However, the analysis of the trends of real prices and the speculative bubble, lets predict the existence of a disconnection of the prices of fundamental and a continuation of the positive tendency of the bubble. For this purpose and to avoid a radical deflation of the bubble, it is convenient to lead preventive policies being able to mitigate the negotiable instruments of a crash landing of the prices on the real estate market.

# NOTES

1. The arbitrated prices are those formed in a situation of absence arbitration (Fama, 1965).
2. Bubble on the shares of the Company of Mississippi and those of South Sea Company (Company of the South Seas) in London.
3. It is the assumption according to which or the exit resale price with tendency to cancel itself with very long run. Then it is supposed that the investor holds the financial credit during one long life and what interests it is rather the yield and not the appreciation. The theory of the fundamental value, as solution to the equation of Euler is based on this assumption.

4. Thus, one can define a speculative bubble as the difference between the real price of a financial credit and its fundamental value. According to Blanchard and Watson (1982) the existence of a resale price within the model of determination of the fundamental value is at the origin of the emergence of speculative bubbles. In other words, the possibility of negotiating and of renegotiating its assets on a resale market is at the origin of the speculative bubbles. However, if this assumption of renegotiation was eliminated, only the behavior qualified as "corporate," according to Keynes, should exist.

5. Anticipation Self-fulfilling is a form of rational anticipation which constitutes a form of answer as for the indetermination of the future of the economic world and which describes the beliefs of the individuals.

6. This condition is however not implemented in the case of the bubbles defined within the framework of the model of hyperinflation of Cagan (1956). Indeed, in this case the variable indicate to bubble represents the logarithm of the price level which can take negative securities without for as much the price level is negative.

7. These approaches based on the implementation of the unit tests of roots and co-integration were largely criticized by authors Charemza and Deadman (1995) and Evans (1991) because of their incapacity to collect deflations of bubbles. Indeed, in the event of existence of periodic or seasonal bubbles, the unit tests of roots can reject their existence in favor of a perfect co-integration between the intrinsic prices and variables.

8. Artificial Neural Network *ARCH*.

9. Homm and Breitung (2012) also affirm, using simulations Monte Carlo, the supremacy of the test of PWY (2011).

10. See Blanchard (1979, p. 115) and Gourieroux, Laffont, and Monfort (1982), and McCallum (1983).

11. With $Y_{t+i} = A^i Y_t$ a form of capitalization.

12. We suppose in this formulation that the cov $(\eta, \mu)$ is null.

13. According to Peters *Fractal Market Analysis* (1994), this persistence indicates a sensitivity to the initial conditions to feed the assumption according to which the agents will tend to have irrational behaviors while continuing to believe for one long life in the rise of the prices.

# REFERENCES

Al-Anaswah, N., & Wilfling, B. (2011 May). Identification of speculative bubbles using state-space models with Markov-switching. *Journal of Banking & Finance, 35,* 1073–1086.

Bachelier, L. (1900a). Théorie de la spéculation (PDF). *Annales Scientifiques de l'École Normale Supérieure, 3*(17), 21–86.

Barlevy, G. (2007). Economic theory and asset bubbles. *Economic Perspectives Publisher: Federal Reserve Bank of Chicago, 3*(31).

Bhargava, A. (1986). On the theory of testing for unit roots in observed time series. *Review of Economic Studies, 53,* 369–384.

Blanchard, O. J. (1979). Speculative bubbles, crashes and rational expectations. *Economic Letters, 3,* 387–389.

Blanchard, O. J., & Watson, M. W. (1982). Bubbles, rational expectations, and financial markets. In P. Wachtel (Ed.), *Crisis in the economic and financial structure* (pp. 295–315). Lexington, MA: Lexington Books.

Brunnermeier, M. K. (2009). Deciphering the liquidity and credit crunch 2007-2008. *Journal of Economic Perspectives, 23*(1), 77–100.

Busetti, F., & Taylor, A. M. R. (2004). Tests of stationarity against a change in persistence. *Journal of Econometrics, 123*, 33–66.

Cagan, P. (1956). The monetary dynamics of hyperinflation. In M. Friedman (Ed.), *Studies in the quantity theory of money*. Chicago, IL: University of Chicago Press.

Charemza, W. W., & Deadman, D. F. (1995). Speculative bubbles with stochastic explosive roots: The failure of unit root testing. *Journal of Empirical Finance, 2*, 1453–1463.

Chung, H., & Lee, B.-S. (1998). Fundamental and nonfundamental components in stock prices of Pacific-Rim countries. *Pacific-Basin Finance Journal, 6*(3–4), 321–346.

Campbell, J. Y., & Shiller, R. J. (1988). The dividend-price ratio and expectations of future dividends and discount factors. *Review of Financial Studies, 1*(3), 195–228.

Davis, E. P. (1997). Population ageing and retirement income provision in the European Union. In B. Bosworth & G. Burtless (Eds.), *Ageing societies, the global dimension*. Washington, DC: Brookings Institution Press, (also Special Paper, Royal Institute of International Affairs, London).

Dezhbakhsh, O., & Demirguc-Kunt, A. (1990). On the presence of speculative bubbles in stock prices. *Journal of Financial and Quantitative Analysis, 25*, 101–112.

Diba, B. T., & Grossman, H. I. (1988). Explosive rational bubbles in stock prices? *American Economic Review, 78*(3), 520–530.

Evans, G. W. (1991). Pitfalls in testing for explosive bubbles in asset prices. *American Economic Review, 81*(4), 922–930.

Fama, E. (1965). The behavior of stock market prices. *Journal of Business, 38*, 34–105.

Fama, E. F. (1970). Efficient capital markets: A review of theory and empirical work. *The Journal of Finance, 25*, 383–417.

Fama, E. F., Lawrence, F., Jensen, M. C., & Richard, R. (1969). The adjustment of stock prices to new information. *International Economic Review, 10*(1), 1–21.

Fisher, I. (1932). *Booms and depressions: Some first principles*. New York, NY: Adelphi Company.

Froot, K., & Obstfeld, M. (1991). Intrinsic bubbles: The case of stock prices. *American Economic Review, 81*, 1189–1214.

Garber, P. M. (2000). *Famous first bubbles: The fundamentals of early manias* (p. 175). Cambridge: MIT Press.

Glen, D. R., & Kamstra, M. (1996). A new dividend forecasting procedure that rejects bubbles in asset prices: The case of 1929's stock crash. *Review of Financial Studies, 9*(2), 333–383 (Summer).

Gourieroux, C., Laffont, J. J., & Monfort, A. (1982). Rational expectations in dynamic linear models: Analysis of the solutions. *Econometrica, 50*, 409–425.

Hamilton, J. D. (1994). *Time series analysis*. Princeton, NJ: Princeton University Press.

Hamilton, J. D. (2005). *What's real about the business cycle?* NBER Working Paper No. 11161.

Homm, U., & Breitung, J. (2012). Testing for speculative bubbles in stock markets: A comparison of alternative methods. *Journal of Financial Econometrics, 10*(1), 198–231.

Keynes, J. M. (1933). National self-sufficiency. *The Yale Review, 22*(4), 755–769.

Keynes, J. M. (1936). The postulates of the classical economics. The General Theory of Employment, Interest and Money.

Kim, C.-J., & Nelson, C. R. (1999). *State space models with regime switching.* Cambridge: MIT Press.

Kim, T. H., Leybourne, S., & Newbold, P. (2002). Unit root test with a break in innovation variance. *Journal of Econometrics, 109,* 365–387.

Kindleberger, C. P. (1978). *Manias, panics and croshes.* New York, NY: Basic Books.

Koustas, Z., & Serletis, A. (2005). Rational bubbles or persistent deviations from market fundamentals? *Journal of Banking and Finance, 29*(10), 2523–2539.

LeRoy, S. F., & Porter, R. D. (1981). The present-value relation: Tests based on implied variance bounds. *Econometrica, 49,* 555–574.

McCallum, B. T. (1983). On non-uniqueness in rational expectations models: An attempt at perspective. *Journal of Monetary Economics, 11,* 139–168.

Minsky, H. P. (May 1957). Central banking and money market changes. *Quarterly Journal of Economics, 71,* 171–187.

Muth, J. F. (1961). Rational expectations and the theory of price movements. *Econometrica, 29,* 315–335.

Peters, E. (1994). *Financial fractal analysis: Applying chaos theory to investment and economics.* Hoboken, NJ: Wiley Finance.

Phillips, P. C. B., Shi, S., & Yu, J. (2011). *Testing for multiple bubbles.* Unpublished Manuscript. Singapore Management University.

Phillips, P. C. B., & Yu, J. (2009). *Limit theory for dating the origination and collapse of mildly explosive periods in time series data.* Unpublished Manuscript. Singapore Management University.

Phillips, P. C. B., Wu, Y., & Yu, J. (2011). Explosive behavior in the 1990s Nasdaq: When did exuberance escalate asset values? *International Economic Review.*

Phillips, P. C. B., Wu, Y., & Yu, J. (2012). *Testing for multiple bubbles.* Cowles foundation discussion Paper No. 1843.

Samuelson, P. (1965). Proof that properly anticipated prices fluctuate randomly. *Industrial Management Review, 6,* Spring 41–49.

Shiller, R. J. (1981). Do stock prices move to much to be justified by subsequent changes in dividends? *American Economic Review, 71,* 421–436.

Van Norden, S., & Vigfusson, R. (1996). *Regime-switching models: A guide to the bank of Canada gauss procedures.* Working Paper No. 96-3, Bank of Canada.

Van Norden, S., & Vigfusson, R. (1998). Avoiding the pitfalls: Can regime-switching tests reliably detect bubbles? *Studies in Nonlinear Dynamics and Econometrics, 3,* 1–22.

Vayanos, D., & Wang, T. (2003). *Search and endogenous concentration of liquidity in asset markets.* Working Paper.

West, K. (1987). A specification test for speculative bubbles. *Quarterly Journal of Economics, 102,* 553–580.

Wu, Y. (1995). Are there rational bubbles in foreign exchange markets? Evidence from an alternative test. *Journal of International Money and Finance, 14,* 27–46.

Wu, Y. (1997). Rational bubbles in the stock market: Accounting for the US stock-price volatility. *Economic Inquiry, 35,* 309–319.

Wulf, G., Lee, T. D., & Schmidt, R. A. (1994). Reducing knowledge of results about relative versus absolute timing: Differential effects on learning. *Journal of Motor Behavior, 26,* 362–369.

Yiu, M. S., Yu, J., & Jin, L. (2013). Detecting bubbles in Hong Kong residential property market. *Journal of Asian Economics, 28,* 115–124.

# CORPORATE GOVERNANCE
# INDEX IN EMERGING MARKETS:
# PERUVIAN LISTED COMPANIES ☆

## Edmundo R. Lizarzaburu, Luis Berggrun
## and Kurt Burneo

## ABSTRACT

*Companies are wishing to incorporate good corporate governance practices into their organization in order to be more attractive to investors, knowing whether this influences their financial indicators and profitability or not. This, in fact, is beneficial for investors so they know that a company who applies the principles of corporate governance (CG) presents best management practices and transparent information, safeguarding the interests of all its stakeholders, which helps their investment decision; reducing market uncertainty, making it more efficient and liquid. The research focuses on the companies listed in the Stock Exchange of Lima that had implemented CG strategies in their organizations.*

**Keywords:** Corporate governance; financial scandals; principles of corporate governance; corporate governance index; Lima Stock Exchange

---

☆The paper had the collaboration of Nathalie Nogueira, Esan Student.

---

The Spread of Financial Sophistication Through Emerging Markets Worldwide
Research in Finance, Volume 32, 311−336
Copyright © 2016 by Emerald Group Publishing Limited
ISSN: 0196-3821/doi:10.1108/S0196-382120160000032013

# INTRODUCTION

For a long time, managers' primary goal was to increase the wealth of its shareholders by ensuring the expected return on their investments. This is why, some companies, in order to align the objectives of managers with the company's, gave them shares as while performing their duties they also increase their wealth. Friedman, 1983, who publicly supported this management model, claimed that if the manager implements social responsibility actions with shareholders' money, this would be unethical, as this do not generate financial benefits to the company. This management model dominated for a while; however, as several financial scandals became known, primarily caused by short-term vision generated by this model of government, it was when the model of stakeholders emerged. Besides, the model in which the company not only concerned with the interests of shareholders but also gives importance to all stakeholders that influences the development of their activities (Friedman, 1983).

All this learning process in which managers realized that what really matters is the long-term sustainability of the company both in the financial sector, and socially.

Brammer and Millington (2008) note, "Corporate philanthropic activities provide a highly transparent insight into corporate strategy in the context of social responsiveness because philanthropic activities are subject to the control of the main board of directors in most companies, have a high degree of external visibility and thus play a key role in shaping the perceptions of the company in the eyes of external stakeholders."

Stakeholder management had become an important part of a firm's strategic planning as the stakeholders' perceptions may affect operating and financial performance. As Starbuck (2014) notes, widespread but incorrect myths say corporations operate for the benefit of stockholders and are subordinate to local and national governments, and that other stakeholders should have no voice in corporate governance. Reality says that some other stakeholders have stronger voices in corporate governance than stockholders.

# LITERATURE REVIEW

*Shareholder Models and Stakeholder Model*

The first decade of the twentieth century was remembered for many perpetrated frauds and financial scandals by giant companies; and is renowned as some of the famous cases: Enron, Wolrdcom, Madoff, and others. These scandals showed how vulnerable was the market to managers whose reward are linked to short-term performance and a growing adequate capacity of governmental supervision, principally in the case of financial firms. It will go on to describe the differences between these two management models.

Therefore, Dalton, Daily, and Cannella (2003) define governance as the determination of the board uses to which organizational resources are going to be used and the resolution of conflicts among the main stakeholders. This definition stands for many years, where researches have focused on the control of executive self-interest and the protection of shareholders' interest. New researches have given many insights about the manager-shareholder conflict. The main differences between these models are whether they focus only the stakeholders' interest or they consider other stakeholders as important for the company sustainability.

*The shareholder model*
The main objective of the senior managers of these companies is to obtain the highest possible return for shareholders at all costs, which is called the "shareholder model," a governance philosophy whose only goal is to maximize profits of shareholders. In 1970, Friedman argued that the manager's main responsibility is to maximize profit for shareholders while aligned with the laws and society ethics, and should not pursue social responsibilities.

Sawayda (2013) attributed the shareholder model as the best way to run a business in order to make a business more competitive, this is why the shareholders' money and investors is used for, instead of meeting social responsibilities, which does not help financially. Starbuck (2014) says that there have been many examples of current executives who have extracted personal short-run benefits to the disadvantage of other current stakeholders (employees, customers, suppliers, neighbors).

The survival and success of individual business firms may well prove harmful from a long-run global perspective, and what matters for the world at large is the distribution of evolving capabilities across the entire population of business firms. Consequently, this philosophy was neither viable in the long term, because the managers prefer to make decisions for improving the situation of the company in the short term. But, eventually came to light financial scandals that generated huge losses and so rattled financial markets sensitive and vulnerable to this type of risk that for those effects are operational and reputational. "Contemporary corporations gain considerable advantages from focusing on a unitary goal: corporate profits.

Pursuit of profit is not simple, of course, in that profit integrates many sub goals, some of which contradict others" (Starbuck, 2014).

*The stakeholder model*
What the market learned of these situations was that it had a major vulnerability and weakness referred to companies' internal and external control practices; as a result, the shareholder model became replaced by stakeholder model, a governance philosophy that focuses wealth creation in the care of the interests of all groups involved within the company.

The stakeholders are defined as all those groups who are affected directly or indirectly by the business' activities development, and therefore have the ability to directly or indirectly affect the development of these (Freeman & Reed, 1983). This was the first definition of stakeholder on his book "Stockholders and Stakeholders: A New Perspective on Corporate Governance."

The Manual for the practice of relations with stakeholders (2006) says that to define whose the main stakeholders of a company are: First, it is necessary to analyze the concept's evolution and how it has been gaining strength and impact on how companies develop their strategies, as they have a strong impact on how business is conducted today.

The definition of stakeholder has evolved in tandem with the definition of business strategy. Currently, Johnson and Scholes (2001) define "strategy is the direction and scope of an organization long term, while at the same time, allows achieving benefits for the organization through its configuration of resources in a changing environment, to meet the needs of markets and meet the expectations of stakeholders." That is when the question "what are the main stakeholders of a company?" becomes crucial, as most companies have begun to perceive.

Wheeler and Sillanpää (1997) "made the distinction between main and secondary. Among the major include shareholders, employees, customers, suppliers and local communities where the company operates. Among the side mentioned: the media, government and regulatory bodies, government organizations, unions, competitors, etc. At the end of the day, what matters is that the company made a map of all stakeholders involved with the organization."

Stakeholder management goes close to CG practices as Lizarzaburu, Berggrun, and Burneo (2014) note that a CG help improve access to new capital, allowing the firm raise a lower interest rate, which is translated on lower risk company. Besides, CG helps identify the distribution of rights and responsibilities among different participants in the company (stakeholders) and includes the rules and procedures for making decisions on corporate affairs.

Under this preamble, several organizations assume an important role in determining actions and guidelines that allow businesses being able to apply better practices with all stakeholders on the business' development.

*Stakeholder's Mapping*

One organization that issued guidelines on how to apply corporate responsibility was the International Organization for Standardization by its ISO 26000, which provides guidance for companies regarding Social Responsibility issues. According to ISO 26000: Project Overview (2010), "The International Standard ISO 26000, Guidance on social responsibility, provides an harmonized relevant global guide for private and public sector organizations and of all kinds, based on international consensus among expert representatives of the key stakeholders, and encourages the implementation of best practices in social responsibility worldwide."

One of the main purposes of this guidance is to help organization in the identification and commitment among their stakeholders. Consequently, making a general mapping of stakeholders can be identified as follows; however, each company must do this exercise, because depending on the business in which it is found, it has specific stakeholders to concentrate in, which may differ from other companies or from this general map in Fig. 1.

So taking the guidance provided by the ISO of a general stakeholders' mapping, now we move to a stakeholder map provided by the Lima Stock Exchange, which is applied by the Peruvian companies that voluntarily wish to implement Corporate Governance Practices issued by the Superintendency of Securities Market (SMV: Superintendencia del Mercado de Valores) in 2002.

As a result, the Lima Stock Exchange (BVL for its acronym is Spanish) and its presentation of Good Corporate Governance Index in 2008 introduced the following map of the stakeholders (Fig. 2).

The market was rocked by several financial scandals, some more serious than others, before realizing that the model only focused on the interests of shareholders was not viable in the long term. The impact they had on the market made necessary having measures in order to prevent these things from happening again. So implementing best practices in corporate governance was a key aspect to consider.

*Fig. 1.* ISO 26000 Stakeholders' Mapping. *Source*: ISO 26000.

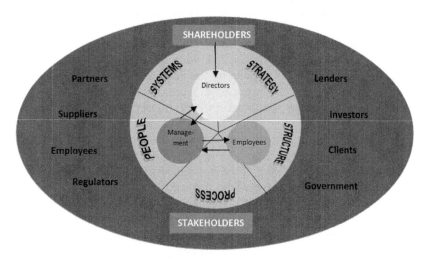

*Fig. 2.* Lima Stock Exchange, IBGC – Stakeholders' Mapping. *Source*: BVL.

## International Standards

There was a time when financial scandals sent warning signals to the market about the weaknesses they had regarding the management of corporations and transparency of financial information presented to investors, by not making the best decisions as the information was manipulated. These people kept a widespread "greed is good" mentality in the business world, only worrying about the impact of their decisions primarily in their pockets and not in the collateral damage that these would cause to stakeholders. Besides the Latin American Development Bank (2012) develop the CG triangle, that it is shown in Fig. A1.

For instance, Enron according to the BBC Mundo (2006), Skilling was the former CEO of the company, was charged with 28 counts of fraud, conspiracy, lying to auditors, and improper conduct handling of confidential information. Furthermore, Enron made US$31,800 million in debt, its shares lost all value, and 21,000 people worldwide became unemployed. Enron emerged from bankruptcy protection in 2004, and it continues to sell its remaining assets to pay creditors.

Worldcom was the largest accounting manipulation of US history, even higher than Enron, about US$3,850 million causing the crash in the stock markets, the Dow Jones and Nasdaq, falling dollar, massive layoffs and a series of damage to the shareholders and public pension funds. The fraud consisted of presenting as capital investments what was spending, so that substantial profits of US$1,400 million at the end of 2001 showed, when in fact they were generating losses.

Another case was Madoff Investment Securities, whose president was arrested by the FBI after confessing that his business was a "Giant Ponzi scheme." According to Beekman (2014), Madoff would have caused losses of US$40,000 million customers whereby the promised returns were paid by the entry of new customers.

It is important to analyze how Madoff could sustain this pyramid for 20 years. He passed inspections by the Securities Exchange Commission (SEC) that could not detect anything illegal, there were complaints against bad business practices, but their customers were not interested in investigating, as yields offered were very tempting; which shows a clear conflict of interest in the case. The impact they had both financially and on implementing measures to counteract these bad governance practices in companies are clear the following. We think that an additional factor that explains all of these cases was an adequate official capacity to supervision.

## The Sarbanes-Oxley Act

As more of these scandals arose, the market had the need to have some generally accepted guidelines to be implemented by companies and banks, so now investors were the ones to require corporations to put in practice guidelines that helped restore some confidence raised by fear felt in the market for that period. Under these conditions, mainly arose two entities that took the lead in this issue and these are the Organization for Economic Co-operation and Development (OECD) and the law proposed by Deputy Michael G. Oxley and Senator Paul S. Sarbanes in American Congress named Sarbanes-Oxley (SOX).

In July 2002, the US government passed the Sarbanes-Oxley Act as a mechanism to tighten controls of companies and restore lost confidence. The legal text covers issues such as corporate governance, accountability of managers, transparency, and other important limitations to the work of auditors.

According to Gámiz (2012), SOX was born to protect shareholders' equity, which would be of great benefit to be incorporated into the legislation and regulations for trading activities in Peru, but there will be necessary an adequate adopting process because there are several differences in the local legislation.

Some of the requirements include:

- Publish all financial and non-financial reporting.
- Certification of financial reporting and internal control by the chief executive officers (CEO) and chief financial officers (CFOs).
- Update investors with all the latest internal organizational changes, both financial and non-financial.
- The CEO and CFO must certify that they are responsible for implementing and maintaining controls and procedures publications.
- Hiring independent legal counsel and public accounting firm.
- Choosing a professionally competent board, truly independent, both psychologically and legally independent.

SOX Act requires the CEO to perform a series of certifications regarding the accuracy of accounting records and the adequacy of internal controls. The most relevant items are known as SOX Sections 302 and 404.

Section 302 establishes liability for financial reporting. The Security Exchange Commission (SEC) implemented SOX requirements stating that the CEO, CFO, or senior executives of a firm contributor, quarterly, and annually shall certify that:

- Are responsible for establishing and maintaining controls and procedures disclosures published.
- They have designed these controls and procedures publications so that they ensure they have taken cognizance of all material information.
- Evaluated the effectiveness of controls and procedures.
- Revealed to the auditors, the audit committee and the board's firm any significant deficiencies in controls, fraud and whether or not there were significant changes in the controls.

Section 404 requires the SEC to adopt rules requiring each annual report of firms contains a statement of its management accepting responsibility for establishing and maintaining a system of internal controls and procedures for the issuance of financial statements; and an assessment of the effectiveness of such internal controls and procedures. It also requires the external auditor to verify and report on management's statement on the effectiveness of internal controls and procedures. To implement this section, the SEC defined internal control over financial reporting as "the process established by CEO, CFO and head of the firm, to provide reasonable assurance regarding the reliability of financial reporting and the preparation of financial statements for third, and include policies and procedures covering:

- Accounting records sufficiently detailed and appropriate, to reflect the transactions and assets of the company.
- Provide reasonable assurance that transactions are register in ways that enable the preparation of financial statements are issued in accordance with accounting principles, and that receipts and expenditures of the company are made only in accordance with authorizations of management and the board.
- Provide reasonable assurance regarding timely prevention detection of expenses use, or unauthorized disposal of assets that may have had a material effect on the financial statements."

## *The OECD*

Uses its vast and rich information on a wide variety of topics to help governments so that they help promote prosperity and fight poverty through economic growth and financial stability. They help ensure that all implications for economic and social development are taken into account. OECD'S way of working is shown in Fig. 3.

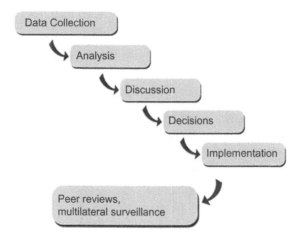

*Fig. 3.* OECD's Way of Working. *Source*: OECD

The work of the organization is based on continuous monitoring of events among member countries, in addition to non-OECD countries, including projections of short to medium-term economic development (OECD, 2014).

*Definition of the Principles of Good Corporate Governance*
They were created in 1999 by the ministers of the OECD, and since then have become international reference standards for policies makers, investors, corporations, and other stakeholders worldwide both OECD and non-members; moreover, was adopted as one of the 12 key standards for Sound Financial Systems by the Financial Stability Forum (OECD, 2004).

According to OECD (2004), policymakers are now more aware of the contributions that corporate governance makes to financial market stability, and growth in investment and economic. In addition, companies have a better understanding of how good corporate governance contributes to their competitiveness.

Principles are a living instrument offering non-binding standards and best practices; as well as implementation guidance, that can be adapted to specific circumstances of countries and regions. These principles are subject to periodic review by identifying trends and seeking remedies to new challenges.

*Good Practices of Corporate Governance?*
According to OECD (2004), Corporate Governance is a key factor for improving economic efficiency and growth; besides increasing investor confidence. Corporate governance involves a set of relationships between managers managing the company, its directors, shareholders, and other stakeholders (OECD, 2004).

The presence of an effective corporate governance system, within an individual company and the economy as a whole, helps to provide a necessary degree of confidence for the function of a market economy. Resulting on a lower cost of capital and encouraging companies to become more efficient using resources, making growth sustainable. Kocourek et al. (2003) quoted by Moudud-Ul-Huq (2014), "Corporate governance is an important effort to ensure accountability and responsibility and is a set of principles which should be incorporated into every part of an organization."

The effectiveness of an organization's corporate governance structure has far-reaching effect on its proper functioning. Corporate governance essentially involves balancing the interests of the many stakeholders in a company; its shareholders, management, customers, suppliers, financiers, government, and the community.

Corporate governance is affected by the relationships among participants in the system, these are the shareholders (including individuals, families, block alliances, other companies, etc.) and their own organization structure that can influence the company claiming best practices, can happen that individual shareholders do not demand this, and however, they are very concerned about getting equal treatment. Fund providers play an important role and can serve as external monitors of corporate governance.

Employees and other stakeholders also play an important role in contributing to the success of the company in the long term; while governments establish the legal and institutional framework for corporate governance. An additional issue related to good practices of corporate governance is the particular social and economic context in a developing country as Peru. Indeed, the current regressive income distribution defines with most priority the need to have a growing number of firms with good practices of corporate governance.

*OECD's Principles of Corporate Governance*
According to OECD (2004), the degree to which companies embrace the principles of good corporate governance is because they have earned an international relevance within the flow of investments. International capital flow allow businesses to obtain financing from a wider range of investors,

so they need to be internationally recognized as companies implementing credible corporate governance practices accepted by international standards. While the company does not resort to foreign investors for funding, this will help build confidence among local investors, reduce its cost of capital, supporting the function of financial markets, and ultimately induce more stable funding sources.

The principles are as follows, and are divided into seven categories: Ensuring the basis for an effective corporate governance framework, the rights of shareholders and key ownership functions, and the equitable treatment of shareholders, the role of stakeholders in Corporate Governance, disclosure and transparency, and the Responsibilities of the Board.

## CORPORATE GOVERNANCE INSIGHTS

Studies related to corporate governance are providing more guidance on the subject and how this affects different aspects and variables in the company. It had been studied how the corporate governance influences the management of a company's revenues, variables such as capital structure, the shareholders' participation, board members, and their relationship with the company and senior management (González & García-Meca, 2013), showing that when exists a legal system that promotes ethical behavior; compliance with rules and effectiveness of government, increases the quality and transparency of the presented information. Furthermore, according to Pooja and Sharma (2014), CG practices help establishing a name for the company, as these gives confidence to investors and stakeholders on the company. On the other hand, board composition, its compensation, and its relationship between stakeholders; in addition to established accounting and audit committees to monitor critical governance practices, are factors that cannot be measured quantitatively, since it would not be fair enough, so these are aspects that measurements must be made qualitative.

Consequently, Lacker (2004) cited by Pooja and Sharma (2014) examine the relationship between the various factors of Good Corporate Governance with different measures of organizational thinking and performance. However, there are several studies in which the relationship between CG and performance of the company are mainly measured as profitability ratios like ROE and ROA (Pooja & Sharma, 2014). Finally, Coughlan and Schmidt (1984), in their research, the board of directors controls the actions of management, making compensations related to stock return, and the results obtained were the expected as they were related. For instance, Fig. 4 shows the compared performance of the Lima Stock Exchange indexes. In early 2014, the IBGC maintains a spread of 36% from the INCA Total.

## PERU: LIMA STOCK EXCHANGE

According to González and García-Meca (2013), the case of Latin America and other countries characterized by weak legal system to protect the interests of minority shareholders, plus a concentration on shareholding structure, since a company can be controlled by several firms that are part of a larger conglomerate that operates in the region, which does not happen in countries like the United States or Europe, where there is a larger and more diversified market.

In the case of Peru, the principles of Good Corporate Governance were applied since 2002, as no one could leave out the situation that had been taking a lot of strength in recent years from the First Declaration of Principles of the OECD.

It was decided to implement the principles in the Peruvian market because it was considered important for the market, since it was possible to achieve more efficient and reliable markets, generating more value, strength and efficiency for businesses, contributing to the transparency that showed by listed companies (Stakeholders Publicaciones, s.f.); actually Peru is in course to accomplish several policy OECD requirements, because it is interesting to be member in the future of this international institution.

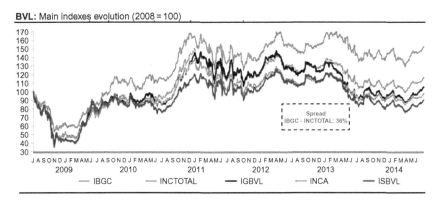

*Fig. 4.* Corporate Governance Index versus Others. *Source*: BVL.

The application of companies to join the Corporate Governance Index is voluntarily. A new Code of Good Corporate Governance for Peruvian Companies had its basis in the following proposals and publications. Tables 1 and 2 show the several publications in Peru related to CG codes and rules

The timeline in Fig. 5 shows the history of Corporate Governance in the Peruvian Market.

*Involved Parties*

"The Code of Good Corporate Governance for Peruvian Companies was prepared by the Updating Committee on the Principles of Good Governance for Peruvian Companies established in February 2012, with the financial support of CAF-Development Bank of Latin America." (Deloitte, 2013), so in this line, Table 3 shows the entities that participate in the elaborations of CG recommendations that should be implemented and followed by the Peruvian companies.

*Principles of Corporate Governance Followed by Listed Companies in Peru*
The corporate governance principles applied in Peru were born on the international standard published by the OECD in 1999 and have been revised in line with new trends. While based on the OECD principles, in our case in particular, the principles were adapted to fit best to our reality and better

*Table 1.*   Main Publications Use on the CG Code for Peruvian Companies.

| Main Basis |
| --- |
| Comisión Nacional del Mercado de Valores de España (CNMV), "Código unificado de buen gobierno de las sociedades cotizadas," 2006 |
| Comité de Supervisión bancaria de Basilea, "La mejora del gobierno corporativo en organizaciones bancarias," 2006 |
| Corporación Andina de Fomento (CAF), "Lineamientos para un Código Andino de Gobierno Corporativo," 2006 |
| European Commission, "Green Paper: Corporate Governance Framework," 2011 |
| Ibargüen, Alfredo, "Propuesta de modificación de los Principios de Buen Gobierno de las Sociedades Anónimas Peruanas," 2005 |
| New York Stock Exchange (NYSE), "Corporate Governance Rules," 2003 |
| OCDE, "Principios de Gobierno Corporativo de la OCDE," 2004 |

*Source*: Deloitte.

***Table 2.*** Complementary Basis on the CG Code for Peruvian Companies.

| Complementary Basis |
|---|
| Asociación de Supervisores Bancarios de las Américas (ASBA), "Gobierno Corporativo en instituciones bancarias," 2009 |
| Corporación Andina de Fomento, "Lineamientos para el buen gobierno corporativo de las empresas del estado," 2010 |
| Corporación Financiera Internacional, "Manual IFC de Gobierno de empresas familiares," 2008 |
| De Aldama y Miñon, Enrique y demás comisionados, "Informe de la Comisión especial para el fomento de la transparencia y seguridad en los mercados y en las sociedades cotizadas," España, 2003 |
| Deloitte, "The Dodd – Frank: Act´s impact on public companies," 2011 |
| Global Corporate Governance Forum, "Toolkit: Developing Corporate Governance Codes of best practice," 2005 |
| Gómez, Gonzalo y López, Maria Piedad, "El Gobierno Corporativo y la Ley Sarbanes-Oxley," 2005 |
| Instituto de Consejeros – Administradores, "Principios de Buen Gobierno Corporativo," 2004 |
| Institute of International Finance, "Policies for Corporate Governance in emerging markets: revised guidelines," 2003 |
| OCDE, "Fortaleciendo el gobierno corporativo latinoamericano: el papel de los inversionistas institucionales," 2011 |
| OCDE, "Guidelines on Corporate Governance of state – owned enterprises," 2005 |

*Source*: Deloitte.

implementation in the Peruvian stock market showing a low trading volume compared with their peers in the region. The OECD principles are divided into six principles (categories such as those applied in Peru) and 31 subprinciples versus 4 categories in which our 26 principles are divided.

Until 2002, the BVL classified the principles into four categories: (i) Shareholders' rights, (ii) equitable treatment of shareholders, (iii) Disclosure and transparency, and (iv) Board responsibilities, shown in Table 4.

*The Corporate Governance Index in Lima Stock Exchange*
*(IBGC for Its Acronym in Spanish)*
According to the BVL, The Good Corporate Governance Index, IBGC is a statistical indicator for the performance of securities of issuers that adequately fulfill the principles of good corporate governance for Peruvian Companies and additionally possess a minimum level of liquidity established by the Lima Stock Exchange. The IBGC is a capitalization ratio, whereby the weights of the shares in the portfolio are obtained based on

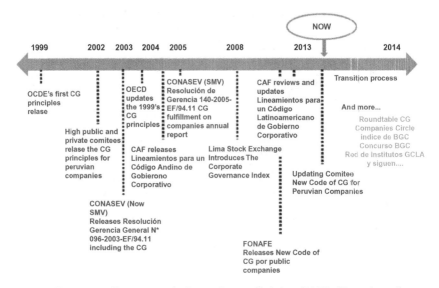

*Fig. 5.*   Corporate Governance in Peru. *Source*: Deloitte (2013). From http://www. procapitales.org/

***Table 3.***   Parties Involved Corporate Governance Code.

| Involved Parties on the Elaboration of the CG Code for Peruvian Companies |
| --- |
| Superintendencia del Mercado de Valores |
| La Asociación de Empresas Promotoras del Mercado de Capitales (PROCAPITALES) |
| Ministerio de Economía y Finanzas (MEF) |
| Superintendencia de Banca, Seguros y Administradoras Privadas de Fondos de Pensiones (SBS) |
| Fondo Nacional de Financiamiento de la Actividad Empresarial del Estado (FONAFE) |
| Bolsa de Valores de Lima S.A. (BVL) |
| CAVALI S.A. Institución de Compensación y Liquidación de Valores |
| Asociación de Sociedades Agentes de Bolsa del Perú |
| Asociación de Bancos (ASBANC) |
| Comité de Fondos Mutuos de ASBANC |
| Asociación de Administradoras Privadas de Fondos de Pensiones (AAFP) |
| Confederación Nacional de Instituciones Empresariales Privadas (CONFIEP) |
| Instituto Peruano de Auditores Independientes (IPAI) |
| Mercados de Capitales, Inversiones y Finanzas Consultores S.A. (MC&F) |

*Source*: Deloitte (2014).

***Table 4.***    Categories of the CG Principles.[a]

| Shareholders' Rights | Equitable Treatment of Shareholders | Disclosure and Transparency | Board Responsibilities |
|---|---|---|---|
| The framework of corporate governance must protect the rights of shareholders. | The corporate governance framework should ensure the equitable treatment of all shareholders, including minority and foreign shareholders. All shareholders should have the opportunity to obtain effective redress for violation of their rights | The framework of corporate governance should ensure that information accurately and regularly appears on all matters regarding the corporation, including the results, financial situation, ownership and corporate governance. | The framework of corporate governance should ensure the strategic guidance of the company, effective monitoring of management by the board of directors and responsibility toward the company and its shareholders. |

*Source*: BVL. Elaboration: The authors'.
*Note*: [a]For more details, go to Table B1.

the market capitalization of the "free-float" of these shares, adjusted for the level of corporate governance obtained. The higher the market capitalization of the free-float share, the greater the weight that will have a share in the index. The IBGC was launched by the Lima Stock Exchange on July 1, 2008 and its importance lies in that it benefits both companies and investors, because it allows better visibility of these and it is an important tool in making investment decisions. The securities in the portfolio of IBGC are valid for one year, considered from the first working day of July of the previous year to the last business day of June of the recalculation of the portfolio (Tables 5).

Other companies that also have good corporate governance practices, but for trading volume factors do not have been considered in the index are listed in Tables 6.

*Requirements and Procedures*

The BVL has published on its website information on what companies should do to join the Corporate Governance Index. According to the BVL (2009), those companies that are interested in being recognized by the Lima Stock Exchange (BVL) as companies adopting, at an appropriate level, the practices of good corporate governance, may participate in the evaluation

EDMUNDO R. LIZARZABURU ET AL.

*Table 5.* IBGC Portfolio as of September 5, 2014.

| No. | Company | Ticker |
| --- | --- | --- |
| 1. | Credicorp Ltd. | BAP |
| 2. | Alicorp S.A.A. | ALICORC1 |
| 3. | BBVA Banco Continental | CONTINC1 |
| 4. | Graña Y Montero S.A.A. | GRAMONC1 |
| 5. | Ferreycorp S.A.A. | FERREYC1 |
| 6. | Compañía De Minas Buenaventura S.A.A. | BVN |
| 7. | Cementos Pacasmayo S.A.A. | CPACASC1 |
| 8. | Compañía Minera Milpo S.A.A. | MILPOC1 |
| 9. | Edegel S.A.A. | EDEGELC1 |
| 10. | Refinería La Pampilla S.A.A. – Relapa S.A.A. | RELAPAC1 |

*Source*: BVL.

*Table 6.* Other Companies with CG Practices.

| Companies |
| --- |
| A.F.P Integra S.A. |
| AFP Habitat S.A. |
| Cavali S.A. I.C.L.V. |
| Corporación Financiera de Desarrollo S.A. – COFIDE |
| Corporación Lindley S.A. |
| Diviso Grupo Financiero S.A. |
| Empresa Electricidad del Perú – Electroperú S.A. |
| Manufactura de Metales y Aluminio "Record" S.A. |
| Prima AFP S.A. |
| Profuturo A.F.P. |
| Rimac Seguros y Reaseguros |
| Seguros Sura |
| Sociedad Minera el Brocal S.A.A. |
| Telefónica del Perú S.A.A. |
| Unión de Cervecerias Peruanas Backus y Johnston S.A.A. |

*Source*: BVL.

that the BVL develop annually. Will be considered in the selection process companies listed on the stock exchange and those who submitted voluntarily to the BVL a document where the company self-rated their level of adoption of these practices.

The Auto-evaluation has to be validated by a consulting firm that has been previously approved by the BVL to perform this work, following the minimum parameters of Evaluation of Corporate Governance Practices.

The validation service mentioned only will be offered by those consulting firms approved by the BVL for it. In this sense, the purpose of the consultancy is to validate the self-rating of good corporate governance practices of the companies listed on the Lima Stock Exchange.

The selected values will be part of the portfolio of IBGC during the period July assessment year and June of the following year. However, the weight of each security in the portfolio will be recalculated every six months. Also, the market name companies that have obtained an appropriate level of corporate governance practices but were not selected on the IBGC by other factors (low liquidity, etc.) will be published. This list of companies will be posted on the website of the Lima Stock Exchange.

The procedure to be part of the IBGC of the Lima Stock Exchange is shown in Fig. 6.

Accredited companies validating the survey are shown in Table 7.

## CONCLUSION AND COMMENTS

In recent years, a crisis of companies considered big and strong that these "could not fail" has had occurred. However, the reality showed the case of

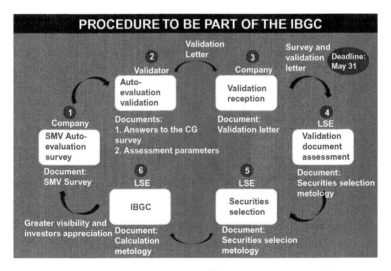

*Fig. 6.*   Procedure to Be Part of the IBGC. *Source*: BVL.

*Table 7.*   Validating Companies.

| No. | Company |
|-----|---------|
| 1. | Grant Thornton S.A.C. |
| 2. | Deloitte |
| 3. | MC&F-Mercado de Capitales, Inversiones y Finanzas |
| 4. | PCR – Clasificadora de Riesgo Pacific Credit Rating |
| 5. | Ernst & Young |
| 6. | PricewaterhouseCoopers |

*Source*: BVL.

Enron (2001) whose main engine was a series of deceptions, partnerships with other banks, agency problems, and manipulated financial disclosures did not reflect the current reality of the bank in order to continue attracting more investors for purchasing its shares. When the situation could no longer be held and the real situation of the company were met, the scandal caused in the market for this event was catastrophic, not only for the amount of money lost, but also because it showed the vulnerability of stakeholders to the weaknesses and the absence of a system of internal control and governance principles that were aligned with the interests of all stakeholders.

As the Enron case, we can mention several other cases such as Barings Bank (1995) in which the bank's internal controls failed to detect Nick Leeson operations; the case of telecommunications giant WorldCom (2002) who made up their financial statements in order to hide losses and obtain financing; or the case of Madoff Scam with his company Madoff Investment Securities (BMIS, 2008), with its pyramid scheme to make money, and in which it was outrageous how it passed unnoticed for inspections regulators and the Securities Exchange Comission (SEC), auditors and rating agencies. These are just a few examples of how the lack of control, transparent communication with shareholders, lack of ethics, and best practices affecting stock markets generated large losses, showing the market the lack of attention to this issue, and then a risk for consequence is to overregulate the financial system, originating a less response capacity in front an adverse macroeconomic environment change.

In Peru, since 2002 we have implemented the Code of Corporate Governance for Peruvian companies and since 2008 the Corporate Governance Index on the Lima Stock Exchange. That helped the market become more liquid; allowing local and foreign investors make better decisions, thanks to all the parties involved that worked to adapt the international standards of corporate governance to Latin American reality, moreover, specifically for Peruvian companies that promptly adopted these principles knowing and embracing the importance of this practices to gain more visibility and attract more investors, maintaining in-ceteris parabus-condition the macroeconomic factors.

# REFERENCES

BBC Mundo. (2006, Mayo 25). *BBC Mundo.com*. Retrieved from http://news.bbc.co.uk
Beekman, D. (2014). Madoff victim fund claims rise to nearly 52,000, total more than $40 billion in losses. *Daily News*, 13 de May de.
Bolsa de Valores de Lima. (2009). Corporate report.
Brammer, S., & Millington, A. (2008). Does it pay to be different? An analysis of the relationship between corporate social and financial performance. *Strategic Management Journal, 29*(12), 1325−1343.
Coughlan, A., & Schmidt, R. (1984). *Executive compensation, management turnover and firm performance*. New York, NY: University of Rochester.
Dalton, D. R., Daily, C. M., & Cannella, A. A. (2003). Corporate governance: Decades of dialogue and data. *Academy of Management Review, 28*(3), 371−382.
Davies, M., & Schlitzer, B. (2008). The impracticality of an international "one size fits all" corporate governance code of best practice. *Managerial Auditing Journal, 23*(6), 532−544.
Deloitte. (2013, October). *Procapitales*. Obtenido de http://www.procapitales.org/
Deloitte. (2014). Corporate report.
Freeman, R. E., & Reed, D. L. (1983). Stockholders and stakeholders: A new perspective on corporate governance. *California Management Review, 25*(3), 88−106.
Friedman, B. M. (1983). Pension funding, pension asset allocation, and corporation finance: Evidence from individual company data. In Z. Bodie & J. Shoven (Eds.), *Financial aspects of the United States pension system*. Chicago, IL: University of Chicago Press.
Gámiz, F. (2012). *Sarbanes-Oxley y la Protección de Los Accionistas en Perú*. Lima: KPMG.
González, J. S., & García-Meca, E. (2013). Does corporate governance influence earnings management in Latin American markets? *Journal Business Ethics, 121*(3), 419−440.
Johnson, G., & Scholes, K. (2001). *Exploring corporate strategy text and cases* (6th ed.). London: Prentice Hall.
Lacker, J. M. (2004). Payment system disruptions and the federal reserve following September 11, 2001. *Journal of Monetary Economics, 51*(5), 935–965.
Lantin American Development Bank – World Bank Group Edition. (2012). *World development indicators 2012*. World Bank Publications.
Lizarzaburu, E., Berggrun, L., & Burneo, K. (2014). Corporate governance in emerging markets and its impact on finance performance. *Corporate Ownership & Control, 12*, 625−632.
Moudud-Ul-Huq, S. (2014). Corporate governance practices in banking and non-banking financial institutions of Bangladesh. *IUP Journal of Corporate Governance, 13*(4), 61−70.
OCDE. (2014, September 6). *Organización para la Cooperación y Desarrollo Económicos*. Retrieved from http://www.oecd.org/

OECD. (2004). *OECD principles of corporate governance*. París: OECD Publications Service.

Pooja, G., & Sharma, A. M. (2014). A study of the impact of corporate governance practices on firm performance in Indian and South Korean companies. *Procedia – Social and Behavioral Sciences, 133*(2014), 4–11.

Sawayda, J. (2013). *The debate over the shareholder model of corporate governance*. Daniels Fund Ethics Initiative – University of New Mexico.

SMV. (2013). *Código del Buen Gobierno Corporativo para las sociedades peruanas*. Lima.

Stakeholders Publicaciones. (s.f.). Sobre el Índice del Buen Gobierno Corporativo. Suplemento Especial – BVL.

Starbuck, W. H. (2014). Why corporate governance deserves serious and creative thought. *Academy of Management Perspectives, 28*(1), 15–21. doi:10.5465/amp.2013.0109

The International Organization for Standardization. (2010). ISO 26000: Project Overview.

Wheeler, D., & Sillanpää, M. (1997). *The stakeholder corporation: A blueprint for maximizing stakeholder value*. London: Pitman Publishing.

# APPENDIX A

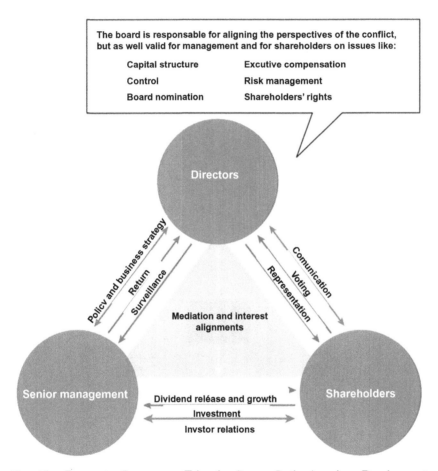

*Fig. A1.* Corporate Governance Triangle. *Source*: Latin American Development Bank (2012).

# APPENDIX B

**Table B1.** The 26 Principles of Corporate Governance for Peruvian Listed Companies.

| Pilars | | | |
|---|---|---|---|
| Shareholders' Rights | Equitable Treatment of Shareholders | Disclosure and Transparency | The Responsibilities of the Board |
| Do not include generic issues on the agenda, being stressed talking points so that each topic is discussed separately, facilitating its analysis and avoiding the joint resolution of issues on which you can have a different opinion. | Should choose a sufficient number of directors capable of exercising independent judgment to tasks where there is a potential conflict of interest, being able, for this purpose, and taking into consideration the participation of shareholders lacking control. | While generally external audits are focused on expressing opinions on financial information, they may also refer to opinions or specialized reports on the following aspects: accounting expertise, operational audits, systems audits, project evaluation, evaluation or implementation cost systems, tax audits, or other special services. It is recommended that such services are performed by different auditors or, if auditors handle themselves; do not affect the independence of opinion | Evaluate, approve, and guide corporate strategy; setting objectives and targets as well as major plans of action, policy monitoring, control and risk management, annual budgets, and business plans; monitor the implementation thereof; and overseeing major capital expenditures, investments, acquisitions, and disposals — Monitor the effectiveness of the governance practices under which it operates and making changes as they become necessary — Following clearly established and defined policies, the board may decide to engage the services of specialized expertise required by the company for decision-making |
| The venue of the General Meetings should be set so that the attendance of shareholders to them is facilitated | Independent directors are those selected for their professional prestige and who are not connected with the administration of the society or major shareholders of it | Attention to particular requests for information by shareholders, investors in general or stakeholders related to the company, must be made through an instance and/or personnel responsible designated for that purpose | Select, monitor, and, when necessary, replacing key executives and to fix their remuneration — Supervise information policy — New directors should be instructed on their powers and responsibilities as well as the characteristics and organizational structure of society |

It should establish procedures that the board continues in choosing one or more replacements, if no alternate directors and the vacancy of one or more directors occurs, in order to complete their numbers for the remaining period when there is no provision for different treatment in the statute

The directors may form special bodies according to the needs and size of the company, especially one that assumes the audit function. Also, these special bodies may be, inter alia, the functions of appointment, retribution, control, and planning

Evaluate the compensation of top executives and board members, ensuring that the procedure for electing directors is formal and transparent

The cases of doubt on the confidential nature of the information requested by shareholders or stakeholders related to the company must be resolved. The criteria should be adopted by the board and ratified by the General Meeting and included in the statute or rules of society. In any case, the disclosure of information should not jeopardize the competitive position of the company or be likely to affect the normal development of the activities

The company should have internal audit. The internal auditor, in the exercise of their duties, must relate to professional independence from the company that hires. Should act and observe the same principles of diligence, loyalty, and confidentiality at board and management are required

Monitor and control of possible conflicts of interest of management, board members, and shareholders, including misuse of corporate assets and abuse in transactions between interested parties

The membership of the board of a company should ensure plurality of opinions within it, so that decisions taken therein are the result of appropriate deliberation, always looking after the best interests of the company and shareholders

The functions of the Chairman, if applicable Executive Chairman and the CEO should be clearly defined in the statute or the rules of society in order to avoid duplication of functions and possible conflicts

Shareholders should have the opportunity to enter items to be discussed within a reasonable limit on the agenda of the General Meetings

It is recommended that the issuing of investment shares or other equity securities without voting rights, society offer their holders the opportunity to exchange for common shares voting or providing for this possibility at the time of issue.

## Table B1. (Continued)

| | Pilars | | |
|---|---|---|---|
| Shareholders' Rights | Equitable Treatment of Shareholders | Disclosure and Transparency | The Responsibilities of the Board |
| | | | Ensuring the integrity of accounting systems and financial statements of the Company, including the independent audit, and the existence of appropriate control systems, in particular, financial risk control and non-financial and law enforcement | Information concerning the matters to be discussed at each meeting must be made available to the directors with sufficient notice to enable them to review, except when dealing with strategic matters that are confidential, in which case it will be necessary to establish mechanisms enabling the directors to properly evaluate such matters | The organizational structure of the company should avoid concentrating functions, powers, and responsibilities to the people of the Chairman, the Executive Chairman of the case, the General Manager, and other officials with management responsibilities |
| | | | | | It is recommended that the Management receives at least part of their compensation based on the results of the company, so that compliance with the objective of maximizing corporate value for shareholders is ensured |

*Source:* SMV (2013).

# OPTIMAL ARBITRAGE PATH IN THE FOREIGN EXCHANGE MARKET

Reza Habibi

## ABSTRACT

*This chapter is concerned with finding the optimal arbitrage path in a foreign exchange market. First, an algorithm for the optimal arbitrage path is derived. Then, the Markov chain solution to the problem of most profitable path is given. Also, a game theory perspective to the problem is given.*

**Keywords:** Largest eigenvalue; exchange rate matrix; triangular arbitrage opportunities

## INTRODUCTION

Ma (2008) detected arbitrage opportunities in a foreign exchange market containing $n$ currencies. He used a linear transformation maximum eigenvalue of the exchange rates matrix of $A = (a_{ij})$, that is,

$$\Lambda = \frac{\lambda_{\max} - n}{n - 1}$$

The Spread of Financial Sophistication Through Emerging Markets Worldwide
Research in Finance, Volume 32, 337–343
Copyright © 2016 by Emerald Group Publishing Limited
All rights of reproduction in any form reserved
ISSN: 0196-3821/doi:10.1108/S0196-382120160000032014

as the arbitrage leading indicator. Here, $a_{ij}$ is the exchange rate of $i$th currency with respect to the $j$th currency, $i, j = 1, 2, ..., n$. Let $w_i$ be the intrinsic price of $i$th currency. Then, the market has no arbitrage opportunities if $a_{ij} = \frac{w_i}{w_j}$, for all $i, j = 1, 2, ..., n$. The price discrepancy of a specified asset at two different markets motivates investors to provide a zero risk arbitrage profit by buying the asset low and selling it high, simultaneously. The no arbitrage assumption (No-Arb) is a fundamental equilibrium principle for pricing the financial assets such as financial derivatives (Bjork, 2009). Moosa (2003) exploited the arbitrage opportunities in several kinds of markets. Soon and Ye (2011) considered the currency arbitrage detection using a binary integer programming model. Zhang (2012) proposed a neural network model for currency arbitrage detection. There are several types of arbitrage. The above No-Arb assumption $a_{ij} = \frac{w_i}{w_j}$ yields several types of No-Arbs, such as three-point arbitrage (triangular arbitrage). It is the possibility of arbitrage because of differences in the price of an asset between three markets. It happens in the foreign exchange market due to cross exchange rate discrepancies among three or more different currencies. In a formal way, it is written as

$$a_{ij} = a_{ik}a_{kj}, \quad \text{for all} \quad i, j = 1, 2..., n$$

If the above conditions hold, the matrix $A$ is consistent (Analytic Hierarchy Process, AHP, see Saaty (1980). Chacholiades (1971) showed that the necessary and sufficient condition to remove any type of arbitrage such as four- or five-point arbitrage is removing the triangular arbitrage. Ma (2008) argued that $\Lambda$ is an arbitrage indicator. When there is an arbitrage, then $a_{ij} = \frac{w_i}{w_j}\varepsilon_{ij}$ for some $i, j$. Hao (2009) detected the applied method of Ma's foreign exchange market considering the bid-ask transactions. The rest of this chapter is organized as follows. The section "The Arbitrage Path" contains derivation of the optimal arbitrage path. The section "Markov Chain Solution" gives a Markov chain solution to the problem of most profitable path.

# THE ARBITRAGE PATH

Dijkstra (1959) also proposed a solution for the problem based on the shortest-path algorithm. Ma (2008) argued that the bridge between the maximum of $\varepsilon_{ij}$ and minimum of $\varepsilon_{ij}$ is the optimal arbitrage path and studied that arbitrage path in two-, three-, and four-point arbitrage cases. If $\varepsilon_{ij}$ is one or very close to one, then the No-Arb is satisfied. Saaty (1980) proved that

$$\Lambda = \frac{\sum_{i=1}^{n} \sum_{j=1}^{n} \left(\varepsilon_{ij} - 1\right)}{n(n-1)}$$

When the matrix $A$ is consistent (there is no arbitrage opportunity), then $\lambda_{\max} = n$ (other eigenvalues are zero) and $\Lambda = 0$. In case of the existence of arbitrage $\lambda_{\max} > n$ and other, eigenvalues are negative. Therefore, the

$$\lambda_{\max} > n \quad \text{or} \quad \varepsilon_{ij} > 1$$

are indicators of the arbitrage opportunities. The $\varepsilon_{ij} - 1$ implies the excess return(er) of buying the $i$th currency with the $j$th currency, since

$$\text{er}_{ij} = \frac{\varepsilon_{ij} - (w_i/w_j)}{w_i/w_j}$$

It can be shown that

$$\Lambda = \frac{\sum_{i=1}^{n} \varepsilon_{ij}}{n-1}$$

Indeed, $\Lambda$ is the mean excess return if the investor buys all currencies using a specified currency. If there is no arbitrage, then this additional return is zero, and $\Lambda$ is the mean of all excess returns. In practice, $\text{er}_{ij}$ are bounded and the central limit theorem may be applied to approximate a normal frequency distribution for $\Lambda$ see Ferguson (1996). The $\text{er}_{ij}$ is gain if it is positive and loss if it is zero or negative. Therefore, the optimal arbitrage path is a path like $i_1 \to i_2 \to \cdots \to i_m \to i_1$ such that the following maximum is attained:

$$\max_{1 \leq i_1 \leq \cdots \leq i_m} \left(a_{i_1 i_2} a_{i_2 i_3} \ldots a_{i_{(m-1)} i_m} a_{i_m i_1}\right) = \max_{1 \leq i_1 \leq \cdots \leq i_m} \left(\varepsilon_{i_1 i_2} \varepsilon_{i_2 i_3} \ldots \varepsilon_{i_{(m-1)} i_m} \varepsilon_{i_m i_1}\right)$$

The above discussion shows that by choosing a suitable $i_1$ (it will be discussed in the section "Markov Chain Solution"), it is enough to select the maximum of $\varepsilon_{i,j}$. The above argument can be presented in other way, given as follows:

$$\max_{1 \le i_1 \le \cdots \le i_m} \left( \varepsilon_{i_1 i_2} \varepsilon_{i_2 i_3} \cdots \varepsilon_{i_{(m-1)} i_m} \varepsilon_{i_m i_1} \right)$$

$$= \max_{1 \le i_1 \le \cdots \le i_m} \left( \exp \left( \ln(1 + \varepsilon_{i_1 i_2} - 1) + \cdots + \ln(\varepsilon_{i_m i_1} - 1 + 1) \right) \right)$$

$$\approx \exp \left( \max_{1 \le i_1 \le \cdots \le i_m} \left( \varepsilon_{i_1 i_2} - 1 + \cdots + \varepsilon_{i_m i_1} - 1 \right) \right)$$

That is, the subsequence of like $i_1 \to i_2 \to \cdots \to i_m \to i_1$ such that has the maximum among positive excess returns $er_{ij}$ of $\Lambda$ to construct the optimal arbitrage path. There is a similar argument based on *Bellman's* principal of optimality, which yields the same conclusions. The last term is true because for small $x$, then $\ln(1 + x) \approx x$. As follows, the optimal arbitrage path is given through a portfolio management perspective. Let $i = 1$ be fixed. Then, a portfolio containing $n_j$ units of the $j$th currency is well diversified by the following maximization:

$$\max_{n_j} \sum_{j=1}^{n} n_j \left( a_{1j} - \frac{w_1}{w_j} \right)$$

with respect to $\{n_j\}_{j=1,2,\ldots,n}$ such that $\sum_{j=1}^{n} n_j = N$. It is equivalent to the following maximization:

$$\max_{x_j} \sum_{j=1}^{n} x_j (\varepsilon_{1j} - 1)$$

such that $\sum_{j=1}^{n} x_j = 1$. The equivalent form is the maximization of $\max_{x_j} \sum_{j=2}^{n} x_j (\varepsilon_{1j} - 1)$, when $\sum_{j=2}^{n} x_j < 1$. The dual linear program is given by $\min(y)$, for $y \ge \max_{j \ge 2} (\varepsilon_{1j} - 1)$. The minimum is attained at $x_{j^*}$, where $j^* = \text{argmax}_j (\varepsilon_{1j} - 1)$. In the above strategy, short selling is not allowed. To consider this operation, it is enough to define $j^* = \text{argmax}_j (|\varepsilon_{1j} - 1|)$. Indeed, it is enough to select the maximum of $\varepsilon_{i_1 i_2} - 1$ for $i_1$th row. A natural question arises is how to select $i_1$ where this will be answered by a game theory approach. The following algorithm finds the optimal arbitrage path (if short selling is not allowed). This algorithm will be modified in the last section.

**Algorithm 1.** *Finding the arbitrage path.*

1. *Set $i_1 = 1$.*
2. *Find $j_2^* = \text{argmax}_j(\varepsilon_{1j} - 1)$ and let $i_2 = j_2^*$.*
3. *Continue to find time points $i_3, \ldots, i_m$.*
4. *Compute $a_{i_1 i_2} a_{i_2 i_3} \ldots a_{i_{(m-1)} i_m} a_{i_m i_1}$.*
5. *Set $i_1 = 2$ and repeat steps 2,3,4.*
6. *Find the maximum of $a_{i_1 i_2} a_{i_2 i_3} \ldots a_{i_{(m-1)} i_m} a_{i_m i_1}$. It is the optimal arbitrage path.*
7. *In each step, the $\varepsilon_{ij} - 1$ with be replaced by its absolute value if short selling is allowed.*

## MARKOV CHAIN SOLUTION

Here, we consider a Markov chain solution for finding the subsequence of the section "The Arbitrage Path." Let $I_t$ denotes the currency the investor has at time $t \in \{1, 2, \ldots, n\}$. Then the probability of buying the $j$th currency at time $t + 1$ using currency $i$ is given by

$$p_{ij} = P(I_{t+1} = j | I_t = i) = \frac{a_{ij}}{a_{i+}}$$

where $a_{i+} = \sum_{j=1}^{n} a_{ij}$. It is easy to see that $I_t$ is a Markov chain (Billingsley, 1995) and its transition matrix is given by

$$P = \begin{pmatrix} \frac{a_{11}}{a_{1+}} & \cdots & \frac{a_{1n}}{a_{1+}} \\ \vdots & \ddots & \vdots \\ \frac{a_{n1}}{a_{n+}} & \cdots & \frac{a_{nn}}{a_{n+}} \end{pmatrix}$$

Under the No-Arb assumption, then the risk neutral probability measure is given by

$$Q_{ij} = \frac{1/w_i}{\sum_{k=1}^{n} 1/w_k} = \frac{1}{a_{i+}}$$

Under $Q$, this chain has stable distribution given by $\pi_i = \frac{1}{a_{i+}}$. Let $U_{ij}$ be the utility denote the utility achieved to investor by passing from state $i$ to state $j$, that is $U_{ij} = a_{ij}$. Given state $i$, it is seen that

$$E_p(U_{ij}) = E_Q\left(U_{ij}^2\right)$$

Under the risk neutral probability measure $Q$,

$$E_Q(U_{ijk}) = E_Q(U_{ij})$$

which shows the martingale properties of $U_{ij}$. Similarly, given states $i_1, i_2, \ldots, i_m$ then

$$E_p\left(U_{i_1, i_2, \ldots, i_{m,i_1}}\right) = E_Q\left(U_{i_1, i_2, \ldots, i_{m,i_1}}^2\right)$$

The most profitable path for investor may be found by maximization of $E_Q\left(U_{i_1, i_2, \ldots, i_{m,i_1}}^2\right)$. The algorithm gives the solution.

**Algorithm 2.** *Finding the most profitable path.*

1. *Set $i_1 = 1$.*
2. *Find $j_2^* = \mathrm{argmax}_j\left(\varepsilon_{1j} - 1\right)$ and let $i_2 = j_2^*$.*
3. *Continue to find time points $i_3, \ldots, i_m$.*
4. *Compute $E_Q\left(U_{i_1, i_2, \ldots, i_{m,i_1}}^2\right)$.*
5. *Set $i_1 = 2$ and repeat steps 2,3,4.*
6. *Find the maximum of $a_{i_1 i_2} a_{i_2 i_3} \ldots a_{i_{(m-1)} i_m} a_{i_m i_1}$. It is the optimal arbitrage path.*

## GAME THEORETIC APPROACH

A natural question arises is which row of $A$ should be selected? Here, based on game theory, solution is proposed. That is, a randomized strategy $\{q_j\}_{j=1}^n$ (probability measure) is designed such that for each row the expectation of *investor's* profit is maximized. The necessary condition to this end is

$$\sum_{j=1}^n q_j a_{1j} = \cdots = \sum_{j=1}^n q_j a_{nj}$$

where a matrix equivalent form is $Aq = a*1$, for some arbitrary $a*$ where $q$ is the vector of probabilities. When there is an arbitrage opportunity, then the largest eigenvalue is $n$ and others are negative. If all of them are non-zero, then the inverse of matrix $A$ exists and $q = a**A^{-1}1$. Therefore, the algorithm 1 is revisited as follows (step 1 is replaced by 1'):

**Algorithm 3.** *Finding the arbitrage path.*

1. *Find $i_1$ as described above.*
2. *Find $j_2^* = \text{argmax}_j(\varepsilon_{1j} - 1)$ and let $i_2 = j_2^*$.*
3. *Continue to find time points $i_3, ..., i_m$.*
4. *Compute $a_{i_1i_2}a_{i_2i_3}...a_{i_{(m-1)}i_m}a_{i_mi_1}$.*
5. *Set $i_1 = 2$ and repeat steps 2,3,4.*
6. *Find the maximum of $a_{i_1i_2}a_{i_2i_3}...a_{i_{(m-1)}i_m}a_{i_mi_1}$. It is the optimal arbitrage path.*
7. *In each step, the $\varepsilon_{ij} - 1$ with be replaced by its absolute value if short selling is allowed.*

# REFERENCES

Billingsley, P. (1995). *Probability and measure.* New York, NY: Wiley.
Bjork, T. (2009). *Arbitrage theory in continuous time.* Oxford: Oxford University Press.
Chacholiades, M. (1971). The sufficiency of three-point arbitrage to ensure consistent cross rates of exchange. *Southern Economic Journal, 38,* 86–88.
Dijkstra, E. W. (1959). A note on two problems in connexion with graphs. *Numerische Mathematik, 1,* 269–271.
Ferguson, T. S. (1996). *A course in large sample theory.* USA: Chapman & Hall.
Hao, Y. *Foreign exchange rate arbitrage using the matrix method.* Technical Report. Chulalongkorn University, Bangkok.
Ma, M. (2008). *Identifying foreign exchange arbitrage opportunities through matrix approach.* Technical Report. School of Management and Economics, Beijing Institute of Technology.
Moosa, I. A. (2003). *International financial operations: Arbitrage, hedging, speculation, financing and investment.* New York, NY: Palgrave Macmillan.
Saaty, T. L. (1980). *The analytic hierarchy process.* New York, NY: McGraw Hill.
Soon, W., & Ye, H. Q. (2011). Currency arbitrage detection using a binary integer programming model. *International Journal of Mathematical Education in Science and Technology, 42,* 369–376.
Zhang, Z. (2012). A neural network model for currency arbitrage detection. *Advances in neural networks* (Vol. 73, pp. 64–71). Lecture Notes in Computer Science. USA: Springer.

# THE MISALIGNMENT PHENOMENA IN THE FOREIGN EXCHANGE MARKET: EVIDENCE FOR THE TUNISIAN DINAR

Salima Ben Ezzeddine and Kamel Naoui

## ABSTRACT

*The aim of this chapter is to assess the real exchange rate misalignments. A smooth transition autoregressive model (STAR) is used for Tunisian exchange market. This model allows us to see whether these differences are temporary or persistent over the period 1975–2012. We start by defining the exchange rate's fundamental determinants to provide the equilibrium exchange rate value. Then, we study the observed exchange rate adjustment toward its equilibrium level. Vector autoregressive model and vector error correction model are applied to characterize the joint dynamics of variables in the long run. The results indicate a long-run relationship between variables. In order to consider the nonlinearity for better results, we will move to nonlinear smooth transition model. We found there is a high degree of exchange rate misalignment.*

The Spread of Financial Sophistication Through Emerging Markets Worldwide
Research in Finance, Volume 32, 345–360
Copyright © 2016 by Emerald Group Publishing Limited
ISSN: 0196-3821/doi:10.1108/S0196-382120160000032015

*We recognized that this difference decreases in the long run and disappears at the end.*

**Keywords:** Real exchange rate; misalignment phenomena; nonlinear model; Logistic Smooth Transition Auto-Regression; LSTAR

**JEL classifications:** C23; F31; F62; F65; G15

# INTRODUCTION

The financial markets have a high disequilibrium level over the last two decades. The interrogation that exchange rates can spend long periods away from their fundamentals values implied a revival of interest in the study of exchange rate equilibrium. Any deviation from the equilibrium level is temporary. There are forces ensuring quickly mean-reverting dynamics (Mignon, Dufrénot, Lardic, Mathieu, & Feissolle, 2008). However, Dufrénot, Lardic, Mathieu, Mignon, and Péguin-Feissolle (2004) thought that this idea was very idealistic. The exchange rate deviation from the equilibrium value is exchange rate misalignments.

Our aim is to find out if the misalignments Tunisian real exchange rates have temporary deviations from the fundamentals. If not, they must be associated with significant persistent dynamics. We choose the Tunisian Dinar and Euro (TND/EUR) for European influences reasons. By the end of the 20th century, the US dollar is the world's most dominant reserve currency, that's why we will considerate the TND/USD. The period of our sample is 1975−2012.

The standard macroeconomic view links the exchange rate misalignment to the macroeconomic fundamentals. The most useful fundamental models are: (1) The purchasing power parity (effective in the long run) (Cassel, 1918), (2) The fundamental equilibrium exchange rate (FEER) (Williamson, 1994), (3) The behavioral equilibrium exchange rate (BEER) as proposed by Clark and MacDonald (1998). The first model does not describe the convergence to the equilibrium but gives, for known period, the exchange rate misalignment degree. The second model controls the exchange rate misalignment with a behavioral model. The problem with models is that the size of previous misalignments affects the deviations. The dependence of the time proves that the adjustment may not be constant rate, like in linear models (VAR, linear cointegration test, linear VECM, etc.). This means that in practice, when disequilibrium appears, prices do not quickly move to bring the real exchange rate to its equilibrium level. Using nonlinear cointegration is more suitable than the standard linear cointegration. For this chapter, we will use a nonlinear model approach with smooth transition auto-regression, STAR.

The goal is to provide a better understanding of the adjustment that underlies the misalignments of the Tunisian exchange rates. We will explore the cointegration between exchange rates and their fundamentals. This chapter is structured as follows: The next section is "Literature Review". The section "Data and Methodology" describes the STAR model, the data and cointegration tests. The section "Results and Discussion" describes the results and interpretation. The section "Conclusion" ends the chapter.

# LITERATURE REVIEW

The equilibrium of exchange rates aroused interest of the economists for long time. There are many methods to describe the evolutions. The fundamentals' influence on the exchange rates has been amply considered in the economic literature (Edwards, 1994; Isard, 2007; Ricci, Milesi-Ferretti, & Lee, 2008). The issue is that the economic fundamentals often fail to explain short-term misalignment in exchange rates (see Meese & Rogoff, 1983). Transitory shocks dominate exchange rate variations, while permanent shocks dominate the variations in economical fundamentals (Chen & Chou, 2015). The economists used annual data from 1880 to 2011 for Finland, France, Italy, Portugal, Spain, and Switzerland.

The standard models, such as the target zone models (Krugman, 1991; Tronzano, Psaradakis, & Sola, 2003), transaction costs (Dumas, 1992; Imbs, Mumtaz, Ravn, & Rey, 2003; Obstfeld & Taylor, 1997; O'Connell & Wei, 1997; Sercu, Uppal, & Van Hulle, 1995), heterogeneity of buyers and sellers (Taylor & Allen, 1992), speculative attacks on currencies (Flood & Marion, 1999), heterogeneity of central banks' interventions (Dominguez, 1998), and heterogeneous behaviors model (De long, Shleifer, Summers, & Waldmann, 1990), show the prices move quickly. However in practice, when there is disequilibrium, prices do not quickly move to bring the exchange rate to its long-run equilibrium. Agreeing with this line, Mignon, Coudert, and Couharde (2015) analyzed the impact of terms of trade on real exchange rates. They inferred that only advanced oil-exporter's currencies are sensitive to changes in terms of trade in the short run, especially when volatility is high on commodity markets. Tang (2015) considered between the real exchange rate and the economic growth in China applying the cointegrated VAR (CVAR).

Sallenave (2010) looked into the misalignment impact on economic growth. The results showed that misalignments have a negative influence on the economic growth. As a note, a correct exchange rate policy would close the gap between real exchange rates and their equilibrium level.

Further, nonlinear models (Nonlinear GARCH models, Markov switching models, multifactor GARCH models, threshold autoregressive models (TAR), etc.), become very suitable to describe the misalignment phenomena. The assigned model for works of Dufrénot, Guéguan, and Péguin-Feissole (2005) was the self-exciting TAR (SETAR) by a long memory. The results suggest the model offers an interesting alternative competing to describe the persistent in modeling the powers of the returns (Chan & Tong, 1986). In this chapter, we will focus on TAR models (Tong & Lim, 1980; Tong, 1990) by exposing the misalignment switching by a nonlinear model with smooth regression STAR. The latter describes the persistent shocks on future misalignments. STAR models are more suitable for nonparametric variables (Stock & Watson, 1999; Teräsvirta, van Dijk, & Medeiros, 2005). The most important argument of choosing STAR instead of SETAR is in fitting turbulent variable (see Teräsvirta, 1995). In this case, Mignon et al. (2008) opted for STAR model, after many tests. The unit root test shows that all the series are not stationary, except the interest rate. This variable was, moreover, dropped in the long-run relation. On the other hand, the cointegration test points out the existence of two relationships: between $q_{i,t}$, $NFA_{i,t}$, and $RPI_{i,t}$ and between $q_{i,t}$, $NFA_{i,t}$, $RPI_{i,t}$, and $tot_{i,t}$. Their result showed the real exchange rate convergence process in the long run is characterized by nonlinearities for emerging economies, whereas industrialized countries present linear pattern. Besides, there exists an asymmetric behavior of the real exchange rate when facing an over- or an undervaluation of the domestic currency. The real exchange rate may be unable to unwind only global imbalances.

Coudert, Mignon, and Couharde (2013) studied the associationship between terms of trade and real exchange rates of commodity producing Commodity currencies, countries in both the short and the long run. They explored the dominant role played by oil among commodities by researching the potential nonlinear effect exerted on the oil market on the real exchange rate − terms of trade link. To this end, they relied on the panel smooth transition regression method to estimate the adjustment of the real effective exchange rate to its equilibrium value depending on the oil market volatility. They chose panel of 52 commodity exporters and 17 oil exporters over the 1980−2012 period. They found the exchange rates are mostly sensitive to changes in terms of trade when oil price variations exceed a certain threshold. The commodity-currency property is thus at play in the short run only for important variations of the oil price.

The equilibrium exchange rates literature has focused on country-by-country estimations of equilibrium exchange rates (Clark & MacDonald, 1998) or on consistent estimations of equilibrium exchange rates for a set of industrial economies (Williamson, 1994; Wren-Lewis & Driver, 1998). Béreau, Mignon, and Villavicencio (2010) takes the G-20 group as a sample which includes both developing and industrial economies. Our research concerns the case of developing country, the Tunisia's currencies. Most of the conclusions of the large literature show a time-varying smooth vector error correction model (Bierens & Martins, 2010), which was generalized by Park and Hahn (1999). They included the purchasing power parity theory of international prices and nominal exchange rates. They verified if the cointegrating vector provides a solution to the disequilibrium path in the long-run money demand. Many authors have deduced the misalignment by the FEER approach like Saadaoui (2012), Jeong, Mazier, and Saadaoui (2010), Cline and Williamson (2012), and Carton and Hervé (2012). Indeed, since 1999 the real exchange rates did not stop evolving. The misalignment is important because of the wide difference between the real exchange rate and the Fundamental Equilibrium Exchange Rate. Despite these obvious facts, it is important to know that misalignment eventually converges on its equilibrium value, thanks to economic strengths.

## DATA AND METHODOLOGY

Mignon et al. (2008) studied the real exchange rate toward the fundamentals of five European countries, using STAR model:

$$y_t = \left(\alpha_0 + \alpha_1 y_{t-1} + \cdots + \alpha_p y_{t-p}\right) + \left(\beta_0 + \beta_1 y_{t-1} + \cdots + \beta_p y_{t-p}\right) G(S_t; \gamma, c) + \varepsilon_t \quad (1)$$

where $G(S_t; \gamma, c)$ is the transaction function from state to another one such as: $0 \leq G \leq 1$; $\gamma$ is the slope, more it is high more the transition is rough and fast; $S_t$ is the transition variable; $c$ is the located parameter; and $\varepsilon_t$ is the random error having no average and constant variance.

The authors assumed if the difference between the real exchange rates answers symmetrically past positive or negative deflections then the exponential smoothly autoregressive models of transition (ESTAR) are more convenient. However, if the adjustment toward the fundamental value (positive or negative shocks) rather asymmetric, the models Logistic STAR (LSTAR) are best. However, the nonlinear tests lead to reject the case of an asymmetric adjustment of logistic type. Thus, they did estimate the ESTAR.

$$G(S_t; \gamma, c) = \left(1 - \exp(-\gamma(S_t - c))^2\right), \quad \gamma > 0 \qquad (2)$$

The transition variables are chosen in the tests of linearity. It is about a clear signal of nonlinear dynamic return to the equilibrium for the Netherlands, the United Kingdom, and Portugal, despite the unit root presence. Coudert, Couharde, and Mignon (2011) used the STAR model to study the impact of global financial turmoil on the exchange rate policies in emerging countries. Spillovers from advanced financial markets to currencies in emerging countries are exacerbated during crisis periods. To test this theory, we assess the exchange rate policies by currencies volatility and explore their relationship to a global financial stress sign, measured by global markets volatility. They introduced the possibility of nonlinearities by running smooth transition regressions over a sample of 21 emerging countries from January 1994 to September 2009. The results confirm that exchange rate volatility does increase more than proportionally with the global financial stress, for most countries in the sample. They also evidence regional contagion effects spreading from one emerging currency to other currencies in the neighboring area.

*Data, Normality Test and Unit Root Test*

We use yearly data over the period 1975–2012 (37 years) for the following parities: TND/EUR and TND/USD. The data are obtained from World Bank website www.worldbank.org

According to Grossmann and Orlov (2012) and Béreau et al. (2010), our fundamentals are represented as follows: (1) Real exchange rate (RER) is, our endogenous variable, defined as the ratio of the domestic consumer price index to the foreign consumer price index. It is constructed as the trade weighted average of the exchange rates, where the weights are based on bilateral trade share; (2) GDP is the gross domestic product; (3) TOT is an indicator of the terms of trade, defined as the ratio of export price index to import price index; (4) IDE is a variable of foreign direct investments; and (5) NFA is a variable of net foreign assets.

As first step, we will test the theory of a normal distribution by Jarque-Béra test. The null hypothesis is the normal distribution against the alternative, non-normal distribution. To find out the order of integration of our sample, we will apply unit root test Augmented Dickey-Fuller (ADF). The null hypothesis: the data need to be differenced to make it stationary against the alternative that the data are stationary and do not need to be differenced. We will do both the tests for each of our sample. The results of Jarque-Béra and ADF tests are condensed in Table 1 which shows the accepting or rejecting the null by probability values.

In line with the Jarque-Béra test, we reject the null against the alternative. Our distributions are non-normal at the level of 10% except for terms of trade (TOT). The latter will be rejected because of non-significance.

Just as ADF test, the null is rejected at 10% level for all time series. It means RER, for example, does not have a unit root problem and the RER series is a stationary series at 1%, 5%, and 10% significant level (same results for America and Tunisia).

*Cointegration Test, Var, Vecm*

Once our time series are from non-normal distribution and do not have a unit root problem, we can test linear cointegration using both Trace Test and Maximum likelihood test. Our results extracted from E-view are ambiguous at 5% level for Tunisia and France but clear for the United States which indicates that there is no cointegration. Therefore, Table 2 pointed out the linear tests used to confirm robustness for American time series (Vector Autoregressive) and correct ambiguities for the other part of time series (Vector Error Correction Model).

Estimation of VAR model:

$$X_t = c + A_1 X_{t-1} + \cdots + A_p X_{t-p} + \varepsilon_t \qquad (3)$$

***Table 1.*** Jarque-Béra and ADF Test.

|              | RER        | GDP        | IDE        | NFA        | TOT        |
|--------------|------------|------------|------------|------------|------------|
| Jarque-Béra  | 35.911     | 1642.3     | 5.067      | 5.793      | 3.6        |
| $p$-Value    | 0.0000***  | 0.0000***  | 0.0793*    | 0.0552*    | 0.1652     |
| ADF test     | −5.36      | −4.105     | −5.414     | −3.361     | −5.661     |
| $p$-Value    | 0.0006***  | 0.014**    | 0.0005***  | 0.0766*    | 0.0000***  |

*Notes*: Those values are extracted from E-views. Significance is detected by the value of probability. Values of Jarque-Béra detect the nature of the distribution, if it is a normal or abnormal time series. Values of ADF allow us to deduce if our time series sample has or not a unit root. ***, ** and * indicate significance at 1%, 5%, and 10% levels, respectively.

***Table 2.*** VAR Model and VECM Model.

|  | $t$-Statistic | $p$-Value |
|---|---|---|
| *VAR (USD)* | | |
| RER(−3) | −3.37 | 0.0001*** |
| RER(−4) | 3.885 | 0.0002*** |
| *VECM (EUR)* | | |
| CointEq1 | −0.896 | 0.06* |
| *VECM (TND)* | | |
| CointEq1 | −0.026 | 0.048** |

*Notes*: The VAR tests past values influence of RER on the current values. The significance can be detected by $p$-value. If the variable is significant, we say there is an influence. The VECM corrects the errors happened in cointegration test and shows the causality between variables in the long run. If the variable is significant and negative then there is long-run causality. Values of ADF allow us to deduce if our time series sample has or not a unit root.
***, ** and * indicate significance at 1%, 5%, and 10% levels, respectively.

where $X_t$ is a dimension vector ($n \times 1$), $n$ is an endogenous variable, $A_i$ is a time-invariant ($n \times n$) matrix, $c$ is the vector of constants, $p$ is the lag, $\varepsilon_t$ is white noise. Estimation of VECM:

$$\Delta y_t = \gamma \Delta x_t + \delta(y_{t-1} - ax_{t-1} - b) + \varepsilon_t \text{ avec } \delta < 0 \qquad (4)$$

When $y_{t-1} > (ax_{t-1} + b)$, in the long run there is not forces ensuring mean-reverting dynamics only if $\delta$ is significantly negative.

Where $y_t$ and $x_t$ are two series nonstationary and cointegrated, $(1 - a - b)$ is the cointegration vector, $b > 0$, $\varepsilon_t$ is residue.

We can deduce:

$$\varepsilon_t = y_t - ax_t - b \qquad (5)$$

The dependent variable RER with 3 and 4 lags are significant as we can see in Table 2. We may say that the past value of RER influence the present RER watched. We have summarized the results in this table, but E-views shows us the same results for the other independent variables (e.g., GDP(−3) and IDE(−4) are significant at 5% level). Thus, according to Mignon et al. (2008), the independent variables have an important influence on the RER value. The Wald coefficient test allows us to verify if there is a joint influence on RER. RER(−3) and RER(−4) jointly can influence RER (same thing for all the other variables except for TOT).

After selecting the optimum lag which is 3 and verifying that all variables are stationary at first difference, we estimated the VECM. The error correction model suggests the validity of the equilibrium relationship indicating the existence of market forces that operate to restore long-run equilibrium. We found, similar to Poon, Choong, and Habibullah (2005), the values are negative and significant. RER(−3) for TND have *t*-statistic negative and significant (−0.776). There is a long-run relationship between RER(−3) and RER. For Euro, RER(−4) have a *t*-statistic equal to (−0.337). There is a long-run causality running the RER(−4) to the RER. The RER, GDP, TOT, and NFA have long-run associationship for both Tunisia and France. There are forces which delete the volatility of exchange rate and adjust it toward the equilibrium values.

## *Star Model*

The results of previous cointegration tests are mixed because of the presence of nonlinearity in the adjustment process toward the equilibrium value. Various modeling approaches have been proposed, which include the smooth transition autoregressive models (STAR).

Generally two types of STAR models are considered. If one assumes that the current deviation of the real exchange rates responds symmetrically to either positive or negative past deviations, then the exponential smooth transition autoregressive models (ESTAR) are convenient. If the adjustment toward the fundamental value in response to positive or negative shocks is instead asymmetric, logistic STAR models (LSTAR) are more appropriate. Therefore, the difference between the two transition function is that the logistic one changing monotonically from 0 to 1 with the transition variable $S_t$ in spite of the symmetrical changing at $c$ with $S_t$ of the exponential function.

In this chapter, LSTAR is more appropriate than ESTAR for our investigation:

$$G(S_t; \gamma, c) = (1 + \exp(-\gamma(S_t - c)))^{-1}, \gamma > 0 \qquad (6)$$

where $G(S_t; \gamma, c)$ transition function bounded between 0 and 1, $S_t$ is "smooth transition variable" between regimes ($S_t = \varepsilon_t$ means that the past values affect the current misalignment), $\gamma$ is the slope parameter which shows how rapid is the transition between the two deviations. It determines the smoothness of the change in the value of the logistic function and, thus, the smoothness of the transition from one regime to the other. $c$ is the located parameter (where the transition occurs). When the speed of transition aims toward the infinity ($\gamma \to \infty$), the transition becomes rough and LSTAR becomes confused with the nonsmooth model TAR (Transition autoregressive). On the contrary, when the transition's speed aims toward zero ($\gamma \to 0$), the model is transformed into a linear model because the transition function is equal to 0.5.

## RESULTS AND DISCUSSION

We will follow the procedures given by Teräsvirta (1994); we carry out the linearity test against the STAR model, discover the delay parameter, and choose between the LSTAR model and the ESTAR model. Linearity test verify if there is nonlinearity in the model. Besides, he allows identifying the transition variable. Since the LM test fails for LSTAR and ESTAR adjustment test, therefore Teräsvirta (1994) develops framework which can detect the presence of nonlinear behavior. This method is used to determine whether series are best modeled as an LSTAR or ESTAR process. Thus, we will test the presence of LSTAR or ESTAR behavior by estimating an auxiliary regression (JMulTi). The test for linearity is identical to testing the joint restriction that all nonlinear terms are zero. The results from the estimated model suggest the STAR model is better performing than the linear autoregressive model.

The model supposes the null hypothesis that the time series is linear against the alternative which detects the STAR type. The regression function:

$$y_t = \beta_0' z_t + \sum_{j=1}^{3} \beta_j' \bar{z}_t s_t^j + \mu_t^* \tag{7}$$

where $z_t = (1, \bar{z}_t)$

$H_0$: $\beta_1 = \beta_2 + \beta_3 = 0$ on JMulTi the linearity test is checked by the Fisher statistics $F$ with the traditional critical values. If linearity is rejected, the choice between LSTAR1 and LSTAR2 is based on three tests: (1) Test $F_4$: $\beta_3 = 0$, (2) Test $F_3$: $\beta_2 = 0 | \beta_2 = 0$, and (3) Test $F_2$: $\beta_1 = 0 | \beta_2 = \beta_3 = 0$.

The results on JMulTi rejected the null against the alternative. It means our series have to be modeling with STAR test. Whereas, we did some restrictions to have better results; we have excluded the variable real exchange rate to avoid the auto-regressions; the model is estimated by only a constant.

The results are formulated in Table 3. It suggests the model is nonlinear and LSTAR1 is more specific to our sample. Teräsvirta (1994) said that if the model is logistic then the results will be good. Then, we can estimate our model by doing the grid research on JMulTi with the aim to extract the first values of slope parameter and location parameter. To estimate the STAR model, there are some restrictions as: (1) $\theta_i = -\phi_i$ if $G(\gamma, c, s_t) = 1$, (2) $\phi_i = 0$ if $G(\gamma, c, s_t) = 0$, and (3) $\theta_i = 0$ only linear part will be considered. The parameter will disappear undoubtedly only for the third restriction when the parameter will be considered.

Thus the model will begin with $\gamma = 9,019$ and $c = 118,46$, for the first combination. While for the second combination, STAR will begin with a $\gamma = 10$ and $c = 112.4$ (Table 3).

As we can see in the table 4 the nonlinear part is significant because both parameters are significant at the 5% level. The $\gamma$ probability is equal to 0.0107 for TND/EUR and 0.0708 for TND/USD. The location parameter probability is 0.000 and 0.0005, respectively, for TND/EUR and TND/USD. Further, values in linear part are all positive whereas some of the nonlinear part values are negative. We deduce there are two growth regimes depending of the exchange rate variation; over or under-evaluation (Grossmann & Orlov, 2012). On the whole, there is a different adjustment of the exchange rate toward its equilibrium value, depending on misalignment's size and sign. This nonlinear variation of the real exchange rate is explained by a lot of factors like the trade barriers, the market inefficiency, interest rate, inflation, etc. This misalignment is watched, analyzed and governmentally manipulated for the only reason that the exchange rates play a vital role in a country's level of trade.

Fig. 1 shows the transition function evolution of TND/EUR, which describes clearly the adjustment through the first or second regime.

Fig. 2 represents the transition function of TND/USD.

We notice that as $y_{t-1}$ (euro real exchange rate value) increases, $G$ increase slowly until it is equal to 1 in the long run. So, we are still in the first regime in the Fig. 1. In the opposite, the transition function of the combination TND/USD decreases slowly from 1 to zero in the long run. Thus, we are in the regime number 2 in this graph. Indeed, when $\gamma$ is small, as the case of our test, the process of adjustment is very slowly made. The

***Table 3.*** Star Grid Research.

| Transition variable | TND/EUR (RER($t-1$)) | TND/USD (RER($t-1$)) |
|---|---|---|
| Transition function STAR grid research | LSTAR | LSTAR |
| $\gamma$ | 9.019 | 10 |
| Located parameter $c$ | 118.46 | 112.4 |

The table exposed the transition function which is the Logistic STAR. The $\gamma$ and $c$ are the first values from which the model begins.

***Table 4.***  STAR Model Estimation.

| Variables | Start Value | Estimate | $t$-Stat. | $p$-Value |
|---|---|---|---|---|
| *TND/EUR* | | | | |
| Linear part | | | | |
| Constant | 101.673 | 99.469 | 42.256 | 0.0000*** |
| Nonlinear part | | | | |
| Constant | 912.01 | 3671.1 | 0.5945 | 0.5564 |
| Rer($t-1$) | −7.178 | −28.873 | −0.5903 | 0.5591 |
| $\gamma$ | 9.019 | 1.476 | 2.711 | 0.0107*** |
| $c$ | 118.46 | 129.28 | 15.392 | 0.0000*** |
| *TND/USD* | | | | |
| Linear part | | | | |
| Constant | 102.6 | 126 | 4.756 | 0.0000*** |
| Nonlinear part | | | | |
| Constant | −102.6 | −126 | −4.756 | 0.0000*** |
| Rer($t-1$) | 0.9669 | 0.9502 | 8.343 | 0.0000*** |
| $\gamma$ | 10 | −0.4636 | −1.867 | 0.0708* |
| $c$ | 135.9 | 149.8 | 3.867 | 0.0005*** |

*Notes*: The model reports the linear and nonlinear specifications. Positive values in linear part expose the adjustment toward the average. Some values in nonlinear part are negative because of the over or under-valuations of the exchange rate. The fourth column reports the results of the estimation test. ***, ** and * indicate significance at 1%, 5%, and 10% levels, respectively.

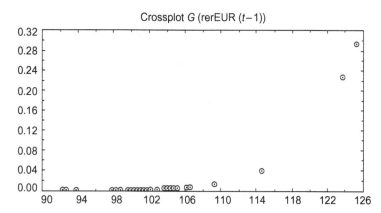

*Fig. 1.*   Transition Function (TND/EUR) $G(y_{t-1}; \gamma, c)$. *Source*: JMulTi.

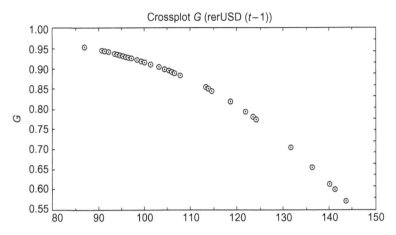

*Fig. 2.* Transition Function (TND/USD) $G(y_{t-1}; \gamma, c)$. *Source*: JMulTi.

exchange rate fits its mean-reverting only in the long run. This means the misalignment is characterized by a mean-reverting in the long run.

We close the exchange rate is far from equilibrium for many reasons, but there are forces ensuring the exchange rate to the equilibrium. Mignon et al. (2008) got the same observation; their works let them think that this misalignment is described by a long memory. In the long run, this volatility decreases until the exchange rate adjustment to its equilibrium. Grossmann and Orlov (2012) had similar conclusions. They support the idea of the force which aligns the exchange rate with its equilibrium. This strength is the state intervention on exchange market and they give the example of the Plaza Agreement.

# CONCLUSION

In this chapter, we have studied the volatility of Tunisian real exchange rate and its adjustment toward fundamentals. We have chosen the most dominant currencies for Tunisia's Economy, which are the American Dollar and the Euro. To this end, we have started by testing linearity of our sample from 1975 to 2012 by the E-views software. We found the misalignments must be modeled by a nonlinear model to defeat the incompetence of the linear tests. The model LSTAR was used to describe the annual exchange rate evolution. About these tests, we confirmed the presence of nonlinearity adjustment of the real exchange rate to its equilibrium value. Because of the inefficiency of financial markets, trade barriers, and sunk costs of the international arbitrage, the adjustment shows asymmetric behavior. Additionally, the technological shocks affect the real exchange rate by their impact in terms of trade or report of the prices of the non-traded goods over those of the traded goods. Saadaoui (2012) testified an important misalignment caused by strong inflations, degradation of the net outside position, relative productivity which did not progress enough to check depreciating exchange rates.

On the other hand, we find that any deviation of the exchange rate from the equilibrium level is viewed as temporary since there are forces, in the long run, ensuring mean-reverting. This result agrees with Mignon et al.'s (2008) and Grossmann and Orlov's (2012) results. The exchange rate cannot be always far from its equilibrium. There are big strengths which bring it back to the average. Much as we achieve the goal of this chapter with satisfied results that suited to the same subject articles of our investigation. Our model has some weaknesses, like Teräsvirta (1994) said; the slope transition parameter cannot be significant. Inclusion of this item in empirical exchange rate models could be a useful future direction for research.

# REFERENCES

Béreau, S., Mignon, V., & Villavicencio, A. L. (2010). Nonlinear adjustment of the real exchange rate towards its equilibrium value: A panel smooth transition error correction modelling. *Economic Modelling*, 27(1), 404–416.

Bierens, H. J., & Martins, L. F. (2010). Time varying cointegration. *Econometric Theory*, 26, 1453–1490.

Carton, B., & Hervé, K. (2012). Désajustements des taux de change effectifs réels dans la zone euro, No. 319, avril, la Lettre du CEPII.

Cassel, G. (1918). Abnormal deviations in international exchanges. *Economic Journal*, December 28, pp. 413–415.

Chan, K. S., & Tong, H. (1986). On estimating thresholds in autoregressive models. *Journal of Time Series Analysis*, 7, 179–190.

Chen, S., & Chou, Y. (2015). Revisiting the relationship between exchange rates and fundamentals. *Journal of Macroeconomics*, 46, 1–22.

Clark, P., & MacDonald, R. (1998). *Exchange rates and economics fundamentals: A methodological comparison of BEERs and FEERs*. IMF Working Paper No. 98/67. International Monetary Fund.

Cline, W. R., & Williamson, J. H. (2012). Estimates of fundamental equilibrium exchange rates. Policy Brief 12–14. Peterson Institute for International Economics.

Coudert, V., Couharde, C., & Mignon, V. (2011). Exchange rate volatility across financial crises. *Journal of Banking and Finance*, 35(11), 3010–3018.

Coudert, V., Mignon, V., & Couharde, C. (2013). Les Mésalignements de Taux de Change Réels à l'Intérieur de la Zone Euro, Banque de France, CEPII et EconomiX-CNRS, Université Paris Ouest, pp. 35–56.

De Long, J., Shleifer, A., Summers, L., & Waldmann, R. (1990). *Noise trader risk in financial markets. Journal of Political Economy, 98*(4), 703–738.

Dominguez, K. (1998). Central bank intervention and exchange rate volatility. *Journal of International Money and Finance, 17*(1), 161–190.

Dufrénot, G., Guéguan, D., & Péguin-Feissolle, A. (2005). Long-memory dynamics in a SETAR model: Applications to stock markets. *Journal of International Financial Markets, Institutions and Money, 15*, 391–406.

Dufrénot, G., Lardic, S., Mathieu, L., Mignon, V., & Péguin-Feissolle, A. (2004). Cointégration entre les taux de change et les fondamentaux: Changement de régime ou mémoire longue? *Revue Economique, 55*(3), 449–458.

Dumas, B. (1992). Dynamic equilibrium and the real exchange rate in a spatially separated world. *Review of Financial Studies, 5*, 153–180.

Edwards, S. (1994). Real and monetary determinants of real exchange rate behavior: Theory and evidence from developing countries. In J. Williamson (Ed.), *Estimating equilibrium exchange rates* (pp. 61–92). Washington, DC: Institute for International Economics.

Flood, R., & Marion, N. (1999). Perspectives on the recent currency crisis literature. *International Journal of Finance & Economics, 4*(1), 1.

Grossmann, A., & Orlov, A. G. (2012). Exchange rate misalignments in frequency domain. *International Review of Economics and Finance, 24*, 185–199.

Imbs, J., Mumtaz, H., Ravn, M., & Rey, H. (2003). Nonlinearities and real exchange rate dynamics. *Journal of the European Economic Association, 1*(2–3), 639–649.

Isard, P. (2007). *Equilibrium exchange rates: Assessment methodologies.* IMF Working Paper No. 07/296. International Monetary Fund.

Jeong, S., Mazier, J., & Saadaoui, J. (2010). *Exchange rate misalignements at world and European levels: A FEER approach.* CEPN Working Papers 2010-03. University of Paris Nord, France.

Krugman, P. (1991). Target zones and exchange rate dynamics. *Quarterly Journal of Economics, 18*, 231–254.

Meese, R. A., & Rogoff, K. (1983). Empirical exchange rate models of the seventies: Do they fit out-of-sample? *Journal of International Economics, 14*, 3–24.

Mignon, V., Coudert, V., & Couharde, C. (2015). On the impact of volatility on the real exchange rate – Terms of trade nexus: Revisiting commodity currencies. *Journal of International Money and Finance, 58*(November), 110–127.

Mignon, V., Dufrénot, G., Lardic, S., Mathieu, L., & Feissolle, A. P. (2008). Explaining the European exchange rates deviations: Long memory or non-linear adjustment? *Journal of International Financial Markets, Institution and Money, 18*(3), July, 207–215.

Obstfeld, M., & Taylor, A. (1997). Nonlinear aspects of goods–market arbitrage and adjustment: Heckscher's commodity points revisited. *Journal of the Japanese and International Economics, 11*(4), 441–479.

O'Connell, P., & Wei, S. (1997). *The bigger they are, the harder they fall. How price differences across US cities are arbitraged.* NBER Working Paper No. 6089.

Park, J. Y., & Hahn, S. B. (1999). Cointegrating regressions with time varying coefficients. *Econometric Theory, 15*, 664–703.

Poon, W. C., Choong, C. K., & Habibullah, M. S. (2005). Exchange rate volatility and exports for selected East Asian countries: Evidence from error correction model. *Asean Economic Bulletin, 22*, 144–159.

Ricci, L. A., Milesi-Ferretti, G. M., & Lee, J. (2008). *Real exchange rates and fundamentals: A cross-country perspective.* IMF Working Paper No. 08/013. International Monetary Fund.

Saadaoui, J. (2012). *Déséquilibres globaux, taux de change d'équilibre et modélisation stock-flux cohérente*. Unpublished PhD thesis, Paris Nord University, Paris, France.

Sallenave, A. (2010). *Real exchange rate misalignments and economic performance for the G20 countries*. EconomiX Working Papers 2010-1.

Sercu, P., Uppal, R., & Van Hulle, C. (1995). The exchange rate in the presence of transactions costs: Implications for tests of purchasing power parity. *Journal of Finance, 50*, 1309–1319.

Stock, J. H., & Watson, M. W. (1999). A comparison of linear and nonlinear univariate models for forecasting macroeconomic time series. In R. F. Engle & H. White (Eds.), *Cointegration, causality and forecasting* (pp. 1–44). A Festschrift in Honour of Clive W.J. Granger. Oxford: Oxford University Press.

Tang, B. (2015). Real exchange rate and economic growth in China: A cointegrated VAR approach. *China Economic Review, 34*, 293–310.

Taylor, M., & Allen, H. (1992). The use of technical analysis in the foreign exchange market. *Journal of International Money and Finance, 11*, 304–314.

Teräsvirta, T. (1994). Specification, estimation, and evaluation of smooth transition autoregressive models. *Journal of the American Statistical Association, 89*, 208–218.

Teräsvirta, T. (1995). Modeling nonlinearity in U.S. Gross National Product 1889–1987. *Empirical Economics, 20*, 577–597.

Teräsvirta, T., van Dijk, D., & Medeiros, M. C. (2005). Smooth transition autoregressions, neural networks, and linear models in forecasting macroeconomic time series: A re-examination. *International Journal of Forecasting, 21*, 755–774.

Tong, H. (1990). *Non-linear time series: A dynamical system approach*. Oxford: Oxford University Press.

Tong, H., & Lim, K. S. (1980). Threshold autoregression, limit cycles and cyclical data (with discussion). *Journal of the Royal Statistical Society, Series B, 42*, 245–292.

Tronzano, M., Psaradakis, Z., & Sola, M. (2003). Target zones and economic fundamentals. *Economic Modelling, 20*, 791–807.

Williamson, J. (1994). *Estimates of FEERS*. Washington, DC: Peterson Institute for International Economics.

Wren-Lewis, S., & Driver, R. (1998). *Real exchange rates for the year 2000*. Washington, DC: Institute for International Economics.